D1744382

Multichannel Integrations of Nonverbal Behavior

Multichannel Integrations of Nonverbal Behavior

Edited by

Aron W. Siegman
Stanley Feldstein
University of Maryland Baltimore County

LAWRENCE ERLBAUM ASSOCIATES, PUBLISHERS
1985   Hillsdale, New Jersey   London

Lawrence Erlbaum Associates, Inc., Publishers
365 Broadway
Hillsdale, New Jersey 07642

Library of Congress Cataloging in Publication Data
Main entry under title:

Multichannel integrations of nonverbal behavior.

Includes bibliographies and indexes.
1. Nonverbal communication (Psychology)
I. Siegman, Aron Wolfe. II. Feldstein, Stanley,
1930–   . [DNLM: 1. Nonverbal Communication.
HM258   M961]
BF637.C45M85   1985   153.6   85-12867
ISBN 0-89859-566-5

Printed in the United States of America

10   9   8   7   6   5   4   3   2   1

*To my father, Mendel (1899–1982) and to
my grandson, Daniel Mendel (1983–   )*
                                        AWS

To my children, Heather and Judd
                                     SF

Contents

List of Contributors

Peter A. Anderson, *California State University, Long Beach*
Bruce L. Brown, *Brigham Young University*
Joseph N. Cappella, *The University of Wisconsin*
Robert E. Driver, *University of Rochester*
Stanley Feldstein, *University of Maryland Baltimore County*
Amy G. Halberstadt, *Vassar College*
Judith A. Hall, *Harvard University*
Robert Rosenthal, *Harvard University*
Aron Wolfe Siegman, *University of Maryland Baltimore County*
C. Terry Warner, *Brigham Young University*
Richard N. Williams, *Brigham Young University*
Miron Zuckerman, *University of Rochester*

Prologue

Aron W. Siegman
Stanley Feldstein

Considering the many books on nonverbal behavior that have been published during the recent past, one could justifiably ask: Why another book on the same topic? This challenge is particularly salient in light of the fact that the editors of this book have only recently finished revising their earlier book: *Nonverbal Behavior and Communication* (2nd ed., in press). Unlike many earlier texts—including our own initial effort in this area—in which the material is organized around specific channels of communication, this book takes a multichannel perspective. The first three chapters are written from a distinctly functional perspective: the function of nonverbal behavior on interpersonal attraction, in the expression of emotions and in the control of conversations. They are followed by two topically organized chapters, namely, the role of nonverbal behavior in interpersonal expectancies and deceptive communications. They, in turn, are followed by a process-oriented discussion of the nature of nonverbal behavior. The book concludes with two contributions concerned with the demography of nonverbal behavior: the role of gender, class, and ethnicity (with the latter viewed from a cultural perspective). In each case, however, the chapter is organized, to the extent possible, from a multichannel perspective. During the early years of research on nonverbal behavior, the single-channel approach represented the most reasonable way of organizing the available data. With the proliferation of sophisticated research in this area, and with the field having come into its own, it is now possible to organize the data around specific functions and psychologically meaningful topics. Some investigators have even started developing theories or mini-theories of nonverbal behavior and communication. This is not to imply that a multichannel perspective is superior to the single-channel perspective. Each provides a different perspective on the available data, and both are necessary.

In addition to the multichannel perspective, many of the chapters in this book also provide an update of earlier reviews. Given the vigorous research activity in this growing field, such updates are necessary, and occasionally require a reformulation of accepted conclusions. These two considerations, a multichannel perspective and up-to-date reviews, are the guidelines that were provided to the contributors of this book. In the light of these guidelines, Anderson's chapter provides a very appropriate opening contribution to this book.

Anderson examines very systematically the contribution of all the nonverbal channels of behavior to the interpersonal communication of warmth or intimacy, although he calls the communication *immediacy* because the term carries less connotative baggage than other possible terms. Immediacy cues are defined as those behaviors that: (1) signal physical and/or psychological approaches; (b) signal availability for communication; (c) increase sensory stimulation; and (d) communicate interpersonal warmth and closeness. The contributions to immediacy involve, at the least, the use of personal space and distance, interpersonal touch and other forms of tactile communication, facial expressions and body movement, gaze behavior, and vocal behavior. There are no doubt other behaviors that fit the definition of an immediacy cue. But Anderson stresses that the encoding and decoding of immediacy cues operate within an interpersonal gestalt and that investigations of immediacy need require designs that recognize its multidimensional nature.

If time is treated as a commodity, it can be used as an immediacy cue. Thus, spending more or less time with someone communicates more or less interest, respectively. Spending time with another person is also a statement of the extent to which one individual is available to another. Even promptness or lateness can be used within an interpersonal context to convey immediacy or its absence. It appears that few investigators other than Anderson have attempted to test the viability of *chronemics*—concern with the interpersonal use of meaning and time—as an immediacy cue.

Interpersonal synchrony (congruence, accommodation, etc.) has been used in the literature (Cappella, 1981; Feldstein & Welkowitz, 1978; Gils, 1980) to refer to the simultaneous or sequential coordination and/or matching of a variety of behaviors, among which are body movements, body position, conversational time patterns, vocal intensity, and speech accents. Anderson suggests that such interactional synchrony may ". . . operate to build rapport, warmth, and immediacy" (p. 11). It may well be, however, that synchronous or congruent behavior is an outcome of immediacy behaviors, rather than an immediacy behavior itself. The distinction has not been examined systematically.

After reviewing behaviors that can be identified as immediacy cues and behaviors that are potential immediacy cues, the chapter briefly discusses the issue of measurement. The three methods proposed all involve human judgments or scales used to assess "overall immediacy." It might be noted that this reliance upon human observers severely limits the amount of data that can be analyzed and,

as an almost certain consequence, the number of research studies that are conducted. What may ultimately prove to be a more fruitful approach is the development of a set of immediacy cues (behaviors) that can be detected automatically
by a specially designed hardware and/or software system. There are, for example,
a number of systems now available (e.g., Dabbs, Ruback, & Evans, in press;
Jaffe & Feldstein, 1970; Martz & Welkowitz, 1977) that automatically detect
and measure the conversational rhythms of dyads and small groups.

Anderson asserts that in order to understand the mechanism underlying the
operation of immediacy in interpersonal contexts, the relation of immediacy to
arousal must be clear. More specifically, there appears to be evidence that
immediacy is arousing, but the evidence is controversial. Thus, the chapter
presents brief but cogent reviews and critiques of four of the major theories of
the relation between nonverbal behaviors (including those that can be considered
immediacy cues) and arousal, and ends with an "arousal-valence" theory of
immediacy exchange proposed by the author. The theory incorporates some of
the features of the previous theories and attempts to answer the criticisms to
which they have been subjected. Although not presented in great detail, the
theory is clearly provacative and now needs to be tested.

In its classical pre-modern and pre-empirical phrase, the field of nonverbal
behavior was almost exclusively associated with the expression of emotion. This
approach to nonverbal behavior had its roots in Darwin's classical work, *The
Expression of Emotions in Man and Animals* (1872/1904), and was reinforced
by psychoanalysis with its emphasis on people's affective experiences, especially
repressed emotions that somehow find expression in their nonverbal behavior.
The contemporary interest in nonverbal behavior is marked by a shift of emphasis
to its *regulatory* and *communicative* functions, and by what some consider to
be a neglect of its expressive functions. In fact, *Nonverbal Behavior and Communication* (Siegman & Feldstein, 1978), was criticized by some for precisely
such a benign neglect of the expressive aspects of nonverbal behavior. It is of
interest to note that the contemporary emphasis on the communicative functions
of nonverbal behavior parallels psychology's increasing concern with language
and information processing, which may very well have influenced the new look
in nonverbal behavior research.

Most recently, there have been signs of a renewed interest on the part of
psychologists in the role of emotions, which hopefully will influence nonverbal
behavior research. On the other hand, the expressive tradition of nonverbal
behavior research was never entirely abandoned. Siegman's chapter summarizes
the research on the expressive correlates of three affective states and traits:
anxiety, depression, and anger. His review is limited to the veridical correlates
of experimentally manipulated and naturally occurring affective experiences, and
excludes the expressive correlates of acted-out emotions, which tend to be con-
taminated by people's stereotypes of emotional behavior. Whether accurate or
not, such stereotypes certainly influence our interpretations of other people's

nonverbal behavior—this attributional process is discussed in the Brown, Werner, and Williams chapter—but, if our interest is in the veridical expressive correlates of emotions, then to the extent that such stereotypes are not accurate, they are a source of error. Most of the research reviewed by Siegman deals with the expressive correlates of anxiety and depression—with a focus on vocal behavior. There has been much research on the expression of specific emotions in the face (for a recent comprehensive review, the reader is referred to Fridlund, Ekman, & Oster in press). Most of the studies have been acted-out emotions, and such research was excluded from Siegman's summary. According to Siegman, the recent interest in coronary-prone behavior, especially in the role of anger and hostility, has spurred research that is likely to enhance our understanding of their expressive correlates.

A recurring theme in Siegman's chapter is that the assumption, held by some theorists, that expressive nonverbal behavior represents immediate, "pure" correlates of affective experiences, uncontaminated by secondary cognitive processes and copying mechanisms, is not supported by the evidence. At the same time, nonverbal behaviors are not to be viewed as indirect signs of affect states but as the very substance of the affective experience—a point of view discussed at some length in a subsequent chapter by Brown, Turner, and Williams in the context of personality.

Cappella's chapter is concerned with the more recent emphasis on the regulatory functions of nonverbal behavior. Conversational interaction enables the acquisition of interpersonal power and the management of interpersonal impressions. "Power can be achieved," asserts Cappella (this volume), ". . . by controlling one's own and others' ability to present information" (p. 70). In conversation, such control is exerted by controlling access to the floor, i.e., by regulating the availability and duration of the speaker turn. Moreover, the adequacy with which access to the floor is regulated determines, to an important extent, not only the impressions that others form about the speaker, but also the impressions that the speaker forms about him or herself. To achieve control of the floor, and, thereby, the conversation, requires a knowledge of the rules of turn-taking. Indeed, if conversational control influences interpersonal and self-perceptions, then the knowledge of how to achieve such control must be considered an important interpersonal skill.

Cappella begins to support his position by critiquing the sequential-functional model of nonverbal communication offered by Patterson (Edinger & Patterson, 1983; Patterson, 1982, in press). The model proposes that the meaning or function of a particular nonverbal behavior depends on the motivation of the individual who exhibits it. Thus, different nonverbal behaviors can serve the same function and the same behavior can serve different functions at different times. Cappella's criticism is that motivational states are unobservable; they must be inferred somehow from the context of the interaction and/or the report of the person engaging in the behavior. As such, they offer an essentially post hoc explanation.

Cappella agrees that the meanings of nonverbal behaviors derive from the functions they serve but suggests that those functions can be identified empirically by the impressions of the persons to whom the behaviors are directed or who observed the behaviors. Thus, if observers interpret a particular behavior as hostile, then that interpretation must be considered to be its meaning or function, regardless of the presumed intent of the actor. He argues that there exist well-established procedures for identifying and analyzing interpersonal perceptions/ impressions. He also contends, on the basis of a brief review of the relevant literature, that people are apt to view others mostly in terms of dominance or power, and social evaluation or affiliation. In other words, interpersonal perceptions appear to be limited primarily to two, "and probably no more than four" (Cappella, p. 74) categories. If that is indeed the case, is it also the case that the functions of nonverbal behavior are similarly limited? Can it be that the myriad of nonverbal behaviors serve primarily to communicate degrees of power and affiliation (potency and evaluation)?

Having stated his position, Cappella devotes much of the chapter to a review of studies that are concerned specifically with the cues involved in "getting and holding the floor," and the relation between holding the floor and interpersonal perception. One intriguing question that he examines is whether there is a curvilinear relation between amount of talkativeness and the perception of power. Perhaps, however, the most important section of the chapter is that part dealing with the hypothesis that one of the primary determinants of turn regulation and participation is *cognitive load*. The literature that Cappella reviews strongly suggests that the construct, cognitive load, provides a telling, if not total, explanation of the frequency and duration of pauses and switching pauses in a conversation, gaze aversion, hesitant speech, and body-focused gestures. All of the behaviors singly and, to some extent, jointly influence the frequency with which turns are taken and exchanged in a conversation.

Three chapters in this book, the chapters by Zuckerman and Driver, Hall, and Halberstadt, are review articles in which the authors use a meta-analytic approach in order to summarize the results of many diverse studies. In each case, however, the chapter goes beyond a simple summary of the results, and adopts the meta-analytic approach in order to test different theoretical interpretations of their respective materials.

The chapter by Zuckerman and Driver deals with the verbal and nonverbal correlates of deception. If is of interest to note that although the accuracy of lie detection is above chance, it is nevertheless fairly low, i.e., from .45 to .60 in most studies when chance accuracy is .5. Presumably more accurate knowledge about the veridical correlates—both verbal and nonverbal—of lying should enhance our lie detection ability. Their review includes 45 published and unpublished studies, in contrast to 21 studies included in a previous review by Kraut (1980) and 32 studies in a previous review by Zuckerman, DePaulo, and Rosenthal (1981).

Proceeding from the assumption that four factors, or processes, namely, need for control, arousal, negative affects, and cognitive complexity—are involved in the telling of lies, the authors identified 24 specific verbal and nonverbal behaviors that should discriminate between deceptive and nondeceptive communications. They found that 14 out of the 24 (58%) behaviors distinguished reliably between truth- and lie-telling, which is substantially above what could be expected by chance. Of course, there may be other specific behaviors that were not included in this analysis, but that also may discriminate between truth- and lie-telling. It is frequently assumed that the nonverbal cues that are not readily controlled, such as voice characteristics and body movements, are more likely to disclose deception than verbal content, presumably because the latter is readily controlled. Surprisingly, the accuracy of detecting deception from verbal content (i.e., the transcript) was relatively high. Apparently, although the semantic *content* of speech may be quite controllable, the semantic *structure* may be as leaky as the body and tone of voice. Nonverbal behaviors associated with deception were pupil dilation, blinking, facial segmentation (negatively), adaptors, body segmentation, pitch, speech length (negatively), hesitation, and speech errors.

One additional analysis conducted by the authors involves the classification of the studies by level of motivation to deceive. The results of this analysis indicate the deceptive messages of highly motivated deceivers are associated with a different pattern of verbal and nonverbal behaviors than those of individuals with a low motivation to deceive. Apparently, different types of lies are associated with different behavioral cues, and future studies will need to take this into consideration.

Serious questions have been, and continue to be, raised about the extent to which nonverbal behavior can be considered communicative. The issue is discussed in some detail in the introduction to our earlier book. It is a definitional issue that is explicitly articulated in the writings of many of those who investigate nonverbal behavior. Thus, for example, Anderson in his chapter in this book, points out that "Though various definitions of nonverbal communication have been offered, ranging from restrictive to inclusive, this essay takes the position that any behavior performed in the presence of a receiver is potentially communicative" (p. 2). There is, however, one area of research that appears to have little difficulty demonstrating that nonverbal behavior is communicative. It is the area that is concerned with what Rosenthal calls "interpersonal expectancy effects." These effects, he suggests, are mediated by nonverbal cues. The purpose of his chapter is to describe what has been, and might be learned about nonverbal behavior with respect to the area of expectancy effects. Thus, the chapter presents a review of several of the classical and important current studies of the experimenter-bias, or self-fulfilling prophesy phenomenon.

Rosenthal also proposes what he calls (somewhat facetiously, perhaps, but with clear empirical justification) a "10-arrow model" to account for the influence of interpersonal expectancy. It consists of three classes of variables: independent and dependent variables and those that mediate between them and are essentially process variables. The classes of independent and dependent variables are each divided into proximal and distal variables which include, for the independent class, stable participant characteristics and manipulated interpersonal expectancy, and for the dependent class, the short and long-term expectancy efforts. The arrows that tie together the classes and types of variables delineate the relationships that are critical to an understanding of these effects.

The chapter than reviews studies of various nonverbal behaviors that have been implicated as cues in the mediation of expectancy effects. It further describes four factors that seem to account for much of the influence of interpersonal expectancy (the Pygmalion effect) in teacher–student (and similar types of) interactions.

The systematic study of interpersonal expectancy began actively with Rosenthal's investigations of experimenter-bias effects almost 3 decades ago. Since that time, the issue has been pursued with increasing energy not only by Rosenthal and his students, but also by many other investigators. The influence of their work has affected, in various ways, the conduct of almost all psychological research and has extended well beyond psychological research. Given such influence, the chapter provides a very clear statement of the issue and reviews the highlights of its examination.

Related to the issue of which nonverbal behaviors can be considered communicative is the problem of distinguishing among *nonverbal behavior, nonverbal communication*, and *paralinguistics*. Elsewhere (Siegman & Feldstein, 1978), we have taken the position that nonverbal communication refers to all nonverbal behaviors, including the nonintended nonverbal behaviors, that are part of an *intended* communication. Brown, Warner, and Richards in their chapter, however, prefer to limit the term *nonverbal communication* strictly to intended nonberbal messages, with the term *paralinguistics* covering the nonintended components. "Paralinguistic information is a subset of this more general nonintended behavior, but it has special properties. Although it is not intentionally communicated by the speaker, it is not unrelated to the meaning of his behavior either. It is instead a manifestation of his purposes, motives, and intentions in acting as he does. It can even divulge information about him that he would resist" (p. 151).

Unconscious processes are frequently invoked in order to explain how people convey information about themselves of which they are unaware would resist acknowledging. Brown, Warner, and Richards, however, reject such explanations because of what they perceive to be unresolved conceptual paradoxes that characterize the construct of the unconscious. In order for a person to repress information—and unconscious information always involves repression—the person must be aware of that which he represses.

The Brown, Warner, and Williams chapter is an ambitious project. They attempt to show that paralinguistic research and theory is at the heart of the major theoretical and conceptual problems in psychology, drawing together areas as diverse as interpersonal perception, psychodynamic theory, contemporary information processing psychology, existential philosophy, and psychophysics. A major part of the chapter is devoted to showing that the information processing approach to cognition is fundamentally Freudian in its way of dealing with "processing without awareness," and as such is guilty of many of the same fallacies and falls prey to many of the same paradoxes as the psychodynamic explanation of human behavior. After reviewing some of the research and theory on divided attention and showing its conceptual similarity to the phenomena and explanations found in the subliminal perceptual and perceptual defense literature and even the psychodynamic literature, they argue that the theorists have not given a conceptually coherent account of the observations and research findings, although they think they have. Brown et al. reject the information-processing approach to cognition on the basis of its mechanical passivity, its unnecessary and excessive mentalism and its conceptual inability to deal with a broad range of phenomena.

They propose that there is a common core of principles running through the ecological perception theory of J. J. Gibson, the psychology of skills proposed by the philosopher, Michael Polanyi, and miscellaneous findings connected with contemporary psychophysics, that can much more adequately handle these phenomena and bring a conceptual unity to these diverse subject matters within psychology. This common set of principles is referred to by them as "transparency theory," taking its name from Polanyi's argument for the "transparency of language," the way in which words are in subsidiary awareness as we focus through them to the total pattern of meaning that groupings of words constitute.

In addition to all of the other areas of contemporary psychology and philosophy surveyed within the chapter, they propose ways in which vocal paralinguistic research can "unlock the science of personality" and similarly clarify our understanding of emotion. Grandiose to say the least. But central to their argument is the proposition that psychophysics, personality, emotion, cognition, attention, psychodynamics, nonverbal communication, and so on are really only different levels of analysis of human functioning with a great deal of historical accident and arbitrariness in the way the boundaries have been drawn, so that an adequate understanding of any one of them will have reverberations throughout the rest.

A recurrent finding in nonverbal behavior and communication research is that of gender differences. Some of these differences—for example that females typically interact at closer distances (Patterson, 1978) and maintain higher levels of gaze toward others than males (Exline & Fehr, 1978)—are by now well established. The evidence regarding some other alleged gender difference is less consistent, and needs to be carefully assessed before definitive conclusions can be reached. Such an assessment, based on a meta-analysis of the available data, is provided in the chapter by Judith Hall. The topics covered include gender differences in encoding and decoding skills, facial expressiveness, smiling and frowning, gaze, interpersonal distance, body orientation, touch, movements, and gestures. The only major channel of nonverbal communication not covered in this review is the vocal channel, which is covered elsewhere (Hall, this volume; Siegman, in press). The review is uniquely comprehensive not only in terms of the variety of behaviors that are considered, but also in terms of the number of studies that provide the data base for meta-analysis. The results of some of these analyses require that we modify accepted conclusions. For example, the accepted expert consensus, based on a limited number of studies, is that the much touted advantage of women over men in decoding skills is nothing but a myth. However, the more comprehensive review conducted by Hall leads her to agree with the popular view that females are indeed better decoders than men.

In some of the analyses, the available studies could be grouped in terms of population characteristics, i.e., children versus adults, or in terms of an experimental variable, i.e., whether the nonverbal behavior occurs in a social or a nonsocial context. Whenever such groupings could be made, the author conducted additional analyses in order to compare the effects of gender in the different groups, or in the different conditions. The results of such supplemental analyses allow the author to assess the validity of different explanations that have been offered to account for gender differences in nonverbal communication. The author concludes that there is no consistent evidence for any one of the existing theories, and calls for more theoretical research. She also points out that gender differences in nonverbal communication may be overdetermined, and that not all such differences are similarly determined.

Given the pervasive gender differences in nonverbal communication, it would seem reasonable to include gender routinely as an independent variable in nonverbal communication research. Moreover, given that the gender of the receiver of a communication frequently affects the sender's behavior, it would seem that the gender of both sender and receiver should be systematically varied whenever possible.

Halberstadt uses, as does Hall in her chapter on gender differences in nonverbal communication, a meta-analytic approach to evaluate the role of ethnicity and class in nonverbal communication. Her review makes it abundantly clear that both ethnicity and class affect nonverbal communication, and that typically the differences between blacks and whites parallel those between the lower and the middle class. Clearly, there is a confounding between ethnicity and class, and a good many of the ethnic differences can be attributed to class differences. However, her analyses also suggest that at least part of the differences between blacks and whites reflect cultural rather than class differences.

This chapter, like the previous chapter by Hall, demonstrates that meta-analysis can be an extremely useful tool, especially when there are numerous studies with contradictory findings. For example, in a seminal work, Edward Hall (1966) hypothesized that blacks in the United States participate in a closer, more sensorially involved culture than whites. It follows that blacks would be more likely to maintain closer interpersonal distances than whites. The available empirical evidence is clearly inconsistent. By first classifying the available studies in terms of the participants' age level, and then subjecting them to a meta-analysis, Halberstadt was able to demonstrate that although the accepted wisdom of closer spatial interactions among blacks, rather than whites, is indeed true for children, the reverse relationship prevails for adolescents and adults. Parallel findings prevail for the class variable. The author offers the interesting hypothesis that the differences in proxemic norms among adult blacks and whites and across classes may be a function of the different destiny that is experienced by these respective groups in their day-to-day living conditions. Individuals who have less spacious housing and urban life experience a sense of crowdedness, which in turn leads to a need for more personal space. The results of other meta-analyses indicate that blacks engage in *less* direct body orientation, and *less* gazing during interpersonal interactions than whites. Taken together, the findings indicate that Hall (1966) was correct in hypothesizing that blacks and whites indeed inhabit different sensory worlds—but in the opposite direction of that which he predicted.

Given the previous ethnic and class differences in nonverbal communication behavior, it is not surprising to find that black and lower class children are less skilled than white and middle-class children in a variety of visual decoding studies in which the encoder is a middle-class white. Of course, the reverse should also be true, but apparently there are not enough appropriate studies to test this hypothesis. Although black children are less skilled than white youngsters in visual decoding tasks, in adulthood, blacks surpass the skill of whites. To account for this finding, Halberstadt invokes Weitz's (1974) oppression hypothesis, which states that in order to survive oppressed people because especially skilled in recognizing what the more powerful people think.

Of special interest is Halberstadt's analysis of class differences in the relative use of verbal versus nonverbal channels of communication. She finds that lower class individuals make greater use of nonverbal channels than members of the middle class. This leads Halberstadt to a reassessment of Bernstein's (1962a, 1962b) claim that lower class communications lack the elaboration of meaning and intent that characterize middle and upper class communications. Halberstadt suggests that in the lower class, the elaboration of intent and meaning is encoded in the nonverbal channel of communication. Therefore, its relative absence in the verbal channel should not be interpreted to mean that the members of the lower class are limited to a restricted, or non-elaborated, code.

Also of significance are the findings of class differences in nonverbal turn-taking cues. Halberstadt observes "that the regulatory patterns favored by the two classes rarely overlap" (p. 000). Clearly, such major differences can only contribute to difficulties in cross-class communications. The chapter concludes with an appeal for more studies that look simultaneously at the effects of ethnicity and class as well as age level—and one might add gender—on nonverbal communication behavior. Needless to say that such studies must control for these same demographic variables for the sender as well as for the receiver of the communications.

In that we have used this prologue in the place of a preface, it behooves us to provide at least two pieces of information we would have included in a preface: for whom the book is intended and to whom we are indebted. The book is intended for the use of advanced undergraduate and graduate courses in nonverbal behavior and/or communication. It is also intended for graduate students and professionals who want or need to know the directions that investigators are taking to integrate, in terms of the interpersonal functions they serve, the many dimensions of an increasingly important area of psychological knowledge.

We are indebted to, and wish to thank, the contributors for their forbearance with the long gestation period of the book. We are also especially grateful to Ms. Madelon Kellough for the excellence of her secretarial skills. Her ability to remain "cool" under the inevitable pressures that attend the production of a book made it a pleasure to work with her!

REFERENCES

Bernstein, B. (1962a). Linguistic codes, hesitation phenomena and intelligence. *Language and Speech, 5,* 31–46.

Bernstein, B. (1962b). Social class, linguistic codes and grammatical elements. *Language and Speech, 5,* 221–240.

Dabbs, J. M., Ruback, R. B., & Evans, M. S. (in press). "Grouptalk": Sound and silence in group conversation. In A. W. Siegman & S. Feldstein (Eds.), *Nonverbal behavior and communication* (Revised Edition). Hillsdale, NJ: Lawrence Erlbaum Associates.

Darwin, C. (1904). *Expression of emotion in man and animals.* London: John Murray (Originally published 1872).

Edinger, J. A., & Patterson, M. L. (1983). Nonverbal involvement and social control. *Psychological Bulletin, 93,* 30–56.

Exline, R. V., & Fehr, B. J. (1978). Applications of semiosis to the study of visual interaction. In A. W. Siegman & S. Feldstein (Eds.), *Nonverbal behavior and communication* (pp. 117–158). Hillsdale, NJ: Lawrence Erlbaum Associates.

Fridlund, A. J., Ekman, P., & Oster, H. (in press). Facial expressions of emotions: Review of literature, 1970–1983. In A. W. Siegman & S. Feldstein (Eds.), *Nonverbal behavior and communication* (Revised Edition). Hillsdale, NJ: Lawrence Erlbaum Associates.

Hall, E. T. (1966). *The hidden dimension.* New York: Doubleday.

Jaffe, J., & Feldstein, S. (1970). *Rhythms of dialogue.* New York: Academic Press.

Kraut, R. E. (1980). Human as lie detectors: Some second thoughts. *Journal of Communication, 30,* 209–216.

Martz, M. J., & Welkowitz, J. (1977). WELMAR—computer programs to analyze dialogic time patterns. *Perceptual and Motor Skills, 45,* 531–537.

Patterson, M. L. (1978). The role of space in social interaction. In A. W. Siegman & S. Feldstein (Eds.), *Nonverbal behavior and communication* (pp. 265–290). Hillsdale, NJ: Lawrence Erlbaum Associates.

Patterson, M. L. (1982). A sequential-functional model of nonverbal exchange. *Psychological Review, 89,* 231–249.

Siegman, A. W. (in press). The telltale voice: Nonverbal messages of verbal communications. In A. W. Siegman & S. Feldstein (Eds.), *Nonverbal behavior and communication* (Revised Edition). Hillsdale, NJ: Lawrence Erlbaum Associates.

Siegman, A. W., & Feldstein, S. (Eds.) (1978). *Nonverbal behavior and communication.* Hillsdale, NJ: Lawrence Erlbaum Associates.

Siegman, A. W., & Feldstein, S. (Eds.) (in press). *Nonverbal behavior and communication* (Revised Edition). Hillsdale, NJ: Lawrence Erlbaum Associates.

Zuckerman, M., DePaulo, B. M., & Rosenthal, R. (1981). Verbal and nonverbal communication of deception and honesty. *Advances in Experimental Social Psychology, 15,* 378–396.

1 Nonverbal Immediacy in Interpersonal Communication

Peter A. Andersen
California State University, Long Beach

Fascination with nonverbal communication has permeated the academic community and their general population during the last two decades. Though the sophistication of their questions sets them apart, both groups have been captured by a need for greater understanding of the subtleties of communication. People are almost universally captivated by the prospect of gaining insight into their own messages and the messages of others. Researchers in psychology, communication, and a score of other disciplines have demonstrated their interest with a veritable explosion of research on nonverbal communication. Almost two decades ago, as interest in nonverbal communication was accelerating, Watzlawick, Beavin, and Jackson (1967) maintained that communication is a *conditio sine qua non* for human life and social order and that much of communication was communicated at subtle nonverbal levels.

No function of nonverbal communication is more central to human interaction than the process of communicating warmth or intimacy to one another. Though called by a variety of names (intimacy, warmth, affect, immediacy, etc.), the exchange of harmonious messages is of importance in every human interaction, across a variety of contexts. Friends, parents, teachers, businesspeople, lovers, and leaders color each verbal message with affective meaning that comments on both that message and the relationship between the communicators. There is no affectively neutral message; every communication tells something about our interpersonal relationship.

The term *immediacy* is used to describe these messages because it is less connotative than warmth, intimacy, or some other terms that have wider possible interpretations (J. F. Andersen, 1984; Schaefer & Olson, 1981). Immediacy

1

behaviors simultaneously communicate several complementary interpersonal messages:

1. *Immediacy behaviors are approach behaviors.* These actions signal other individuals that we are closer to them physically or psychologically. Sometimes such approach behaviors are blatant approaches as in the case of kisses, long gazes, or the large amounts of time spent with another person. Other times, immediacy is communicated in abbreviated forms of approach (Mehrabian, 1971a). A wave is an abbreviated hug. An open body position is an open invitation to come closer. The opposite of these displays communicates avoidance by blocking stimuli and increasing distance.

2. *Immediacy behaviors signal availability for communication.* Avoiding another's eyes, closing an office door, or facing away from another person nonverbally tells another person the channel is closed and that communication will be difficult. The opposite behaviors, such as eye contact, closer distances, and open positions, invite and almost force another person to realize that communication is commencing. Goffman (1964) maintained that these behaviors come in sets that signal social availability.

3. *Immediacy behaviors increase sensory stimulation.* Literally dozens of interpersonal cues can individually or simultaneously stimulate another individual psychologically or physiologically. Later in this report the physiological evidence is reviewed in more depth (see Table 1.1.). Central to the issue of immediacy is that the senses are interpersonally stimulated by immediacy messages that are typically multichanneled (Mehrabian, 1971a).

4. *Immediacy behaviors communicate interpersonal warmth and closeness.* A number of researchers (J. F. Andersen, P. A. Andersen & Jensen, 1979; Exline & Winters, 1965; Mehrabian, 1971a) have noted that immediacy behaviors generally reduce psychological distance and create feelings of interpersonal closeness in positive relationships. In less positive or over-stimulated interactions, immediacy cues can have the opposite effect and can be overwhelming, suffocating, or viewed as a threat. The conditions that produce these reactions are discussed in some detail throughout this essay.

Immediacy can be communicated verbally (Wiener & Mehrabian, 1968) as well as nonverbally through word choice and sentence structure. In this essay our consideration of immediacy cues is confined to nonverbal expressions of immediacy. Nonverbal messages are communicated nonlinguistically and analogically and involve neurophysiological processes different from those of verbal messages (P. A. Andersen, Garrison, & J. F. Andersen, 1979). Though various definitions of nonverbal communication have been offered, ranging from restrictive to inclusive, this essay takes the position that any behavior performed in the presence of a receiver is potentially communicative. When the behavior produces a change in the cognitive or behavioral state of a receiver, communication has occurred.

COMPONENTS OF NONVERBAL IMMEDIACY

One problematic issue of the conceptualization and measurement of immediacy involves which nonverbal cues are actually part of the immediacy construct as defined above. Certainly, immediacy is a multidimensional, multichanneled construct embracing a number of different behaviors. Likewise, a cue that functions to communicate immediacy and interpersonal closeness in one context or relationship may communiate interest, aggression, or a host of other meanings in other circumstances. Nonverbal cues rarely have arbitrary, singular meanings and are not neatly conceptualized using verbal or linguistic models (P. A. Andersen, Garrison & J. F. Andersen, 1979). In the following section, each behavior that is discussed has been identified as part of the immediacy construct. Although theories of immediacy exchange are discussed in a subsequent section of this essay, representative effects on receiver attitudes are also examined. An assumption of this section is that immediacy cues are being exchanged in positive to neutral relationships as opposed to negative or hostile relationships. In most of our initial encounters with others (Coutts, Schneider, & Montgomery, 1980) strangers are perceived positively or neutrally. However, some individuals or some contexts may make strangers potentially threatening. As we see later, when approach behaviors are employed in negative or hostile relationships they will not be perceived as immediacy cues at all but will most likely generate negative affect and compensating responses.

Proxemics

Proxemics, the use of interpersonal space and distance, has been one of the most widely studied immediacy cues. At least four proxemic behaviors satisfy our definition of an immediacy behavior and have been researched as immediacy cues: physical distance, body angle or orientation, communicating on the same physical plane, and forward leaning.

Physical distance. Argyle (1972) maintained that intimacy (immediacy) is primarily a function of five nonverbal cues, the first being physical proximity. Considerable research has shown that interpersonal attraction is manifested by closer distances. Likewise, closer distances typically result in more interpersonal attraction. For example, Mehrabian and Friar (1969) reported that communicators interact at closer distances to people they like than to those they dislike. Similarly, Mehrabian and Ksionzky (1970) reported several studies that show that closer distances result in more positive attitudes. Kleck (1970) found more nonverbal agreement responses by receivers when a speaker stood at a closer interpersonal distance. Indeed, one report found that closer residential distance elicited greater friendship and liking in college dormitories (Priest & Sawyer, 1967).

The relationship between proximity and attraction is strongest among friends, less powerful for new acquaintances, and nonexistent or negative for enemies or persons with threat potential. Morton (1977) has shown that although acquainted dyads prefer close interpersonal distances, unacquainted pairs were more comfortable and intimate at intermediate distances. In a series of studies, Burgoon reported more compliance for rewarding communications (i.e., more attractive, credible, or of higher status) at distances closer than ordinary proxemic norms. Nonrewarding communicators were not positively perceived at intermediate distances (Burgoon, 1978; Burgoon & Aho, 1982). Studies of negative and positive interactions show an intensification effect. Closer distances make a negative interaction more negative, whereas positive interactions are more positive at closer distances (Schiffenbauer & Schiavo, 1976).

Body Orientation.   A second proxemic behavior that signals immediacy is body angle or orientation. Several studies report that more immediacy is communicated when interactants face one another (J. F. Andersen, P. A. Andersen, & Jensen, 1979; Mehrabian, 1971a). Less immediacy is conveyed in side-to-side positions and least immediacy in a back-to-back position. Several studies have shown that close proxemic positions are often compensated with less direct body orientations (Harper, Wiens, & Matarazzo, 1978; Patterson, 1973b, 1977).

The Physical Plane.   Several reports suggest that communicating on the same physical plane increases perceptions of immediacy. P. A. Andersen and J. F. Andersen (1982) suggested this is particularly important for elementary school teachers and parents who tower over children thereby decreasing availability for communication and immediacy. Likewise, tall adults communicating with shorter adults may decrease immediacy while standing erect. Brown (1965) has suggested that interacting on the same plane is a manifestation of interpersonal solidarity, a construct referencing interpersonal closeness. Little empirical research has examined the physical plane so its centrality to the immediacy construct is not fully known.

Forward Leans.   Mehrabian (1971a) first suggested that forward leans are immediacy cues. Recently, empirical support for the inclusion of postural leans as part of the immediacy construct has been reported by Trout and Rosenfeld (1980). They found that although forward leans communicate greater rapport and immediacy, backward leans communicate no less immediacy than the upright position. In a recent study, Burgoon, Buller, Hale, and DeTurck (1984) found that forward leans communicated greater immediacy than backward leans.

Haptics

Haptic or tactile communication involves physical contact between people. Although dependent on cultural norms and the interpersonal relationship (Jourard, 1966; Trenholm & Petrie, 1980), normative touch is usually perceived as a warm, intimate behavior. Considerable research has included tactile messages as an important part of the immediacy construct (J. F. Andersen, 1979; J. F. Andersen, P. A. Andersen, & Jensen, 1979; Heslin, 1974; Heslin & Boss, 1980; Mehrabian, 1971a; Patterson, 1977). In a study of touching in an initial therapeutic relationship Pattison (1973) reported that clients who were touched more engaged in more depth of self-exploration with a therapist. This finding may be limited to therapeutic relationships since P. A. Andersen and Leibowitz (1978) found no substantial relationship ($r<.22$) between five dimensions of self-disclosure and tendency to approach, rather than to avoid touch.

In an interesting study of inconspicuous touches by college librarians, Fisher, Rytting, and Heslin (1976) found that females' responses to touch were uniformly positive. Although some males also had a positive response, there was no significant difference for males between the touch no-touch condition. In a study of compliance gaining with strangers, Willis and Hamm (1980) reported that touch was more effective in getting a petition signed or survey completed than was no touch. The effect was strongest for same-gender compliance. In a bogus ESP experiment, Boderman, Freed, and Kinnucan (1972) reported their subjects (college women) found their partner more responsive, likable, and attractive and wanted the same partner in the future in the touch condition as opposed to the no-touch condition. A replication by Breed and Ricci (1973) that added a cold-warm manipulation found no effect of touch on the same dependent variables over and above the cold-warm manipulation. They concluded that touch may indeed increase liking but only if it is done in such a way as to communicate a sense of warmth and openness. In the school environment several recent books have reported the beneficial effects of appropriate touch in the elementary classroom (P. A. Andersen & J. F. Andersen, 1982; Bassett & Smythe, 1979; Hurt, Scott, & McCroskey, 1978; Thompson, 1973).

In intimate relationships touch seems to operate as a powerful immediacy cue. Heslin and Boss (1980) reported data collected during arrivals and departures at a major airport that showed a large correlation (.89) between the rated intimacy of touch and the subsequent self-reported intimacy of the relationship. In a videotape of actors posing as engaged couples, Kleinke, Meeker, and Fong (1974) found that observers perceived greater intimacy for the touching couples than for the nontouching couples. Beier and Sternberg (1977) in a field study of married couples reported those couples who experienced the least disagreement touched themselves less and each other more than couples who frequently disagreed.

Although the findings indicate generally positive effects and correlates of interpersonal touch, some qualifications on these results should be noted. DeWever (1977), in a study of hospital patients, found that patients were most uncomfortable if touched by a male nurse or if any nurse put an arm around their shoulder. It should be noted that DeWever gathered data only on the negative and not on the positive effects of touch. Several recent studies of the trait touch avoidance found some individuals react quite negatively to touch in general. These findings generalize to college students, elementary teachers, high school teachers (P. A. Andersen & Liebowitz, 1978) and nurses (Lower, 1980). Touch avoiders, unlike most individuals, rarely find interpersonal touch rewarding.

Kinesics

Although in some early writings the term *kinesics* was synonymous with all forms of nonverbal communication, in this essay it refers to communication through body movement. Thus, the study of kinesics incorporates intentional and unintentional body behaviors including facial expressions, walking, bodily tension and relaxation, head positions and movements, and hand gestures. Some researchers include eye behavior in the kinesic system, though in this essay it is examined in the next section on the oculesic communication system. Several kinesic cues are powerful indicators of interpersonal immediacy.

Smiles.   One of the cues most central to the immediacy construct is the smile. Indeed, Bayes (1970) found the frequency of smiles was the best single predictor of perceived interpersonal warmth. Likewise, other researchers have classified smiles as a crucial component of immediacy (J. F. Andersen, P. A. Andersen, & Jensen, 1979; Mehrabian, 1971a; Patterson, 1978b), intimacy (Argyle, 1972), and warmth (Reece & Whitman, 1962). In a study of therapeutic communication, Reece and Whitman (1962) found smiles produced substantial benefits, including an increase in interpersonal acceptance. Several studies have found smiling to be one of the primary ways interpersonal affiliation is communicated (Mehrabian, 1971b; Mehrabian & Ferris, 1967; Rosenfeld, 1966a, 1966b). Several studies have found that smiles are frequently reciprocated (Kendon, 1967; Rosenfeld, 1966a, 1967). Gutsell and J. F. Andersen (1980) reported experimental data that higher, as oppposed to lower, levels of smiling were a predictor of immediacy, affiliation, and behavioral intention to attend a college party. Similarly, Burgoon, Buller, Hale and DeTurck (1984) found absence of smiling communiated significantly less immediacy than smiling in dyadic interactions.

Head Nods. In western culture head nods are an indication of agreement and rapport. Eibl-Eibesfeldt (1974) contends that originally both primates and human beings used head nods as ritual bowing gestures to signal submission and friendliness. Head nods have been found to communicate warmth and agreement particularly when used as listener responses to a speaker (Dittmann, 1972). When Rosenfeld (1966a, 1966b) asked subjects to simulate approval-seeking behaviors, they nodded more frequently. Rosenfeld also found that as two communicators became more acquainted, head nods were reciprocated during communication. In several studies (Mehrabian, 1971b; Mehrabian & Ksionzky, 1970) conducted in waiting rooms, strangers communicated affiliation by using more head nods.

Gestures. Several studies have shown that increases in gestural activity communicate more affiliativeness (Mehrabian, 1971b) and immediacy (J. F. Andersen, P. A. Andersen, & Jensen, 1979). In Rosenfeld's (1966a, 1966b) studies of simulated approval seeking, approval seekers displayed more overall gestural activity. Finally, Mehrabian and Williams (1969) found that when feamales used more gestures, they were perceived by others and by themselves as more persuasive.

Bodily Relaxation. Relaxation communicates immediacy to another interactant by demonstrating freedom from tension and stress. Excessive tension is viewed negatively since it may be perceived as a buildup to an aggressive release of tension (Eibl-Eibesfeldt, 1974). In a study of therapist behavior, Reece and Whitman (1961) found warmth to be partly a function of relaxed, nonaggressive behavior. Reece and Whitman (1962) included "still relaxed hands" as one of four behaviors operationalizing warmth. Similarly, Mehrabian (1968a) included relaxed postures as a component of immediacy. Likewise, in a series of factor analytic studies of immediacy behaviors, J. F. Andersen, P. A. Andersen, and Jensen (1979) found reduced tension and relaxation were an important part of an immediacy dimension.

Additional research has demonstrated that relaxed communicators are perceived more positively and are more successful than tense communicators. Mehrabian (1968b, 1969) found that relaxed, as opposed to tense, body positions communicated more liking. Jensen and P. A. Andersen (1979) also found relaxation to be predictive of more credibility and attraction between communicators.

Open Body Positions. Generally open body positions communicate more openness, warmth, and immediacy. Morris (1977) describes a set of gestures and positions called barrier signals, which communicate defensiveness and avoidance in social situations. In childhood these positions are quite blatant, as in the case of a child hiding behind a parent's legs. Later in life these gestures become more subtle and take the form of folding arms, crossing hands, adjusting one's cuffs, and crossing one's legs. Mehrabian (1969) reported that females who used more open arm and leg positions communicated more positive attitudes to receivers. In a study of the nonverbal behavior of married couples, Beier and Sternbeng (1977) found that "close" couples who reported less conflict and disagreement more frequently used open leg positions than couples experiencing conflict. Generally, folding one's arms and holding one's legs tightly together communicate defensiveness and coldness rather than immediacy.

Oculesics

The study of messages sent by the eyes is called oculesics. This area is often considered part of the kinesic system, but such abundant research is now available on visual interaction that oculesics is deserving of its own area of research and theory. Though this area embraces research on eye contact and gaze, pupil dilation, conjugate lateral eye movements, and eye blinks, the last two areas have limited relevance to immediacy cues and are not discussed.

Eye Contact and Gaze.   Eye contact is an invitation to communicate and a powerful immediacy cue. Since numerous researchers have examined gaze behavior, it is impossible to review more than a small part of the available research. Exline and Fehr (1978) provide a more comprehensive review of this area. Argyle (1972) reported that perceptions of intimacy were, in large part, a function of increased eye contact. More recently, in a factor analytic study of immediacy behaviors, J. F. Andersen, P. A. Andersen, and Jensen (1979) found that increased eye contact is an important part of immediacy both in interpersonal and teaching contexts. Eye contact performs a monitoring function that communicates to other individuals that you are "taking account of them" (Kendon, 1967). This is the reason that eye contact so clearly signals a person's "availability" for communication.

Eye contact usually produces positive perceptions in receivers. Goldberg, Kiesler, and Collins (1969) found that people who spent more time gazing at an interviewer received higher socioemotional evaluations. Mehrabian (1968b, 1970, 1971b) reported that increased eye contact communicated a more positive interpersonal attitude and increased affiliative behavior. In a videotaped study of actors playing engaged couples, Kleinke et al. (1974) found subjects rated gazing couples more positively on all evaluative dimensions. In a study of the effects of eye contact, posture, and voice, Beebe (1980) found increased eye contact was associated with greater perceived dynamism, likability, and believability. Indeed, the eye contact manipulation accounted for more than a third of the variance in perceived dynamism. Several studies have shown that eye contact is *not always* perceived more positively. Exline, Ellyson, and Long (1975) discussed an intriguing paradox in the shared glance. Although considerable research indicates glances are affiliative, under certain circumstances (e.g., prolonged gaze, gaze accompanied by anger display) glances are perceived as threat displays. Additionally, Scherwitz and Helmreich (1973) reported data that show that eye contact interacts with verbal content such that with positive verbal content or personal positive evaluations less eye contact communicates more liking. With negative content or with impersonal positive evaluation more eye contact communicates more liking. These studies indicate that eye contact is not, under all circumstances, an affiliative, immediate cue.

A good deal of research has linked eye contact with attraction and friendship. For example, when Mehrabian and Friar (1969) asked experimental subjects to role-play liking for an interactant, they used substantially more eye contact than usual. Exline and Winters (1965) found both males and females showed more mutual glancing at a liked confederate as opposed to a disliked confederate. Coutts and Schneider (1976) reported that friends engage in longer and more frequent mutual and individual gaze than do strangers.

The positive effects of eye contact generalize to several diverse human contexts. J. F. Andersen (1979) found eye contact to be an important part of teacher immediacy and effectiveness. Reece and Whitman (1961) reported that therapist warmth was related to an increased number of glances at patients. A study of married couples by Beier and Sternberg (1977) showed that couples who experienced less conflict and disagreement looked at each other more ferquently and for longer time periods.

Finally, it should be noted that individual differences may cause atypical reactions to eye gaze. In a study of high, moderate, and low communication apprehensives, P. A. Andersen and Coussoule (1980) found that low and moderate communication apprehensives conformed to the typical pattern of response to gaze reported in other studies. Specifically, low and moderate communication apprehensives perceived an interviewee using almost continuous gaze as more competent, extroverted, sociable, homophilous, and immediate than interviewees using averted gaze. Conversely, high communication apprehensives perceived no differences between the continuous and averted gaze conditions on any of those five dimensions including *immediacy*. On a sixth dimension, high communication apprehensives perceived an interviewee in an averted gaze condition as having more honesty and good character than in the continuous gaze condition. This study indicates the importance of assessing the effects of communicator traits and predispositions in combination with immediacy cues.

Pupil Dilation.   The study of pupil dilation, or pupilometrics, was pioneered by Hess (1965, 1975). Research indicates that a number of variables are correlated with amount of pupil dilation (Goldwater, 1972). For a number of years it has been known that pupil dilation is a correlate of interpersonal attraction (Hess & Goodwin, 1973; Hess & Polt, 1960). P. A. Andersen, Todd-Mancillas, and DiClemente (1980) found that pupil dilation was perceived as increasing a target person's social and physical attraction but not their task attraction. In an imaginative experiment, Hess and Goodwin (1973) showed subjects two pictures of a mother with her infant. As in previous experiments, the photos were retouched so that in one photo the mother's pupils appeared dilated and in the other, constricted. Subjects unanimously perceived that the mother with the dilated pupils loved her baby more. Interestingly, few subjects indicated the eyes made a difference. Most pointed to other facial characteristics as the basis of their choice, which had remained unchanged in the two pictures. Pupil dilation is probably an immediacy cue that is processed at very low levels of awareness.

Vocalics

Vocalics or paralinguistic communication deals with the nonverbal components of the human voice. All spoken communication contains a verbal or linguistic element and a vocalic or paralinguistic element that are inseparable in ordinary conversation but can be studied separately or together. Furthermore, some nonverbal vocal utterances (e.g., mmm, uh-huh, sss) have meaning even though they may take place separately from verbal communication.

Vocalic cues are certainly a part of the general construct of immediacy as well as other affective aspects of communication. In a series of publications (Mehrabian, 1971a; Mehrabian & Ferris, 1967), it was reported that interpersonal liking is in large part a function of vocal and facial cues rather than verbal cues. In a series of factor analytic studies, J. F. Andersen, P. A. Andersen, and Jensen (1979) found vocal expressiveness to be an important part of immediacy. Indeed, the vocal expressiveness items had the highest loadings of any behavior on the immediacy factor. In a creative experiment employing a Moog synthesizer to electronically vary pitch, amplitude, duration, and speed (tempo) of nonverbal sounds, Scherer (1979) found that the best emotional and affective cues were the result of changes in pitch and tempo. A study of pitch variation by Beebe (1980) revealed that greater vocal inflection had no effect on perceived dynamism or believability but did have small effect on perceived likability. Thus, limited research indicates that vocal variations and perceived vocal expressiveness are immediacy cues.

Another vocalic behavior that probably acts to increase interpersonal immediacy is the use of the mm-hmm by listeners. Matarazzo, Wiens, and Saslow (1965) found that the listener mm-hmm belongs to a general class of reinforcing nonverbal stimuli and acts to increase the durations of interviewer utterances.

Several other studies are suggestive of the value of vocalic cues. Milmoe, Rosenthal, Blane, Chafetz, and Wolf (1979) found that the doctor's paralinguistic cues were significant postdictors of successful referrals for alcohol treatment. Specifically, doctors with anxious but not angry voices were most successful in their referrals. Content of the doctor's referral had no effect. In a study of mother-child interactions, Milmoe, Novey, Kagan, and Rosenthal (1974) found that ratings of warmth and pleasantness in content-filtered voices produced more attentiveness in 13-month-old children. In a summary of research on paralanguage, Burgoon and Aho (1982) concluded that pleasantness elements of the voice including greater fluency, pleasantness, clarity, variety, and slower speaking have been shown to enhance credibility, including sociability.

Interaction Synchrony and Congruence

In recent years much has been written about interactional synchrony, the extent to which interactants simultaneously coordinate and imitate one another's movements. Studies have examined postural congruence, limb correspondence, conversational synchronization, pause matching, and a number of additional variables. A full discussion of these issues is beyond the scope of the present essay. Indeed, in a recent article Cappella (1981) suggested little data clearly support the existence of movement synchrony and urges direct tests of these issues. Nonetheless, some limited evidence seems to suggest that congruent behavior during interaction may operate to build rapport, warmth, and immediacy. J. F. Andersen (1984) suggested that body congruence may constitute "relational immediacy" but also urged additional research to confirm or falsify this notion. Feldstein and Welkowitz (1978) reported research that shows interactants match pause time, speech rates, vocal intensity, and conversational rhythm. They also reported that participants with congruent switching pauses were rated by independent observers as manifesting more warmth. Scheflen (1972) suggested that congruence may signal affect in therapeutic settings. Similarly, Trout and Rosenfeld (1980) reported that in client-therapist interactions more forward leans and congruent limb positions were significant contributors to perceptions of rapport. LaFrance and Mayo (1978), in their summary of research on synchrony, reported that posture sharing between students and instructors produced higher levels of interpersonal rapport. A recent study by Woodall and Burgoon (1981) found that when confederates simulated congruent kinesic movements they were perceived as more competent, composed, trustworthy, extroverted and sociable, as opposed to less congruent confederates. Moreover, the congruent confederates were less distracting and more persuasive, and produced higher recall in receivers. Morris (1977), in his discussion of postural echoes, asserted that synchrony may produce the "good vibes" mentioned in American slang. Although much research remains to be done on interaction synchrony, it certainly needs to be considered as a potential part of the nonverbal immediacy construct.

Chronemics

Chronemics is the study of the use and meaning of time in interpersonal interaction. Time is viewed as a commodity in America that can be wasted, saved, spent, and used much as if it were money. Several recent essays have maintained that immediacy can be communicated through chronemic cues (J. F. Andersen, 1984, P. A. Andersen & J. F. Andersen, 1982; Burgoon & Aho, 1982).

Spending time with someone communicates closer psychological distance, increased availability, and interpersonal approach. Mehrabian (1967) maintained communication that is ongoing rather than past or present is more immediate. Likewise, spending time with someone communicates immediacy. J. F. Andersen, P. A. Andersen, and Jensen (1979), in a factor analysis of 22 potential immediacy behaviors, reported that spending more time with someone was a component of communicated immediacy. Burgoon and Aho (1982) suggested that the amount of time spent in conversation presumably indicates more interest because of the premium placed on time in our culture. Additionally, Todd-Mancillas (1982) suggested that pause-time is an immediacy cue, particularly in classroom interaction. Inadequate pausing prevents interpersonal responses and probably increases psychological distance.

Finally, late arrivals probably also communicate avoidance, interpersonal distance, and a lack of immediacy. Baxter and Ward (1975) found that secretaries perceived late arrivers to be incompetent, to lack composure, and to communicate less friendliness and sociability.

General Immediacy Behaviors

Certainly, additional behaviors will be added to this taxonomy of immediacy behaviors. Some evidence indicates that sociopetal environments that reduce barriers and facilitate communication are probably immediacy cues (P. A. Andersen, J. F. Andersen, 1982; Todd-Mancillas, 1982). Any behavior meeting the four definitional criteria provided at the beginning of this essay should be added to this taxonomy.

It is important to realize that immediacy behaviors operate in an interpersonal gestalt. Though this essay has attempted to fragment this immediacy system into constituent parts for careful analysis, actual communicators view immediacy as a conceptual gestalt. Indeed, J. F. Andersen, P A. Andersen, and Jensen (1979) suggested that in terms of reliability and predictive validity a general measure of immediacy might be superior to the behavioral measure. J. F. Andersen (1979) used both types of measures to examine teacher behavior. Her data demonstrate an even stronger relationship between the general immediacy scale and student affect than with the behavioral indicants of immediacy scale. It is quite clear that receivers do not count individual behaviors when judging the warmth and immediacy of interactants. Some sort of gestalt impression of immediacy is doubtlessly how receivers operate in real interactions. Which immediacy cues are most important and how conflicting cues are weighted are an important topic for future research.

Encoding of immediacy probably operates in a gestalt as well. Although some of us may be mindful of the need to gaze or smile in certain interactions, it is unlikely that we have conscious control over the dozens of immediacy cues discussed in this essay. What is most likely is that immediacy is usually a mindless expression of our underlying set or affective state. A few years go, when this author was training experimental confederates to use continuous (90%) or averted (15%) gaze, an interesting and troubling experience occurred. The validations of our manipulations revealed that confederates in the continuous gaze condition used more forward leans, more vocal enthusiasm, and more smiles. Only after considerable training were some confederates able to suppress these collateral immediacy cues. Some were unable to suppress immediacy in other channels and weren't used in the experiment. Other researchers have reported similar problems. Bakken (1978a) suggested that one "source of bias in immediacy experiments lies in the inability of confederates to deviate from their usual pattern of behavior without in some way compensating in other aspects of their behavior." Beebe (1980) suggested that some experiments produce inconsistent combinations of cures, such as constant eye contact and limited vocal inflections, that are perceived as incredulous by receivers. The point is that immediacy cues are encoded and decoded as a conceptual, behavior gestalt. Studies continuing to manipulate one or two cues in isolation may miss the true nature and impact of interpersonal immediacy.

Several researchers have called for studies that preserve the gestalt, multidimensional nature of immediacy. Patterson (1978c), in his review of space in social interaction, maintained that nonverbal processes in social interaction necessarily involve a multidimensional appraoch. Many behaviors must be weighed in combination to properly evaluate what is communicated nonverbally in an interaction. Bakken (1978a) argued that it is presumptive to limit the number of dependent variables to one or two of the possible components of nonverbal immediacy. Though using more variables may increase the complexity of an experiment, such an approach may reduce the likelihood of negative experimental findings. This is particularly true for studies of reciprocity and compensation discussed later in this essay.

MEASUREMENT OF NONVERBAL IMMEDIACY

Most of the studies reported in this essay have manipulated one or more immediacy behaviors and measured the resulting effect. On occasion, particular immediacy behaviors are measured as a manipulation check. Some studies of immediacy exchange have measured one or several immediacy cues as a dependent variable to ascertain whether reciprocity or compensation was occurring. Since many scholars have argued that immediacy is probably multidimensional and processed as a gestalt (J. F. Andersen, P. A. Andersen, & Jensen, 1979; Bakken, 1978b; Patterson, 1978a), the most fruitful approach is to measure overall immediacy in some way.

There are three primacy approaches that can be employed to measure overall immediacy. First, one can employ trained observers to count or code individual nonverbal behaviors that are part of the taxonomy of immediacy behavior. For example, one could count numbers of head nods, degree of body orientation, amount of smiling, and so on. Then weighted combinations of these observations could be used to indicate the level of overall immediacy.

Second, immediacy can be measured by recording perceptions of the extent to which each immediacy behavior is generally manifested. This can be accomplished either by the interactants themselves or by trained raters. The difference between this approach and the previous approach is that this one relies on overall perception of each behavior (e.g., overall touch, overall closeness of the other interactant). This second method may be superior to the first because real interactants do not carefully count the occurrence of each behavior but may note that the other person stood close or touched a lot.

A third method of measuring overall immediacy is to rate a purely subjective gestalt or holistic impression without reference to any particular behavior. Again, either trained raters or the actual interactants can complete scales to assess overall immediacy.

Scales to assess immediacy by the second and third methods are available in an article by J. F. Andersen, P. A. Andersen, and Jensen (1979). Feldman and Lobata-Barrera (1979) designed a four-item scale that employs a version of the first method discussed above.

All three methods can be employed to measure immediacy either by trained observers or by the communicators themselves, though the first method probably works best with a trained observer. J. F. Andersen (1979) found that outside observers' and interactants' perceptions of immediacy were fairly well correlated (.80). She also found that perceptions of individual immediacy (method 2) and overall perceptions of immediacy (method 3) correlated moderately well (.67). Studies of how well individual immediacy behaviors (method 1) correlate with the other two methods still need to be conducted.

IMMEDIACY AND AROUSAL

To understand how immediacy operates in interpersonal interaction it is essential to understand the effect of increases in immediacy on arousal, particularly physiological arousal. This is true for several reasons. First, considerable evidence indicates a curvilinear relationship between arousal and affect (Cappella & Greene, 1982; Eysenck, 1976) such that moderate arousal will be experienced neutrally or positively. Large increases in arousal, regardless of the source of arousal, tend to be aversive. Second, since several models described later in this essay assume that immediacy behaviors are arousing, it is crucial to establish this link or these models must be falsified.

This essay summarizes studies that report 24 statistical relationships between immediacy increases and arousal. The research generally supports a positive relationship between immediacy increases and increases in arousal. Seventeen of the 24 studies show that increased immediacy is associated with increases in arousal (see Table 1.1). Four of these studies have failed to demonstrate such a relationship; one shows increased immediacy decreases arousal; and two show mixed results with different patterns for males and females.

Gaze and Arousal

The most powerful support for the immediacy-arousal relationship is for eye contact or gaze. Seven of eight relationships reported are positive and only one found no significant effect. One study found increases in gaze produced increases in galvanic skin response (GSR; Nicholas & Champness, 1971). Another study reported that increased gaze produced increased heart rate (Kleinke & Pohlem, 1971). The effect of gaze on electroencephalographic activity has been supported by one study (Gale, Lucas, Nissim, & Harpham, 1972) and not supported in another study (Martin & Gardner, 1979). Two studies have found a positive relationship between increased gaze and nervous movements and self-manipulations (Schaeffer, 1979; Schaeffer & Patterson, 1980). The same two studies reported a significant positive relationship between increased gaze and self-reports of arousal.

Distance and Arousal

A number of studies have examined the impact of closer interpersonal distance on arousal and show a mixed result. Of eight findings, four showed an increased arousal effect, two showed no significant effect, one showed decreased arousal for closer distances, and one showed a pattern of mixed results for males and females. Specifically, one study (McBride, King, & James, 1965) found an effect for closer distance on GSR, and one study found that closer distance resulted in shorter minetration duration and time to minetration (Middlemist, Knowles, & Matter, 1976). Efron and Cheyne (1974) found no effect for closer distances on heart rate, and Dabbs (1971) found no effect on palmar sweat. Fisher and Byrne's (1975) study of self-reported arousal found males aroused by frontal invasions but not side invasions and females aroused by side invasions but not frontal invasions. Of three studies that examined the effect of closer distances on nervous movement and self-manipulations, two found increases (Burgoon & Aho, 1982; Kleck, 1970) and one decreases (Mahoney, 1974) in arousal.

TABLE 1.1 Immediacy and arousal responses.

Arousal Measure	Immediacy Behaviors							
	Increased Gaze	Closer Distance	Direct Body Orientation	Density	Smiles	Touch	Combination of lean, touch and gaze	Combination of gaze, smile & direct orientation
Galvinic Skin Response	Nichols & Champness (1971) +	McBride, King & James (1965) +	McBride, King & James (1965) +	Aiello, Epstein & Karlin (1975) + Schaeffer & Patterson (1980) 0			Patterson, Jordan, Hogan & Frerker (1981) +	Coutte, Schneider & Montgomery (1980) +
Heart Rate	Kleinke & Pohlen (1971) +	Efron & Cheyne (1974) 0						
Electroencephalograph	Gale, Lucas, Nissim & Harpham (1972) + Martin & Gardner (1979) 0				Martin & Gardner (1979) +			
Nervous Movements and self-manipulators	Schaeffer & Patterson (1980) + Schaeffer (1979) +	Burgoon & Abo (1982) + Kleck (1970) + Mahoney (1974) −						
Self-Reports	Schaeffer & Patterson (1980) + Schaeffer (1979) +	Fisher & Byrne (1975) #						
Palmer Sweat		Daba (1971) 0						
Blood Pressure						Whitcher & Fisher (1979) #		
Duration or and time of minetration		Middlemist, Knowles & Matter (1976) +						

NOTE: + indicates a positive statistical relationship
0 indicates no significant statistical relationship
− indicates a negative statistical relationship
# indicates a mixed statistical relationship

Other Immediacy Behaviors and Arousal

Few studies have examined the effects of other immediacy behaviors on arousal. McBride et al. (1965) reported that face-to-face body orientation produced an increase in galvanic skin response. Two studies of interpersonal density found contrary results. Aiello, Epstein, and Karlin (1975) found an increase in G.S.R. as a result of more interpersonal density but Schaeffer and Patterson (1980) failed to replicate that finding. A significant increase in electroencephalographic activity in response to smiling was reported by Martin and Gardner (1979). One study of the effect of touch on arousal (Whitcher & Fisher, 1979) found touch produced a decrease in blood pressure for women and an increase for men. Two studies have shown positive increases in arousal for groups of simultaneous immediacy cues. Patterson, Jordan, Hogan and Frerker (1981) found a combination of forward leans, touches, and interpersonal gazes resulted in increased galvanic skin response. Likewise, Coutts, Schneider, and Montgomery (1980) reported a combination of increased gaze, smiles, and more direct body angle created faster heart rates in experimental subjects.

AFFILIATIVE-CONFLICT THEORY

The most famous theory of immediacy exchange was proposed nearly two decades ago by Argyle and Dean (1965). Affiliative-conflict, or equilibrium theory as it is more commonly known, posits that for a given interaction a comfort or equilibrium level is established. Excessive immediacy will be compensated as the interactant seeks to restore the previously established level of immediacy. Reductions in immediacy are also compensated for with greater immediacy to restore the previous level of equilibrium. Since the original equilibrium level is probably partly a function of cultural and individual norms and situational factors, Argyle and Cook (1976) modified the original theory to allow for fluctuations in equilibrium over the course of an interaction.

Criticisms of Affiliative-Conflict Theory

Because affiliative-conflict theory was the first powerful theory of immediacy exchange, it has been the subject of more research and criticism than any other position. The numerous criticisms of affiliative-conflict theory can be collapsed into several main arguments. First, equilibrium theory was developed to account for compensatory and not reciprocal responses (Cappella & Greene, 1982). Reciprocity remains generally unaccounted for despite considerable empirical evidence indicating immediate behavior produces reciprocal responses. Since relational needs are not accounted for, the model is perceived as insufficient to explain the variety of responses that are commonly observed. Argyle and Cook

(1976) have modified the theory to account for changes in equilibrium during interaction. The theory is indeterminate as to how or why the equilibrium levels change (Cappella & Greene, 1982). A second related problem with affiliative-conflict theory suggested by Cappella and Greene (1982) is that the theory is a poor explanation of activity-related behaviors (i.e., kinesic behaviors, verbal immediacy).

The most severe criticism of affiliative-conflict theory is that many well-conducted empirical studies have failed to confirm the theory's predictions. Several excellent reviews have concluded that empirical studies are likely to find reciprocity effects or no effect more frequently than the predicted compensation effects (Coutts, Schneider, & Montgomery, 1980; Firestone, 1977; Patterson, 1978a). Indeed, a number of recent studies have failed to show any compensation effect at all. Stephenson, Rutter, and Dore (1973) found that neither the duration of looking nor the number of interpersonal looks was significantly affected by a 2-, 6-, and 9-foot distance manipulation, though mutual looking did increase with distance. Russo (1975) failed to find that the mean length of eye contact increased with distance as predicted by affiliative-conflict theory, though the percentage of time in eye contact did increase with distance. D. R. Anderson (1978) failed to find any relationship between topic intimacy and eye contact. In the stranger conditions, some dyads did show less eye contact but an equal number engaged in more eye contact. Two recent studies failed to find any adjustment in subjects' immediacy behavior as a result of coactors' decreased gaze (Coutts, Irvine, & Schneider, 1977; Coutts & Schneider, 1976). These nonsignificant findings cast severe doubt on the generality of affiliative-conflict theory. However, since immediacy is a multidimensional set of behaviors, compensation may have occurred in other behaviors beyond the scope of these particular studies.

An even more severe threat to the viability of affiliative-conflict theory is the numerous studies that have found a reciprocity effect where the theory would have predicted a compensatory effect. Rosenfeld (1965) reported that in response to approval cues including many immediacy cues (smiles, head nods, gestures, and verbal acknowledgments) subjects emitted significantly *more* smiles and head nods than in disapproving or nonresponsive conditions. Breed (1972) manipulated intimacy with simultaneous forward leans, constant gaze, and direct front-facing body positions. Instead of using compensatory responses to this set of immediacy behaviors, subjects reciprocated with increased eye contact, more forward leans, and more positive self-reported attitude scores. Word, Zanna, and Cooper (1974) found that decreased immediacy by one person in job interviews produced less total immediacy by the other person, including greater proxemic distances. Bakken (1978c) found that similar or uninformed subjects increased their own immediacy and *matched* the others' level of immediacy. These data supported an interactive model of immediacy exchange rather than a compensatory model. Wilson (1979), in a test of affiliative-conflict theory, found that, contrary to his prediction, subjects engaged in more self-disclosure in the close rather than the distant proximity condition, though this difference was not significant.

In addition to the nonsignificant and reciprocity effects unsupportive of the theory, Aiello has found significant sex differences in several studies. In a test of affiliative-conflict theory, Aiello (1972) found a linear relationship between distance and two gaze measures, amount of looking and average gaze length, for males but not for females. Furthermore, in the highly immediate face-to-face condition, females actually maintained longer glances. In two additional tests of the theory, Aiello (1977a, 1977b) found that although males compensated with increased gaze at extended distances, females failed to compensate and actually engaged in less eye contact at extended distances. Thus, a number of nonsignificant findings, reports of reciprocated findings, and individual differences in equilibrium responses have cast doubt on the viability of affiliative-conflict theory.

Despite these problems in a number of studies, several well-conducted studies support affiliative-conflict theory. Patterson, Mullens, and Romano (1971), in a study of spatial invasions in libraries, found evidence of compensatory responses including backward leans, blocking responses, and rapid departure. Carr and Dabbs (1974) found that excessive verbal intimacy produced compensation behaviors including more response latency, less talk, and fewer eye contacts. As predicted by affiliative-conflict theory, Coutts and Ledden (1977) reported that closer distances by an interviewer resulted in increased compensation including less looking and smiling. Additionally, when the interviewer increased distance, subjects smiled more, used more forward leans and more direct body orientation. A study by Sundstrom (1978) showed that both friends and strangers compensated with less facial regard and fewer gestures to increased topic intimacy. Finally, a recent study of infant-adult interaction by Peery and Crane (1980) found that both adults and infants withdrew proxemically to spatial approaches by the other.

Though the preceding group of studies have offered support for affiliative-conflict theory, they are criticized on three grounds. First, as indicated by Patterson (1978b), virtually all studies supporting affiliative-conflict theory use excessive manipulations of immediacy. This is true of the preceding group of studies. Extreme spatial invasions were employed by Patterson et al. (1971), Sundstrom (1978), and Coutts and Ledden (1977). Carr and Dabbs (1974) manipulated verbal immediacy by asking female subjects about their favorite sexual fantasy, first sexual encounter, or most exciting sexual experience. It may be that compensations are most likely only in cases of *excessive* interpersonal immediacy. Second, this is particularly true when most studies supportive of affiliative-conflict theory employ strangers (LaFrance & Mayo, 1978; Patterson, 1978a). This is true of all five supportive studies reviewed above. Finally, Patterson (1973a, 1978a, 1978b) argued correctly that nonsignificant findings are far less likely to get published, probably inflating the published support for affiliative-conflict theory.

Although there can be little doubt that affiliative-conflict theory has had important heuristic value and has generated considerable research, the data show equivocal support at best for its predictions.

EXPECTANCY NORM THEORIES

An alternative to the affiliative-conflict models of immediacy exchange are expectancy norm theories. Bakken (1978b), after reviewing both affiliative-conflict theory and arousal-labeling theory, proposed a model of "intimacy regulation by intimacy norms." He maintained that this model is superior because, unlike the other popular models, the norm model doesn't rely on intrapsychic processes such as approach-avoidance equilibrium or physiological arousal. Bakken argued that the norm model is more parsimonious and explains intercultural differences and sex differences that are fairly stable within a culture but vary greatly among cultures. Since immediacy and intimacy take place between people in communication, not within people in isolation, he argued that the norm model is more appropriate to the study of communicative interactions. Although the model has definite merit, subsequent tests have not appeared in the literature, so its usefulness remains unknown at this time.

A second expectancy norm-based theory was independently proposed by Burgoon and Jones (1976). Though limited to violations of personal space, the authors argued that space expectations were defined by social norms and the known idiosyncrasies of the particular interactants. Burgoon's model posits that if persons are rewarding (high status, attractive, etc.) they will be perceived more positively at distances closer than the norm, until a threshold is reached. Conversely, a punishing interactant will create more positive impressions in receivers at the expected distance, and less positive perceptions as a function of violations at either closer or farther distances (Burgoon, 1978; Burgoon, Stacks, & Woodall, 1979).

The Burgoon model has received some inconsistent support in empirical tests. In a laboratory study of the model, Burgoon (1978) manipulated the interpersonal reward value of interactants through positive and negative feedback and partially supported the model. Spatial norm violations by rewarding communicators produced more positive outcomes than by punishing communicators, and the relationships were generally curvilinear as predicted. In an application of the model to persuasive communication, Stacks and Burgoon (1979) generally failed to support the model, with the exception of the finding that between two rewarding group members the one who deviates from the expected distance is more persuasive, attractive, and credible than the one who conforms to distancing expectations. Burgoon, Stacks, and Woodall (1979) tested the model in a laboratory setting by employing race, sex, and physical attractiveness as the reward manipulation. Again, the model received partial confirmation. The authors warned that the reward value of an interaction cannot be ascertained by fixed attributes such as race and sex. In general, they found that rewarding individuals are more successful if they deviate from the norm, regardless of direction, whereas nonrewarding individuals are most successful if they conform to the norm. Recently, Burgoon and Aho (1982) reported three tests of the model in a field setting. In experiment 1, reward was operationalized as a combination of status, attractiveness and purchasing power. Partial support for the model was obtained. High reward confederates could improve others' reactions through distance violations. In experiment 2, reward was manipulated with amount of intended purchase in a retail setting. Again, only partial support for the model was obtained. In the third study reward was manipulated with academic status and success, but individual confederate variability precluded a successful test of the model.

Although Burgoon and her associates have formulated a complex, well-thought-out model and subjected it to a number of tests, several factors prevent it from contributing very much to the general issue of intimacy exchange. First, as indicated above, support for the model has been partial and inconsistent. Second, the model is sufficiently complex that it is not unusual to have numerous confounding or interacting variables preventing a firm conclusion as to the model's viability. It may be that human communication is as complex as these tests, but if so, then the already complex Burgoon model is probably lacking enough complexity. Third, it was intended as a model of *distance* violations only. Although many dependent variables have been employed in the research, the only predictor variable has been space violations. Finally, except for Burgoon and her associates, the model has failed to generate much research. This may be due to the complexities of the model, which make replication a painstaking process.

AROUSAL-LABELING THEORY

A major alternative to affiliative-conflict theory and other models of immediacy exchange has been proposed by Patterson (1976). The model holds that sufficient changes in one person's immediacy level produces arousal changes in the receiver. Although these changes typically involve an increase in physiological arousal, Patterson (1978a) clearly emphasized that the changes can be *either* arousal increases or decreases. The receiver then labels the arousal change positively or negatively depending on cognitive factors such as situational cues, past experiences, or the relationship between the interactants (Patterson, et al., 1981). Positively labeled arousal, according to the model, should result in reciprocity or matching responses by the receiver. Negatively labeled arousal, on the other hand, should result in compensatory responses that decrease immediacy.

As reported earlier in this essay, the majority of studies show that increased immediacy by one communicator does produce significant increases in arousal for the other communicator. Indeed, critics of the arousal-labeling model rarely dispute this part of the theory.

Although some good empirical support for the arousal-labeling model has been reported, the findings are not unequivocally supportive. D. R. Anderson (1978) reported findings that failed to support the affiliative-conflict model but may have provided some support for the arousal model. He found that at close distances stranger dyads engaged in either a little or a great deal of eye contact, whereas intimates reciprocated eye contact. He suggested that these differences may be a function of the way in which the observed arousal was labeled. In a more direct test of the arousal-labeling model in children, Foot, Chapman, and Smith (1977) found that friends as opposed to strangers in an arousal condition reciprocated immediacy cues including laughing, smiling, and looking at the companion. In a study of intimacy, arousal, and crowding, Schaeffer (1979) reported that his results strongly supported the intimacy-arousal model proposed by Patterson. Specifically, he found that arousal, regardless of how it was measured, was greater when subjects encountered highly intimate as opposed to normally intimate others. Also, as predicted, increased intimacy/arousal produced more feelings of crowding when manipulated cues were negative as opposed to positive.

A study by Janik (1980) tested whether or not Patterson's (1976) model held for televised immediacy. In addition to a positive and negative affect manipulation, the televised image appeared large or small, to create an impression of

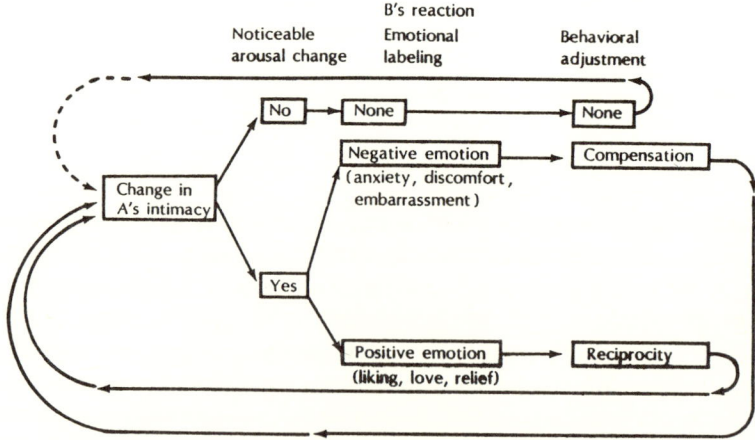

FIG. 1.1 Diagram of the arousal model of interpersonal intimacy from An Arousal Model of Interpersonal intimacy by M. L. Patterson, *Psychological Review*, 1976, *83*, 235–245. Copyright 1976 by The American Psychological Association. Used by permission.

closeness or distance. Some support for arousal labeling was reported and no support was found for the affiliative-conflict model. There was a tendency for subjects to avert gaze in the closer manipulation confounded by a three-way interaction. Coutts et al. (1980) tested the arousal model and found definite increases in physiological arousal as a function of increased immediacy. However, results showed only a tendency to support a relationship between arousal change and immediacy change. Positive correlations between the change in the respondents' immediacy and their heart rate (the measure of arousal) were all in the hypothesized direction. Unfortunately, only frequency and duration of gaze reached statistical significance. Low statistical power is certainly one possibility since the samples were very small ($n = 20$).

Finally, Patterson et al. (1981) tested the model by comparing a control group with two intimacy conditions that consisted of combinations of eye contact, leans, and touch. Results showed a definite change in arousal as a result of the immediacy manipulation. However, the results for behavioral adjustment were mixed. In one of the sequences immediacy-induced increases in physiological arousal were related to weak trends for reciprocated increases in eye contact and talking.

Criticisms of Arousal-Labeling Theory

Since arousal-labeling theory has emerged as the primary alternative explanation to affiliative-conflict theory, it also has been widely criticized. The major criticisms can be summarized in the following arguments.

First, arousal labeling (and all other models of intimacy exchange) assumes that increases in immediacy are *perceived* by interactants as they occur. Decoding is an elementary part of most communication models (Berlo, 1960) yet is absent from the arousal-labeling model. Limited research (P. A. Andersen & Coussoule, 1980) suggests that socially anxious or apprehensive individuals fail to recognize immediacy cues altogether. Rosenthal, Hall, DiMatteo, Rogers, & Archer (1979) reported dozens of variables related to insensitivity to nonverbal cues, including introversion. It is quite unlikely that either arousal increases or cognitive labeling can occur in the absence of a receiver perceiving changes in the interactant's behavior (P. A. Andersen, 1984). An improved model would account for individual variation in sensitivity to immediacy cues (J. F. Andersen, 1984). Such an improvement might account for the fact that some experiments and individuals fail to perform in the manner predicted by the theory.

A second criticism is that the arousal-labeling theory must be extended to behaviors of generalized involvement (activity) and not be restricted to affiliative behaviors alone (Cappella & Greene, 1982). Expansion to include other behaviors probably is not an inherent limitation of the theory. Moreover, as a theory of immediacy exchange the Patterson (1976) model is probably quite adequate, since immediacy is an indication of activity and affiliation (J. F. Andersen, P. A. Andersen, & Jensen, 1979).

A third criticism of the theory is that the conditions that produce positive labeling and ones that produce negative labeling are not specified (Bakken, 1978b; Cappella & Greene, 1982). This is a valid criticism that researchers need to devote more attention to. Later in this essay an arousal-valence model is presented that discusses the conditions for labeling or valencing in more detail.

Fourth, since the basis of arousal-labeling theory is the controversial Schachter and Singer (1962) studies, the entire labeling process in the model is in doubt (Cappella & Greene, 1982; Marshall & Zimbardo, 1979; Maslach, 1979; Schachter & Singer, 1979). Although the details of this controversy are beyond the scope of the present report, it is undeniable that the Schachter and Singer findings have been overstated since the original experiment. Even if the original Schachter and Singer findings were totally invalidated, some other theories may explain Patterson's model (i.e., Bem's 1967 self-perception theory). Patterson's model should be evaluated on its own merit rather than on the merits or demerits of its theoretical grandparents.

Fifth, Cappella and Greene (1982) argued that the cognitive emphasis of arousal-labeling theory prohibits its extension to infant-adult interactions. It is uncertain that the same model can or should account for the same processes in both infants and adults. It may be that separate theories of immediacy exchange are required for infants and adults. Also, Stern (1977) argued that by the second or third month of life, an infant is becoming more of a cognitive than a sensory animal. Labeling affect may not be such a heavy cognitive process that infants are incapable of accomplishing it. This, of course, remains to be examined.

A sixth problem is that arousal-labeling is incapable of explaining intermittent periods of reciprocation and compensation. It is argued that the labeling process should remain relatively constant so long as the circumstantial cues of a situation remain constant (Cappella & Greene, 1982). Of course, since communication is dynamic, the situation and relationship could change during an interaction. Tactile contact may be positively labeled in a crowded room by an unwarranted intimacy cue when the crowd leaves. Likewise, aspects of verbal or nonverbal communication acts could permit sudden relabeling of both the immediacy cues and of the arousal. Although this may need to be elaborated in the model, it does not seem to be an inherent limitation.

Seventh, the arousal-labeling model is criticized as inadequate since no degree of expressed involvement by the other person would be experienced as too intense (Cappella & Greene, 1982). Recent research by Coutts, Schneider, and Montgomery (1980) suggested that the Patterson model may require modification to incorporate the degree of arousal. Coutts et al. found that "the greater the subject's arousal following the accomplice's increase in immediacy, the more extreme the adjustments in gaze" (p. 559). This is a valid criticism of the original model that may require some modification for the degree of arousal.

Eighth, it must be demonstrated that arousal-labeling theory's heavy cognitive load and reaction time requirements are compatible with the rapid changes that occur in speaker switches (Cappella & Greene, 1982). This is a strong criticism that goes to the heart of the labeling process. It may be that arousal labeling is best suited for mean responses over the course of an interaction or a relationship and not for sudden shifts that can occur verbally or nonverbally during communication interactions. However, it may be that interactants stereotype the responses of others and may often fail to cognitively process the immediately preceding cue. I'm sure we have all had that feeling of foolishness when we've responded not to the interactant's actual behavior but to what we predicted he or she would say. This question should not be taken lightly, since it is at the center of an important question regarding communication, namely, how well are a typical individual's cognitive processes able to handle the speed and complexity of face-to-face interaction?

Finally, arousal-labeling theory is criticized for its complexity. Norm models may be more parsimonious because they do not require explanations of complex processes within the individual (Bakken, 1978b; LaFrance & Mayo, 1978). Norm theories rely on cues available in the interaction rather than complex intrapsychic processes.

It is clear that arousal-labeling theory has provided an exciting theoretical position that has stimulated both research and controversy. Additional research is necessary before many of the claims of arousal theory can be confirmed. Likewise, modifications in the original model will most likely be the result of additional debate and research.

DISCREPANCY-AROUSAL THEORY

An alternative to arousal-labeling theory has recently been proposed by Cappella and Greene (1982). This model is an expansion of Stern's (1977) discrepancy-arousal hypothesis as applied to mother-infant interaction. Basically, this model proposes that the discrepancy between person A's expectation of person B's behavior leads to arousal (see Fig. 1.2). If the arousal is moderate, positive affect will result. If the arousal is high, then negative affect will result. The direction of the affect will, in turn, determine A's response. Although this model is similar to arousal-labeling theory, it places the cognitive component prior to the arousal component, the reverse of arousal-labeling theory. It argues that the discrepancy between expectations and behavior produces arousal which in moderation is reinforcing but at high levels is aversive (Eysenck, 1976). One of the primary advantages of the discrepancy-arousal model is that the cognitive "work"

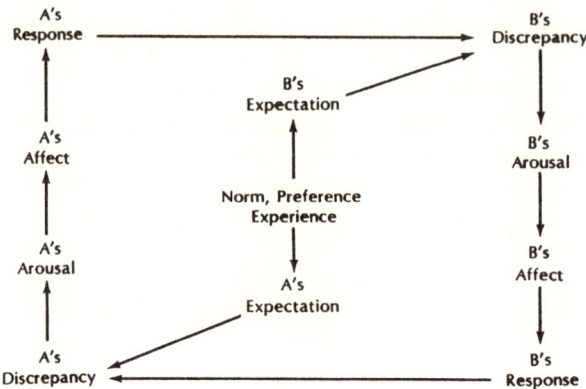

FIG. 1.2 A schematic representation of the linkages among variables for the discrepancy-arousal model.

occurs in perceiving the magnitude of discrepancy between expressed and expected behavior. Second, the model gives a stronger role to arousal as opposed to the arousal-labeling model, which gives a stronger role to labeling. Given the controversy over the Schachter-Singer theory base for arousal-labeling theory, this is probably an advantage (Cappella & Greene, 1982; Marshall & Zimbardo, 1979; Maslach, 1979). Cappella and Greene (1982) called for experiments pitting the rival models against one another to see which one, if either, receives support.

Since the discrepancy-arousal model has only recently been used as an explanation of adult immediacy exchange, little research on the model per se now exists. However, some questions should be raised about the model. First, the model proposes that the primary precursor of affect is arousal. It can be persuasively argued that norms, preferences, and relationship histories are independent precursors of affect without the mediating influence of arousal. If this is true, the relative contribution to affect of arousal versus these other precursors needs to be assessed and the model adjusted accordingly.

The second questionable link in the model is the discrepancy-arousal link. Even if the discrepancy between B's behavior and A's expectation results in arousal, other factors are probably arousing in the absence of discrepancy. One can quickly generate a list of arousers quite independent of discrepancy: sexual arousal with a familiar other, racial prejudice, the sight of someone who is disliked, general anxiety, caffeine and other drug-induced states, and so forth. Again, it seems that additional arousers should be identified and added to the model.

Third, the discrepancy-arousal model assumes that B's response is perceived by A and perceived accurately. Some evidence seems to indicate that certain individuals are relatively oblivious to affect cues (Andersen & Coussoule, 1980; Rosenthal et al., 1979).

Finally, Cappella and Greene (1982) admitted that the discrepancy-arousal position suggested that positive situational cues, positive prior expectations, and personal relationships have a limited ability to induce approach responses. Since each of the variables has generated a considerable body of theoretical and empirical findings, it is incumbent upon proponents of discrepancy-arousal theory to show that violations of one's expectations are more powerful forces than those other factors.

AROUSAL-VALENCE THEORY

Recently P. A. Andersen (1984) proposed an arousal-valence model of immediacy exchange that may have some advantages over other approaches. The model combines the best qualities of several other models (see Fig. 1.3).

The model starts with A's increase in nonverbal immediacy, which is either perceived or not perceived by B. Obviously, if the increase in immediacy is not perceived or processed by B then no compensatory or reciprocal behavior should occur. If A's increased immediacy is perceived by B, then B should experience an arousal change as demonstrated earlier in this essay (see Table 1). If B experiences very high arousal, aversion is the result and compensation will occur (Cappella & Greene, 1982; Eysenck, 1976). If the arousal increases are moderate, then B feels emotionally aroused and valences the arousal accordingly (Patterson, 1976). Positively valenced arousal is reciprocated whereas negatively valenced arousal is compensated. If arousal changes are low, no behavioral change is anticipated.

An often criticized element of arousal-labeling theory is the lack of specificity with regard to the labeling process. Thus, I should briefly mention six factors that lead to positive or negative valencing. The term *valence* is used because it

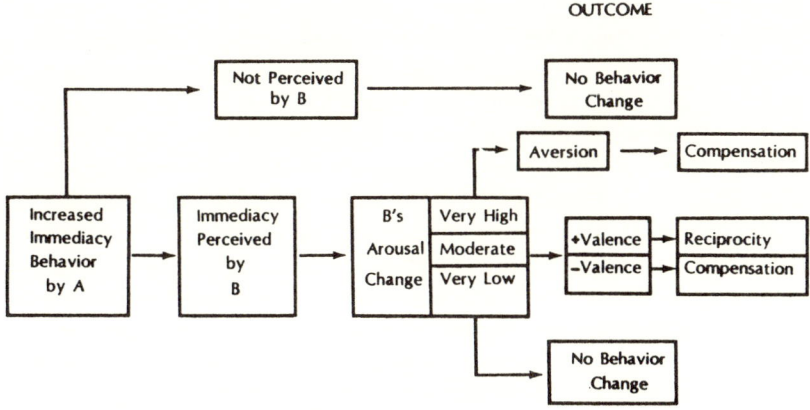

FIG. 1.3 Arousal-valence model.

implies a positive or negative reaction that may not rely on verbal labels (P. A. Andersen, Garrison, & J. F. Andersen, 1975, 1979; Sperry, 1968, 1973).

The first valencing factor consists of social and cultural norms (Bakken, 1978b; Burgoon & Aho, 1982; Burgoon & Jones, 1976). If cultural norms dictate greater spatial boundaries (Aiello & Jones, 1971), less touch (P. A. Andersen & Liebowitz, 1978), and so forth, then individuals from these cultures are likely to valence such norm violations negatively. Parents even articulate immediacy norms with verbal commands (e.g., don't stare, don't push) so that learning of these norms is facilitated.

A second valencing factor is the interpersonal relationship. A large body of literature now shows that a negative relational history has a powerful impact on future communication encounters (Altman & Taylor, 1973; Knapp, 1978). Excessive immediacy by someone with whom you've had confict would be valenced as a threat, not as an affiliative behavior.

Third, even in the absence of a relationship "problem" negative interpersonal perceptions could create negative valencing of immediacy behaviors. Communicator characteristics as perceived by receivers include interpersonal valence (Garrison, Sullivan, & Pate, 1976), credibility (K. Andersen & Clevenger, 1963; McCroskey, 1966), attraction (McCroskey & McCain, 1974), and homophily (P. A. Andersen & Todd-Mancillas, 1978; Rogers & Shoemaker, 1971). Negative valencing on any of these person-perception dimensions could create compensatory effects just as positive valencing could cause reciprocity.

A fourth valencing factor is the environmental context. Close distancing and intimate touching could be valenced positively in a bedroom and valenced negatively at the office. Certainly, spatial immediacy on a dark street at night would be interpreted differently than on the same street during the day.

Fifth, the temporary state of an individual can affect how immediacy cues are valenced. A fight with one's boss, a headache, a raise, a heavy workload, or any number of temporary factors can cause immediacy behaviors to be valenced either more positively or more negatively.

Finally, an abundance of research shows that psychological or communication traits can interact with immediacy displays to cause valencing. Mehrabian (1971b) found that subjects with higher affiliative tendency scores were more responsive to positive immediacy behaviors from a confederate. McCroskey (1977) reported that persons with communication apprehension and anxiety were very likely to avoid social interaction and tended to withdraw from others' attempts to communicate. Indeed, P. A. Andersen and Coussoule (1980) found extremely different reactions from high and low communication apprehensives in response to manipulated gaze behavior. Patterson (1978a) reported that high and low self-monitors had different levels of intimacy expression and reciprocation. P. A. Andersen and Leibowitz (1978) reported that touch-avoidance may be a trait measure of responsiveness to immediacy cues.

Finally, two separate studies have found high levels of intra-individual stability for particular immediacy behaviors. Patterson (1973b) reported high intra-individual stability for immediacy behaviors across a one-week interval. He reported intra-individual correlations for space (.97), body orientation (.90), eye contact (.57), and leans (.64). Similarly, Crouch (1980) had subjects engage in round robin interactions and accounted for stable individual variance of over 50% for eye contact among multiple partners. These data indicate the individuals have stable individual differences in their immediacy behaviors and their valencing of others' immediacy behaviors. High communication apprehensives, low affiliators, low self-monitors, and high touch-avoiders are much more likely to negatively valence arousal in the presence of an immediate communicator.

These sorts of research findings mandate a continuance of multiple methodologies to examine immediacy behaviors. A complete picture of immediacy dictates both laboratory and field studies, theoretical and empirical research efforts, and attention to the many types of data that can be collected. These data should include interaction patterns, communication exchange, cognitive and behavioral models, physiological research, individual differences, personality and traits, and so forth. Moreover, it is imperative that the approaches be integrated into a conceptual whole to paint the most comprehensive picture of message exchange.

ACKNOWLEDGEMENTS

The author would like to thank Dr. Janis F. Andersen for valuable criticism and encouragement in preparing this article and Ms. Cora Cochran for her editorial and typing efforts.

REFERENCES

Aiello, J. R. (1972). A test of equilibrium theory: Visual interaction in relation to orientation, distance and sex of interactants. *Psychonomic Science, 27,* 335–336.

Aiello, J. R. (1977a). A further look at equilibrium theory: Visual interaction as a function of interpersonal distance. *Environmental Psychology and Nonverbal Behavior, 1,* 122–140.

Aiello, J. R. (1977b). Visual interaction at extended distances. *Personality and Social Psychology Bulletin, 3,* 83–86.

Aiello, J. R., Epstein, Y. M., & Karlin, R. A. (1975). *Field experimental research on human crowding.* Paper presented at the Eastern Psychological Association, New York.

Aiello, J. R., & Jones S. (1971). Field study of the proxemic behavior of young children in three subculture groups. *Journal of Personality and Social Psychology, 19,* 351–356.

Altman, I., & Taylor, D. A. (1973). *Social penetration: The development of interpersonal relationships.* New York: Rinehart & Winston.

Andersen, J. F. (1979). The relationship between teacher immediacy and teaching effectiveness. In B. Ruben (Ed.), *Communication yearbook III*. New Brunswick, NJ: Transaction Books.

Andersen, J. F. (1984, April) *Nonverbal cues of immediacy and relational affect*. Paper presented at the Central States Speech Association Convention, Chicago.

Andersen, J. F., Andersen, P. A., & Jensen, A. D. (1979). The measurement of nonverbal immediacy. *Journal of Applied Communication Research, 7*, 153–180.

Andersen, K., & Clevenger, T., Jr. (1963). A summary of experimental research in ethos. *Speech Monographs, 30*, 59–78.

Andersen, P. A. (1984, April). *An arousal-valence model of immediacy exchange*. Paper presented at the Central States Speech Association Convention, Chicago.

Andersen, P. A., & Andersen, J. F. (1982). Nonverbal Immediacy in instruction. In L. L. Barker (Ed.), *Communication in the classroom: Original essays*. Englewood Cliffs, NJ: Prentice-Hall.

Andersen, P. A., & Coussoule, A. (1980). The perceptual world of the communication apprehensive: The effect of communication apprehension and interpersonal gaze on interpersonal perception. *Communication Quarterly, 28*, 44–53.

Andersen, P. A., Garrison, J. P., & Andersen, J. F. (1975, November). *Defining nonverbal communication: A neurophysical explanation of nonverbal information processing*. Paper presented at the annual meeting of the Western Speech Communication Association, Seattle.

Andersen, P. A., Garrison, J. P., & Andersen, J. F. (1979). Implications of a neurophysiological approach for the study of nonverbal communication. *Human Communication Research, 6*, 74–88.

Andersen, P. A., & Leibowitz, K. (1978). The development and nature of the construct touch avoidance. *Environmental Psychology and Nonverbal Behavior, 3*, 89–106.

Andersen, P. A., & Todd-Mancillas, W. R. (1978). Scales for the measurement of homophily with public figures. *Southern Speech Communication Journal, 43*, 169–179.

Andersen, P. A., Todd-Mancillas, W. R., & DiClemente, L. C. (1980). The effects of pupil dilation on physical, social, and task attraction. *Australian Scan of Nonverbal Communication, 7-8*, 89–96.

Anderson, D. R. (1978). Interpersonal relationship and intimacy of social interaction: Re-examining the intimacy-equilibrium model. (Doctoral dissertation, University of South Dakota, 1977.) *Dissertation abstracts International, 38*, 46438.

Argyle, M. (1972). *The psychology of interpersonal behavior* (2nd ed.). London: Penguin Books.

Argyle, M., & Cook, M. (1976). *Gaze and mutual gaze*. Cambridge University Press.

Argyle, M., & Dean, J. (1965). Eye contact, distance, and affiliations. *Sociometry, 28*, 289–304.

Bakken, D. (1978a). Behavioral adjustment in nonverbal immediacy: A methodological note. *Personality and Social Psychology Bulletin, 4*, 300–303.

Bakken, D. (1978b, April). *Intimacy regulation in social encounters*. Paper presented at the meeting of the Eastern Communication Association, Boston, MA

Bakken, D. (1978c). *Nonverbal immediacy in dyadic interactions: The effects of sex and information about attitude similarity*. Paper presented at the meeting of the Eastern Psychological Association.

Bassett, R. E. & Smythe, M. J. (1979). *Communication and instruction* New York: Harper and Row.

Baxter, L. & Ward, J. (1975). Newsline. *Psychology Today, 8*, 28.

Bayes, M. A. (1970). An investigation of the behavioral cues of interpersonal warmth. (Doctoral dissertation, University of Miami, 1970.) *Dissertation Abstracts International, 31*, 2272B.

Beebe, S. A. (1980). Effects of eye contact, posture and vocal inflection upon credibility and comprehension. Australian Scan: *Journal of Human Communication, 7–8*, 57–70.

Beier, E. G., & Sternberg, D. P. (1977). Marital communication: Subtle cues between newlyweds. *Journal of Communication, 27*, 92–97.

Bem, D. J. (1967). Self-perception: An alternative interpretation of the cognitive dissonance phenomena. *Psychological Review, 74*, 183–200.

Berlo, D. K. (1960). *The process of communication*. New York: Holt, Rinehart & Winston.

Boderman, A., Freed, D. W., & Kinnucan, M. T. (1972). Touch me, like me: Testing an encounter group assumption. *Journal of Applied Behavioral Science, 8,* 527–533.

Breed, G. (1972). The effect of intimacy: Reciprocity or retreat? *British Journal of Social and Clinical Psychology, 11* (2), 135–142.

Breed, G., & Ricci, J. S. (1973). "Touch me, like me" artifact. *Proceedings of the 81st Annual Convention of the American Psychological Association,* Montreal, Canada, *8,* 153–154.

Brown, R. (1965). *Social psychology.* New York: The Free Press, 1965.

Burgoon, J. K. (1978). A communication model of personal space violations: Explication and an initial test. *Human Communication Research, 4,* 129–142.

Burgoon, J. K., & Aho, L. (1982). Three field experiments on the effects of violations of conversational distance. *Communication Monographs, 49,* 71–88.

Burgoon, J. K., Buller, D. B., Hale, J. L. & DeTurck, J. L. (1984). Relational messages associated with immediacy behaviors. *Human Communication Research, 10,* 351–378.

Burgoon, J. K., & Jones, S. B. (1976). Toward a theory of personal spaces expectations and their violations. *Human Communication Research, 2,* 131–146.

Burgoon, J. K., Stacks, D. W., & Woodall, W. G. (1979). A communicative model of violations of distancing expectations. *Western Journal of Speech Communication, 43,* 153–167.

Cappella, J. N. (1981). Mutual influence in expressive behavior: Adult-adult and infant-adult dyadic interaction. *Psychological Bulletin, 89,* 101–132.

Cappella, J. N., & Greene, J. O. (1982). A discrepancy-arousal explanation of mutual influence in expressive behavior for adult and infant-adult interaction. *Communication Monographs, 49,* 89–114.

Carr, S. J., & Dabbs, J. M., Jr. (1974). The effect of lighting, distance, and intimacy of topic on verbal and visual behavior. *Sociometry, 37,* 592–600.

Coutts, L. M., Irvine, M., & Schneider, F. W. (1977). Nonverbal adjustments to changes in gaze and orientation, *Psychology, 14,* 28–32.

Coutts, L. M., & Ledden, M. (1977). Nonverbal compensatory reactions to changes in interpersonal proximity. *Jouranl of Social Psychology, 102,* 283–290.

Coutts, L. M., & Schneider, F. W. (1976). Affiliative conflict theory: An investigation of intimacy equilibrium and compensation hypothesis. *Journal of Personality and Social Psychology, 34,* 1135–1142.

Coutts, L. M., Schneider, F. W., & Montgomery, S. (1980). An investigation of the arousal model of interpersonal intimacy. *Journal of Experimental Social Psychology, 16,* 545–561.

Crouch, W. W. (1980, April). *Consistency of selected eye behaviors across conversations with nine different partners.* Paper presented at the meeting of the Eastern Communication Association, Ocean City, Maryland.

Dabbs, J. M., Jr. (1971). Physical closeness and negative feelings. *Psychonomic Science, 23,* 141–143.

De Wever, M. K. (1977). Nursing home patients' perception of nurses' affective touching. *Journal of Psychology, 96,* 163–171.

Dittman, A. T. (1972). Developmental factors in conversation behavior. *Journal of Communication, 22,* 404–423.

Efron, M. G., & Cheyne, J. A. (1974). Affective concomitants of the invasion of the shared space: Behavioral, physiological and verbal indicators. *Journal of Personality and Social Psychology, 29,* 219–226.

Eibl-Eibesfeldt, I. (1974). *Love and hate: The natural history of behavior patterns.* New York: Schocken Books.

Exline, R. V., Ellyson, S. L., & Long, B. (1975). Visual behavior as an aspect of power role relationships. In P. Pliner, L. Arames, & T. Alloway (Eds.), *Nonverbal communication of aggression.* New York: Plenum.

Exline, R. V. & Fehr, B. J. (1978). Applications of semiosis to the study of visual interaction. In

A. W. Siegman & S. Feldstein (Eds.), *Nonverbal behavior and communication.* Hillsdale, NJ: Lawrence Erlbaum Associates.

Exline, R. V., & Winters, L. C. (1965). Adaptive relations and mutual glances in dyads. In S. Tompkins & C. Izard (Eds.), *Affect, cognition, and personality.* New York: Springer.

Eysenck, H. J. (1976). Arousal, learning and memory. *Psychological Bulletin, 83,* 389–404.

Feldman, R. S, & Lobato-Barrera, D. (1979, April). *Attitudes, cognition, and nonverbal communication behavior.* Paper presented at the annual conference of the American Educational Research Association, San Francisco, CA.

Feldstein, S., & Welkowitz, J. (1978). A chronograhy of conversation: In defense of an objective approach. In A. W. Seigman & S. Feldstein (Eds.), *Nonverbal behavior and communication.* Hillsdale, NJ: Lawrence Erlbaum Associates.

Firestone, I. J. (1977). Reconciling verbal and nonverbal models of dyadic communication. *Environmental Psychology and Nonverbal Behavior, 2,* 30–44.

Fisher, J. D., & Byrne, D. (1975). Too close for comfort: Sex differences in response to invasions of personal space. *Journal of Personality and Social Psychology, 32,* 15–21.

Fisher, J. D., Rytting, M., & Heslin R. (1976). Hands touching hands: Affective and evaluative effects of interpersonal touch. *Sociometry, 39,* 416–421.

Foot, H. C., Chapman, A. J., Smith, J. R. (1977). Friendship and social responsiveness in boys and girls. *Journal of Personality and Social Psychology, 35,* 401–411.

Gale, A., Lucas, B., Nissim, R. & Harpham B. (1972). Some EEG correlates of face to face contact. *British Journal of Social and Clinical Psychology, 11,* 326–332.

Garrison, J. P., Sullivan, D. L. & Pate, L. E. (1976, December). *Interpersonal valance dimensions as discriminators of communication contexts: An empirical assessment of dyadic linkages.* Paper presented at the Speech Communication Association Convention, San Francisco.

Goffman, E. (1964). *Behavior in public places,* Glencoe, IL: The Free Press.

Goldberg, G. N., Kiesler, C. A., & Collins, B. E. (1969). Visual behavior and face-to-face distance during interaction. *Sociometry, 32,* 43–53.

Goldwater, B. C. (1972). Psychological significance of pupillary movements. *Psychological Bulletin, 77,* 340–355.

Gutsell, L. M., & Andersen, J. F. (1980). *Perceptual and behavioral responses to smiling.* Paper presented at the convention of the International Communication Association, Acapulco, Mexico.

Harper, R. G., Wiens, A. N., & Matarazzo, J. D. (1978). *Nonverbal communication: The state of the art.* New York: Wiley.

Heslin, R. (1974, May). *Steps toward a taxonomy of touching.* Paper presented at the annual convention of the Midwestern Psychological Association.

Heslin, R., & Boss, D. (1980). Nonverbal intimacy in arrival and departure at an airport. *Personality and Social Psychology Bulletin, 6,* 248–252.

Hess, E. H. (1965). Attitude and pupil size. *Scientific American, 212,* 46–54.

Hess, E. H. (1975). The role of pupil size in communication. *Scientific American, 233,* 110–119.

Hess, E. H. & Goodwin, E. (1973). The present state of pupilometrics. In M. P. Janisse (Ed.), *Pupillary dynamics and behavior.* New York: Plenum Press.

Hess, E. H., & Polt, J. M. (1960). Pupil size as related to interest value of visual stimuli. *Science, 132,* 349–350.

Hurt, H. T., Scott, M. D., McCroskey, J. C. (1978). *Communication in the classroom.* Reading, MA: Addison-Wesley.

Janik, S. W. (1980). Visual adjustments to changes in apparent interactive distance: A test of Patterson's intimacy-arousal model. (Doctoral dissertation, University of Miami, 1979). *Dissertation Abstracts International, 41,* 408B–409B.

Jensen, A. D., & Andersen, P. A. (1979, May). *The relationship among communication traits, communication behaviors, and interpersonal perception variables.* Paper presented at the annual convention of the International Communication Association, Philadelphia.

Jourard, S. M. (1966). An exploratory study of body-accessibility. *British Journal of Social and Clinical Psychology, 5*, 221–231.

Kendon, A. (1967). Some functions of gaze direction in social interaction. *Acta Psychologica, 26*, 22–63.

Kleck, R. (1970). Interaction distance and non-verbal agreeing responses. *British Journal of Social and Clinical Psychology, 9*, 180–182.

Kleinke, C. L., Meeker, F. B., & Fong, C. L. (1974). Effects of gaze, touch, and use of name on evaluation of "engaged" couples. *Journal of Research in Personality, 7*, 368–373.

Kleinke, C. L., & Pohlem, P. D. (1971). Affective and emotional responses as a function of other person's gaze and cooperativeness in a two-person game. *Journal of Personality and Social Psychology, 17*, 308–313.

Knapp, M. L. (1978). *Social intercourse: From greeting to goodbye.* Boston: Allyn & Bacon.

LaFrance, M., & Mayo, C. (1978). *Moving bodies: Nonverbal communication in social relationships.* Monterey, CA: Brooks/Cole.

Lower, H. M. (1980). Fear of touching as a form of communication apprehension in professional nursing students. *Australian Scan: Journal of Human Communication, 7-8*, 71–78.

Mahoney, E. R. (1974). Compensatory reactions to spatial immediacy. *Sociometry, 37*, 423–431.

Marshall, G. D., & Zimbardo, P. G. (1979). Affective consequences of inadequately explained physiological arousal. *Journal of Personality and Social Psychology, 37*, 970–988.

Martin, W. W., & Gardner, S. N. (1979). The relative effects of eye-gaze and smiling on arousal in asocial situations. *Journal of Psychology, 102*, 253–259.

Maslach, C. (1979). Negative emotional biasing of unexplained arousal. *Journal of Personality and Social Psychology, 37*, 953–969.

Matarazzo, J. D., Wiens, A. N., & Saslow, G. (1965). Studies in interviewer speech behavior. In L. Kresner & U. P. Ullman (Eds.), *Research in behavior modification.* New York: Holt, Rinehart & Winston.

McBride, G., King, M. G., & James, J. W. (1965). Social proximity effects of galvanic skin responses in adult humans. *Journal of Psychology, 61*, 153–157.

McCroskey, J. C. (1977). Oral communication apprehension: A summary of recent theory and research. *Human Communication Research, 4*, 78–96.

McCroskey, J. C., & McCain, T. A. (1974). The measurement of interpersonal attraction. *Speech Monographs, 41*, 261–266.

Mehrabian, A. (1967). Orientation behaviors and nonverbal attitude in communicators. *Journal of Communication, 17*, 324–332.

Mehrabian, A. (1968a). Relationship of attitude to seated posture, orientation, and distance. *Journal of Personality and Social Psychology, 10*, 26–30.

Mehrabian, A. (1968b). Inference of attitude from the posture, orientation, and distance of a communicator. *Journal of Consulting and Clinical Psychology, 32*, 296–308.

Mehrabian, A. (1969). Significance of posture and position in the communication of attitude and status relationships. *Psychological Bulletin, 71*, 359–372.

Mehrabian, A. (1970). A semantic space for nonverbal behavior. *Journal of Consulting and Clinical Psychology, 35*, 248–257.

Mehrabian, A. (1971a). *Silent messages.* Belmont, CA: Wadsworth.

Mehrabian, A. (1971b). Verbal and nonverbal interactions of strangers in a waiting situation. *Journal of Experimental Research in Personality, 5*, 127–138.

Mehrabian, A., & Ferris, S. R. Inference of attitudes from nonverbal communication in two channels. *Journal of Consulting Psychology, 31*, 248–253.

Mehrabian, A., & Friar, J. (1969). Encoding of attitude by a seated communicator via posture and position cues. *Journal of Consulting and Clinical Psychology, 33*, 330–336.

Mehrabian, A., & Ksionzky, S. (1970). Models for affiliative and conformity behavior. *Psychological Bulletin, 74*, 110–126.

Mehrabian, A., & Williams, M. (1969). Nonverbal concomitants of perceived and intended persuasiveness. *Journal of Personality and Social Psychology, 13,* 37–58.

Middlemist, R. D., Knowles, E. S. & Matter, C. F. (1976). Personal space invasion in the lavatory: Suggestive evidence for arousal. *Journal of Personality and Social Psychology, 33,* 541–549.

Milmoe, S., Novey, M. S., Kagan, J., & Rosenthal, R. (1974). The mother's voice: Postdiction of aspects of her baby's behavior. In S. Weitz (Ed.), *Nonverbal communication: Readings with commentary,* New York: Oxford University Press.

Milmoe, S., Rosenthal, R., Blane, H. T., Chafetz, M. E., & Wolf, J. (1974). The doctor's voice: Postdiction of successful referral of alcoholic patients. In S. Weitz (Ed.), *Nonverbal communication: Readings with commentary,* New York: Oxford University Press.

Morris, D. (1977). *Manwatching: A field guide to human behavior.* New York: Abrams.

Morton, T. L. (1977). The effects of acquaintance and distance on intimacy and reciprocity (Doctoral dissertation, University of Utah, 1976). *Dissertation Abstracts International, 37,* 3680B.

Nichols, K. A., & Champness, B. G. (1971). Eye gaze and the GSR. *Journal of Social Psychology, 7,* 623–626.

Patterson, M. L. (1973a). Compensation in nonverbal immediacy behaviors: A review. *Sociometry, 36,* 237–252.

Patterson, M. L. (1973b). Stability of nonverbal immediacy behaviors. *Journal of Experimental Social Psychology, 9,* 97–109.

Patterson, M. L. (1976). An arousal model of interpersonal intimacy. *Psychological Review, 83,* 235–245.

Patterson, M. L. (1977). Interpersonal distance, affect, and equilibrium theory. *Journal of Social Psychology, 101,* 205–214.

Patterson, M. L. (1978a). Arousal change and cognitive labeling: Pursuing the mediators of intimacy exchange. *Environmental Psychology and Nonverbal Behavior,* 17–22.

Patterson, M. L. (1978b, October). *Nonverbal intimacy exchange: Problems and prospects.* Paper presented at the second national conference on body language, New York.

Patterson, M. L. (1978c). The role of space in social interaction. In A. W. Siegman & S. Feldstein (Eds.), *Nonverbal behavior and communication,* Hillsdale, NJ: Lawrence Erlbaum Associates.

Patterson, M. L., Jordan, A., Hogan, M., & Frerker, D. (1981). Effects of nonverbal intimacy on arousal and behavioral adjustment. *Journal of Nonverbal Behavior, 5,* 184–198.

Patterson, M. L., Mullens, S., & Romano, J. (1971). Compensatory reactions to spatial intrusion. *Sociometry, 34,* 114–121.

Pattison, J. E. (1973). Effects of touch on self-exploration and the therapeutic relationship. *Journal of Consulting and Clinical Psychology, 40,* 170–175.

Peery, J. C., & Crane, P. N. (1980). Personal space regulation: Approach-withdrawal-approach proxemic behavior during adult-preschooler interaction at close range. *Journal of Psychology, 106,* 63–75.

Priest, R. F., & Sawyer, J. (1967). Proximity and peership: Bases of balance in interpersonal attraction. *The American Journal of Sociology, 72,* 633–649.

Reece, M. M., & Whitman, R. N. (1961). Warmth and expressive movements. *Psychological Reports, 8,* 76.

Reece, M. M. & Whitman, R. (1962). Expressive movements, warmth, and verbal reinforcements. *Journal of Abnormal and Social Psychology, 64* (3), 234–236.

Rogers, E. M., & Shoemaker, F. F. (1971). *Communication of innovations.* New York: The Free Press.

Rosenfeld, H. M. (1965). Effect of approval-seeking induction on interpersonal proximity. *Psychological Reports, 17,* 120–122.

Rosenfeld, H. M. (1966a). Approval-seeking and approval-inducing functions of verbal and nonverbal responses in a dyad. *Journal of Personality and Social Psychology, 4,* 597–605.

Rosenfeld, H. M.(1966b). Instrumental affiliative functions of facial and gestural expressions. *Journal of Personality and Social Psychology, 4*, 65–72.

Rosenfeld, H. M. (1967). Nonverbal reciprocation of approval: An experimental analysis. *Journal of Experimental Social Psychology, 3*, 102–111.

Rosenthal, R., Hall, J. A., DiMatteo, M. R., Rogers, P. L., & Archer, D. (1979). *Sensitivity to nonverbal communication: The pons test.* Baltimore, MD: Johns Hopkins University Press.

Russo, N. (1975). Eye contact, distance and the equilibrium theory. *Journal of Personality and Social Psychology, 31*, 497–502.

Schachter, S., & Singer, J. C. (1962). Cognitive, social, and physiological determinants of emotional state. *Psychological Review, 69*, 379–399.

Schachter, S., & Singer, J. C. (1979). Comments on the Maslach and Marshall-Zimbardo experiments. *Journal of Personality and Social Psychology, 37*, 970–988.

Schaefer, M. T., & Olson, D. H. (1981). Assessing intimacy: The pair inventory. *Journal of Marital and Family Therapy*, 47–60.

Schaeffer, G. H. (1979). The influence of interpersonal intimacy and arousal on the experience of crowding (Doctoral dissertation, University of Missouri, St. Louis, 1978). *Dissertation Abstracts International, 40*, 498B–499B.

Schaeffer, G. H., & Patterson, M. L. (1980). Intimacy, arousal, and small group crowding. *Journal of Personality & Social Psychology, 38*, 283–290.

Scheflen, A. E. (1972). *Body language and social order.* Englewood Cliffs, NJ: Prentice-Hall.

Scherer, K. R. (1979). Acoustic concomitants of emotional dimensions: Judging affect from synthesized tone sequences. In S. Weitz (Ed.), *Nonverbal communication: Readings with commentary.* New York: Oxford University Press.

Scherwitz, L., & Helmreich, R. (1973). Interactive effects of eye contact and verbal content on interpersonal attraction in dyads. *Journal of Personality and Social Psychology, 25*, 6–14.

Schiffenbauer, A., & Schiavo, R. S. (1976). Physical distance and attraction: An intensification effect. *Journal of Experimental Social Psychology, 12*, 274–282.

Sperry, R. W. (1968). Hemispheric deconnection and unity in conscious awareness. *American Psychologist, 23*, 723–733.

Sperry, R. W. (1973). Lateral specialization of cerebral function in surgically separated hemispheres. In F. J. McOwgan & R. A. Schoonover (Eds.), *The psychophysiology of thinking: Studies of covert processes.* New York: Academic Press.

Stacks, D. W., & Burgoon, J. K. (1979, April). *The persuasive effects of violating spatial distance expectations in small groups.* Paper presented at the annual convention of the Southern Speech Communication Association, Biloxi, MS.

Stephenson, G. M., Rutter, D. R., & Dore, S. R. (1973). Visual interaction and distance. *British Journal of Psychology, 64* (2), 251–257.

Stern, D. (1977). *The first relationship: Mother and infant.* Cambridge, MA: Harvard University Press.

Sundstrom, E. (1978). A test of equilibrium theory: Effects of topic intimacy and proximity on verbal and nonverbal behavior in pairs of friends and strangers. *Environmental Psychology and Nonverbal Behavior, 3*, 17–22.

Thompson, J. J. (1973). *Beyond words: Nonverbal communication in the classroom.* New York: Citation Press.

Todd-Mancillas, W. R. (1982). Classroom environments and nonverbal behavior. In L. L. Barker (Ed.), *Communication in the classroom: Original essays.* Englewood Cliffs, NJ: Prentice-Hall.

Trenholm, S., & Petrie, C. R. (1980). Reexamining body accessibility. *Australian Scan: Journal of Human Communication, 7-8*, 33–42.

Trout, D. L., & Rosenfeld, H. M. (1980). The effect of postural lean and body congruence on the judgment of psychotherapeutic rapport. *Jouranl of Nonverbal Behavior, 4*, 176–190.

Watzlawick, P., Beavin, J. H., & Jackson, D. D. (1967). *Pragmatics of human communication.* New York: Norton.

Whitcher, S. J., & Fisher, J. D. (1979). Multi-dimensional reaction to therapeutic touch in a hospital setting. *Journal of Personality and Social Psychology, 37,* 87–96.

Wiener, M., & Mehrabian, A. (1968). *Language within language: Immediacy, a channel in verbal communication.* New York: Appleton-Century-Crofts.

Willis, F. N., & Hamm, H. K. (1980). The use of interpersonal touch in securing compliance. *Journal of Nonverbal Behavior, 5,* 49–55.

Wilson, S. D. (1979). Eye contact and self-disclosure as a function of interpersonal proximity and eye directional classification (Doctoral dissertation, California School of Professional Psychology, Los Angeles, 1978). *Dissertation Abstracts International, 40,* 1434B-1435B.

Woodall, W. G., & Burgoon, J. K. (1981). The effects of nonverbal synchrony on message comprehension and persuasiveness. *Journal of Nonverbal Behavior, 5,* 207–223.

Word, C. O., Zanna, M. P., & Cooper, J. (1974). The nonverbal mediation of self-fulfilling prophecies in interracial interaction. *Journal of Experimental Social Psychology, 10,* 109–120.

2 Expressive Correlates of Affective States and Traits

Aron Wolfe Siegman
University of Maryland Baltimore County

This chapter discusses the expressive, nonverbal correlates of three affective states: anxiety, depression, and anger. Theoretical discussions of emotions typically are concerned with fear rather than with anxiety and with sadness rather than with depression (e.g., Ekman, 1972, 1978). Unfortunately, much of the existing research on the expressive correlates of fear and sadness involves feigned, or simulated, emotions that may tell us more about the theatrical stereotypes associated with these emotions than about their veridical correlates. The number of existing studies on the veridical expressive correlates of fear and sadness are limited, in part because of the ethical problems involved in inducing such negative states. By way of contrast, there are many studies on the expressive correlates of anxiety, and fewer, but still a substantial number of studies, on naturally-occurring depression. Whatever the distinction between anxiety and fear may be—which is a matter of considerable debate—no one questions that anxiety is an affective state. The same is true, of course, about depression.

This review begins with a discussion of the nonverbal correlates of anxiety because there are more empirical data on this topic than there are on the nonverbal correlates of the other two affective states. In fact, the information available on the nonverbal correlates of anger is fairly sparse and of recent vintage.

EXPRESSIVE CORRELATES OF ANXIETY

Historical Background

Anxiety, of course, plays a central role in many theories of psychopathology, and its reduction is a major focus of many psychotherapeutic (including behaviorally oriented) interventions. This provided a strong impetus for the scientific investigation of anxiety. With the advent of Clark Hull's (1943) drive reduction approach to learning, anxiety became a subject of interest to general psychology as well. Spence, a student of Hull, conceptualized anxiety in terms of drive, which inspired numerous studies on the effects of anxiety on a wide range of learning tasks. (For a detailed review see Taylor, 1956). The development of the Taylor (1953) Manifest Anxiety Scale (MAS), a paper-and-pencil instrument for the measurement of predispositional, or trait anxiety, virtually initiated a mass production of anxiety studies. Although these factors created a favorable intellectual climate for studies on the nonverbal correlates of anxiety, the more proximate impetus for such studies was the emergence of affordable audiorecording instruments soon after the end of World War II. The availability of these instruments made it possible to carry out what was known at the time as therapy process research. The authors of this research were primarily interested in the effects of different psychotherapeutic interventions and of different therapist-patient relationships on the patient's responses within the therapy session, not just on ultimate therapeutic outcome. It included studies on the effects of different therapist interventions on their patients' anxiety level, which made it necessary to develop reliable and valid indices of moment-to-moment changes in anxiety level, ideally of a nonintrusive character. This, of course, brought into focus the possible use of the nonverbal correlates of anxiety for such assessment purposes.

Any historical discussion of the intellectual climate that fostered an interest in nonverbal behavior must take into account the post-World War II popularity of ethology. Findings on nonverbal communication in lower species in the context of bonding behavior, agonistic behavior, and the expression of affect brought into focus analogical behaviors in humans and their potential phylogenetic origin and biological bases. It should be noted, however, that these speculations about the role of ethology may be more relevant to the *facial* expression of emotion than they are to the *nonverbal* and *vocal* correlates of emotion.

The Voice of Anxiety

There are many more studies on the vocal correlates of anxiety than there are on the nonverbal correlates of anxiety involving body movements and facial expressions. Perhaps this reflects some kind of folk wisdom that anxiety arousal can be most readily detected by carefully monitoring changes in a speaker's voice. On the other hand, it may simply reflect the fact that vocal parameters lend themselves to quantification more readily than facial expression and body movement. There is also a widely held assumption that one's voice, in contrast to one's facial expressions, is not readily controlled. That the vocal channel is *relatively* less controllable and more "leaky" than facial expressions has been demonstrated by Ekman and Friesen (1974). This, however, does not mean that the former is immune from attempts at impression management—but more about this problem later in this chapter.

Anxiety and Disrupted Speech.   One of the first to empirically investigate the effects of anxiety on speech was George Mahl (1956). His working hypothesis was essentially the clinically derived assumption that anxiety has a disruptive effect on the normal flow of speech. In an attempt to quantify this disruptive effect he developed the Speech Disturbance Ratio (SDR), comprising the following categories: repetition (superfluous repetition of one or more words), sentence incompletion or reconstruction (the speaker stops leaving a sentence unfinished or starts it again), omission (the omission of a whole word or part of a word), tongue slip, stutter, intruding incoherent sounds, and "ahs," and their allied hesitation phenomena ("er," "um," etc.).

In a preliminary study, Mahl (1956) divided a series of therapeutic interviews with a single patient into high-anxiety, high-conflict phases versus low-anxiety, low-conflict phases, and found that the former were associated with a significantly higher SDR than the latter. It should be pointed out that for the purpose of categorizing the interviews into high and low conflict and anxiety phases, he used a typescript from which all speech disturbances had been removed. Additional analyses indicated that anxiety had no effect on the occurrence of "ahs" and similar expressions, which led Mahl to remove this category from the SDR. The basic finding of a positive association between anxiety arousal and the SDR was replicated by Kasl and Mahl (1965) with a group of college students, in which anxiety arousal was manipulated by means of a stress interview. Despite an early failure to replicate Mahl's finding (Boomer & Goodrich, 1961), the results of many subsequent studies provide impressive support for the claim that anxiety arousal is associated with an increase in SDR. Furthermore, Mahl's contention that anxiety arousal has no significant effect on the Ah Ratio (or the Filled Pauses Ratio, as it has been referred to by others) has also been corroborated by the results of three independent investigations (Cook, 1969; Feldstein, Brenner, & Jaffe, 1963; Siegman & Pope, 1965a). All three studies experimentally manipulated their subjects' anxiety level by subjecting them to a stress and a control interview. One caveat about this procedure is that it confounds anxiety arousal with interviewer topical focus, for the interviewer's questions in the stress interview typically concern different topical areas than his questions in the control interview. Since there is evidence that the SDR increases as a function of the cognitive difficulty of the task (Siegman, 1978), it is not unreasonable to argue that interviewer topical focus could be a significant source of variance in interviewees' SDR, independent of anxiety arousal. There is, however, at least one study that suggests that there may be a relationship between anxiety arousal and the SDR, independent of topical focus (Pope, Siegman, & Blass, 1970).

Anxiety and the Temporal Pacing of Speech.   In his study on the effects of anxiety on speech within the context of psychotherapeutic interviews, Mahl (1956) looked not only at its effects on speech-disruption but also on silent pauses. He found that the high-anxiety, high-conflict phases were associated with longer silent pauses than were the low-anxiety, low-conflict phases. Mahl did not pursue this issue further in his subsequent studies, but others who did obtained contradictory findings: In some studies anxiety was associated with longer pauses and generally with a slowing down of speech, and in others with the very opposite pattern. These studies are reviewed in some detail because it is hoped they will help us to develop a model that will let us predict when anxiety is likely to have a generally accelerating or decelerating effect on speech.

One of the early experimental investigations of the effects of anxiety arousal on the temporal structure of speech, including the duration of silent pauses, within the context of the initial interview, is by Siegman and Pope (1965a, 1972). Differential anxiety levels were aroused in the interviewees by means of a topical manipulation. Specifically, interviewees were selected so that questions focusing on their family relations would be more anxiety provoking than questions focusing on their school experiences. A post-interview questionnaire revealed that this objective was achieved, although the topical manipulation produced only mild anxiety arousal. The results show that the anxiety-arousing topic, in contrast to the neutral one, was associated with shorter response latencies, fewer and/or shorter silences, and a faster speech rate, altogether with accelerated rather than with decelerated speech. Using a similar experimental paradigm, Feldstein et al. (1963) also found that the anxiety-arousing interview topics were associated with a faster speech rate (or verbal rate, as they refer to it) than the neutral interview topics. Cook (1969) obtained similar results, but only with low trait-anxiety subjects (i.e., subjects obtaining low scores on inventories measuring chronic anxiety level), whereas the opposite trend was obtained with high trait-anxiety subjects. Perhaps beyond a certain optimum level, anxiety no longer accelerates speech but has the opposite effect—a possibiity that is discussed in greater detail later. If this is so, it may explain why the anxiety manipulation in the Cook study did not produce a facilitating, or accelerating effect in the high trait-anxiety subjects, because for them the manipulation may have produced more than the optimum level of anxiety arousal.

One serious problem with the aforementioned studies is that anxiety arousal was achieved via topical manipulation. As suggested earlier, this confounding between anxiety arousal and topical focus presents a serious methodological problem because one cannot be certain that the results of these studies reflect variations in anxiety arousal rather than variations in topical focus. There are, however, other findings indicating that experimentally produced anxiety arousal is in fact associated with an acceleration in verbal tempo independent of topical focus. Perhaps the most convincing evidence comes from a series of word association studies by Kanfer (1958a, 1958b), in which subjects were administered intermittent electric shocks that were preceded by an auditory warning signal. Subjects showed an increase in post-tone speech rate, i.e., in anticipation of the shock, and a decreae in post-shock speech rate, indicating that anxiety arousal has an accelerating effect on speech. These findings are not especially surprising if we think of anxiety arousal in terms of a heightened drive level. Conceptualizing anxiety in terms of drive, Taylor and Spence (Taylor, 1951;

Taylor & Spence, 1952) hypothesized that anxiety arousal would facilitate simple conditioning and simple serial learning and would interfere with complex serial learning. This hypothesis is based on the Hullian postulate that response strength is a multiplicative function of habit strength and drive. Thus, anxiety arousal should facilitate learning in situations in which the dominant response is the correct one, that is in simple learning tasks, and impede the learning process in situations involving multiple conflicting response tendencies, that is complex learning tasks. The results of a number of investigations have confirmed this hypothesis (e.g., Montague, 1953; Siegman, 1957). By the same token, anxiety arousal should accelerate speech tempo, provided the speaker is not faced with conflicting response tendencies.

Although it is clear that anxiety arousal can have a facilitating and accelerating effect on speech, it is equally true that it can have the opposite effect as well. We have already discussed Mahl's (1956) study, in which he found that anxiety arousal was associated with an increase in silent pauses in speech. We now discuss a number of other studies that found anxiety arousal to be associated with a slowing down effect on speech, and attempt to develop a model allowing us to predict when anxiety is likely to have an accelerating effect and when it is likely to have a decelerating effect.

The Inverted U Hypothesis.   In discussing the energizing-facilitating effects of arousal on behavior, a number of authors have argued that this effect is likely to reach an asymptote with increasing levels of arousal, and that eventually it reverses itself (Duffy, 1962; Fiske & Maddi, 1961; Hebb, 1955). If this is indeed the case, then even if mild and moderate levels of anxiety arousal tend to accelerate speech, very high levels of anxiety arousal should be associated with slower speech, more pauses, and so forth. This hypothesis, although reasonable from a commonsense and perhaps even a theoretical viewpoint, is difficult to test empirically. It is difficult to calibrate levels of anxiety arousal and to identify in advance precisely which anxiety levels will produce a facilitating effect and which will produce the reverse effect. The failure to obtain the hypothesized asymptote or reversal in any particular study can always be attributed, post hoc, to insufficent arousal.

Perhaps the most clear-cut evidence in favor of the inverted *U* hypothesis comes from a study by Fenz and Epstein (1962) in which the authors obtained stories in response to TAT-like stimulus cards from a group of novice parachutists on their day of jumping and from a control group. In addition to the control group of nonparachutists, the parachutists served as their own controls by responding to the cards on a non-jumping day. Subjects always responded to three kinds of cards: neutral (no relevance to parachute jumping), low relevance, and high relevance. The data clearly suggest that anxiety arousal has an activating effect on response latency. Conditions that can be assumed to have aroused mild-to-moderate anxiety were associated with a decrease in response latency, or RT. On the other hand, the one condition that probably aroused very high anxiety levels, namely, the high-relevance cards on the day of jumping, was associated with a steep increase in RT. Pauses in the parachutists' stories on the day of jumping also showed an activation effect, with lower silence ratios in the low-relevance than the neutral cards, and higher silence ratios in the high-relevance than the low-relevance cards. There were no significant differences in the control group. By and large, the results of the Fenz and Epstein study support the inverted *U* hypothesis, as far as anxiety and temporal indices of speech are concerned.

Audience Anxiety and Speech.   Public speaking is an anxiety-arousing situation for many people, and its effects on speech have been investigated in a series of studies by Levin and Paivio and their associates (e.g., Levin & Silverman, 1965; Paivio, 1965; Reynolds & Paivio, 1968). Considering the effects of situational anxiety on speech summarized earlier in this chapter, one would expect public speaking, to the extent that it is in fact anxiety arousing, to be associated with speech disturbances as measured by Mahl's SDR. Second, public speaking should be associated with an accelerated speech tempo if the speaking task is a simple one, and with a reduced speech tempo if the task is a complex one. A review of the literature (Siegman, in press) indicates that high-audience, or public-speaking, anxiety is associated with more frequent and longer silent pauses even if the speech task is a fairly simple one. Perhaps people who know that they become very anxious when they have to speak in public deliberately adopt a slow and careful speech style so as to reduce potential speech disruptions to a minimum. It should be noted that, of the several investigators who looked specifically at the impact of audience anxiety on Mahl's SDR or on its separate major component categories, none obtained the expected disruptive effect (Geer, 1966; Levin & Silverman, 1965; Paivio, 1965; Reynolds & Paivio, 1968). Considering the consistency with which situational anxiety has been found to be associated with an increase in the SDR, this is a rather puzzling finding. All the findings, however, fall into place if we assume that people who suffer extreme stage fright try to cover up their disability by adopting a deliberate, slow and careful speech style. This might also explain why public speaking apparently is associated with reduced productivity (Levin, Baldwin, Gallwey, & Paivio, 1960), rather than with an increase in productivity, as was the case in the Siegman and Pope (1972) interview study. To the extent that a speaker wishes to cover up his anxiety, he or she is, of course, well advised to curtail the length of his or her speech.

Deceptive Speech.   On the assumption that, at least as far as most individuals are concerned, lying is a stressful and anxiety-arousing experience, this research should be of relevance to how anxiety arousal affects the vocal and temporal aspects of speech. The assumption that lying is anxiety arousing for most people has in fact informed many of the hypotheses regarding the nonverbal correlates of deceptive communications. The findings have been summarized in a comprehensive review by Zuckerman, DePaulo, and Rosenthal (1981), and they have been brought up to date in a subsequent review article by Zuckerman and Driver (chapter 5). The conclusions regarding the effects of deception on noncontent, or paralinguistic, speech variables are based on a combination of results obtained in 11 to 17 independent studies, depending on the variable being investigated, except pitch, for which there were only 4 independent studies. Compared to truthful communications, deceptive ones are relatively short, high pitched, contain many speech disruptions, as indexed by Mahl's SDR (1956), and many hesitations (ah's, etc.), with the latter being more strongly and more significantly associated with lying than any other nonverbal measure except pupil dilation. On first glance this is somewhat surprising because other studies have failed to reveal a significant relationship between anxiety and the frequency of ah's and similar hesitation phenomena. As far as the temporal aspect of speech is concerned, no clear-cut pattern seemed to emerge from the various studies. It is possible, however, that for a variety of reasons, these deception studies cannot provide us with critical information about the effects of anxiety arousal on nonverbal behavior. First, in almost all of these studies the subjects are instructed by the experimenter to give truthful responses to some questions and to lie in response to others. To the extent that subjects were instructed by their experimenter to lie, they should have little reason to be anxious about lying, or so it would seem on first glance.

A second problem is that in many of these deception studies, the deceptive communications were obtained from subjects talking into a tape recorder or to a video camera rather than addressing another person. Again, the relevance of such studies to naturalistic lying, which typically is face-to-face—a condition that may be essential for producing the anxiety arousal and the other negative affects usually associated with lying—is open to debate. A third problem is that in many of the deception studies the participants are required to spontaneously make up a fictitious response. The making up of such fictitious responses is cognitively more demanding than simply telling the truth. This may account for the finding in some of the deception studies that lying rather than the truthful response, was associated with slower speech. In fact, when Zuckerman and Driver grouped the deception studies into those in which subjects had no opportunity to plan and rehearse their deceptive communications and into those in which the subjects were given an opportunity for such pre-planning, it was found that in the former set of studies there was a significant negative correlation between lying and speech-rate, whereas in the latter there was a significant positive correlation between the two. A recent study (Reynolds, Siegman, & Demorest, 1983) tried to assess the temporal pacing of speech in deceptive communications using a design that is not subject to any of the above strictures. The lying was unfeigned, it caused subjects to be fairly anxious (it was not sanctioned by the experimenter), it was face-to-face and not particularly cognitively demanding. Nevertheless, lying was found to be associated with relatively long response latencies, relatively frequent and long pauses, and a relatively slow speech rate. The authors suggest that the subjects of this study found themselves in a conflict situation about whether to respond truthfully or to lie, and that this approach-avoidance conflict reversed the otherwise positive association between anxiety arousal and speech. Furthermore, what was noted earlier within the context of audience anxiety, namely, that individuals who suffer from such anxiety frequently try to cover up their anxiety symptoms and in so doing overshoot the mark, may be of relevance in deceitful communications as well. People are likely to want to cover up the nonverbal manifestations of their deceitfulness, and in so doing overshoot the mark. Of course, from a lie detection point of view, it does not matter whether the individual speaks more quickly or more slowly than usual—as long as the deviation is an indication that the person is lying.

At this point, it should be fairly obvious that there are a number of factors that can reverse the otherwise accelerating effect of anxiety arousal on speech including intensity of anxiety level, approach-avoidance conflicts, and the desire to cover up one's anxiety arousal.

On the Controllability of Expressive Behavior. One other finding that was obtained in the deception study previously cited is relevant to the issue of whether people can control, or manage, the expressive correlates of their affective experiences. It has been claimed that whereas verbal behavior is a product of cognitive activity, expressive nonverbal behavior represents a direct expression of affective experience, and therefore is relatively free from cognitive control (Zajonc, 1980). Ekman and Friesen (1974) have argued that although people can readily control the facial expressions that are associated with different affective experiences, it is considerably more difficult to control the vocal characteristics and body movements that are associated with affective experiences. It may very well be that people are more cognizant of and have more experience in controlling their facial expression as compared to other expressive behavior, but this does not make the latter inherently less controllable. In fact, there is evidence that expressive vocal behavior can be readily controlled. A study by Feldstein and Sloan (1984) has shown that people are aware of and can readily control their temporal pacing of speech. In this study a group of extraverts and introverts were asked to speak as they normally do, as extraverts do, and as introverts do. Both extraverts and introverts decreased their pause durations and increased their speech rates when imitating extraverts, and increased their pause durations and decreased their speech rates when imitating introverts, although the extraverts were better at this "acting" task than the introverts. Apparently, people not only have fairly clear stereotypes of the temporal pacing of speech on the part of introverts and extraverts, but they can also readily manage their own pacing of speech to match their stereotypes. This, of course, does not mean that they are equally capable of managing their temporal pacing of speech under conditions of affective arousal, but there is evidence that this, too, is the case. As part of the aforementioned deception study, Siegman and Reynolds (1983) investigated the relationship between personality variables and lying skills, with the latter operationally defined as the ability to control one's temporal pacing of speech so that it would be nearly the same when lying as when telling the truth. There were three indices for measuring the participants' lying skills, based respectively on their reaction times, silent pauses, and speech rates when lying as compared to their truthful responses. The lower the discrepancy, the better one's lying skill. Of particular interest was the relationship between Snyder's (1974) Self-Monitoring Scale (SMS) and lying skills, because this scale was designed to measure the ability to control, or to regulate, one's expressive, self-presentation behavior. Although subjects' overall SMS scores correlated significantly with only one out of the three indices measuring lying skills, their scores on two SMS subscales—Extraversion and Acting Skills—correlated significantly with all three indices designed to measure lying skills. Specifically, extraverts and subjects with good acting skills were more successful liars than introverts and individuals with poor acting skills. These findings suggest that people can and do regulate their expressive nonverbal behavior, even when emotionally aroused, and that this ability involves specific social skills. It would seem that what Ekman (1972, 1978) proposed about the expression of emotion in the face—that such expressions reflect biologically programmed responses that can be modified by cultural display rules and personal learning experiences—is probably true of expressive behavior in general.

Trait Anxiety and Speech.   A number of investigators have looked at the relationship between dispositional anxiety, or trait anxiety, as measured by Taylor's MAS and similar measures, and some of the speech parameters discussed earlier, and have drawn implications about the effects of anxiety on speech. It is by no means clear, however, that one can generalize from trait anxiety to state anxiety. In fact the evidence indicates that the two have different effects on a number of speech parameters. For example, although situational anxiety and stress have consistently been found to be associated with speech disruptions, as measured by Mahl's SDR, there is no evidence for a similar positive correlation between trait anxiety and SDR (Cook, 1969; Kasl & Mahl, 1965; Siegman & Pope, 1972). As far as the relationship between trait anxiety and the temporal pacing of speech is concerned, the evidence is somewhat contradictory and puzzling. A review article by Murray (1971) cites 6 studies that correlated measures of trait anxiety and response latency. All 6 correlations were negative, 3 significantly so. Given this negative correlation between trait anxiety and response latency—which is consistent with a drive conceptualization of anxiety—one would expect a similar negative correlation between trait anxiety and within-response silent pauses, because the evidence suggests a moderate positive correlation between RT and within-response silent pauses (e.g., Siegman, 1979). In our laboratory, however, trait anxiety consistently correlates positively with the duration of within-response silent pauses, a finding that has been confirmed by Helfrich and Dahme (1974) in Germany, although they suggest that this correlation obtains only in high anxiety-arousing situations. To complicate matters further, Preston and Gardner (1967) obtained *negative* correlations between various indices of trait anxiety and the frequency of pauses 1.5 seconds and over, but also *positive* correlations between the same indices and the average duration of all pauses 1.5 seconds and over.

These findings may not be as paradoxical as they appear to be at first glance if we assume that high trait-anxiety scorers pause relatively infrequently, but when they do pause, it is for a relatively long period of time. As pointed out earlier, if we think of anxiety in terms of arousal and drive level, it should not be surprising that high trait-anxiety scorers respond more quickly and with fewer silent pauses than do low trait-anxiety scorers. Although under these circumstances, high trait-anxiety individuals should also exhibit more nonfluencies than low trait-anxiety individuals, given their lack of planning time, this is not the case. Perhaps one strategy that high trait-anxiety individuals have learned to use in order to avoid excessive nonfluencies is to do their planning during a few, but relatively long, silent pauses. In other words, the relatively long pauses of high trait-anxiety speakers may serve to compensate for their relatively short latencies and generally accelerated speech tempo under conditions of high-anxiety arousal. Scherer (1979), on the other hand, suggests that high trait-anxiety scorers are excessively sensitive to other people's evaluations, and that their accelerated speech tempo represents an attempt to avoid negative evaluations from their listeners. Of course, by the same token, they should avoid engaging in long silent pauses. According to Scherer, they fail to do this for one of two reasons. One reason is that because of their sensitivity to listener evaluations, unexpected listener signals such as a frown of doubt or disapproval interferes with their ongoing thought processes, requiring long silent pauses to reorient and restructure their cognitive planning. An alternative explanation is in terms of cognitive overload and the compensatory mechanism mentioned earlier. To test these alternate explanations one would need fairly complex interaction oriented designs. So much seems fairly clear, however, that in addition to the factors mentioned earlier in this chapter as moderators between anxiety arousal and speech, one also needs to consider the individual's learned strategies to cope with anxiety arousal and stress.

Anxiety and Speech: Some General Observations.   In the early literature on anxiety and speech, especially in the clinical literature, it was assumed that the effects of anxiety on speech are exclusively of a disruptive and disorganizing nature. If the authors of this literature had major reservations about this generalization, they certainly were not very explicit about them. The experimental data indicate that the picture is much more complex than is suggested by the aforementioned literature. In fact, conceptualizing anxiety in terms of drive and arousal, it was suggested that anxiety arousal per se is associated with an accelerated speech pattern. There are, however, a number of factors that can moderate or even reverse this relationship. For example, one implication of conceptualizing anxiety in terms of drive, in the Hullian sense, is that the effects of anxiety on speech are a function of task difficulty, a variable that has all but been ignored in the literature on anxiety and speech. Clearly, we need more studies to clarify the effects of task difficulty, of anxiety level, and of the interaction between these two variables on speech.

Another factor affecting the relationship is the level of anxiety arousal, with very high levels reversing the relationship from a positive to a negative one. Also, anxiety arousal, even in mild or moderate degrees, is likely to decelerate rather than accelerate speech if the anxiety produces an approach-avoidance conflict. Also, for a variety of reasons, people may want to cover up the fact that they are anxious. Under such circumstances, anxiety arousal may produce paradoxical behavior, i.e., a deliberate and slow pacing of speech, relatively few speech disruptions, and reduced productivity. The very intensity of subject's anxiety arousal may motivate the subject to hide it, which may be yet another reason why the usual positive relationship between anxiety arousal and speech tempo tends to break down under extreme arousal.

Finally, any model for the effects of anxiety arousal on speech should allow for individual differences, that is, for different learned response tendencies to anxiety. There is evidence that although the speech behavior of chronically anxious individuals parallels the speech behavior produced by situational anxiety arousal in some respects (e.g., short response latencies), there are also exceptions to this parallelism. First, the speech of chronically anxious individuals apparently tends to be punctuated by relatively long silent pauses, and second, it has no more speech disruptions than the speech of nonanxious individuals. It was suggested that perhaps chronically anxious individuals have learned to compensate for their accelerated speech tempo with few but relatively long silent pauses so as to avoid too many speech disruptions.

Other Expressive Correlates of Anxiety

Scherer (1981) has reviewed the effects of stress on vocal behavior. Although not all the studies reviewed in that chapter are of relevance to the effects of anxiety, some clearly are. An example of the latter are the naturalistic studies involving air-to-ground communication in aviation and space flights under dangerous conditions. These studies show an increase of fundamental frequency (F_0), which is perceived as pitch, with increasing danger. In fact, according to Scherer, the only solid finding, as far as the effect of stress on vocal behavior is concerned, is that stress is associated with an increase in fundamental frequency. But even as far as this relationship is concerned, there are considerable individual differences. Some individuals respond with a decrease in fundamental frequency even in conditions where one can assume extreme anxiety. Scherer suggests that these individual differences can be accounted for in terms of personality variables. For example, he cites the results of a pilot study on the effects of viewing slides of accidents on fundamental frequency. Only repressors (who tend to verbally deny being stressed but generally show higher autonomic reactivity) showed the expected increase in F_0. There was no such effect among the sensitizers (who verbalize their stress openly but show lower physiological reactivity). Apparently, then, the effect of stress and anxiety on vocal behavior is a function of one's coping mechanism.

It is widely assumed that anxiety is associated with an increase in fidgeting and motor activity. There are only few studies on the effects of anxiety on motor behavior, probably because of the difficulties involved in quantifying body movements. Nevertheless, there is one study that seems to support the assumed relationship between anxiety and fidgetiness. Ekman and Friesen (1972a) have distinguished between three categories of hand movement: emblems, illustrators, and adaptors. An emblem can usually be replaced with a word or two, or perhaps a phrase, and is known as such to all the members of a culture. For example, the symbol used by hitchhikers when they solicit a ride is an emblem. Illustrators are movements directly tied to speech. They illustrate what is being said verbally. Adaptors are movements used to satisfy bodily or emotional needs. Scratching or playing with one's ring are examples of adaptors. Ekman and Friesen (1972b) found a significant positive correlation (.38) between the anxiety scales on the Overall and Gorham (1962) Brief Psychiatric Rating Scale and self-adaptor activity.

Expressive Correlates of Depression

Vocal Correlates of Depression

Although there are fewer studies on the nonverbal correlates of depression than there are on the nonverbal correlates of anxiety, the results of the depression studies are more consistent than are the results of the anxiety studies. Given the general motor retardation of depressed persons, one would expect the temporal pacing of their speech to reflect this general retardation. Furthermore, given their reduced energy level and social withdrawal, one would also expect them to speak less (i.e., to be less voluble) than nondepressed individuals. The reduced level of social involvement would also lead one to expect less mutual gazing on the part of depressed than nondepressed individuals. Finally, one would expect fewer gestures and slower body movements. By and large, the empirical investigations have confirmed these expectations, which is not terribly surprising because, at least in part, the diagnosis of depression is based on these very signs, i.e., low productivity, slow speech and avoidance of mutual gaze, and few and slow movements. Perhaps what needs explanation are the negative findings. This is discussed later in this chapter.

A study by Kanfer (1960) is one of the first to yield empirical information on the speech rate associated with depression. In a group of patients with varying psychiatric diagnoses, Kanfer obtained a significant negative correlation between their scores on the Depression scale of the MMPI and their speech rates. In another early study, Aronson and Weintraub (1967, 1972) compared depressed patients with other patient groups, and with normal controls, on several content-oriented as well as extralinguistic-speech variables. The depressed group could be clearly distinguished from all others on the basis of their slower speech rate, long silent pauses, and reduced overall productivity levels. Aronson and Weintraub (1972) point out, however, that "agitated depressives differ from other depressives in the direction of their scores. The agitated depressives demonstrate a noticeably higher rate and high quantity of speech" (p. 275). A study conducted in England by Hinchliffe, Lancashire, and Roberts (1971), comparing 10 depressed patients and 10 controls, confirmed the Aronson and Weintraub findings, as far as speech rate is concerned. However, these authors also report 3 of the depressed patients spoke unusually fast. They do not, however, give any further clues as to a possible reason for these exceptions.

A study by Pope, Blass, Siegman, and Raher (1970) examined the effects of depression on the temporal pacing of speech in 6 psychiatric, hospitalized patients. Each morning, for the entire period of their hospitalization, these patients spoke into a tape recorder, describing their experiences during the preceding day. A team of specially trained nurses made daily ratings of each patient, which included a number of depression scales. The audio-recordings obtained from each patient during the 8 most depressed days were compared with those made during the 8 least depressed days, on a number of temporal indices. The expectation that the speech samples obtained during the high-depression days would be associated with slower speech rates than would those obtained during the low-depression days was fully confirmed. A person's speech rate is a function of his or her articulation rate and the frequency and/or duration of his or her silent pauses. The relatively slow speech rate of the depressed patient could, therefore, be a function of a slowing down in articulation rate, or of an increase in the frequency and/or duration of silent pauses, or both. The general motor retardation of the depressed patients could slow down their articulation rates, and the intrusion of depressed thoughts could be responsible for an increase in silent pauses. However, in this study, it was found that only the index measuring relatively long pauses (2 sec and over), but not the index measuring relatively brief pauses and articulation rate, discriminated between the high- and low-depression days. It would seem, therefore, that the intrusion of depressed thoughts, rather than the slowing down of articulation, is responsible for the depressed patient's slow speech rate. Moreover, the patients' Filled Pauses, or "Ah" ratios, which can be taken as an index of cautious and hesitant speech (Goldman-Eisler, 1968), did not discriminate between the depressed and nondepressed speech samples. Thus, the relatively slow speech rates during states or experiences of depression are not an indication of cautious speech, but instead seem to reflect the instrusion of distracting, depressed thoughts. Finally, in this study depression had no significant effect on the Mahl's Speech Disturbance (or non-Ah) ratio, which is an index of anxiety arousal (Siegman & Pope, 1965a). It should be noted that in contrast to previous studies that used dialogues, the study by Pope and associates (Pope et al., 1970) involved monologues. This is significant in that it rules out the possibility that the increase in silent pauses and the resultant slow speech rate of the depressed patients are merely a consequence of their lack of social responsiveness or lack of concern with being interrupted.

The evidence is less satisfactory as far as depression and verbal productivity are concerned. The expected inverse relationship between depression and verbal productivity was confirmed by the Aronson and Weintraub (1972) study, and at a lesser level of significance, by the longitudinal study conducted by Ellgring, Wagner, and Clarke (1980). In the latter study, the productivity level of the depressed patients increased as their depression decreased, the difference being significant at less than the 5% level in a one-tailed test. However, in a study by Rutter and Stephenson (1972a), the depressed patients were more productive than the nondepressed psychiatric controls, and less productive than the non-psychiatric controls, with neither of these differences being significant. More about this study is discussed later in this section.

With the exception of Scherer and his co-workers, very few, if any, investigators have looked systematically at the effect of depression on loudness and pitch. Scherer (1981) reports that depressive patients speak with higher F_0 and higher proportion of energy above 500 Hz at admission to a psychiatric hospital as compared to the time of their discharge, when they feel much less depressed.

A number of investigators have reported that depression has the effect of reducing the level of eye contact during interviews and conversations, apparently both when speaking and when listening (Hinchliffe, Lancashire, & Roberts, 1970, 1971; Rutter & Stephenson, 1972a). Findings reported by Ellgring et al., (1980) also suggest that depression is associated with reduced eye contact, although their evidence is less than overwhelming. Theirs is a longitudinal investigation of the speech and gaze behavior of 5 male and 4 female depressed patients, all of whom were considered to have an endogenous depression and showed considerable improvement in their subjective state of well being during their treatment. A comparison of the interviews conducted when the patients first came for treatment, with subsequent interviews conducted when they felt much improved, showed that for the group as a whole there was an increase in eye contact over these two periods. The difference was significant at less than the 5% level in a one-tailed test, which seems justified given previous findings. The authors point out, however, that not all patients showed the expected change in eye contact. In fact, 3 out of the 9 patients *decreased* their level of eye contact from the depressed to the nondepressed period. The authors speculate that this was because of these patients' high initial level of eye contact. In fact, however, this explanation applies only to two of the three exceptions. The one clear-cut exception to the above findings is a follow-up study by Rutter and Stephenson (1972b) that failed to confirm their earlier finding of reduced eye contact in depressed patients. On first glance, then, it would appear that the evidence for reduced eye contact in depression is not as strong as it is for a slow speech rate in these patients. Such a conclusion, however, may be premature given the very limited number of studies involving eye contact. Moreover, the one study (Rutter & Stephenson, 1972a) with clear-cut negative findings is suspect since in that study there was also no evidence for depression influencing speech rate. In fact, in that study, the depressed patients were also *more* productive than the controls, although the difference was not significant. One cannot help but wonder about the nature of this depressed sample, and whether it did not include a significant number of agitated patients.

Although there are not too many studies on gestures and body movements in depression, the results of the available studies are clearly consistent with expectations. Ekman and Friesen (1972b) report a negative correlation between depressed patients' scores on the depressive mood subscale of the Overall and Gorham Brief Psychiatric Rating Scale and the frequency of illustrative gestures in a psychiatric interview ($r = -.51$ at admission and $-.39$ at discharge). Furthermore, there was an increase in illustrators from admission to discharge, but this difference was significant only for the psychotic depressives, and not for the neurotic depressives. Although Ekman and Friesen (1972b) apparently found no relationship between depression and self-adaptor activity, Freedman (1972) reports a very high level of such activity in depressives, although he refers to it as body focused activity. Perhaps the most impressive findings on depression and nonverbal behavior are reported in a study by Fisch, Frey, and Hirsbrunner (1983). Thirteen patients (9 female, 4 male) with a diagnosis of a primary affective disorder, retarded subtypes, were interviewed on admission, when they were rated as highly depressed, and upon discharge, when they were rated as recovered. All interviews were videotaped. The movements of head, trunk, shoulders, upper arms, hands, upper legs, and feet were transcribed as a series of positions over time for the first 3 minutes of each doctor-patient interview. The data matrix yields a number of parameters, including mobility, complexity and dynamic activation. Mobility is defined as the sum of time periods when at least one part of the body is in motion. Complexity indicates the degree to which the various parts of the body are simultaneously involved in movement activity. Dynamic activation measures the swiftness with which movement shifts to different levels of activation or deactivation. For a more detailed description of this objective method for the description and quantification of body movement, the reader is referred to Hirsbrunner, Frey, and Crawford (in press). The results of this study revealed a significant increase in all three parameters as the patients emerged out of their depression. Moreover, there was a very strong relation between the patients' complexity scores in the second interview and the doctors' ratings of the patients' recovery ($r = .85$, $p < .01$). When the patients were grouped according to four different levels of recovery, average complexity scores increased from one category of recovery to the next in steps of almost equal size. It should be noted, however, that in relation to all three parameters, there were considerable individual differences. For example, there were patients who, even in depression, spent more than 50% of the observation time in motion, and there were patients who spent less than 25% of the time in motion even when they had recovered. Clearly, it is the within-subjects design of this study that accounts for the impressive findings. Of interest is the finding that the doctors' mobility and complexity of movement also increased significantly from the first to the second interview. However, the negligible correlations between the doctors' and the patients' behavior indicate that the increase in the patients' activity had little relation to the increased activity of the doctors.

Clearly, more studies are needed on the expressive correlates of depression. However, it is important that such studies use sufficiently large samples and that the nature of the patient's depression be carefully identified. Current clinical thinking distinguishes between unipolar versus bipolar depression and between exogenous versus endogenous depression. These different types of depression may be associated with different clinical symptoms. They may also have different expressive correlates. Evidence already exists that some of the expressive vocal correlates of depression, such as a slow speech rate and a low productivity level, do not apply to agitated depressives (Ellgring et al., 1980; Starkweather, 1967). The same may be true of the other expressive behaviors as well. On the whole, expressive behavior seems to be an exceedingly good index of patients' level of depression, as determined by psychiatrists' judgments, provided one is dealing with a clinically homogeneous group. Suffice it to cite the Fisch, Frey, and Hirsbrunner (1983) study, in which an index of the complexity of the patients' movements correlated .85 with their recovery from depression, as determined by their psychiatrists' clinical judgments. Finally, there is evidence to suggest that changes in expressive behavior actually precede clinical improvements (e.g., Ellgring et al., 1980).

EXPRESSIVE CORRELATES OF ANGER

Compared to anxiety, and even depression, there are very few studies on the expressive correlates of spontaneous anger. Even in the days when psychologists showed little reluctance to experimentally create anxiety, they apparently were reluctant to create depression or anger, even in the absence of American Psychological Association guidelines. Naturalistically occurring depression provided the opportunity to investigate the nonverbal correlates of that affective state but anger is too fleeting an experience for careful laboratory study. With the exception of about 3 or 4 studies, the early investigations on the expressive correlates of anger involve feigned or simulated anger. The results of such studies are open to the criticism that they may reflect theatrical stereotypes rather than veridical correlates of anger. The handful of exceptions are not very helpful either because the findings are based on clinical judgments rather than on careful measurements and/or involve single subjects. Nevertheless, these findings, which have been reviewed by Scherer (1981), should be summarized, even if only briefly. They consistently show that anger is associated with an increase in speech rate, loudness, and pitch. The last is of special interest, because it represents the only data available on pitch.

New information on the expressive correlates of anger has become available over the past 2 decades as a result of the research on the Type A behavior pattern (TABP). The TABP has been defined as an action-emotion complex consisting of hard-driving job involvement, competitiveness, time urgency, hostility, and a low threshhold for anger (Friedman & Rosenman, 1974; Rosenman, 1978), and has been shown to be an independent risk factor for coronary heart disease (Rosenman, Friedman, Straus, Wurm, Kositchek, Hahn, & Werthessen, 1964; Rosenman, Brand, Jenkins, Friedman, Straus, & Wurm, 1975). The TABP can be assessed by means of either objective paper-and-pencil questionnaires, the most important of which appears to be the Jenkins Activity Survey (JAS) (Jenkins, Rosenman, & Friedman, 1967), or a structured interview (SI) (Chesney, Eagleston, & Rosenman, 1980; Rosenman, 1978). At best, the two (i.e., the JAS and the SI) correlate only about .4 (Siegman, Feldstein, Barkley, Simpson, & Kobren, 1984) and there is evidence to suggest that the SI is a better predictor of CHD than the JAS (Dembroski & MacDougall, 1982).

The questions that comprise the SI focus on the behaviors that constitute the TABP, such as ambition, competitiveness, impatience, and a low threshold for anger. What distinguishes the SI from a conventional clinical interview is that in the SI the questions are asked in a challenging and provocative manner (Chesney et al., 1980). The determination of a person's behavior pattern is based not so much on the content of one's responses to the SI questions as it is on one's expressive behavior, or stylistics. Factor analyses of the SI have shown that a single factor consisting of the respondents' vocal stylistics and the clinical ratings of the respondents' potential for hostility and anger account for over half of the variance of the SI-derived behavior type scores (Musante, MacDougall, Dembroski, & Van Horn, 1983). Given that both the potential for hostility and anger and speech stylistics define the factor that accounts for most of the variance of the SI-derived Type A behavior pattern, it would seem that of the various components of the TABP (i.e., competitiveness, time urgency, job involvement, etc.), it is the potential for hostility and anger that may account for the Type A's unique speech style. Support for this hypothesis comes from a study conducted by Siegman and associates (Siegman, Feldstein, Barkley, Simpson & Kobren, 1984).

In this study, 85 undergraduates, 43 males and 42 females, were administered the SI, which served as the basis for assigning each participant a potential for hostility and anger score (Dembroski & MacDougall, 1983), and for determining each participant's speech style in response to challenge and provocation. Additionally, a conventional clinical interview provided the basis for determining the participants' speech styles in a nonchallenging situation. The participants' responses in both interviews were scored for the following stylistic variables: average response latencies, or RTs, average duration of within response silent pauses, PCR, which is an index of speech rate (Feldstein, 1976), frequency of simultaneous interruptive speech, and loudness, with all but the latter computer scored. In the challenging and provocative interview (i.e., in the SI), males with high potential for hostility and anger scores spoke more loudly, more quickly, and interrupted their interviewer more often than did low-anger scorers. It is of interest to note that respondents with high potential for anger scores interrupted their interviewer more often than low scorers even in the nonchallenging interview (Table 2.1). The speech correlates of anger arousal[1] in males, especially the loud and accelerated speech style, are exactly what one would expect on the basis of previous findings with simulated anger. However, these expressive correlates of anger arousal apparently are attenuated in females (Table 2.1). Although anger arousal raised the level of loudness in both males and females, its accelerating effect on speech was limited to males. Given our cultural norms, which expect women to control their anger, it is not surprising that the expressive vocal correlates of anger are less pronounced in females than in males. It must be remembered that in addition to their expressive functions, nonverbal cues also serve communicative as well as regulatory functions (Siegman, 1978). Speakers can either amplify or attenuate the expressive manifestations of their anger, depending on the impression that they wish to communicate to the listener. In any one specific interaction, it is most difficult, if not impossible, to disentangle the different functions of nonverbal behavior.

In addition to potential for anger scores, the participants were also assigned covert anger, or anger-in scores, according to criteria developed by Dembroski and MacDougall (1983). The correlations between the participants' anger-in scores and their vocal behavior in the challenging and nonchallenging interview, indicate that the associations between anger arousal and speech that have been

---

[1]The participants indicated that they felt more angry in the challenging interview (the SI) than in the nonchallenging, clinical interview. The findings, then, indicate how individuals with a propensity for anger and hostility (trait) respond to anger arousal (state).

TABLE 2.1

Correlations Between Male and Female Interviewees' Anger and Hostility Scores and Their Vocal Behavior in the SI and a Clinical Interview

Anger and Hostility Measures	Sex	Vocal Indices[a] in SI					Vocal Indices[a] in Clinical Interview				
		APD	Lat	PCR	FISS	Loudness	APD	Lat	PCR	FISS	Loudness
Potential for anger and hostility	M	-118	-136	348*	396**	373**	-118	058	167	296*	443**
	F	-142	-071	150	-078	309*	-274+	-198	164	123	142
Anger-in	M	006	-013	-131	-359	076	-051	-177	-071	-183	-286+
	F	098	-039	-061	005	-120	-103	038	066	-349*	-185

[a]The legend for the vocal indices is: APD = average pause duration, Lat = latency, PCR = proportionality constant ratio (a speech rate index), and FISS = frequency of interruptive simultaneous speech.
+p < .10 *p < .05 **p < .01

noted thus far are limited to overt anger, and do not hold for covert anger, or anger-in. In fact, there were significant negative correlations between anger-in and frequency of interruptions for both males (in the challenging interview) and females (in the nonchallenging interview). Also, in the nonchallenging interview, males with high anger-in scores spoke more softly than low scorers (Table 1). By and large, the speech style associated with anger-in was in the opposite direction from that associated with anger-out. There are two ways that one can interpret these findings. One is basically that anger manifests itself in a loud, accelerated, and interruptive speech style. However, such behavioral manifestations can be inhibited, and this is what we see in covert anger, or anger-in. Alternatively, it can be argued that loud and accelerated speech is no more a direct manifestation of anger arousal than is a more subdued speech style; each simply represents a different coping mechanism with anger. According to this print of view, expressive behavior—vocal or otherwise—is not to be seen as an immediate manifestation of affective experiences, unencumbered by cognitive processes, but rather as the manifestation of an individual's coping style. In fact, there is evidence to suggest that this is so not only on the behavioral level but on the physiological level as well. Thus, Diamond (1982) cites evidence that overt anger, or anger-out, and covert anger, or anger-in, are associated with different cardiovascular responses, with the cardiovascular correlates of covert anger resembling those of anxiety and fear more than those of overt anger. These data suggest that even the physiological correlates of anger may reflect one's coping strategies, which influence one's affective experiences on the most fundamental level.

The Facial Expression of Anger

Ekman (1972, 1978) has identified a specific set of facial expressions associated with anger that distinguish it from other affective experiences. It should be noted, however, that with one exception the studies by Ekman on the facial expression of affect involve feigned affect. In one study using an experimental manipulation of affect, the affect involved was fear not anger (Ekman, 1972). Nevertheless, a study by Ekman, Levenson, and Friesen (1983) has exceedingly important implications for understanding the relationship of expressive behavior and affective experiences. In this study professional actors and scientists were instructed (1) to construct the facial stereotypes that in previous studies were found to be associated with anger, fear, sadness, happiness, surprise, and disgust, and (2) to relive a past experience involving each of these experiences. The dependent variables were various indices of autonomic nervous system (ANS) activity, including heart rate and finger temperature. Heart rate discriminated between the negative affects of fear and anger on the one hand and happiness on the other, and finger temperture discriminated between anger and fear, with higher temperature readings in the anger, rather than in the fear, condition. These findings challenge the widely accepted notion that the ANS correlates of the different affective experiences, such as anger, fear and happiness, are essentially the same and that the phenomenological distinctions between emotions reflect secondary cognitive rather basic physiological processes (Schachter & Singer, 1962). Of course, data challenging this assumption and indicating that the different emotions, and sometimes the very same emotion, are associated with different ANS correlates depending on one's coping strategy, have been around for some time (Ax, 1953; Funkelstein, King, & Drolette, 1954; for a summary, see Diamond, 1982). The recent findings by Ekman and his associates merely confirm the earlier findings.

The novel and exciting feature of these recent findings by Ekman et al. (1983) is that the conscious manipulation of facial expressions produces ANS correlates paralleling those associated with subjective emotional experiences. It suggests that expressive behavior should be viewed not as an indirect index of one's affective state, but rather as an integral part of it. From an applied perspective, these findings have exceedingly important therapeutic implications. The ANS correlates of anger have been implicated in the relationship between the Type A behavior pattern and coronary heart disease (Dembroski & MacDougall, 1982; Matthews, 1982; Rosenman & Chesney, 1982). Current attempts to change the Type A behavior pattern involve psychodynamically oriented, psychotherapeutic interventions (Roskies, 1980), or major lifestyle modifications (e.g., Friedman, Thoresen, Gill, Ulmer, Thompson, Powell, Price, Elek, Rabin, Breal, Piaget, Dixon, Bourg, Levy, & Tasto, 1982; Suinn, 1979); both of which require considerable investment of time and effort. The findings by Ekman and associates raise the possibility that if one could learn to control the expressive correlates of one's anger, it could very well shortcircuit the pathogenic process that produces CHD. As was pointed out earlier in this chapter, it is widely assumed that although it is relatively easy to control one's facial expressions, other expressive behaviors, including those that involve the vocal channel, are difficult to control. The evidence, however, indicates that although facial expressions may be easier to manage than expressive behavior in the vocal channel, the latter, too, can be readily controlled. Feldstein and Sloan (1984) have shown this to be the case with the temporal pacing of speech, and there is evidence that this applies to loudness as well. More importantly, the results of one study conducted in our laboratory indicate that simple instructions to reduce loudness and speech rate reduced blood pressure levels significantly. We are now looking at the effects of such modifications of speech rate and loudness—both increases and decreases—on the cardiovascular responses of experimentally provoked Type A and Type B subjects. Ultimately, of course, we need a study on the long-range effects of anger control techniques, i.e., interventions that focus on modifying the expressive correlates of anger, on the incidence and recurrence of CHD.

The discussion so far has focused on the expressive vocal correlates of anger in the vocal channel and in the face. There is some evidence that other nonverbal behaviors such as gestures and body movements, may also be affected by anger, but so far most of this evidence is clinical and anecdotal. Nevertheless, this evidence needs to be reviewed, if only very briefly.

Psychomotor Correlates of Anger

Earlier, it was mentioned that the Structured Interview, or SI, is the major instrument for the assessment of the Type A behavior pattern. Friedman et al. (1982) have developed a method for administering and scoring the SI, which varies in some ways from that developed by Rosenman (1978). The Friedman interview, unlike the Rosenman interview, is videotaped and, hence, the emphasis by Friedman on psychomotor (i.e., gestural and body movement) variables in the behavior typing process. Also, according to Friedman, behavior typing is based on the diagnostic indicators of only two components of the TABP: time urgency and anger and hostility. In addition to an explosive and staccato speech style and characteristic facial expressions (involving eye and jaw muscles as well as a tic-like drawing back of the corner of the lips, almost exposing the teeth), the nonverbal indicators of anger and hostility are said to include an excessively forceful use of hands and fingers and the use of clenched fists. We know of only two studies on the relationship between the Type A behavior pattern and psychomotor behavior (Friedman, Hall, & Harris, in press; Hughes, Jacobs, Schucker, Chapman, Murray, & Johnson, 1983), the results of which tend to confirm some of the expected relationships. We are now beginning to investigate the effects of anger on body movements and gestures. One interesting finding in the two studies previously cited is that the expected relationships between the Type A behavior pattern and expressive motoric behavior occurred even in a nonchallenging, nonprovocative context, something noted earlier in relation to the Type A and expressive vocal behavior, and subsequently in relation to anger and expressive vocal behavior (Feldstein, Siegman, Simpson, Barkley, & Kobren, 1984; Siegman, Feldstein, Barkley, Simpson, & Kobren, 1984). Similarly, Friedman et al. (1982) report that individuals with a low-anger threshold tend to display the typical facial expression of anger even when they are not being provoked or angered. Apparently, the expressive correlates of anger, and perhaps of other affective experiences as well, if they occur often enough, tend to generalize and to become part of one's general communicative style, or personality.

THE ROLE OF ANGER AND HOSTILITY AND VOICE STYLISTICS IN CHD

In the preceding section, it was pointed out that the TABP, as measured by the SI, has been implicated as a significant risk factor for CHD. It is apparent, however, that only a fraction of those identified as Type A's develop CHD, and that we need to distinguish between the A's that are at risk and the A's that are not. Elsewhere (Siegman, in press), it has been noted that the very same expressive vocal characteristics that define the SI-defined TABP, i.e., short response latencies, accelerated speech and a loud voice also characterize the speech style of extraverted individuals. There is no reason to assume, however, that extraversion in the sense of being socially outgoing puts one at risk for CHD. To the extent that an accelreated and vigorous speech style contributes to the SI-defined TABP—and there is evidence that it accounts for over half of the variance in the SI-defined TABP (Howland & Siegman, 1982; Schucker & Jacobs, 1977; Sherwitz, Berton, & Leventhal, 1977)—it may pick up a good number of healthy, noncoronary-prone extraverts. It comes as no surprise, therefore, that positive correlations have been found between the SI-defined Type A diagnosis and extraversion (e.g., Chesney, Black, Chadwick, & Rosenman, 1981). Similarly, Friedman, Hall, and Harris (in press) have noted an overlap between the Type A speech style and what they refer to as "charismatic" speech. Clearly, if we want to improve the ability of the TABP construct to predict CHD, we need to develop a scoring procedure that will exclude from the coronary-prone diagnosis the healthy, noncoronary-prone extravert and charismatic speaker.

Others have pointed out that the TABP construct consists of many components, such as competitiveness, job involvement, time urgency, hostility and anger proneness, not all of which are necessarily pathogenic of CHD (e.g., Dembroski & MacDougall, 1983). In fact, Matthews and associates (Matthews, Glass, Rosenman, & Bortner, 1977) reanalyzed some of the SI protocols of the Western Collaborative Group Study and found that only some of the components of the TABP were related to the incidence of CHD. They were potential for hostility, competitiveness, impatience, irritability and vigorous voice stylistics. On the other hand, speed of activity, job involvement, and achievement orientation were not related to CHD. Dembroski and MacDougall (1983) developed a component scoring system for the SI that includes speech stylistics, potential for hostility and anger-in, or suppressed anger. In an angiographic study, they found that only potential for hostility and anger-in were related to severity of coronary artery disease (CAD) (Dembroski, MacDougall, Williams, Heney, & Blumenthal, in press). Of course, anger and hostility have always played a key role in speculations about coronary-prone behavior, but that the supression of anger is also implicated in CAD is somewhat surprising, although it has been implicated before in hypertension (Diamond, 1982). On the basis of repeated significant correlations between patients' scores on the Cook-Medley (C-M) Hostility scale from the MMPI (Cook & Medley, 1954) and the severity of coronary atherosclerosis, Williams (1983; Williams, Barefoot, & Shekelle, 1984), like Dembroski, has identified hostility as a significant behavioral risk factor in CHD. It is not at all certain, however, that Dembroski's potential for hostility ratings and the C-M Hostility scale are measuring the same behavior, their common label (hostility) notwithstanding. Whereas Dembroski's ratings seem to measure the potential for anger and hostility, the C-M scale seems to tap cynical attitudes (Williams et al., 1984). It is not surprising, therefore, that the correlation between these two measures was not significant in one study that was conducted in our laboratory, and significant but weak ($r(84) = .324, p < .01$) in another. They may represent, then, related but different behavioral risk factors in CHD. Clearly, research on the role of anger and hostility in CHD is stymied by the lack of adequate measuring instruments for these constructs. More information about the nonverbal correlates of anger and hostility should help the development of such instruments. This is not to suggest that the paper-and-pencil instruments should be replaced with nonverbal indices. Discrepancies between the two types of measurements would provide valuable information about how people cope with anger arousal.

Earlier it was noted that Dembroski et al. (in press) failed to confirm a significant relationship between vocal stylistics and CAD. It should be pointed out, however, that in order to assess the role of vocal stylistics in CHD, these investigators use a global vocal stylistics score, rather than discrete indices of expressive vocal behavior. Furthermore, in that study, as in all current scoring approaches to the SI, subjective judgments served as the basis for determining the participants' vocal stylistics. There is evidence, however, that in the case of speech rate and volume, such impressionistic judgments are of doubtful validity (Bond & Feldstein, 1982). Contrary to the findings by Dembroski et al., preliminary evidence obtained in our laboratory indicates that selected indices of expressive vocal behavior may show a significant relationship with the severity of CAD (Siegman & Feldstein, 1985). In this study, 37 patients undergoing diagnostic coronary arteriography were administered an expanded version of the SI, one half of which was administered in a challenging manner, the other half in a nonchallenging manner. Both halves were scored for loudness, response latency, duration of within-response silent pauses, frequency of interruptive simultaneous speech, and frequency of noninterruptive simultaneous speech. With the exception of loudness, all measurements were obtained by objective, automated procedures. The problem with loudness judgments is that they are confounded with the speaker's speech rate. In the present study, however, speech rate served as a covariate for the loudness judgments. Additionally, each patient was assigned a global behavior type score, based on the patient's responses to the complete interview. The patients' arteriograms were scored according to the Gensini (1975) method. As in some previous studies, there was no significant relationship between the patients' global TABP scores and severity of coronary occlusion. On the other hand, loudness and frequency of interruptive simultaneous speech in the nonchallenging part of the interview accounted for 31% of the variance in the patients' occlusion scores. Noninterruptive simultaneous speech and loudness in the challenging part of the interview accounted for 32% of the variance in the patients' occlusion scores. Two traditional risk factors, excessive weight and high blood pressure, accounted for another 21% of the patients' severity of occlusion scores. As was mentioned earlier, both loud speech and frequent interruptions were significant correlates of anger arousal. Thus, the results of the present study can be viewed as supporting the hypothesis that anger proneness is one of the components of the TABP construct to CAD. Of course, this is not intended to exclude the possibility that some of the other components of the TABP, such as competitiveness and perhaps impatience and irritability, are also involved. On the other hand, the temporal indices which contributed significantly to our patients' global Type A scores (as much as 27% of the variance) had no significant relationship with their occlusion scores. Clearly, then, only some of the behaviors that are included in the TABP construct, and perhaps some that are not (e.g., repressed anger), are related to CAD.

Since the very inception of the TABP construct, expressive behavior has played a critical role in its conceptualization and assessment. Yet, work on the TABP construct has proceeded without paying much attention, if any, to the theoretical and empirical literature on nonverbal (including vocal) expressive behavior. To this day, the scoring of vocal stylistics in the SI is done impressionistically, although the technology for the objective, automated measurement of the vocal variables involved in the scoring of the SI is now available (Feldstein & Welkowitz, 1978; Jaffe & Feldstein, 1970). The use of this technology for scoring the SI could place the assessment of the TABP on a much more objective and reliable footing than is now the case. In fact, Howland and Siegman (1982) have already shown that patients subjectively arrived at Type A diagnosis can be readily identified on the basis of a few objective, semi-automatic, computer scored indices of the patients' vocal behavior in the SI. Furthermore, the results of the angiographic study suggest that a careful analysis of the expressive vocal behavior associated with CAD and CHD may be of help in identifying the behaviors that are coronary-prone.

Clearly, the technology and conceptual perspective of nonverbal behavior research has much to offer to the understanding of coronary-prone behavior. But the benefits of an integration of these two research areas do not all flow in one direction. The TABP and coronary-prone behavior research has directed our focus to anger and hostility, that, until now, received very little attention from nonverbal behavior researchers. Furthermore, the SI provides a useful paradigm for investigating the expressive correlates of anger arousal and hostility.

CONCLUDING REMARKS

There was a time when many psychologists thought that a physiological approach is the key for identifying the basic human emotions. Today, psychologists are much less sanguine about psychophysiology being the royal highway for the understanding of emotions, primarily because of the results of two research programs. First, there is the research by Lacey (1967) indicating that there are considerable individual differences in the specific physiological indices that are assocated with anxiety arousal. This, of course, presents serious difficulties for research paradigms that are based on group comparisons. Second, and potentially more damaging to the psychophysiological approach, are the findings by Schachter and Singer (1962) suggesting that beyond general autonomic system arousal, there are no specific physiological correlates for the different emotions. As pointed out earlier, however, this pessimistic assessment may have been premature, in light of the more recent evidence suggesting specific physiological correlates for fear as opposed to anger, and for overt anger as opposed to covert anger.

More recently, an increasing number of psychologists have been suggesting that expressive behavior may hold the key for a taxonomy of emotions. Perhaps the greatest encouragement for this point of view comes from Ekman's laboratory, where it has been shown that the different emotions are associated with specific patterns of facial expressions. Perhaps, then, the same can be demonstrated in the other channels of nonverbal behavior as well. Also encouraging was the early work by Mahl suggesting the existence of specific expressive, vocal markers for anxiety. One assumption underlying this new expressive, nonverbal behavior approach to emotion is that such behaviors represent primary, unmediated correlates of emotion, uncontaminated by cognition, not unlike the physiological correlates of emotion (Zajonc, 1980). The evidence reviewed in this chapter suggests that this is not the case. Instead, it suggests that expressive behavior is very much a function of one's coping strategies. In fact, it was suggested that such strategies probably influence one's physiological responses as well. The search for "pure" correlates of affect, uncontaminated by secondary cognitive processes, may be illusory for the simple reason that coping strategies and cognitive processes are an integral part of the affective experience. Be that as it may, the evidence reviewed in this chapter suggests that the expressive correlates of anxiety are very much a function of one's coping strategies and that the same is probably true of the expressive correlates of depression and anger as well.

Is there any evidence in support of the hypothesis that different emotional states such as anxiety, depression, and anger, are associated with distinct patterns of expressive behavior? It should be pointed out that the evidence collected by Ekman (1972) that people can readily discriminate between the facial expressions of various emotions does not answer this question, because their findings are not based on naturally occurring emotional experiences. The research reviewed in this chapter, nearly all of which is based on naturally occurring affective experiences, suggests that at least depression is associated with a distinct pattern of expressive behavior, that distinguishes it from anxiety and anger. However, much more research is needed before one can tell whether anxiety can be readily distinguished from anger.

Given the evidence reviewed in this chapter, it should be exceedingly difficult to identify a person's level of anxiety, or depression, or anger on the basis of that person's expressive behavior, without knowledge of that person's baseline expressive behavior, especially if one has only one variable to go on. The evidence suggests that the same kind of individual response specificity that is characteristic of the somatic correlates of emotion is true of some expressive correlates as well. For example, although the level of motoric mobility is very sensitive to changes in depression, there are wide differences in baseline levels. Judgments of emotional arousal should be greatly facilitated, however, by knowing a person's baseline response. Judgments of affective arousal should also be facilitated by having access to more than one expressive variable. Unfortunately, most of the research on the expressive correlates of emotion is single channel research. More multichannel research is clearly necessary in order to resolve these issues.

Evidence was cited suggesting gender differences in the expressive, vocal correlates of anger arousal, with these correlates being more attenuated in females than in males. Given our cultural norms, which expect women to control their anger, it is not surprising that the expressive, vocal correlates of anger are less pronounced in females than in males. It was pointed out that in addition to its expressive function, nonverbal behavior (including the nonverbal, vocal aspects of speech), also have communicative and regulatory functions. If someone wishes to cover-up or to exaggerate their anger, or their anxiety, or their depression, they can do so by attenuating or amplifying the appropriate nonverbal cues.

A review of the literature indicates that the expressive, vocal correlates of trait anxiety are not identical with those of state anxiety. On the other hand, the state and trait dimensions of depression and anger seem to show considerable correspondence, as far as expressive behavior is concerned.

In the beginning of this chapter it was pointed out that the widely acknowledged role of anxiety in the neuroses prompted much of the research on the expressive correlates of anxiety arousal. The same is true of the research on the expressive correlates of depression. Much of this research was prompted by the search for objective indices of depression. The recent findings that anger and hostility may play a significant role in CHD and in hypertension, have already stimulated research on the nonverbal correlates of this affective state. More importantly, these findings suggest that affective arousal is involved not only in psychopathology, but also in diseases such as CHD and hypertension, with anxiety arousal playing the primary role in the neuroses, and anger and hostility in the cardiovascular diseases.

REFERENCES

Aronson, H., & Weintraub, W. (1967). Verbal productivity as a measure of change in affective status. *Psychological Reports, 20,* 483–487.

Aronson, H., & Weintraub, W. (1972). Personal adaptation as reflected in verbal behavior. In A. W. Siegman & B. Pope (Eds.), *Studies in dyadic communication* (pp. 265–279). New York: Pergamon.

Ax, A. F. (1953). The psychophysiological differentiation between fear and anger in humans. *Psychosomatic Medicine, 15,* 433–442.

Bond, R. N., & Feldstein, S. (1982). Acoustical correlates of perception of speech rate: An experimental investigation. *Journal of Psycholinguistic Research, 11,* 539–557.

Boomer, D. S., & Goodrich, D. W. (1961). Speech disturbance and judged anxiety. *Journal of Consulting Psychology, 25,* 160–164.

Chesney, M. A., Black, G. W., Chadwick, J. H., & Rosenman, R. H. (1981). Psychological correlates of the Type A behavior pattern. *Behavioral Medicine, 4,* 217–229.

Chesney, M. A., Eagleston, J. R., & Rosenman, R. H. (1980). The type A structured interview: A behavioral assessment in the rough. *Journal of Behavioral Assessment, 2,* 255–272.

Cook, M. (1969). Anxiety, speech disturbances and speech rate. *British Journal of Social and Clinical Psychology, 8,* 13–21.

Cook, W. W., & Medley, D. M. (1954). Proposed hostility and pharisaic-virtue scales for the MMPI. *Journal of Applied Psychology, 38,* 414–418.

Dembroski, T. M. & MacDougall, J. M. (1982). Coronary-prone behavior, social psychophysiology, and coronary heart disease. In J. R. Eiser (Ed.), *Social psychology and behavioral medicine* (pp. 39–62), New York: Wiley.

Dembroski, T. M., & MacDougall, J. M. (1983). Behavioral and psychophysiological perspectives on coronary-prone behavior. In T. M. Dembroski, T. H. Schmidt, & G. Blümchen (Eds.), *Biobehavioral bases of coronary heart disease* (pp. 106-129), New York: Karger.

Dembroski, T. M., MacDougall, J. M., Williams, R. B., Haney, T., & Blumenthal, J. (in press). Components of Type A, hostility and anger-in: Relationship to angiographic findings. *Psychosomatic Medicine.*

Diamond, E. L. (1982). The role of anger and hostility in essential hypertension and coronary heart disease. *Psychological Bulletin, 92,* 410–433.

Duffy, E. (1962). *Activation and behavior.* New York: Wiley.

Ekman, P. (1972). Universals and cultural differences in facial expressions of emotion. In J. K. Cole (Ed.) *Nebraska Symposium on Motivation, 1971* (pp. 207–284). Lincoln: University of Nebraska.

Ekman, P. (1978). Facial expression. In A. W. Siegman & S. Feldstein (Eds.), *Nonverbal behavior and communication* (pp. 97–116). Hillsdale, NJ: Lawrence Erlbaum Associates.

Ekman, P., & Friesen, W. V. (1972a). Hand movements. *Journal of Communication, 22,* 353–374.

Ekman, P., & Friesen, W. V. (1972b). Nonverbal behavior and psychopathology. In R. J. Friedman & M. M. Katz (Eds.), *The psychology of depression: Contemporary theory and research.* Washington, DC: U. S. Government Printing Office.

Ekman, P., & Friesen, W. V. (1974). Detecting deception from the body or face. *Journal of Personality and Social Psychology, 29,* 288–298.

Ekman, P., Levenson, R. W., & Friesen, W. V. (1983). Autonomic nervous system activity distinguishes among emotions. *Science, 221,* 1208–1210.

Ellgring, H., Wagner, H., & Clarke, A. H. (1980). Psychopathological states and their effects on speech and gaze behavior. In H. Giles, W. P. Robinson, & P. M. Smith (Eds.), *Language: Social psychological perspectives* (pp. 267–273). Oxford: Pergamon.

Feldstein, S. (1976). Rate estimates of sound-silence sequences in speech. *Journal of the Acoustical Society of America, 60* (Suppl. 1), 546. (Abstract)

Feldstein, S., Brenner, M. S., & Jaffe, J. (1963). The effect of subject sex, verbal interaction, and topical focus on speech disruption. *Language and Speech, 6,* 229–239.

Feldstein, S., Siegman, A. W., Simpson, S., Barkley, S., & Kobren, R. (1984 April). *Assessing coronary prone behavior from the temporal structure of speech.* Paper read at the Eastern Psychological Association, Baltimore.

Feldstein, S., & Sloan, B. (1984). Actual and stereotyped speech patterns of extraverts and introverts. *Journal of Personality, 52,* 188–204.

Feldstein, S., & Welkowitz, J. (1978). A chronography of conversation: In defense of an objective approach. In A. W. Siegman & S. Feldstein (Eds.), *Nonverbal behavior and communication* (pp. 329–378). Hillsdale, NJ: Lawrence Erlbaum Associates.

Fenz, W. D. J., & Epstein, S. (1962). Measurement of approach-avoidance conflict among a stimulus dimension by a thematic apperception test. *Journal of Personality, 30,* 613–632.

Fisch, H. U., Frey, S., & Hirsbrunner, H. P. (1983). Analyzing nonverbal behavior in depression. *Journal of Abnormal Psychology, 92,* 307–318.

Fiske, D. W., & Maddi, S. R. (Eds.) (1961). *Functions of varied experience.* Homewood, IL: Dorsey.

Freedman, N. (1972). The analysis of movement behavior during the clinical interview. In A. W. Siegman & B. Pope (Eds.), *Studies in dyadic communication* (pp. 153–175). New York: Wiley.

Friedman, H. S., Hall, J. A., & Harris, M. J. (in press). Type A behavior, nonverbal expressive style and health. *Journal of Personality and Social Psychology.*

Friedman, M., & Rosenman, R. (1974). *Type A behavior and your heart.* New York: Knopf.

Friedman, M., Thoresen, C. E., Gill, J. J., Ulmer, D., Thompson, L., Powell, L., Price, V., Elek, S. R., Rabin, D. D., Breal, W. Piaget, G., Dixon, T., Bourg, E., Levy, R. & Tasto, D. L. (1982). Feasibility of altering type A behavior pattern after myocardial infarction. *Circulation, 66,* 83–92.

Funkelstein, D. H., King, S. H., & Drolette, M. E. (1954). The direction of anger during a laboratory stress-inducing situation. *Psychosomatic Medicine, 16,* 404–413.

Geer, J. H. (1966). Effects of fear arousal upon task performance and verbal behavior. *Journal of Abnormal Psychology, 71,* 119–123.

Gensini, G. G. (1975). *Coronary arteriography.* Mt. Kisco, NY: Future.

Goldman-Eisler, F. (1968). *Psycholinguistics: Experiments in spontaneous speech.* New York: Academic.

Hebb, D. O. (1955). Drives and the C.N.S. (conceptual nervous system). *Psychological Review, 62,* 243–254.

Helfrich, H., & Dahme, G. (1974). Sind Verzögerungsphänomene beim spontanen Sprechen Indikatoren persönlichkeitsspezifischer Angstverarbeitung. *Zeitschrift fur Socialpsychologie, 5,* 55–65.

Hinchliffe, M., Lancashire, M., & Roberts, F. J. (1970). Eye contact and depression: A preliminary report. *British Journal of Psychiatry, 117,* 1712.

Hinchliffe, M., Lancashire, M., & Roberts, F. J. (1971). A study of eye contact changes in depressed and recovered psychiatric patients. *British Journal of Psychiatry, 119,* 213–215.

Hirsbrunner, H. P., Frey, S., & Crawford, R. (in press). Movement in human interaction: Description, parameter formation, and analysis. In A. W. Siegman, & S. Feldstein (Eds.), *Nonverbal behavior and communication* (2nd ed.). Hillsdale, NJ: Lawrence Erlbaum Associates.

Howland, E. W., & Siegman, A. W. (1982). Toward the automated measurement of the type-A behavior pattern. *Behavioral Medicine, 5,* 37–54.

Hughes, J. R., Jacobs, D. R., Schucker, B., Chapman, D. P., Murray, D. M., & Johnson, A. (1983). Nonverbal behavior of the type A individual. *Journal of Behavioral Medicine, 6,* 279–289.

Hull, C. L. (1943). *Principles of behavior.* New York: Appleton-Century-Crofts.

Jaffe, J., & Feldstein, S. (1970). *Rhythms of dialogue.* New York: Academic.

Jenkins, C. D., Rosenman, R. H., & Friedman, M. (1967). Development of an objective psychological test for the determination of the coronary-prone behavior pattern in employed men. *Journal of Chronic Diseases, 20,* 371–379.

Kanfer, F. H. (1958a). Effect of a warning signal preceding a noxious stimulus on verbal rate and heart rate. *Journal of Experimental Psychology, 55,* 78–80.

Kanfer, F. H. (1958b). Supplementary report: Stability of a verbal rate change in experimental anxiety. *Journal of Experimental Psychology, 56,* 182.

Kanfer, F. H. (1960). Verbal rate, eyeblink, and content in structured psychiatric interviews. *Journal of Abnormal and Social Psychology, 61,* 341–347.

Kasl, S. V., & Mahl, G. F. (1965). The relationship of disturbances and hesitations in spontaneous speech to anxiety. *Journal of Personality and Social Psychology, 1*, 425–433.

Lacey, J. I. (1967). Somatic response patterning and stress: Some revisions of activation theory. In M. H. Appley & R. Trumbull (Eds.), *Psychological stress* (pp. 14–37). New York: Appleton-Century-Crofts.

Levin, H., Baldwin, A. L., Gallwey, M., & Paivio, A. (1960). Audience stress, personality, and speech. *Journal of Abnormal and Social Psychology, 61*, 469–473.

Levin, H., & Silverman, I. (1965). Hesitation phenomena in children's speech. *Language and Speech, 8*, 67–85.

Mahl, G. F. (1956). Disturbances and silences in the patient's speech in psychotherapy. *Journal of Abnormal and Social Psychology, 53*, 1–15.

Matthews, K. A. (1982). Psychological perspectives on the type A behavior pattern. *Psychological Bulletin, 91*, 293–323.

Matthews, K. A., Glass, D. C., Rosenman, R. H., & Bortner, R. W. (1977). Competitive drive, pattern A, and coronary heart disease: A further analysis of some data from the Western Collaborative Group Study. *Journal of Chronic Diseases, 30*, 489–498.

Montague, E. K. (1953). The role of anxiety in serial learning. *Journal of Experimental Psychology, 45*, 91–96.

Murray, D. C. (1971). Talk, silence and anxiety. *Psychological Bulletin, 75*, 244–260.

Musante, L., MacDougall, J. M., Dembroski, T. M., & Van Horn, A. E. (1983). Component analysis of the Type A coronary-prone behavior pattern in male and female college students. *Journal of Personality and Social Psychology, 5*, 1104–1117.

Overall, J. E., & Gorham, E. R. (1962). The brief psychiatric rating scale. *Psychological Reports, 10*, 799–812.

Paivio, A. (1965). Personality and audience influence. In B. A. Maher (Ed.), *Progress in experimental personality research* (Vol. 2) (pp. 127–173). New York: Academic.

Pope, B., Blass, T., Siegman, A. W., & Raher, J. (1970). Anxiety and depression in speech. *Journal of Consulting and Clinical Psychology, 35*, 128–133.

Pope, B., Siegman, A. W., & Blass, T. (1970). Anxiety and speech in the initial interview. *Journal of Consulting and Clinical Psychology, 35*, 233–238.

Preston, J. M., & Gardner, R. C. (1967). Dimensions of oral and written language fluency. *Journal of Verbal Learning and Verbal Behavior, 6*, 936–945.

Reynolds, A., & Paivio, A. (1968). Cognitive and emotional determinants of speech. *Canadian Journal of Psychology, 22*, 164–175.

Reynolds, M. A., Siegman, A. W., & Demorest, M. E. (1983). *The voice of deception: The temporal pacing of speech in unfeigned lying.* Unpublished manuscript, University of Maryland Baltimore County.

Rosenman, R. H. (1978). The interview method of assessment of the coronary-prone behavior pattern. In T. Dembroski, S. Weiss, J. Shields, S. Haynes, & M. Keinleib (Eds.), *Coronary prone behavior* (pp. 55–69). New York: Springer Verlag.

Rosenman, R. H., Brand, R. J., Jenkins, C. D., Friedman, M., Straus, R., & Wurm, M. (1975). Coronary heart disease in the Western Collaborative Group Study: Final follow-up experience of 8½ years. *Journal of the American Medical Association, 233*, 872–877.

Rosenman, R. H., & Chesney, M. (1982). Stress, Type-A behavior, and coronary disease. In L. Goldberg & S. Breznitz (Eds.), *Handbook of stress* (pp. 547–565). New York: Free Press.

Rosenman, R. H., Friedman, M., Straus, R., Wurm, M., Kositchek, R., Hahn, W., & Werthessen, N. T. (1964). A predictive study of coronary heart disease: The Western Collaborative Group Study. *Journal of the American Medical Association, 189*, 15–22.

Roskies, E. (1980). Considerations in developing a treatment program for the coronary-prone (Type A) behavior pattern. In T. O. Davidson & S. M. Davidson (Eds.), *Behavioral medicine: Changing health life styles* (pp. 299–333). New York: Brunner/Mazel.

Rutter, D. R., & Stephenson, G. M. (1972a). Visual interaction in a group of schizophrenic and depressive patients. *British Journal of Social and Clinical Psychology, 11,* 57–65.

Rutter, D. R., & Stephenson, G. M. (1972b). Visual interaction in a group of schizophrenic and depressive patients: A follow-up study. *British Journal of Social and Clinical Psychology, 11,* 410–411.

Schachter, S., & Singer, J. E. (1962). *Psychological Reviews, 69,* 379.

Scherer, K. R. (1979). Personality markers in speech. In K. R. Scherer & H. Giles (Eds.)., *Social markers in speech* (pp. 147–209). Cambridge: Cambridge University.

Scherer, K. R. (1981). Speech and emotional states. In J. K. Darby (Ed.), *Speech evaluation in psychiatry* (pp. 189–220). New York: Grune & Stratton.

Schucker, B., & Jacobs, D. R. (1977). Assessment of behavioral risk for coronary disease by voice characteristics. *Psychosomatic Medicine, 39,* 219–228.

Sherwitz, L., Berton, B. S., & Leventhal, H. (1977). Type A assessment and interaction in the behavior pattern interview. *Psychosomatic Medicine, 39,* 229–240.

Siegman, A. W. (1957). *Some relationships of anxiety and introversion-extraversion to serial learning.* Unpubished doctoral dissertation, Columbia University.

Siegman, A. W. (1978). The telltale voice. In A. W. Siegman & S. Feldstein (Eds.), *Nonverbal behavior and communication* (pp. 183–243). Hillsdale, NJ: Lawrence Erlbaum Associates.

Siegman, A. W. (1979). The voice of attraction: Vocal correlates of interpersonal attraction in the interview. In A. W. Siegman & S. Feldstein (Eds.), *Of time and speech: Temoral speech patterns in interpersonal contexts* (pp. 89–113). Hillsdale, NJ: Lawrence Erlbaum Associates.

Siegman, A. W. (1984). *The role of nonverbal behavior in predicting coronary heart disease or what has gone wrong with the structured interview?* Unpublished manuscript, University of Maryland Baltimore County.

Siegman, A. W. (in press). The telltale voice. In A. W. Siegman & S. Feldstein (Eds.), *Nonverbal behavior and communication* (2nd ed.). Hillsdale, NJ: Lawrence Erlbaum Associates.

Siegman, A. W. & Feldstein, S. (1985). *The relationship of expressive vocal behavior and severity of coronary artery disease.* Symposium paper presented at the annual meetings of the Society for Behavioral Medicine, New Orleans.

Siegman, A. W., Feldstein, S., Barkley, S., Simpson, S., & Kobren, R. (1984). *Expressive speech correlates of anger and hostility and their relation to the Type A behavior pattern.* Unpublished manuscript, University of Maryland Baltimore County.

Siegman, A. W., & Pope, B. (1965a). Effects of question specificity and anxiety producing messages on verbal fluency in the initial interview. *Journal of Personality and Social Psychology, 4,* 188–192.

Siegman, A. W., & Pope, B. (1965b). Personality variables associated with productivity and verbal fluency in the initial interview. *Proceedings of the 73rd Annual Convention of the American Psychological Association,* 273–274.

Siegman, A. W., & Pope, B. (1972). The effects of ambiguity and anxiety on interviewee verbal behavior. In A. W. Siegman & B. Pope (Eds.), *Studies in dyadic communication* (pp. 29–68). New York: Pergamon.

Siegman, A. W., & Reynolds, M. A. (1983). Self-monitoring and speech in feigned and unfeigned lying. *Journal of Personality and Social Psychology, 45,* 1325–1333.

Snyder, M. (1974). Self-monitoring of expressive behavior. *Journal of Personality and Social Psychology, 30,* 526–537.

Starkweather, J. A. (1967). Vocal behaviour as an information channel of speaker status. In K. Salzinger & S. Salzinger (Eds.), *Research in verbal behaviour and some neurophysiological implications* (pp. 253–262). New York: Academic.

Suinn, P. M. (1979). Type-A behavior pattern. In R. B. Williams & W. D. Gentry (Eds.), *Behavioral approaches to medical treatment* (pp. 55–65). Cambridge: Ballinger.

Taylor, J. A. (1951). The relationship of anxiety to the conditioned eyelid response. *Journal of Experimental Psychology, 41,* 81–92.

Taylor, J. A. (1953). A personality scale of manifest anxiety. *Journal of Abnormal and Social Psychology, 48,* 285–290.

Taylor, J. A. (1956). Drive theory and manifest anxiety. *Psychological Buletin, 53,* 303–321.

Taylor, J. A., & Spence, K. W. (1952). The relationship of anxiety level to performance in serial learning. *Journal of Experimental Psychology, 44,* 61–64.

Williams, R. B., Jr. (1983). Behavioral correlates of angiographic findings. In T. M. Dembroski, T. H. Schmidt, & G. Blumchen (Eds.), *Biobehavioral bases of coronary heart disease* (pp. 39–54). New York: Karger.

Williams, R. B., Jr., Barefoot, J C., & Shekelle, R. B. (1984). The health consequences of hostility. In M. A. Chesney, S. E. Goldstein, & R. H. Rosenman (Eds.), *Anger, hostility and behavioral medicine.* New York: Hemisphere/McGraw Hill.

Zajonc, R. B. (1980). Feeling and thinking: Preferences need no inferences. *American Psychologist, 35,* 151–175.

Zuckerman, M., DePaulo, B. M., & Rosenthal, R. (1981). Verbal and nonverbal communication of deception. In L. Berkowitz (Ed.), *Advances in experimental social psychology* (Vol. 14) (pp. 2–59). New York: Academic.

3 Controlling the Floor in Conversation

Joseph N. Cappella
University of Wisconsin-Madison

When large groups of people assemble for the purpose of making a collective decision, they usually adopt some rules of procedure to govern how contributions to the decision-making process are made. These may be an implicit set of rules requiring that all attend to each speaker, that everyone be permitted to have a say, that debate may not be closed off, and that the decision be made by majority rule. They may be an explicit set of rules such as Robert's Rules of Order. Regardless of the informality or formality of the deliberative body, rules of procedure will exist (or, of course, they may evolve over the course of deliberation). These rules will govern the two important phases of deliberation: the information-gathering phase and the decision-making phase.

Not all human gatherings are concerned with deliberation and decision making. But all human encounters in one way or another are concerned with the transfer of information, its generation and reception. If we were capable of both generating and receiving information simultaneously and without limit, there would be no need for rules of procedure for regulating generation and reception. We could speak and listen simultaneously regardless of the complexity, familiarity, uncertainty, and load that the information presented.

Although we can do some simultaneous processing in the listening and speaking modes, it is an axiom of cognitive psychology and a painfully true common experience that people have finite information-processing capacity (Kahneman, 1973; Norman, 1976; Taylor & Fiske, 1978). The consequence is that all human gatherings must be governed by some rules of procedure that control the flow of information and signal when speaking and listening roles are to be switched. That is the topic of this chapter.

The language of "control" and "order" of the previous paragraphs has not been chosen idly. In large gatherings the person who understands, can manipulate, and can operate smoothly within the rules of procedure is not merely competent but, indeed, can be powerful. Power can be achieved in deliberative contexts by controlling one's own and others' ability to present information. It pays to know the rules of parliamentary procedure. The thesis of this chapter is that knowing the rules of turn-taking in conversation is as important a consideration in interpersonal power as knowing the rules of procedure in large deliberative assemblies. Both sets of rules are concerned with access to the floor for the purpose of presenting information. Both are necessary because of the limitations with which we must live as human information processors. Interpersonal power, status, competence, and attraction depend, at least in part, upon our ability to control speaking and listening roles.

My claim that access to the floor, that is to the role of speaker, is important in the exercise of interpersonal power and the perception of liking rests on two assumptions. The first is that interpersonal power and interpersonal attraction variously labeled status, dominance, superiority, or control and affiliation, liking or associativity are an important dimension of the evaluation and perception of other persons. If we do not view others in terms of their power or their attractiveness on a regular basis, then it makes little sense to even suppose that an innocuous set of actions such as who talks when could affect our fundamental perceptions about others. The literature that is reviewed in the next section shows unequivocally that people in relationships view one another in terms of power and attraction categories across a wide variety of situations.

The second assumption is that part of the basis for judgments of who is more powerful and attractive in an interpersonal situation is based upon who controls the floor during conversation. One approach to studying control of the floor has been to treat the back-and-forth flow of information as a problem of regulating whose conversational turn it is (Duncan & Fiske, 1977; Sacks, Schegloff, & Jefferson, 1974). The language of "regulation" implies that "who has the floor for how long" is merely a technical problem of sequencing that, once solved, permits communication to take place more or less smoothly. Such an approach is, indeed, reasonable. The problem of how to avoid a continual sequence of simultaneous speakers or simultaneous listeners must be solved for the community of interactants before communication can proceed.

But it is time to recognize that the regulation of interaction can have significant implications for our impressions of who is in control of a situation, who is a competent social actor, who is friendly, and who is shy. Indeed, the ability or the inability to participate in discussion may have serious consequences on the self-esteem of conversationalists (Zimbardo, 1977). The second section considers the evidence for this second assumption: Does control of the floor have a significant effect on our perceptions of social actors?

Let us not be naive in answering questions about conversational control. The study of conversational regulation per se has been and will continue to be an important domain of research. That control of the floor has implications for a variety of interpersonal perceptions is a complement to the current research traditions. However, the research on the regulation of conversation must begin to participate in theories of interpersonal relations. Such participation comes about with the recognition that the regulation of conversational turns is the regulation of a cherished resource, the floor. The allocation of this resource has profound ramifications on the perceptions that others have of its possessors. Additionally, perceptions of interpersonal power depend upon a variety of factors, only one of which is participation as speaker. Nevertheless, without the ability to participate equally (or more) in conversations, the opportunity to persuade, argue, influence, decide, and lead does not exist. Participation in conversation may not guarantee power but nonparticipation guarantees powerlessness.

The final thesis to be explored in this chapter is a pragmatic one. If conversational control influences perceptions of power and associativity, then the means of achieving conversational control is an important interpersonal skill. Teaching such skills requires knowing how conversational control operates, not merely in its superficial manifestations, the cues of control, but in its less obvious causal forces. Put simply, explaining the operation of conversational control has important implications for training persons in the control of their own conversations. To anticipate the result of this inquiry, the explanation of turn-taking proposed by Duncan and Fiske (1977) will be found wanting. It will be replaced by an explanatory mechanism with significantly different implications for skill training.

THE FUNCTIONS OF INTERPERSONAL COMMUNICATION

In a series of recent papers, Miles Patterson (1982a, 1982b; Eidinger & Patterson, 1983) has argued that researchers and theorists must begin to understand the functions of nonverbal behaviors, and to use such functions as the basis for grouping rather than the more convenient channel categories. He has organized his functional classification around five categories: providing information, regulating interaction, expressing intimacy, and two less common categories of social control and service-task functions. Patterson has shown these categories to be useful in organizing the research literature, and, when treated as motivations of subjects, for explaining their behavior in sometimes parsimonious ways. For example, Ickes, Patterson, Rajecki, and Tanford (1982) found that persons smiled more at confederates whom they expected to be friendly *and* unfriendly (compared to control confederates) even though they rated the friendly confederates more positively and the unfriendly confederates more negatively after their discussions. The reason for the same behavioral reactions to the different confederates is found in the different functions or motivations of subjects. In the interaction that subjects expected to be friendly, they were motivated to express intimacy. With the unfriendly confederate the subjects were motivated to reduce potential hostilities by smiling and seeming friendly themselves. That is, they tried to manage the situation, exerting social control.

In Patterson's conception, the function or meaning of the exhibited behavior depends upon the motivational state of the sender at the time that the behavior is being exhibited. In the crudest sense, the behavior means what the sender's motivational state is. Since there are no a priori constraints on what motivations can produce what nonverbal behaviors, then any attempt to construct a dictionary of functions for nonverbal behaviors requires a close monitoring of the motivational states of senders while they are emitting nonverbal behaviors. I believe that such close monitoring of an unobservable state is beyond our current measurement technology.

Nevertheless, I believe that Patterson is quite right to abandon the channel categorization of nonverbal behavior in favor of the functional categorization. A functional approach recognizes that various behaviors can serve the same function and the same behavior can serve several functions. Thereby, the error of assuming a one-to-one correspondence is avoided. For example, eye gaze can be a sign of affiliation. In studies of territorial invasion by strangers, subjects sometimes look more at the closer invaders than the distant ones (Patterson, Mullens, & Romano, 1971). Such looking is probably more related to attentiveness to a threat than to the expression of positive affect. Moreover, a functional approach encourages researchers to study multiple nonverbal indicators of the same function, avoiding the single channel or single behavior approach of most earlier research. For example, the vast majority of studies of responses to self-disclosure show that even very high disclosure is reciprocated rather than avoided (Cappella, 1981). These studies seldom measure other nonverbal behaviors that might exhibit the expected patterns of avoidance under the high disclosure of confederates.

Most importantly, however, the functional approach makes an explicit linkage between the domain of microscopic nonverbal behaviors and the macroscopic variables of theories of interpersonal relations. In Patterson's approach, the nonverbal behaviors are linked to interpersonal motives such as expressing intimacy or managing impressions (social control). The importance of this step, even acknowledging its incompleteness, should not be minimized. Theories of interpersonal communication and studies of interaction, although paying lip service of the significance of one to the other (Hinde, 1979), have proceeded independently for the most part. The explicit linkage of interaction behaviors to their interpersonal function recognizes and reduces the de facto independence of the two domains.

An alternative to Patterson's grouping of nonverbal behavior by their moti-vational function is to group them by the perceptions that they create in observers. Instead of selecting a behavior and identifying the motivations associated with its expression in various circumstances, the behaviors emitted could be linked to the perceptions that they produce in observers. The *function* of the behavior would then be found in the set of perceptions for which the behavior accounts.

For example, Shrout and Fiske (1981) coded 49 nonverbal behaviors from 8 behavior families for target persons who had interacted for a brief time. Observers rated the target persons on a version of the Adjective Checklist (Gough & Heilbrun, 1965). It was found that five nonverbal variables (smile number, filled pause rate, nod rate, gaze number, and short back-channel rate) explained sub-stantial portions of the variance in observers' ratings of overall sociability from the adjective checklist. The common function of these behaviors, then, is found in the impressions that they create in observers.

Patterson's approach to identifying functions is to suggest that the meaning of a behavior is found in the motivation of the user. This is like classic theories of word meaning that are user-centered: The meaning (in this case function) of a word (in this case nonverbal behavior) is found in the purpose and intention of the sender (in this case the motivation). My approach is more a decoding approach, maintaining that the meaning (function) of a word (nonverbal behavior) is found in the systematic pattern of response of receivers (perceptions). I would maintain that this approach is preferable to Patterson's for a variety of reasons: (1) The measurement technology for identifying interpersonal perceptions is straightforward and well established, whereas the identification of individual motivations is extremely difficult to ascertain or to manipulate. (2) Not only can perceptions be easily identified but the methodologies for establishing associa-tions between nonverbal behaviors and perceptions are also well established (Poole & Folger, 1981; Wish, D'Andrade, & Goodnow, 1980). The criteria for how well shared is the meaning of the nonverbal behavior are also a straight-forward measure of variance explained. (3) Although motivations are obvious candidates for explaining why certain behaviors are emitted or why the same behavior is emitted in two different circumstances, the meaning of a group of behaviors must be evaluated by how those behaviors are perceived in the context of their occurrence by the community of observers. The functions or meanings of the behaviors, identified by perceptions of observers, directly account for the reactions of the community of observers to the sender of the behavior. My approach insists that nonverbal behaviors be grouped in meaning categories not by the motivation of the sender but by the effects systematically produced.

The two approaches are not likely to produce the same groupings of behaviors. My approach requires empirical investigation and Patterson's requires theoretical interpretation and artful conceptualization. Because of the emphasis on systematic observer reactions, my approach emphasizes the communicative function of nonverbal behavior whereas Patterson's may be more useful in accounting for idiosyncratic uses and person-specific motivations. Finally, variations in the functional categorization of nonverbal behaviors are likely to depend upon individual differences in Patterson's approach and upon situational differences in my approach. The reason for this is that Patterson's approach is sender-centered and mine is receiver-centered.

Categories of Interpersonal Perception

If we are to identify the functions of nonverbal behaviors with the perceptions they create in observers, then we must discover what perceptions people have of others in interpersonal encounters. This question has a long and rich history under the title of dimensions of interpersonal perception. Obviously, the set of possible perceptions of others in interpersonal encounters is very large, if not infinite. If the elements of this set group in some identifiable, consistent and generalizable way, then the set of perceptions into which behaviors could map would be simpler than the mass of possible perceptions.

The study of the dimensions of interpersonal perception has produced an unmistakable conclusion: Across a variety of methods, situations, and analysis procedures people group their perceptions of interpersonal behavior in at least two, and probably no more than four, categories, including always a dimension of association, friendliness, or social evaluation and a dimension of superiority, dominance, or power. Additional dimensions reflecting intensity of relationships and reflecting the formality of relationships also arise (Wish & Kaplan, 1977; Wish, Deutsch, & Kaplan, 1976).

Much of the early work in interpersonal relations was aimed at developing personality types whose fit or failure to fit would spell success (or the lack of it) for the relationship. Schutz (1958) isolated three basic interpersonal needs for inclusion, control, and affection from his review of earlier literature. Self-report questions for each of these needs as expressed by the person or as wanted from others were developed. Results from factor analyses of the six categories (three needs each in "expressed" or "wanted" forms) indicate considerable correlation beween the inclusion wanted and the inclusion expressed items and considerable correlation between the affection wanted and expressed scales. These correlations suggest not six separate dimensions of perceived interpersonal needs but three: control wanted, control expressed, and inclusion-affection.

At about the same time, Leary (1957) and the Kaiser group postulated 16 basic personality types in interpersonal behavior based upon their observations of therapy groups. These 16 types were positioned around a circle spanned by the dimensions of love–hostility and dominance–submission. Psychometrically more acceptable tests of personality developed by Edwards (1953) in the Edwards Personality Preference Scale also located personality dimensions of dominance, deference, and affiliation. Bales' (1970) observations of small group behavior led him to the discovery (on weak grounds empirically) that persons in groups should be characterized by their dominance (which he labeled as Up or Down), by their sociability (labeled Positive or Negative), and by their contribution to the task (Forward or Backward). Each of these diverse studies of the structure of interpersonal behavior produced two categories in common, despite their insistence on different category names and the noncomparability of scales, items, methods, and procedure.

More recently, Wish and his colleagues (Wish, Deutsch, & Kaplan, 1976; Wish & Kaplan, 1977) have reopened the question of interpersonal perception. Wish et al. (1976) had people rate 25 typical interpersonal relationships and 19 of their own relationships each on 25 bipolar scales (such as friendly–hostile). A profile of dissimilarity for each pair of interpersonal relationships across the 25 bipolar scales was formed and analyzed statistically for subgroupings. Four subgroupings emerged representing the friendly–hostile category, the equal–unequal category and two others concerned with intensity and with formality. This study differed from the earlier ones reported because it was concerned with the subjects' perceptions of a variety of relationships and not just a report on their own or a specific other's relationship. Despite this substantial reorientation in perspective, two categories of interpersonal perception remained constant.

In an important followup study Wish and Kaplan (1977) asked whether the situational context of the relationship (e.g., discussing a controversial issue, compromising on opposing goals, etc.) would alter the structure of interpersonal perception. Subjects evaluated 12 relationships in 10 different contexts each on 14 bipolar scales. Statistical analyses indicated five dimensions of interpersonal perception with the friendly, dominant, and intense categories emerging as in the previous study and the formality dimension splitting into two dimensions. The different situations did not seem to appreciably affect the groups of inter- personal perceptions. People seem to perceive relationships along similar dimen- sions regardless of the type of relationship or context of the relationship.

Even though these studies indicate that interpersonal perception is relatively well structured across relationships and situations, one might worry that group- ings of perceptions based on bipolar adjective pairs would be different from groupings based on interpersonal *behaviors,* even if they are self-report. Such a concern proves to be unfounded. Triandis and his associates (Triandis & Vassiliou, 1972; Triandis, Vassiliou, & Nassiakou, 1968) had Greeks and Amer- icans indicate the appropriateness of 60 different behaviors (command, marry, fight, etc.) for 100 different pairs of interpersonal relationships in their own culture. Four groupings emerged as common to both cultures: the two well- known groups of association–dissociation, and superordinate–subordinate and two others. In a comprehensive review of the studies on the dimensions of social behaviors Triandis, Vassiliou, Vassiliou, Tanaka, and Shanmugana (1972) con- cluded that four dimensions of these behaviors consistently appear in the literature including association, superordination, intimacy, and an overt–covert factor describing feelings versus behavior.

Some studies have focused more narrowly on the dimensions of reported communication behaviors in interpersonal encounters rather than more general behaviors. Bochner, Kaminski, and Fitzpatrick (1977) had subjects rate themselves and a best-liked other on 140 statements of manifest interpersonal behavior. Five groupings of behaviors emerged across both sets of ratings and included a control dimension, a detachment-affiliation dimension, and three others. Norton (1978) sought to develop a measure of communicator style by having subjects rate their agreement and disagreement with statements descriptive of their style of communication (e.g., "As a rule, I *openly* express my feelings or emotions"). In two studies the 51 statements exhibited clusters, which he identified as attentive-friendly-open and dominant-contentious.

The studies of the dimensions of interpersonal behaviors above ask subjects to report their perceptions of social appropriateness of the behaviors, or how characteristic the behaviors are of themselves or close associates. Wish, D'Andrade, and Goodnow (1980) took the next step asking subjects to evaluate on 18 bipolar scales each actor in 20 brief scenes taken from the television documentary, "An American Family." The structure of these responses once again produced a dominance dimension and a positive-negative dimension, as well as a task and an intensity grouping. This study comes closest to a structural analysis of interpersonal perception because judges are evaluating the immediate behavioral actions of persons in interaction.

The results of the few studies that have been considered here are, I think, rather convincing.[1] Whether people are evaluating televised scenes, socially appropriate behavior, hypothetical relationships in hypothetical circumstances, their own styles, behaviors of their friends, and so on, these evaluations tend to fall into only a few groups with two of the groups being associativity and power perceptions. The importance of this pattern of results for a functional approach to nonverbal behavior cannot be overstated. Although we have a variety of perceptions of people in relationships, two categories of perception emerge again and again. These perceptions, in turn, must arise from the actions of the persons being observed.[2] To establish the functions of nonverbal behavior requires that research empirically map the coded nonverbal actions into the sets of perceptions that observers have of actors. What we now know is that the perceptions of observers are rather well structured. A first step, then, in a functional analysis is to determine which nonverbal behaviors produce fundamental perceptions of affiliation and of dominance in various interpersonal settings.

---

[1]The review of interpersonal perception has been selective of necessity. Numerous other studies exist and are discussed in Bochner et al. (1977) and in Triandis et al. (1972). These additional results only strengthen the case made here.

[2]Some argue that the structure of interpersonal perceptions arise from the structure of the language used to test those perceptions and not from the structure of perceptions themselves. Even if this alternative were true, language, being the medium of mental life, marks it as the means through which perceptions are recorded, stored, and retrieved.

Mehrabian's research took steps in this direction (Mehrabian, 1971; Mehrabian & Ksionzky, 1970, 1972). A large number of nonverbal behaviors of people were coded while they waited with confederates who were instructed to act in a slightly positive or slightly negative manner toward the subject (Mehrabian, 1971). The behaviors and their groupings are presented in Table 3.1. The groupings (using Mehrabian's labels) include groups of affiliative, intimate, and relaxation behaviors. Although these behaviors were not correlated with observers' perceptions of the subjects' degree of associativity or power, other analyses by Mehrabian (summarized in Mehrabian, 1972, chapters 1 and 2) indicate that the behaviors grouped into the affiliative and intimate groups are associated with positive attitude toward the person being addressed, and behaviors in the relaxation group are associated with power differences between the sender and receiver. Besides the Mehrabian studies and the study of Shrout and Fiske (1981) discussed earlier, there have been no systematic efforts to study the functional relationships between categories of nonverbal behavior and categories of interpersonal perceptions. Mehrabian's studies indicate that nonverbal behaviors can be grouped by the usual methods of factor analysis. Studies of interpersonal perception show that these perceptions can also be grouped into a few consistent domains. The task of future research will be to map the behavioral domain into the perceptual

TABLE 3.1
Nonverbal and Vocal Behaviors and their Groupings According to
Mehrabian

Behavior	Category Study I	Category Study II
Statements per minute	Affiliative	Affilitative
Questions per minute	Affiliative	Ingratiation
% duration speech	Affiliative	Affiliative
% duration gaze	Affiliative	Affiliative
Head nods per minute	Affiliative	Affiliative
Pleasant face expressions	Affiliative	Affiliative
# verbal reinforcers	Affiliative	Ingratiation
Positive verbal content	Affiliative	Affiliative
Gestures per minute	Affiliative	Affiliative
Pleasant vocal expressions	Affiliative	Ingratiation
Vocal activity	Responsiveness	Responsiveness
Speech volume	Responsiveness	Responsiveness
Speech rate	Responsiveness	Responsiveness
Leg-Foot per minute	Relaxation	Relaxation
Rocking motion per minute	Relaxation	Relaxation
Body lean	Relaxation	Relaxation
Shoulder orientation	Intimacy	Intimacy
Distance	Intimacy	Intimacy

domain in the hope of establishing consistent functional relationships between nonverbal behaviors and the perceptions that they create.

The Functions of "Holding the Floor"

The remainder of this chapter focuses upon a particular vocal behavior: getting and holding the floor in conversation. "Holding the floor" refers to the duration of time that a person is in the speaker rather than the auditor state. By speaker is meant "a participant who claims the speaking turn" (Duncan & Fiske, 1977, p. 177); by auditor is meant "a participant who does not claim the speaking turn" (Duncan & Fiske, 1977, p. 177). A "claim" is not so much a motivational state as the emission of one or more particular behavioral cues. Some of these cues have been discovered empirically by Duncan and Fiske and are discussed later. Holding the floor does not consider the manner in which the floor is held. For example, the speaker might be fluent or hesitant, might be gesturally active or inactive, might be boisterous or soft-spoken, might be intellectually astute or utterly inane. Holding the floor is a naked and simple index of participation in a conversation.

Even before considering the research on how talkative and quiet persons are perceived, simple reflection tells us that the ability to get a full share of the conversation is important. Without the opportunity to participate, the opportunity to persuade, to agree or disagree, to flatter, ingratiate, or impress, to contribute, evaluate, and refine, to apologize and accuse, and, in short, to act in conversation at all is unavailable. Even good listening requires participation. All the prescriptions for competent listening (Athos & Garbarro, 1978; Wolvin & Coakley, 1982) require clarification, feedback, restatement, or astute questioning. Participation in conversation is at least a necessary, if not sufficient, condition for achieving conversational goals.

The question that shall be asked of the research literature is how observers perceive people who vary systematically in their degree of participation in a conversation. More specifically, we shall focus on observers' perceptions in the two central categories of perceptions of association (attraction, friendliness, and positive evaluation), and perceptions of power.

Lustig (1977) reviewed much of the literature on the perceptions of talkative and quiet persons concluding:

Talkative persons were found to be more productive (Norfleet, 1948), more task-oriented (Strodtbeck & Mann, 1956; Knutson, 1960), more leader like (Bass, 1949, 1951; French, 1950; Borgatta & Bales, 1956; Jaffee & Lucas, 1969), more influential (Strodtbeck, 1951; Reichen, 1958; Bales, 1953), more socially adept (Muir, 1964; Steward, 1968; Knutson, 1960; Phillips, 1965, 1968), and better liked (Strodtbeck & Hook, 1961; Bavelas, Hastorf, Gross, & Kite, 1965; Bales, 1956) than their less verbal counterparts. (p. 3)

Lustig's review would support the general claim that those who hold the floor longer would tend to be perceived as more associative and powerful interpersonally. Let us consider some research not included in Lustig's review.

Most of the research relating holding the floor and interpersonal power has operationalized power as perceptions of leadership. Kirscht, Lodahl, and Haire (1959) had groups of three persons select a leader to represent their views in subsequent discussions. The leaders so selected tended to have talked 44.8% of the time compared to 27.6% for those not selected. The correlation between time talked and leadership was .54. Shaw and Gilchrist (1956) had their groups solving problems by writing letters to the group members. Those ranked more highly in leadership sent more letters and more pieces of information than those ranked lower. Slater (1955) found substantial correlations (.75 and .51) between talkativeness and perceptions of leader behaviors of guidance and organization in a group discussion for both more and less well structured groups.

These studies of leadership and talkativeness are correlational so that one cannot conclude that greater talkativeness leads to perceptions of leadership and power. Other behaviors could have produced the perception of leadership, which, in turn, led the person so perceived to be talkative. A series of studies have explicitly manipulated talkativeness by confederates and obtained leadership and perceived power ratings after the discussions. Regula and Julian (1973) found that their more talkative confederates were perceived as more influential and more active than their less talkative counterparts. Surprisingly, these same two perceptions (plus the perception of increased potency) were obtained when confederates who made many low quality suggestions were compared to those making only a few high quality suggestions. The talkativeness effect overwhelmed the content of the comments! In an impression formation study, Stang (1973) had people rate persons in a group on the basis of audiotapes of their discussions. The tapes were structured so that the three speakers' times of holding the floor were in a 3:2:1 ratio. As floor time increased so did perceptions of leadership ability and perceptions of the person's importance to the group. Sorrentino and Boutellier (1975) manipulated both the quantity and the quality of the comments of their confederates. Group members rated the influence, leadership, competence, and confidence of the more talkative confederates higher than the less talkative confederates at each level of quality of the comments. No interactions between quality and quantity were observed for these perceptions. The aforementioned studies clearly show that talkativeness produces the perceptions of power both for observers of the discussion and for participants.

Experiments that have manipulated the talkativeness of confederates have still employed reasonable percentage of the total time available to the group. If the confederate were to approach a monopolization of the floor, would perceptions of the person's power and influence continue to increase, level off, or actually become less pronounced? Daly, McCroskey, and Richmond (1977) asked people to report their perceptions of a hypothetical person who talked 0%, 5%, . . . ,

95% of the time in a five-person group discussion. Perceptions of power, influence, and competence increased up to about 60% and then leveled off and may have actually taken a significant down turn.[3] Although these findings are based upon imagined behavior, they do show a robust positive, linear relationship between perceptions of power and talkativeness through about 60% of a single person's participation. The importance of this direct increase from 0% to 60% participation can be appreciated when it is realized that in the vast majority of groups the average talkativeness of even the most talkative person is in the 40%-50% range (Reynolds, 1971). Thus, in the vast majority of naturally occurring groups the more talkative the person, the more powerful that person will be perceived to be.

Talkative persons are not only perceived as more powerful but they are also perceived as more friendly and attractive, and in general as more associative. Slater (1955) found that more talkative persons were also better liked, at least in his more cohesive groups. Jurors who spoke more were rated as more attractive by other jurors (Scherer, 1979). In a study by Knutson (1960), public health trainees were placed in groups on the basis of their participation in earlier discussions. This created four classes of groups from very talkative to very quiet. Members of the more vocal groups rated their experience as more positive and satisfying than those in the quiet groups. These more talkative persons also tended to prefer their own to another group.

Davis and Perkowitz (1979) substantially advanced the case for the relationship between participation and perceptions of association in finding that the percentage of responses, independent of their frequency, accounts for these positive perceptions of others. After subjects answered questions, a confederate either responded to the subject's response or did not. By altering the number of trials from 6 to 24, Davis and Perkowitz were able to manipulate the probability of the confederate's response from one third to two thirds at two frequency of response levels (4 and 8). Subjects rated confederates who had a higher probability of response as more likable, easier to get along with, more enjoyable in a conversation, easier to work with, a better potential friend, and as more friendly than the less responsive confederate. No similar effects for the number of responses and no interaction between the probability and frequency of responses were found.

Do these findings suggest that perceptions of associativity will increase throughout the range of talkativeness? Our social intuitions would suggest that those who monopolize conversation or who take much more than their fair share might be viewed less positively than more moderate persons. Hayes and Meltzer (1978) make just this suggestion. If perceptions of associativity become less positive at high as well as low levels of participation, then social actors would

---

[3]These authors report eta values that are larger than the simple product-moment correlations but do no tests of the kind of nonlinearity in their data.

be well advised to moderate their participation in discussions to intermediate levels. In the experiment by Stang (1973) discussed earlier, liking for the moderate talker was greatest and that for the high and low talker least. Hayes and Sievers (1972) found a strong curvilinear (an inverted U) relationship between evaluation and percentage of holding the floor for verbal descriptors of hypothetical persons. These findings were replicated for subject samples in the United States, Great Britain, and Chile. Daley, et al. (1977) also found evidence for decreasing social attractiveness at very high levels of participation. Subjects in both these studies rated hypothetical persons in an imagined group situation.

Although the evidence that the relationship between talkativeness and perceptions of associativity is based to a large extent on subject's evaluations of hypothetical situations, it does agree with some common intuitions about experience and is consistent across studies. It is also an important finding. Unlike the data on talkativeness and power, the point at which perceptions of associativity start to turn downward as participation increases occurs much earlier than the leveling off that occurs in perceptions of power. Figure 3.1 displays the best guess curves relating degree of participation to perceptions of power and of associativity. If power and social-emotional factors are equally important to an individual in a group, then at some point in participation level, power and influence may be bought at the costs of positive social evaluation. However, for a range of talkativeness from about 0% to 45% both perceptions of power as well as those of associativity increase.

It is difficult for most people to accept these findings. Fundamental judgments about other people ought to be based upon actions and behaviors that are more complex and richer than simple possession of the floor. However, programmatic research by Hayes and Meltzer (1972) and by Hayes and Bouma (1976) shows

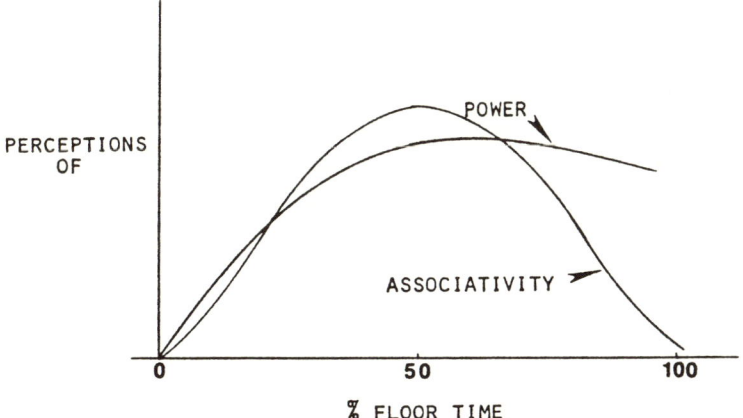

FIG. 3.1. Best guess relationship between perceptions of a speaker's power and associativity and the speaker's percentage of floor time.

that the talkativeness measure accounts for a large portion of the perceptions that observers have of others. In these studies observers see either a videotape of a discussion (with audio) or a series of lights that flash on when a person speaks. They are asked to evaluate the person talking on a series of scales. Across a wide variety of scales and subjects (including 11- to 14-year-old Boy Scouts, college students, middle-aged social psychologists, and French- and English-speaking Canadians), observers gave very similar evaluations of the individuals involved in the video and lights-only conditions. This suggests that all of the verbal content and nonverbal activity contributed only somewhat to the perceptions tapped by the scales used. In the most extreme manipulation, Hayes and Meltzer (1972) had subjects rate group members in the lights condition and other subjects rate the group members after receiving only a single number representing their level of participation in the group. The correlations between these two conditions across the various evaluation scales was .74, .78, and .96 for the three group members. The group members are probably being evaluated on a gross measure of participation and not on the sequencing or patterning of participation.

These results seriously undermine any cynicism about simple floor holding as a basis for important interpersonal perceptions. Certainly, it would be naive to suggest that our perceptions of others are completely determined by their possession of the floor, but one cannot deny that a substantial portion of our perceptions of actors is related to their simple talkativeness.

Conclusions and Implications

This rather long section has tried to make three arguments: (1) Nonverbal behavior should be approached functionally so that behaviors that produce similar perceptions and reactions in observers are treated as functionally equivalent. (2) The interpersonal perceptions of judges are not infinitely complex but rather grouped into broad categories: associativity (attraction, evaluation, friendliness, etc.) and power (dominance, control superiority, etc.). (3) A rather simple variable, possession of the floor during conversation, has substantial effects on interpersonal perceptions in the above two categories. The more a person holds the floor, the greater the perceived power (at least throughout most normal ranges of time of possession). Perceptions of associativity initially increase with increased talkativeness but decrease as talkativeness increases to very high levels.

These arguments are aimed at research on turn-taking, that is, the regulation of possession of the floor. The taking of turns in conversation has important consequences in interpersonal perception above and beyond the control of speaking and listening roles. Turn-taking can have significant effects on who is perceived as more or less powerful and who is perceived as more or less associative. Turn-taking does not merely regulate conversation, it regulates an important *resource* in conversation, access to the floor and the concomitant opportunity to transmit information. Turn-taking can regulate significant portions of interpersonal perceptions as well as speaking and listening roles.

Writers with social sensitivity have recognized the profound personal and social problems that can arise when individuals or social groups are systematically excluded from conversational participation. Zimbardo (1977) tells us that 80% of shy people report that their reluctance to talk is the prime cue of their shyness. With over 80% of those questioned indicating shyness at some point in their lives, individual shyness is a widespread reaction. When shyness, and the concomitant failure to participate, occurs, embarrassment, self-consciousness, and decreased self-esteem result (Zimbardo, 1977). When job and advancement depend upon a positive public image, shyness can be a serious barrier to personal and professional advancement. On a broader scale, Gloria Steinem (1981) portrays the problems of women in male-dominated social groups. Women must bear the (false) reputation of being talkative while at the same time suffering the impotence of being the least talkative with mostly male colleagues in decision-making and social groups. The seemingly trivial actions of simple conversational participation can become a microcosm of the larger social milieu, with the powerless held out of participation and the powerful fully able to exercise their options.

An individual's failure to participate in discussion not only affects the perceptions that others have of the person, but affects the individual's own self-concept and subsequent self-presentation. Being treated as shy, retiring and quiet, deferential and submissive can lead a person to take on these qualities through this reflection through others' responses (Farina, Allen, & Saul, 1968; Farina, Gliha, Boudreau, Allen, & Sherman, 1971).

Once I define myself in these terms, that is, in the terms that others apply to me then it becomes more likely that I will behave in accordance with those traits. The effects can spiral both toward less and toward more participation.

The importance of participation in conversation focuses our attention on how such participation comes about. It is obvious that there is some regularity in the alteration of speaker and listener roles. How people obtain, keep, and relinquish the floor during conversation is not so obvious.

THE CUES FOR TURN-TAKING

Although many researchers have directed their attention to the study of how conversations are organized, structured, and regulated (Goodwin, 1981; Kent, Davis, & Shapiro, 1981; Schenkein, 1978; Wiemann & Knapp, 1975), only the research of Duncan and his associates (Duncan, 1972, 1973, 1974; Duncan, Brunner, & Fiske, 1979; Duncan & Fiske, 1977; Duncan & Niederehe, 1974) has focused on the specific behavioral cues through which speakers and listeners signal their readiness to continue or terminate their speaking and listening roles.

Conversations are organized through a variety of techniques that are only beginning to be understood: rules of transition relevance (Sacks, Schegloff, & Jefferson, 1974), question sequences (Mishler, 1975), vocal amplitude shifts (Goldberg, 1978), specific and general sequencing of comments (Planalp & Tracy, 1980; Tracy, 1982), and so on. But the general organization of conversation is not my concern in this section; the cues associated with the speaker and listener roles are.

Duncan's research has literally defined the study of turn-taking cues.[4] Not only has his research unearthed the specific verbal and nonverbal behaviors that signal smooth transitions from speaker to auditor role but his research has defined the points at which speaker and auditor negotiations of turns take place. On Duncan's analysis, the study of cues for speaker to auditor role switches is only part of the regulation process. In addition, speakers and listeners must regulate their interaction in the presence of "back-channel" actions by the auditor. "Back-channel" actions are verbal and nonverbal behaviors, usually brief, which are not attempts by the auditor to take the floor from the speaker but merely to signal attentiveness or understanding, or to offer brief clarifications, questions, or restatements. Much of Duncan's analysis of turn-taking is directed at the structure of this within-turn interaction, as well as the structure of turn allocation itself.

Turn-Taking Signals[5]

In order to isolate the cues used by speakers and auditors to signal a change of roles, a conversational turn must be defined. Duncan and Fiske (1977) chose not to adopt an objective definition like that of Jaffe and Feldstein (1970) in which any unilateral vocalization by a speaker is a turn beginning for that speaker. The objective definition treats nonverbal and vocal actions by the listener whose purpose is not to wrest the floor from the speaker as if they were actual conversational turns. Duncan and Fiske (1977) define actions with this intent as back channels. Back channels can include nodding, brief vocal insertions such as "yes" and "m-hm," smiles (Brunner, 1979) and longer verbal insertions such as brief restatements, clarifications, questions, and agreements. Despite the fact that this definition of back-channel remarks is ultimately dependent upon the intention of auditor, and, hence, is not directly observable, coders were able to

---

[4]I distinguish Duncan's research of turn-taking cues from Jaffe and Feldstein's (1970) research on turn-taking. Their research concerns the sequence, length, and distribution of crucial interaction parameters such as pause, switching pause, vocalization, and simultaneous speech, not the process of cuing when these switches take place. These two approaches could be integrated with a Markov methodology that uses Duncan's cues as predictors of the transition probabilities from speaker to auditor states (Hewes, 1979). But that is the topic of another paper.

[5]Summaries of the literature on turn-taking cues have appeared in a variety of places (Duncan, 1983; Pelose, 1982; Rosenfeld, 1978) and that literature will not be comprehensively reviewed here.

reliably judge the presence of all types of back-channel actions. The category most likely to produce confusion as to the auditor intent, long back channels, accounted for only 10% of all back-channel actions. Even though Duncan reports no direct test of whether coders could systematically distinguish turns from back channels, the high reliability of each separately is good evidence that they can be reliably distinguished.

Once turns are reliably separated from back-channel actions, then the verbal and nonverbal cues surrounding smooth turn-taking can be isolated. Duncan and Fiske (1977) found that six cues were associated with smooth turn-taking. Duncan (1983) summarizes these cues as follows:

(1) a certain pattern of intonation at the end of phonemic clauses (Traeger & Smith, 1957); (2) a sociocentric sequence (Bernstein, 1962) such as "you know"; (3) the completion of a syntactic clause; (4) a paralinguistic drawl (Traeger, 1958) on the final syllable or the stressed syllable of a phonemic clause; (5) termination of a hand gesticulation or relaxation of a tensed hand position, such as a fist; and (6) decrease of paralinguistic pitch or loudness on a sociocentric sequence. (p. 157)

Remarkably, Duncan and Fiske (1977) report that one or more of these cues by the speaker is present in 261 of 263 smooth turn transitions.

Moreover, gesticulation by the speaker (excluding self-adaptors) while one or more of the above cues is present seems to have a veto effect. Speaker gesticulation greatly suppressed the likelihood that auditors would attempt to take the floor regardless of the number of other turn-yielding cues shown by the speaker. Thus, the six turn-yielding cues plus the speaker gesticulation cue encourage and repress respectively the reversal of speaker and auditor roles.

These data are important not only for what they do find but also for what they fail to find. No single cue seemed to be a more important signal for yielding than the others. No special combination of the cues significantly improved the probability of a smooth turn. No threshold was observed so that, for example, three or more cues predicted turn-taking far better than two cues. In short, the sheer number of cues was the best predictor of the probability of smooth transitions (Duncan & Fiske, 1977).

Other researchers have found one other cue to be of significance in regulating turn-taking: eye gaze. Both Wiemann and Knapp (1975) and Kendon (1967) have claimed that gaze directed at the auditor by the speaker is an important cue for yielding the floor. Duncan and Fiske (1977) do not find that head turns[6] toward the auditor function as a turn-yielding cue. That is, a head turn by the speaker toward the auditor at a time just prior to the auditor smoothly taking the floor does not occur significantly more frequently than when speaker and auditor

_____

[6]Recording procedures did not permit Duncan and Fiske (1977) to study eye gaze per se and they had to settle for head turns.

take simultaneous turns. However, they did find that a shift away in head direction by the auditor approximately at the onset of vocalization by the auditor was much more likely with a turn attempt than with a back channel. In this way, the auditor could signal the speaker that the vocalization was an attempted turn and not a back channel. It was also found that the initiation of gesticulation by the auditor, and to a lesser extent audible inhalation and overloudness, all discriminated between auditor vocalizations that were turn attempts and those that were back channels. Although head shifts do not function as turn-yielding cues, they do have the important role of marking vocal intrusions by the auditor as turn attempts rather than just back-channel actions.

Cegala, Alexander, and Sokuvitz (1979) failed to replicate either the results of Duncan and Fiske (1977) or those of Wiemann and Knapp (1975). Instead, they found that a much greater proportion of speaking turns also had gaze at the other, rather than gaze avoidance, at the initiation of the turn. This finding may have been due to the strict criterion employed in this study. For gaze aversion to have been coded as occurring, the first word of each utterance had to be accompanied by gaze avoidance.

Within-Turn Interaction

If a conversation is to be divided into turns and backchannels, then speakers and auditors not only must negotiate their ways through alternating turns but must also negotiate their ways through back channels during the speaker's turn. The location of back channels and turns is particularly interesting. Duncan and Fiske (1977) studied the distribution of turn attempts and back channels across four different locations in their "units of anlaysis."[7] Three of the locations were within the units and the fourth location was in the pause between units, if any. Of the 319 cases of turn attempts without the speaker's gesticulation signal active, 255 of them occurred in the pause location. Of the 823 cases of auditor back channels (regardless of the speaker's gesturing) 497 of them occurred in the pause location. Duncan and Fiske take no notice of this finding. I think that these frequencies indicate strongly that speaker pauses are the sites of much speaker-auditor activity, marking the location of turn-taking attempts as well as back channels.

Speaker pauses seem to be the primary location for the occurrence of turn attempts and back channel actions by the auditors. Duncan and Fiske (1977) show, however, that other speaker cues can affect the rate of occurrence of such auditor incursions. Gesticulation by the speaker during these pause locations not only severely reduces the number of turn attempts (as might be expected from

---

[7]The units of analysis are particularly difficult to pin down. Duncan and Fiske (1977, p. 169) note that "the boundary of a unit of analysis was considered to be located (a) on the onset of the first syllable; (b) following the end of a phonemic clause . . .; (c) during or immediatley after which at least one of the listed actions occurred." They then list 11 possible actions concluding that "elaborate rules and definitions were not developed and where ambiguity arose . . . decisions were made on the basis of subjective reasonableness" (p. 174).

the earlier results on the gesticulation signal) but also reduces the number of back channels, although the effect is more pronounced with turn attempts than back channels.

Speakers cannot only depress the frequency of back channels but can elicit back channels by using the speaker within-turn cues. These cues include a shift in head direction toward the auditor and completion of a grammatical phrase (Duncan & Fiske, 1977). As the number of these cues increases from 0 to 1 to 2, the proportion of back-channel actions increases proportionately *but only* when these cues occur at pauses or at post-boundary locations, not when these cues occur at speech overlaps or at sociocentric sequences. When speakers generate these within-turn cues, and do get a back-channel response from the auditor, there is a pronounced tendency for the speaker to increase the use of the speaker state cue considerably above baseline (Duncan & Fiske, 1977). In other words, after looking toward the auditor at a brief pause and getting a back-channel response, speakers are much more likely than normal to immediately look away. This look away at the start of a new unit is the display of the important speaker state cue, in a sense notifying the auditor that the speaker still holds the floor.

Simultaneous Turns

The two previous sections treated those cases of speaker-auditor interaction in which no conflict as to who would occupy the speaker state existed. Such conflicts are inevitable and a telling test of Duncan's turn-taking cues would be their ability to predict the "winners" of such competition on the basis of the cues alone. Indeed, Duncan and Fiske (1977) report just such a test. At the points of simultaneous turns, both interactants received a score based on the sum of $+1$ for each speaker state cue (shift away of head direction and initiation of gesticulation) and each gesticulation cue and -1 for each turn yielding cue. The person with the higher score was the predicted winner of the turn competition. In the 67 cases that were not ties, the simple scoring system based on the turn-yielding and speaker state cues predicted correctly in 52 cases.

The only other study of the behavioral cues predictive of the outcomes of simultaneous speaking is that of Meltzer, Morris, and Hayes (1971). Focusing only on amplitude of the voice, they found that successful interruption depended directly on the differences in voice amplitudes at the point of interruption (with the louder person winning the floor) and indirectly on the increase in vocal amplitude by the interrupted party. Duncan and Fiske (1977) did not employ the apparatus necessary to test amplitude differences in interruption.

Turn Regulation and Participation

The motivation for our discussion of turn-taking was laid in the earlier discussion of the importance of conversational participation and judgments of associativity and power. What does turn-taking tell us about participation? Participation in conversation takes two forms: true turns while in the speaker role and back channels while in the auditor role. Duncan's work has isolated some of the behavioral cues associated with terminating the speaker turn, the turn-yielding cues, as well as some of the cues for maintaining the speaking turn, the gesticulation cue, and the speaker continuation cues. On the auditor's side, the speaker state cues indicate attempts at turn-taking rather than back-channel actions, perhaps signaling the speaker that a turn is requested. A very high percentage of these cues of yielding, maintaining, and requesting appear to take place at pauses between units of analysis. These same speaker state and turn-yielding cues are capable of resolving disputes over simultaneous turns and, in combination with vocal amplitude cues, may give a rather complete description of behaviors predictive of the outcomes of simultaneous speaking. In short, the work of Duncan and his associates has made important strides in isolating the specific behaviors that are typically associated with terminating, maintaining, and gaining participation in conversation.

Although I have already drastically simplified the complex of results reported by Duncan and Fiske (1977), I would like to distill them further. Of the great variety of behaviors initially studied, five groups remain as important to participation in conversation: vocal cues associated with the termination of a verbal unit, eye gaze (head shifting), gesticulation, pauses, and possibly vocal amplitude. Of the six cues that function as turn-yielding cues, five (deviation from a certain pitch contour, sociocentric sequences, completion of a grammatical clause, drawl, decreased pitch and/or loudness on a sociocentric sequence) are located at and help designate the completion of a verbal unit (the phonemic clause or grammatical clause). The sixth turn-yielding cue is the termination of gesturing. The gesticulation signal has been found to override the turn-yielding cues as well as to suppress turn attempts and back channels. Head shifting away is an important speaker state cue associated with turn attempts rather than back channels and with speaker continuation after speaker within-turn cues and auditor back channels. Pauses appear to be one of the most likely places in the speaker's speech for turn negotiation to take place. Vocal amplitude signals that vocalizations by the auditor are turn attempts rather than back channels, and relative amplitude, in combination with turn-yielding and speaker state cues, predicts outcomes of simultaneous turns.

Participation in conversation, then, requires an actor to use these five classes of cues in an appropriate way in order to be participative. Implicit knowledge of the cues and the rules must exist. The first group of cues above merely mark the endings of units and, therefore, are the most likely locations for turn attempts or back-channel contributions. These cues mark boundaries more than signal what actions are intended at these boundaries. Clearly, speakers and auditors must be capable of recognizing these boundaries in order to act to continue or terminate their current role. However, the other four cues are much more important because they dictate in some measure what can happen at the ends of verbal units. For example, as the base rate frequency and duration of pauses goes down, so does the opportunity for auditor back channels and turn attempts. If the reticent speaker pauses a great deal, then that person will have more difficulty keeping the floor, simply on the basis of opportunity, than the person who pauses less frequently. If one of the interactants were to maintain an excessively high percentage of gaze aversion, then gaze aversion as a speaker state cue would lose its informativeness. If a person were to employ a high rate of body-focused gestures, especially at points of verbal hesitation, then the usual gesticulation signal would be less available to the apparently fidgety person.

What we do not know about participation and turn-taking is much more extensive than what we do know. We do not know if verbally reticent persons exhibit unusual patterns of turn-taking, employ different turn-taking cues, fail to employ the typical ones, or use the typical cues at inappropriate times. We do not know why the turn-taking process works as it does nor do we have much assurance or detailed knowledge about why reticent persons are reticent. These questions are addressed in the next section in the hopes of showing that the basis of reticent behavior is related to the explanatory basis of turn-taking.

THE BASES OF TURN REGULATION AND PARTICIPATION

Despite our paucity of knowledge concerning the behaviors of reticent conversationalists, this section argues that the most important turn-taking cues are displayed at differential rates by participators and chronic nonparticipators. The argument hinges on the claim that the explanatory basis for turn-taking cues is closely related to the explanatory basis of chronic nonparticipation. If the underlying causes of turn-taking cues and of chronic nonparticipation (which we shall call reticence, Philips, 1968) are similar, then at least some of the reason that reticent persons fail to participate fully in conversations must be a skill deficit in turn-taking.

The Basis for Turn-Taking Cues

Duncan and Fiske (1977) would have us believe that the regulation of conversational turns is nothing more than a coordination problem involving the establishment of mutually compatible expectations between interactants. The bases of these expectations are found in social conventions and not in physiological, perceptual-motor, natural, or genetically coded factors (Duncan & Fiske, 1977). Rather, they are forced to argue, the cues and signals of conversational turns must have grown from arbitrary, tacit agreements among social actors to employ certain nonverbal, vocal, and linguistic cues to govern their interactions. In their view, the cues and rules of turn-taking must be conventional, which, at heart, means that they are arbitrary, so that any other set of cues or rules could have been conventionally adopted to govern conversations.

Such a position defies common sense and ignores significant evidence that pauses, gaze aversion, and body-focused gestures tend to occur at periods of greatest cognitive load. Goldman-Eisler's (1968) work on the cognitive functions of pauses has shown that the more cognitively difficult the information to be encoded, the more pausing in the subject's speech (Goldman-Eisler, 1961a, b). As the difficulty of the material decreases through repetition, the frequency and total duration of pauses also decreases. Despite criticism from Boomer (1970), Goldman-Eisler's findings have been supported in subsequent research by Taylor (1969) on topic difficulty and pauses, by Levin, Silverman, and Ford (1967) on descriptive versus explanatory tasks and pauses, and by Reynolds and Paivio (1968) on abstract noun associates and pause durations. Most pertinent, Siegman (1979) has directly replicated Goldman-Eisler's findings. Recent developments by Butterworth (1975, 1980) and Butterworth and Goldman-Eisler (1979) have identified periods of hesitant and fluent speech presumably associated with periods of planning and execution of that plan respectively. It is presumed that cognitive load during the planning phase is greater than that during the fluent or execution phase.

In interview situations, ambiguous questions elicit longer pauses and switching pauses than do specific questions (Pope, Blass, Bradford, & Siegman, 1971; Siegman & Pope, 1972). When the interviewer behaves in a manner that is warm and attractive, shorter pauses and latencies by the interviewee are observed as compared to the responses to the cold and unattractive interviewer (Pope & Siegman, 1972; Siegman, 1979b). Siegman (1978) has interpreted these latter findings in terms of the added cognitive load that the cold interviewer places on the interviewee. The subjects in the cold condition may be monitoring their verbal choices more closely than those in the warm condition.

Although no study has been conducted using the kind of divided attention task (Norman, 1976) necessary to assess the cognitive load on speakers under the presumed high- and low-load conditions, the interpretation of the results of the above experiments in terms of cognitive load is quite plausible. In many studies of cognitive processes, reaction times are taken as a primary indicator of cognitive load (Anderson, 1980). Pauses and switching pauses are basically measures of reaction time in the domain of speech and, hence, are a reasonable set of indicators of cognitive difficulty and load. Siegman (1978, 1979) has been making just these arguments. The silent pausing associated with ambigious questions, general questions, intimate interactions, interactions with unattractive and cold persons, and with difficult and unfamiliar questions need not be explained by differential appeals to anxiety, and interpersonal attraction, but through the parsimonious mechanism of cognitive decision making. Each of the above conditions requires greater monitoring of one's choice of words and, hence, places the actor under greater congitive load. This decision making takes time resulting in greater pausing.

Gaze aversion may also be associated with higher cognitive load than gaze at the listener during speech. Nielsen (1962) found greater gaze aversion in the preparation of verbal arguments than gaze toward the interlocutor. Exline and Winters (1965) observed more gaze aversion with difficult than easier questions. Kendon (1967) reports more gaze aversion during periods of slow, hesitant speech than periods of fluent speech. Exline, Gray, and Schuette (1965) and Schulze and Barefoot (1974) both coded gaze behavior of persons responding to intimate and nonintimate questions. More gaze aversion by people answering the intimate questions was obtained.

More recent work by Beattie (1978, 1979) supports the cognitive load inter-pretation of gaze aversion. In one study (Beattie, 1979) 1329 fluent word tran-sitions were coded. Of these, 877 were accompanied by gaze with the remainder accompanied by gaze aversion. For nonfluent transitions, there was more gaze aversion during hesitant phases than during fluent phases (this was significant only for clause positions other than the beginning). Beattie (1978) found a nonsignificant tendency for fluent phases of speech to be dominated by gaze at the listener and hesitant phases to be dominated by gaze aversion. The lack of statistical significance may have been due to the excessive scrupulousness of the author who only counted hesitant or fluent phases that had greater than 50% gaze or greater than 50% gaze aversion as supportive of the hypothesis. A direct correlation of degree of hesitancy (measured as the angle of the ratio of pause to phonation time) with the degree of gaze aversion (measured as a percentage) dropping the two extreme cases of total silence along with 100% gaze might have achieved statistical significance. Beattie's data suggest that gaze aversion accompanies periods of planning so that these times of greater cognitive load are indexed by behaviors also associated with cognitive load. Periods of fluency and execution of the planned response exhibit less gaze aversion and more directed gaze, perhaps because of the decreased cognitive load of the execution phase and the desire to monitor its effects.

Cognitive load experienced as social anxiety also seems to be associated with gaze aversion. Jurich and Jurich (1974) rėport high positive correlations between a sweat print measure of anxiety and gaze aversion. In a study by S. Daly (1978), persons identified as more socially anxious exhibited more gaze aversion than less anxious subjects during an interview situation. Although anxiety cannot be equated with cognitive load, anxiety can reduce the available cognitive resources so that the pool of resources that can be marshalled for speech, thought, or other overt or covert activity is thereby reduced (Kahneman, 1973). Together the results on gaze aversion suggest that gaze aversion increased under increased cognitive demands. Anxiety-producing situations may reduce available cognitive resources or may cause actors to reflect upon or weigh their actions more carefully to avoid negative evaluation, embarrassment, or social failure in general. Whatever the function of anxiety in increasing cognitive load, cognitive load is "the most plausible explanation of these forms of gaze aversion" (Argyle & Cook, 1976, p. 171).

In a recent article, Kendon (1983) has argued that on observational, cognitive, and even neurophysiological grounds speech and gesture cannot be separated. We have seen that this is so for conversational regulation. However, to understand the relationship between speech and gesture in turn-taking, the two most common classes of gestures, object-focused (or speech-related) and body-focused (or self-directed), must be separated (Freedman, 1972). Object-focused gestures play an important role in turn-taking as yielding cues, and as attempt-suppressing cues. Body-focused gestures do not.

Body-focused gestures do seem to occur during periods of greatest cognitive load and when the person is anxious or under stress. Dittman and Llewellyn (1969) investigated the relationship between the occurrence of pauses and other body motions. They found that various body motions tended to occur at the beginnings of phonemic clauses just as pauses do. Dittman (1972) noted that the probability of a second movement in nonfluent clauses was greater than that for fluent clauses. Freedman (1972) refined the case somewhat by showing that it was only the body-focused gestures and *not* the object-focused gestures that covaried with pauses.

The crucial finding in the studies above is not that body-focused gestures occur at pauses, but that in nonfluent periods body-focused gestures are associated with the pauses indicative of cognitive load. No single study has investigated both types of gestures at pauses that are in fluent and hesitant phases of the interaction. Object-focused gestures certainly occur during pauses as Duncan and Fiske's (1977) work would lead us to believe. A study by Butterworth and Beattie (1978) helps to solidify, but not to complete, the case. Cycles of hesitancy and fluency in a speech sample were identified. All speech-focused movements and gestures, but no body-focused movements, were recorded, and the speech, as pause or phonation, was also recorded at each gestural movement. The authors found that the (object-focused) gestures were most frequent at pauses during fluent cycles. If the body-focused movements had been studied as well, then they should have occurred most frequently at pauses during hesitant cycles. That study remains to be done.

Gestural activity associated with turn-taking seems to occur primarily at pauses during fluent speech. In this way the gesticulation signal holds off the attempts of the auditor who might intrude in this fluent phase of the speaker's speech. Gestural activity that is body focused also tends to occur during pauses but in periods of hesitant or disfluent speech. These are the periods of greatest cognitive load. These same gestures also tend to occur more frequently under greater stress and anxiety (Jurich & Jurich, 1974; Sainsbury, 1955). When speakers employ body-focused gestures, they cannot easily carry out object-focused gestures at the same time. Thus, under periods of greatest cognitive load or stress and anxiety, speakers are less likely to employ the object-focused gestures necessary to override turn-yielding cues and to suppress turn attempts by the auditor.

In periods of greatest congitive load and/or stress and anxiety, pauses and body-focused gestures increase, decreasing the likelihood of maintaining the floor because the probability of the gesticulation signal is decreased while the opportunities for turn attempts are increased. At the same time, gaze aversion, increasing because of cognitive load, operates as a compensatory mechanism cuing the auditor about the speaker's intent. Its function as a speaker continuation cue mitigates the adverse effects of increased pausing and decreased object-focused gesturing.

A study by Beattie (1979) offers indirect support for this claim. Samples of conversations were coded for periods of hesitancy and fluency and the utterances in each period were coded for the presence of gaze or gaze aversion at the end of the utterance. The duration of the switching pause at the end of the utterance was also coded. Beattie found that speaker switches were fastest when the speaker gazed at the auditor at the conclusion of the utterance but only during the hesitant and not during the fluent cycles. Beattie reasoned that because the hesitant cycles are accompanied by the most gaze aversion, then gaze at the auditor has more information value for the auditor during these periods than during the fluent periods when gaze aversion is much less pronounced. Thus, gaze by the speaker at the end of an utterance successfully cued turn-taking by the auditor during periods of hesitancy.

During periods of less cognitive load, pauses should be fewer and less frequent and be filled with the body-focused gestures typical of speaker continuation and maintenance of the floor. In these fluent periods, gaze at the auditor is more likely than in the less fluent periods, as the speaker is able to monitor the success of his or her speech. The necessity of the speaker continuation cue of gaze away is less because the frequency of pauses is reduced and attempt-suppressing cues of object-focused gesturing are enhanced.

In some ways the system of turn-taking cues that regulates conversations is rather well constructed. As speakers and listeners, we must create what we are going to say, say it, maintain the floor while doing so, and monitor the reactions of our partners in the process. If during the periods of preparation, when we are most vulnerable to interruption, there were no compensatory cues to continuation such as gaze aversion, then as communicators we would suffer interruption before executing our planned segments of speech. Similarly, during periods of execution when the opportunity for interruption by the auditor is diminished, gaze aversion is both unnecessary and counterproductive. Gaze at the auditor permits feedback about the discourse and, as Duncan and Fiske (1977) have shown, is a cue eliciting back-channel responses from the auditor.

I seriously doubt that this rather effective structure permitting cognitive planning while holding the floor, and monitoring during execution of the planned segment of speech, is the result of fortuitous precedents that produced conventions of turn-taking shared among the members of society. The evidence that gaze aversion, pausing, and body-focused gesturing are all associated with situations of greater cognitive load is no accident of social convention. Neither should we conclude that their role in planning and the regulation of conversation is an accident, which social convention has elevated to a well-established, but arbitrary, behavioral regularity. Turn-taking rules are behavioral regularities but not because they are social conventions.

Turn-Taking and the Reticent Person

The chronic nonparticipator in social interaction usually has considerable anxiety and fear over these communication situations. Most self-report measures of reticence have significant components representing general social anxiety. J. Daly (1978) studied the similarity among three classes of measures: performance anxiety, communication anxiety, and general social anxiety. The 14 scales studied included one like Lustig's (1977) measure of verbal reticence whose items are more clearly reports of behavior than measures of anxiety over communication. Nevertheless, J. Daly (1978) concluded that all these scales measure the same basic disposition and that this disposition clearly has an anxiety component. Behnke and Beatty (1981) used a trait measure of communication apprehension and a behavioral measure of heart rate (as a measure of physiological arousal) to predict subject's reports of anxiety on Spielberger's State Anxiety scale (Spielberger, Gorsuch, & Lushene, 1969). Both the trait and the physiological measures correlated very highly with state anxiety, together accounting for 79.6% of the variance in reported anxiety. Schlenker and Leary (1982) also maintain that the variety of measures of fear and anxiety typically produce at least one factor related primarily to social anxiety. Chronic nonparticipators, in addition to their failure to participate, undoubtedly experience considerable anxiety over this failure.

Schlenker and Leary (1982) have argued that social anxiety is the result of cognitive processes activating both arousal and behavior. This approach is unique in that anxiety, social or otherwise, is typically treated as a drive or arousal state activating certain behavioral responses. They single out the cognitive process of self-presentation:

> Social anxiety arises in real or imagined social situations when people are motivated to make a particular impression on others but doubt that they will do so, because they have expectations of unsatisfactory impression relevant responses. (p. 645)

When individuals are in a situation in which the impression they hope to create is important to them or their attempt to do so is hindered "they will engage in a more detailed examination of self, audience, and situation than will otherwise occur" (p.. 656) and will continue to do so as their attempts are frustrated. If they believe they cannot achieve their goals through reassessment, they will seek to withdraw from the situation. But since withdrawal is not always possible, they can become trapped in the assessment and reassessment of their behavior, the situation, and their difficulties in the situation.

Both Zimbardo (1977) and Carver (1979) have noted that socially anxious persons are characterized by this self-conscious evaluation of their own actions and the situation, even in the situation itself. Carver (1979) has called this preoccupation, self-attention. Self-attention must take up a substantial portion of the cognitive resources at the disposal of the anxious person. In focusing on one's self and the situation, the anxious person is considering his or her behaviors, their effectiveness, alternative actions, and so on, thereby increasing his or her own cognitive load. Given the relationship between cognitive load and eye gaze, pausing, and body-focused gesturing, we should expect, on Carver's and Schlenker and Leary's view, that social anxiety would increase gaze aversion, pauses and hesitations in spech, and body-focused gestures. More importantly, these behaviors would result through the mechanism of cognitive load and not through the mechanisms of arousal or anxiety per se. Although Schlenker and Leary (1982) do not make the cognitive load argument, they do claim that the anxiety resulting from the cognitive process of self-attention will lead to an increase in speech disruptions, a decline in productivity, an insensitivity to the cuing functions of the other person's behavior, and a decrease in self-monitoring and control over behaviors (p. 658).

The research literature, although sparse, supports these claims. Socially anxious persons tend to talk less (Cheek & Buss, 1981; Lustig, 1977; Pilkonis, 1977; Sorensen & McCroskey, 1977), have longer latency time to respond (Pilkonis, 1977; Willard & Strodtbeck, 1972), and pause longer while speaking (Pilkonis, 1977) than less socially anxious persons. They also engage in more body-focused gestures (Cheek & Buss, 1981; Pilkonis, 1977) and less eye gaze (Cheek & Buss, 1981; Modigliani, 1971; Pilkonis, 1977). As compared to the socially secure person, the socially anxious use more sociocentric sequences (as rhetorical interrogatives) (Powers, 1977), are less successful interrupters (Natale, Entin, & Jaffe, 1979), and use more back channels such as smiling or nodding (Natale et al., 1979; Pilkonis, 1977). Thus those who are characterized as socially anxious tend to participate less (but more in the back channel), be more hesitant, gaze less, and engage in self-manipulative gestures more than their less anxious counterparts. The behaviors implicated as discriminators between the chronically socially anxious and the socially secure are precisely those behaviors involved in the successful negotiation of turn-taking.

The relationship between turn-taking and participation in conversation, or at least its failure, has been strongly implicated. The crucial behaviors in the regulation of turns and within-turn interaction are also among the significant discriminators of participators and nonparticipators who are known to be socially anxious and socially secure respectively. Beyond the similarity in behaviors manifested, the turn-taking process can be explained through the very same mechanism that social anxiety can be explained. This commonality of explanatory mechanisms suggests strongly that failure to participate in conversation involves a skill deficit in the use of turn-taking cues to obtain, maintain, and yield the floor during conversation.

CONCLUSIONS AND IMPLICATIONS

Participation in conversation is a necessary prerequisite to influence, power, and others' perceptions of attraction and associativity in general. The inability to participate closes important opportunities to individuals or to entire groups within the society.

But why do people fail to participate to their full share? In the view of Schlenker and Leary (1982) socially anxious persons expect that their self-presentational goals will not be met, leading either to withdrawal or to self-attention directed at assessing themselves and the situation. Such self-attention can lead to a greater cognitive load on the actor, and this increased load to greater pausing, self-focused gestures, gaze aversion, sociocentric sequences, and back-channel behaviors. These same cues are the ones that cue turn-taking.

The failure to participate may involve a skill deficit associated with cuing the other about one's intention to obtain, to maintain, or to yield the floor. Since the chronic nonparticipants typically show more pausing and longer latencies to respond, they increase the auditor's opportunities to intrude. By engaging in more sociocentric sequences and body-focused gestures, they offer more turn-yielding cues and fewer attempt-suppressing and speaker continuation cues.

Interestingly, the increased gaze aversion by the socially anxious person seems to act in a direction opposite to that of the other cues. According to Duncan and Fiske (1977), gaze aversion is a speaker continuation cue (but not a turn-yielding cue when in its reversed state [gaze toward]). This claim is controversial, since Kendon (1967) and Beattie (1979) both found more gaze at the auditor toward the end of turns in hesitatnt cycles, but Wiemann and Knapp (1975) cite gaze aversion as a turn-taking cue and Cegala et al. (1979) find gaze accompanying the first words of new turns. The role of gaze as turn-yielding or turn-taking cues remains to be clarified.

Despite this uncertainty, Beattie's (1979) findings remind us that whatever role eye gaze might have, the presence or absence of the state must be informative. If there is a great deal of gaze aversion on the part of an auditor, then a single instance of gaze aversion against the backdrop of extensive periods or high frequencies of gaze aversion is probably not a useful speaker continuation cue. Socially anxious persons employ more gaze aversion than socially secure persons, making their use of gaze aversion less informative than it would otherwise be and, hence, a less useful cue to continuation than it might otherwise be. Beattie (1979) found exactly this. During hesitatnt cycles when gaze aversion was greatest, gaze toward the auditor cued faster speaker switches than when gaze aversion was least during the fluent cycles. Thus, the utility of gaze at or gaze aversion as a cue depends upon the surrounding context which gives the cue its informative value. If the cue blends into the contenxt (e.g., gaze aversion during hesitant periods), then it is a useless cue to the partner. For socially anxious persons, gaze aversion is likely to be a useless cue for speaker continuation because it occurs against the backdrop of higher than normal gaze aversion. Gaze toward the interlocuter would be an informative cue for the partner but is also less likely to be used by the socially anxious rather than the socially secure.

In identifying the inappropriate use of turn-taking cues as one of the reasons for failed participation in conversation, we must not ignore the common explanatory basis of these cues. If socially anxious persons are manifesting nonnormal levels of cues for turn-taking, then one strategy for improving their participation is skills training in the manifestation of the proper levels of these cues in the appropriate locations for obtaining and maintaining the floor (Curran, 1977). But if the reason for the misuse of turn-taking cues is found in the excessive cognitive loads experienced by socially anxious persons, then skills training should be supplemented with training aimed at reducing the self-attention associated with failure in self-presentation. Also, structured experiences should be provided in which cognitive loads on socially anxious persons are reduced by minimizing topic difficulty, topic unfamiliarity, topic ambiguity, topical intimacy, partner aloofness or unresponsiveness, in short, minimizing *any* factor that would add to the cognitive load of socially anxious speakers. The goal of these experiences is to reduce the cognitive load due to factors unrelated to the load due to self-attention. In this way some success experiences might be induced, reducing self-attention and related anxiety.

If the explanation of nonparticipation and of turn-taking is not available to trainers, then techniques for successful training with the socially anxious are limited to treating the symptoms of social anxiety; in this case the symptoms are the failed turn-taking cues. But if social anxiety and turn-taking are mutually implicated through the mechanism of cognitive load and its associated behaviors, then any techniques that reduce excessive congitive load will also reduce abnormalcy in the associated behaviors, induce a modicum of success, reduce the actor's self-attention, reduce the cognitive load, and so on, in a spiral of reduced cognitive load and reduced anxiety. Helping others to act in socially skilled ways, to feel socially secure, and to be perceived as attractive and powerful actors requires elementary knowledge about basic social processes and even esoteric knowledge about the mechanisms explaining social interaction. Separation between the practical and theoretical has never been very useful.

REFERENCES

Anderson, J. R. (1980). *Cognitive psychology and its implications.* San Francisco: Freeman.

Argyle, M., & Cook, M. (1976). *Gaze and mutual gaze.* Cambridge: Cambridge University Press.

Athos, A. G., & Garbarro, J. J. (1978). *Interpersonal behavior.* Englewood Cliffs, NJ: Prentice-Hall.

Bales, R. F. (1953). The equilibrium problem in small groups. In T. Parsons, R. F. Bales, & E. Shils (Eds.), *Working papers in the theory of action.* Glencoe: Free Press.

Bales, R. F. (1956). Task status and likeability as a function of talking and listening in decision-making groups. In L. D. White (Ed.), *The state of the social sciences.* Chicago: University of Chicago Press.

Bales, R. F. (1970). *Personality and interpersonal behavior.* New York: Holt, Rinehart & Winston.

Bass, B. M. (1949). An analysis of leaderless group discussion. *Journal of Applied Psychology, 33,* 527–533.

Bass, B. M. (1951). Situational tests: II. Variables of leaderless group discussion. *Educational Psychology and Measurement, 11,* 196–207.

Bavelas, A., Hastorf, A. H., Gross, A. E., & Kite, R. W. (1965). Experiments on the alternation of group structure. *Journal of Experimental Social Psychology, 1,* 55–70.

Beattie, G. W. (1978). Floor apportionment and gaze in conversational dyads. *British Journal of Social and Clinical Psychology, 17,* 7–15.

Beattie, G. W. (1979). Contextual constraints on the floor-apportionment function of gaze in dyadic conversation. *British Journal of Social and Clinical Psychology, 18.*

Behnke, R. R., & Beatty, J. (1981). A cognitive-physiological model of speech anxiety. *Communication Monographs, 48,* 158–163.

Bernstein, B. (1962). Social class, linguistic codes, and grammatical elements. *Language and Speech, 5,* 221–240.

Bochner, A. P., Kaminski, E. P., & Fitzpatrick, M. A. (1977). The conceptual domain of interpersonal communication behavior. *Human Communication Research, 3,* 291–302.

Boomer, D. S. (1970). Review of F. Goldman-Eisler, Psycholinguistics: Experiments in spontaneous speech. *Lingua, 25,* 152–164.

Borgatta, E. F., & Bales, R. F. (1956). Sociometric status patterns and characteristics of interaction. *Journal of Abnormal and Social Psychology, 43,* 289–297.

Brunner, L. J. (1979). Smiles can be back channels. *Journal of Personality and Social Psychology, 37,* 728–734.

Butterworth, B. (1975). Hesitation and semantic planning in speech. *Journal of Psycholinguistic Research, 4,* 75–87.

Butterworth, B. (1980). Evidence from pauses in speech. In B. Butterworth (Ed.), *Language production* (Vol. 1). London: Academic.

Butterworth, B., & Beattie, G. W. (1978). Gesture and silence as indicators of planning in speech. In R. N. Campbell & P. T. Smith (Eds.), *Recent advances in the psychology of language: Formal and experimental approaches.* New York: Plenum.

Butterworth, B., & Goldman-Eisler, F. (1979). Recent studies on cognitive rhythm. In A. W. Siegman & S. Feldstein (Eds.), *Of speech and time.* Hillsdale, NJ: Lawrence Erlbaum Associates.

Cappella, J. N. (1981). Mutual influence in expressive behavior: Adult-adult and infant-adult dyadic interaction. *Psychological Bulletin, 89,* 101–132.

Carver, C. S. (1979). A cybernetic model of self-attention processes. *Journal of Personality and Social Psychology, 37,* 1251–1281.

Cegala, D. J., Alexander, A. F., & Sokuvitz, S. (1979). An investigation of eye gaze and its relation to selected verbal behavior. *Human Communication Research, 5,* 99–108.

Cheek, J. M., & Buss, A. H. (1981). Shyness and sociability. *Journal of Personality and Social Psychology, 41,* 330–339.

Curran, J. P. (1977). Skills training as an approach to the treatment of hetero social anxiety. *Psychological Bulletin, 84,* 140–157.

Daly, J. A. (1978). The assessment of social-communicative anxiety via self-reports: A comparison of measures. *Communication Monographs, 45,* 204–218.

Daly, J. A., McCroskey, J. C., & Richmond, V. P. (1977). Relationships between vocal activity and perception of communicators in small group interaction. *Western Journal of Speech Communication, 41,* 175–187.

Daly, S. (1978). Behavioral correlates of social anxiety. *British Journal of Social and Clinical Psychology, 17,* 117–120.

Davis, D., & Perkowitz, W. T. (1979). Consequences of responsiveness in dyadic interaction: Effects of probability of response and proportion of content-related responses on interpersonal attraction. *Journal of Personality and Social Psychology, 37,* 534–550.

Dittman, A. T. (1972). The body movement-speech rhythm relationship as a cue to speech encoding. In A. W. Siegman & S. Feldstein (Eds.), *Studies in dyadic communication.* New York: Pergamon.

Dittman, A. T., & Llewellyn, L. G. (1969). Body movement and speech rhythm in social conversation. *Journal of Personality and Social Psychology, 11,* 98–106.

Duncan, S. (1972). Some signals and rules for taking turns in conversations. *Journal of Personality and Social Psychology, 23,* 283–292.

Duncan, S. (1973). Toward a grammar for dyadic conversations. *Semiotica, 9,* 29–46.

Duncan, S. (1974). On the structure of speaker-auditor interaction during speaking turns. *Language in Society, 2,* 161–180.

Duncan, S. (1983). Speaking turns: Studies of structures and individual differences. In J. Wiemann & R. Harrison (Eds.), *Nonverbal interaction.* Beverly Hills, CA: Sage.

Duncan, S., Brunner, L. J., & Fiske, D. W. (1979). Strategy signals in face-to-face interaction. *Journal of Personality and Social Psychology, 37,* 301–313.

Duncan, S., & Fiske, D. W. (1977). *Face-to-face interaction.* Hillsdale, NJ: Lawrence Erlbaum Associates.

Duncan, S., & Niederehe, G. (1974). On signaling that it's your turn to speak. *Journal of Experimental Social Psychology, 10,* 234–247.

Edwards, A. L. (1953). *Manual for the Edwards Personality Preference schedule.* New York: Psychological Corporation.

Eidinger, J. A., & Patterson, M. L. (1983). Nonverbal involvement and social control. *Psychological Bulletin, 93,* 30–56.

Exline, R. V., Gray, D., & Schuette, D. (1965). Visual behavior in a dyad as affected by interview context and sex of respondent. *Journal of Personality and Social Psychology, 1,* 201–209.

Exline, R. V., & Winters, L. C. (1965). Affective relations and mutual glances in dyads. In S. Tomkins & C. Izard (Eds.), *Affect, cognition, and personality.* New York: Springer.

Farina, A., Allen, J. G., & Saul, B. B. (1968). The role of the stigmatized in affecting social relationships. *Journal of Personality, 36,* 169–182.

Farina, A., Gliha, D., Boudreau, L. A., Allen, J. G., & Sherman, M. (1971). Mental illness and the impact of believing others know about it. *Journal of Abnormal Psychology, 77,* 1–5.

Freedman, N. (1972). The analysis of movement behavior during the clinical interview. In A. W. Siegman & B. Pope (Eds.), *Studies in dyadic communication.* New York: Pergamon.

French, R. L. (1950). Verbal output and leadership status in initially leaderless group discussions. *American Psychologist, 5,* 310–311.

Goldberg, J. (1978). Amplitude shift: A mechanism for the affiliation of utterances in conversational interaction. In J. Schenken (Ed.), *Studies in the organization of conversational interaction.* New York: Academic.

Goldman-Eisler, F. (1961a). Hesitation and information in speech. In C. Cherry (Ed.), *Information theory.* London: Butterworth.

Goldman-Eisler, F. (1961b). A comparative study of two hesitation phenomena. *Language and Speech, 4*, 18–26.

Goldman-Eisler, F. (1968). *Psycholinguistics: Experiments in spontaneous speech.* New York: Academic.

Goodwin, C. (1981). *Conversational organization.* New York: Academic.

Gough, H. G., & Heilbrun, A. B. (1965). *The adjective checklist manual.* Palo Alto: Consulting Psychologists Press.

Hayes, D. P., & Bouma, G. D. (1976). Patterns of vocalization and impression formation. *Semiotica, 13*, 113–129.

Hayes, D. P., & Meltzer, L. (1972). Interpersonal judgments based on talkativeness: I. Fact or artifact. *Sociometry, 35*, 538–561.

Hayes, D. P., & Meltzer, L. (1978). *Interpersonal evaluation and participation.* Unpublished manuscript. (Available from Department of Psychology, Cornell University, Ithaca, NY).

Hayes, D. P., & Sievers, S. (1972). A sociolinguistic investigation of the 'dimensions' of interpersonal behavior. *Journal of Personality and Social Psychology, 24*, 254–261.

Hewes, D. E., (1979). The sequential analysis of social interaction. *Quarterly Journal of Speech, 65*, 56–73.

Hinde, R. A. (1978). *Towards understanding relationships.* London: Academic.

Ickes, W., Patterson, M. L., Rajecki, D. W., & Tanford, S. (1982). Behavioral and cognitive consequences of reciprocal versus compensatory responses to pre-interaction expectancies. *Social Cognition, 1*, 160–190.

Jaffe, J., & Feldstein, S. (1970). *Rhythms of dialogue.* New York: Academic.

Jaffee, C. L., & Lucas, R. L. (1969). Effects of rates of talking and correctness of decisions on leader choice in small groups. *Journal of Social Psychology, 79*, 247–254.

Jurich, A. P., & Jurich, A. P. (1974). Correlations among nonverbal expression of anxiety. *Psychological Reports, 34*, 199–204.

Kahneman, D. (1973). *Attention and effort.* Englewood Cliffs, NJ: Prentice-Hall.

Kendon, A. (1967). Some functions of gaze direction in social interaction. *Acta Psychologica, 26*, 22–63.

Kendon, A. (1983). Some recent work on gesture with special reference to its relationship with speech. In J. R. Wiemann & R. Harrison (Eds.), *Nonverbal interaction.* Beverly Hills, CA: Sage.

Kent, G. G., Davis, J. D., & Shapiro, D. A. (1981). Effect of mutual acquaintance on the construction of conversation. *Journal of Experimental Social Psychology, 17*, 197–209.

Kirscht, J. B., Lodahl, T. M., & Haire, M. (1959). Some factors in the selection of leaders by members of small groups. *Journal of Abnormal and Social Psychology, 58*, 406–408.

Knutson, A. L. (1960). Quiet and vocal groups. *Sociometry, 23*, 36–49.

Leary, T. (1957). *Interpersonal diagnosis of personality.* New York: Ronald Press.

Levin, H., Silverman, I., & Ford, B. L. (1967). Hesitation in children's speech during explanation and description. *Journal of Verbal Learning and Verbal Behavior, 6*, 560–564.

Lustig, M. W. (1977). *The relationship between verbal reticence and verbal interaction in triads.* Unpublished doctoral dissertation, Department of Communication Arts, University of Wisconsin, Madison, WI.

Mehrabian, A. (1971). Verbal and nonverbal interaction of strangers in a waiting situation. *Journal of Experimental Research in Personality, 5*, 127–138.

Mehrabian, A. (1972). *Nonverbal communication.* Chicago: Aldine-Atherton.

Mehrabian, A., & Ksionzky, S. (1970). Models for affiliative and conformity behavior. *Psychological Bulletin, 74*, 110–126.

Mehrabian, A., & Ksionzky, S. (1972). Categories of social behavior. *Comparative Group Studies, 3*, 425–436.

Meltzer, L., Morris, W. N., & Hayes, D. P. (1971). Interruption outcomes and vocal amplitude: Explorations in social psychophysics. *Journal of Personality and Social Psychology, 18*, 392–402.

Mishler, E. G. (1975). Studies in dialogue and discourse: II. Types of discourse initiated by and sustained through questioning. *Journal of Psycholinguistic Research, 4,* 99–121.

Modigliani, A. (1971). Embarrassment, facework, and eye-contact: Testing a theory of embarrassment. *Journal of Personality and Social Psychology, 17,* 15–24.

Muir, F. L. (1964). *Case studies of selected examples of reticence and fluency.* Unpublished master's thesis, Washington State University.

Natale, M., Entin, E., & Jaffe, J. (1979). Vocal interruptions in dyadic communication as a function of speech and social anxiety. *Journal of Personality and Social Psychology, 37,* 865–878.

Nielsen, G. (1962). Studies in self confrontation, 1962. Cited in G. W. Beattie, The role of language production processes in the organization of behavior in face-to-face interaction. In B. Butterworth (Ed.), *Language production* (Vol. 1). London: Academic, 1980.

Norfleet, B. (1948). Interpersonal relations and group productivity. *Journal of Social Issues, 2,* 66–69.

Norman, D. A. (1976). *Memory and attention* (2nd ed.). New York: Wiley.

Norton, R. (1978). Foundation of a communicator style construct. *Human Communication Research, 4,* 99–112.

Patterson, M. L. (1982a). A sequential-functional model of nonverbal exchange. *Psychological Review, 89,* 231–249.

Patterson, M. L. (1982b). Personality and nonverbal involvement. In W. Ickes & E. S. Knowles (Eds.), *Personality, roles, and social behavior.* New York: Springer-Verlag.

Patterson, M. L., Mullens, S., & Romano, J. (1971). Compensatory reactions to spatial intrusions. *Sociometry, 34,* 114–121.

Pelose, G. (1982). *Precision timing and turn-taking in conversation: The functions of nonverbal cues, behavioral synchrony and speech rhythm.* Paper presented to the Speech Communication Association Conference, Louisville, KY.

Phillips, G. M. (1965). The problem of reticence. *Pennsylvania Speech Annual, 22,* 22–38.

Phillips, G. M. (1968). Reticence: Pathology of the normal speaker. *Speech Monographs, 35,* 39–49.

Pilkonis, P. A. (1977). The behavioral consequences of shyness. *Journal of Personality, 45,* 596–611.

Planalp, S., & Tracy, K. (1980). Not to change the subject but . . .: A cognitive approach to the management of conversation. In D. Nimmo (Ed.), *Communication yearbook 4.* New Brunswick, NJ: Transactions.

Poole, M. S., & Folger, J. P. (1981). A method for establishing the representational validity of interactional coding systems: Do we see what they see? *Human Communication Research, 8,* 26–42.

Pope, B., Blass, T., Bradford, N. H., & Siegman, A. W. (1971). Interviewer specificity in seminaturalistic interviews. *Journal of Consulting and Clinical Psychology, 36,* 152.

Pope, B., & Siegman, A. W. (1972). Relationship and verbal behavior in the initial interview. In A. W. Siegman & B. Pope (Eds.), *Studies in dyadic communication.* New York: Pergamon.

Powers, W. G. (1977). The rhetorical interrogative: Anxiety or control. *Human Communication Research, 4,* 44–47.

Regula, R. C., & Julian, J. W. (1973). The impact of quality and frequency of task contributions on perceived ability. *Journal of Social Psychology, 89,* 115–122.

Reichen, H. W. (1958). The effects of talkativeness on ability to influence group solutions to problems. *Sociometry, 21,* 309–321.

Reynolds, A., & Paivio, A. (1968). Cognitive and emotional determinants of speech. *Canadian Journal of Psychology, 22,* 164–175.

Reynolds, P. D. (1971). Comment on the 'distribution of participation in group discussions' as related to group size. *American Sociological Review, 36,* 704–706.

Rosenfeld, H. M. (1978). Conversational control functions of nonverbal behavior. In A. W. Sieg-man & S. Feldstein (Eds.), *Nonverbal behavior and communication*. Hillsdale, NJ: Lawrence Erlbaum Associates.

Sacks, H., Schegloff, E. A., & Jefferson, G. (1974). A simplest systematics for the organizaion of turn-taking for conversation. *Language, 50,* 696–735.

Sainsbury, P. (1955). Gestural movement during psychiatric interview. *Psychosomatic Medicine,* 17, 458–469.

Schenkein, J. (Ed.) (1978). *Studies in the organization of conversational interaction.* New York: Academic.

Scherer, K. R. (1979). Personality markers in speech. In K. R. Scherer & H. Giles (Eds.), *Social markers in speech.* Cambridge: Cambridge University Press.

Schlenker, B. R., & Leary, M. R. (1982). Social anxiety and self-presentation: A conceptualization and model. *Psychological Bulletin, 92,* 641–669.

Schulze, R., & Barefoot, J. (1974). Nonverbal responses and affiliative conflict theory. *British Journal of Social and Clinical Psychology, 13,* 237–243.

Schutz, W. C. (1958). *The interpersonal underworld.* Palo Alto, CA: Science Behavior Books.

Shaw, M. E., & Gilchrist, J. C. (1956). Intra-group communication and leader choice. *Journal of Social Psychology, 43,* 133–138.

Shrout, P. E., & Fiske, D. W. (1981). Nonverbal behaviors and social evaluation. *Journal of Personality, 49,* 115–128.

Siegman, A. W. (1978). The telltale voice: Nonverbal messages of verbal communication. In A. W. Siegman & S. Feldstein (Eds.), *Nonverbal behavior and communication.* Hillsdale, NJ: Lawrence Erlbaum Associates.

Siegman, A. W. (1979). Cognition and hesitation in speech. In A. W. Siegman & S. Feldstein (Eds.), *Of speech and time.* Hillsdale, NJ: Lawrence Erlbaum Associates.

Siegman, A. W., & Pope, B. (1972). The effects of ambiguity and anxiety on interviewee verbal behavior. In A. W. Siegman & B. Pope (Eds.), *Studies in dyadic communication.* New York: Pergamon.

Slater, P. E. (1955). Role differentiation in small groups. *American Sociological Review, 20,* 300–310.

Sorensen, G. A., & McCroskey, J. C. (1977). The prediction of interaction behavior in small groups: Zero history versus intact groups. *Communication Monographs, 44,* 73–80.

Sorrentino, R. M., & Boutellier, R. G. (1975). The effect of quality and quantity of verba inter-action on ratings of leadership ability. *Journal of Experimental Social Psychology, 11,* 403–411.

Spielberger, C. D., Gorsuch, R. L., & Lushene, R. E. (1969). *STAI manual for state-trait anxiety inventory.* Palo Alto: Consulting Psychologists Press.

Stang, D. J. (1973). Effect of interaction rate on ratings of leadership and liking. *Journal of Experimental Social Psychology, 27,* 405–408.

Steinem, G. (1981). The politics of talking in groups. *Ms., 9,* 43 and ff.

Steward, L. A. (1968). *Attitudes toward communication: The content analysis of interviews with eight reticent and eight non-reticent college students.* Unpublished doctoral dissertation, Pennsylvania State University.

Strodtbeck, F. L. (1951). Husband-wife interaction over revealed differences. *American Sociological Review, 24,* 468–473.

Strodtbeck, F. L., & Hook, H. (1961). The social dimensions of a twelve-man jury table. *Sociometry, 24,* 397–415.

Strodtbeck, F. L., & Mann, R. D. (1956). Sex role differentiation in jury deliberation. *Sociometry, 19,* 3–11.

Taylor, I. (1969). Content and structure in sentence production. *Journal of Verbal Learning and Verbal Behavior, 8,* 170–175.

Taylor, S. E., & Fiske, S. T. (1978). Salience, attention, and attribution: Top of the head phenomena. In L. Berkowitz (Ed.), *Advances in experimental social psychology* (Vol. 11). New York: Academic.

Tracy, K. (1982). On getting the point: Distinguishing 'issues' from 'events,' an aspect of conversational coherence. In M. Burgoon (Ed.), *Communication yearbook 5*. New Brunswick, NJ: Transaction.

Traeger, G. L. (1958). Paralanguage: A first approximation. *Studies in Linguistics, 13,* 1–12.

Traeger, G. L., & Smith, H. L. (1957). *An outline of English structure*. Washington, DC: American Council of Learned Societies.

Triandis, H. C., & Vassiliou, V. (1972). A comparative analysis of subjective culture. In H. C. Triandis (Ed.), *The analysis of subjective culture*. New York: Wiley.

Triandis, H. C., Vassiliou, V., & Nassiakou, M. (1968). Three cross-cultural studies of subjective culture. *Journal of Personality and Social Psychology, Monograph Supplement, 8,* 1–42.

Triandis, H. C., Vassiliou, V., Vassiliou, G., Tanaka, Y., & Shanmugana, A. (1972). *The analysis of subjective culture*. New York: Wiley.

Wiemann, M., & Knapp, M. L. (1975). Turn-taking in conversations. *Journal of Communication, 25,* 75–92.

Willard, D., & Strodtbeck, F. L. (1972). Latency of verbal response and participation in small groups. *Sociometry, 35,* 161–175.

Wish, M., D'Andrade, R. G., & Goodnow, J. E. (1980). Dimensions of interpersonal communication: Correspondence between structures for speech acts and bipolar scales. *Journal of Personality and Social Psychology, 39,* 848–860.

Wish, M., Deutsch, M., & Kaplan, S. J. (1976). Perceived dimensions of interpersonal relations. *Journal of Personality and Social Psychology, 33,* 409–420.

Wish, M., & Kaplan, S. J. (1977). Toward an implicit theory of interpersonal communication. *Sociometry, 40,* 234–246.

Wolvin, A. D., & Coakley, C. G. (1982). *Listening*. Dubuque, IA: William Brown.

Zimbardo, P. (1977). *Shyness*. Reading, MA: Addison-Wesley.

4

Nonverbal Cues in the Mediation of Interpersonal Expectancy Effects

Robert Rosenthal
Harvard University

The purpose of this chapter is to describe (a) some of what has been learned and (b) some of what might yet be learned about nonverbal communication from the study of the topic of interpersonal expectancy effects. Interpersonal expectancy effects refer to the effects of one person's expectations about the behavior of another person on that other person's behavior. Long before there were experimental studies of this phenomenon, various theorists suggested its operation. Merton (1948), for example, introduced the very useful concept of "the self-fulfilling prophecy." A person prophesies an event, and the expectation of the event then changes the behavior of the prophet in such a way as to make the prophesied event more likely. The late Gordon Allport (1950) applied the concept of interpersonal expectancies to an analysis of the causes of war. Nations expecting to go to war affect the behavior of their opponents-to-be by the behavior that reflects their expectations of armed conflict. Nations who expect to remain out of wars at least sometimes manage to avoid entering into them.

Drawn from the general literature, and the literatures of the healing professions, survey research, educational research, and laboratory psychology, there is considerable evidence for the operation of interpersonal self-fulfilling prophecies. This evidence, ranging from the anecdotal to the experimental, has been reviewed elsewhere (Rosenthal, 1966, 1969, 1976, in press; Rosenthal & Jacobson, 1968; Rosenthal & Rubin, 1978). The best way to get the flavor of research on interpersonal expectancy effects is to consider some illustrative examples.

Some Illustrative Examples

The Case of Clever Hans

Perhaps the paradigm case of interpersonal expectancy effects in the history of experimental psychology is that of Clever Hans (Pfungst, 1911). Although three quarters of a century old, the case is alive enough and important enough that the New York Academy of Sciences held a conference on the topic in May of 1980 (Sebeok & Rosenthal, 1981). Its implications for nonverbal cues as factors in the mediation of interpersonal expectancy effects will be clear from what follows. Hans was the horse of Mr. von Osten, a German mathematics teacher. By means of tapping his foot, Hans was able to add, subtract, multiply, and divide. Hans could spell, read, and solve problems of musical harmony. To be sure, there were other clever animals at the time, and Pfungst tells about them. There was "Rosa," the mare of Berlin, who performed similar feats in vaudeville, and there was the dog of Utrecht, and the reading pig of Virginia. All these other clever animals were highly trained performers who were, of course, intentionally cued by their trainers.

Mr. von Osten, however, did not profit from his animal's talent, nor did it seem at all likely that he was attempting to perpetrate a fraud. He swore he did not cue the animal, and he permitted other people to question and test the horse even without his being present. Pfungst and his famous colleague, Stumpf, undertook a program of systematic research to discover the secret of Hans' talents. Among the first discoveries made was that if the horse could not see the questioner, Hans was not clever at all. Similarly, if the questioner did not himself know the answer to the question, Hans could not answer it either. Still, Hans was able to answer Pfungst's questions as long as Pfungst knew the answer, and was visible to Hans. Pfungst reasoned that the questioner might in some way be signaling to Hans when to begin and when to stop tapping his foot. A forward inclination of the head of the questioner would start Hans tapping, Pfungst observed. He tried then to incline his head forward without asking a question and discovered that this was sufficient to start Hans tapping. As the experimenter straightened up, Hans would stop tapping. Pfungst then tried to get Hans to stop tapping by using very slight upward motions of the head. He found that even the raising of his eyebrows was sufficient. Even the dilation of the questioner's nostrils was a cue for Hans to stop tapping.

When the questioner bent forward more, the horse would tap faster. This added to the reputation of Hans as brilliant. That is, when a large number of taps was the correct response, Hans would tap very, very rapidly until he approached the region of correctness, and then he began to slow down. It was found that questioners typically bent forward more when the answer was a long one, gradually straightening up as Hans got closer to the correct number.

For some experiments, Pfungst discovered that auditory cues functioned additively with visual cues. When the experimenter was silent, Hans was able to respond correctly 31% of the time in picking one of many placards with different words written on it, or cloths of different colors. When auditory cues were added, Hans responded correctly 56% of the time.

Pfungst himself then played the part of Hans, tapping out responses to questions with his hand. Of 25 questioners, 23 unwittingly cued Pfungst when to stop tapping in order to give a correct response. None of the questioners (males and females of all ages and occupations) knew the intent of the experiment. When errors occurred, they were usually only a single tap from being correct. The subjects of this study, including an experienced psychologist, were unable to discover that they were unintentionally emitting nonverbal cues.

Hans' amazing talents, talents rapidly acquired too by Pfungst, serve to illustrate the power of the self-fulfilling prophecy. Hans' questioners, even skeptical ones, expected Hans to give the correct answers to their queries. Their expectation was reflected in their unwitting signal to Hans that the time had come for him to stop his tapping. The signal cued Hans to stop, and the questioner's expectation became the reason for Hans' being, once again, correct.

Other Animal Studies

Some years after Pfungst's work, Rosenthal and Fode (1963a) set out to replicate Pfungst's research; but with horses hard to come by, rats were made to do.

Learning in Mazes.   A class in experimental psychology had been performing experiments with human subjects for most of a semester. Now they were asked to perform one more experiment, the last in the course, and the first employing animal subjects. The experimenters were told of studies that had shown that maze brightness and maze dullness could be developed in strains of rats by successive inbreeding of the well- and the poorly-performing maze runners. Sixty laboratory rats were equitably divided among the 12 experimenters. Half the experimenters were told that their rats were maze-bright while the other half were told their rats were maze-dull. The animal's task was to learn to run to the darker of two arms of an elevated T-maze. The two arms of the maze, one white and one gray, were interchangeable; and the "correct" or rewarded arm was equally often on the right as on the left. Whenever animals ran to the correct side they obtained a food reward. Each rat was given 10 trials each day for 5 days to learn that the darker side of the maze was the one that led to the food.

Beginning with the first day and continuing on through the experiment, animals believed to be better performers became better performers. Animals believed to be bright showed a daily improvement in their performance while those believed to be dull improved only to the third day and then showed a worsening of performance. Sometimes an animal refused to budge from the starting position. This happened 11% of the time among the allegedly bright rats; but among allegedly dull rats it happened 29% of the time. When animals did respond correctly, those believed to be brighter ran faster to the rewarded side of the maze than did even the correctly responding rats believed to be dull.

When the experiment was over, all experimenters made ratings of their rats and of their own attitudes and behavior vis-à-vis their animals. Those experimenters who had been led to expect better performance viewed their animals as brighter, more pleasant, and more likable. These same experimenters felt more relaxed in their contacts with the animals and described their behavior toward them as more pleasant, friendly, enthusiastic, and less talkative. They also stated that they handled their rats more and also more gently than did the experimenters expecting poor performance. In this study, then, differential handling patterns may have served as the nonverbal cues mediating the experimenters' expectations.

Learning in Skinner Boxes.   The next experiment with animal subjects also employed rats, using this time not mazes but Skinner boxes (Rosenthal & Lawson, 1964). Because the experimenters (39) outnumbered the subjects (14), experimenters worked in teams of two or three. Once again about half the experimenters were led to believe that their subjects had been specially bred for excellence of performance. The experimenters who had been assigned the remaining rats were led to believe that their animals were genetically inferior.

The learning required of the animals in this experiment was more complex than that required in the maze learning study. This time the rats had to learn in sequence and over a period of a full academic quarter the following behaviors: to run to the food dispenser whenever a clicking sound occurred; to press a bar for a food reward; to learn that the feeder could be turned off and that sometimes it did not pay to press the bar; to learn new responses with only the clicking sound as a reinforcer (rather than the food); to bar-press only in the presence of a light and not in the absence of the light; and, finally, to pull on a loop which was followed by a light, which informed the animal that a bar-press would be followed by a bit of food.

At the end of the experiment, the performance of the animals believed to be superior was superior to that of the animals believed to be inferior, and the difference in learning favored the allegedly brighter rats in all five of the laboratory sections in which the experiment was conducted.

Just as in the maze learning experiment, the experimenters of the present study were asked to rate their animals and their own attitudes and behaviors toward them. Once again those experimenters who had expected excellence of performance judged their animals to be brighter, more pleasant, and more likable. They also described their own behavior as more pleasant, friendly, enthusiastic, and less talkative, and they felt that they tended to watch their animals more closely, to handle them more, and to talk to them *less*. One wonders what was said to the animals by those experimenters who believed their rats to be inferior.

The absolute amount of handling of animals in this Skinner box experiment was considerably less than the handling of animals in the maze learning experiment. Nonetheless, those experimenters who believed their animals to be Skinner box bright handled them relatively more, or said they did, than did experimenters believing their animals to be dull. The extra handling of animals believed to be brighter may have contributed in both experiments to the superior learning shown by these animals.

In addition to the differences in handling reported by the experimenters of the Skinner box study as a function of their beliefs about their subjects, there were differences in the reported intentness of their observation of their animals. Animals believed to be brighter were watched more carefully, and more careful observation of the rat's Skinner box behavior may very well have led to more rapid and appropriate reinforcement of the desired response. Thus, closer observation, perhaps due to the belief that there would be more promising responses to be seen, may have made more effective teachers of the experimenters expecting good performance.

College Students

We have seen that interpersonal expectancy effects could be demonstrated to occur in horse and rat. Could they be demonstrated in the most common of labortory subjects, the college student?

The First Experiment.   Rosenthal and Fode (1963b) had 10 advanced undergraduate and graduate students of psychology serve as the experimenters. All were enrolled in an advanced course in experimental psychology and were already involved in conducting research. Each student-experimenter was assigned as his or her subjects about 20 students of introductory psychology. The experimental procedure was for the experimenters to show a series of 10 photographs of people's faces to each of their subjects individually. Subjects were to rate the degree of success or failure shown in the face of each person pictured in the photos. Each face could be rated as any value from -10 (extreme failure) to $+10$ (extreme success). The 10 photos had been selected so that, on the average, they would be seen as neither successful nor unsuccessful, but quite neutral, with an average numerical score of zero.

All 10 experimenters were given identical instructions on how to administer the task to their subjects and were given identical instructions to read to their subjects. They were cautioned not to deviate from these instructions. The purpose of their participation, it was explained to all experimenters, was to see how well they could duplicate experimental results that were already well established. Half the experimenters were told that the "well-established" finding was such that their subjects should rate the photos as of successful people (ratings of $+5$) and half the experimenters were told that their subjects should rate the photos as being of unsuccessful people (ratings of -5). Results showed that experimenters expecting higher photo ratings obtained higher photo ratings than did experimenters expecting lower photo ratings. Subsequent studies tended to obtain generally similar results.

The fact that experimenters had all been given the same instructions to read to their subjects suggested that it must have been the nonverbal components of their interaction with their subjects that led experimenters to obtain the results that they had been led to expect. Just because experimenters had been *given* the same instructions to read to their subjects, however, did not mean that in fact they had *read* the same instructions to their subjects. Subsequent studies in which experimenters were filmed during their reading of the instructions suggested that no serious deviations in reading from the written instructions had been occurring (Rosenthal, 1966). The nonverbal cues given off by experimenters remained a likely mechanism serving to mediate the experimenters' expectations.

Experimenters' Voices.   A more direct evaluation of the role of nonverbal cues, auditory cues in particular, was undertaken by Adair and Epstein (1968). They first conducted a study that was essentially a replication of the one just described, and they obtained similar results.

During the conduct of this replication experiment, Adair and Epstein tape-recorded the experimenters' instructions to their subjects. The second experiment was then conducted not by experimenters at all, but by tape-recordings of experimenters' voices reading standard instructions to their subjects. When the tape-recorded instructions had originally been read by experimenters expecting success perception from their subjects, the tape-recordings evoked greater success perception from their subjects. When the tape-recorded instructions had originally been read by experimenters expecting failure perception by their subjects, the tape-recordings evoked greater failure perception from their subjects. Self-fulfilling prophecies, it seems, can come about as a result of the prophet's voice alone. Since, in the experiment described, all experimenters read standard instructions, self-fulfillment of prophecies may be brought about by the tone in which the prophet prophesies.

School Children

The First Pygmalion Experiment.   Studies of interpersonal expectancy effects in which teachers are the expecters and students are the expectees have come to be called "Pygmalion" experiments (Rosenthal & Jacobson, 1966, 1968). In the first of these, all of the children in an elementary school serving a lower class neighborhood were administered a nonverbal test of intelligence, which was disguised as a test that would predict intellectual "blooming." The test was labeled "The Harvard Test of Inflected Acquisition." There were 18 classrooms in the school, three at each of the six grade levels. Within each grade level, the three classrooms were composed of children with above-average ability, average ability, and below-average ability, respectively. Within each of the 18 classrooms, approximately 20% of the children were chosen at random to form the experimental group. Each teacher was given the names of the children from his or her class who were in the experimental condition. The teacher was told that these children had scored on the "Test of Inflected Acquisition" such that they would show surprising gains in intellectual competence during the next 8 months of school. The only difference between the experimental group and the control group children, then, was in the mind of the teacher.

At the end of the school year, 8 months later, all the children were retested with the same test of intelligence. Considering the school as a whole, the children from whom the teachers had been lead to expect greater intellectual gains showed greater gains than did the children of the control group.

In this study we were not able to observe teachers interacting with pupils for whom they held ordinary versus especially high (induced) expectations, though it seemed reasonable to think that teachers treated more favorably, in both verbal and nonverbal channels, those children for whom they held more favorable expectations.

Pygmalion, Galatea, and the Golem.   Among the more recent studies designed specifically to investigate favorableness of treatment of children for whom high versus low expectations are held is that by Babad, Inbar, and Rosenthal (1982). In earlier work, Babad (1979) had shown that teachers' susceptibility to biasing information could be assessed from their scoring of drawings allegedly made by high- versus low-status children. One purpoe of the Babad et al. study was to distinguish between positive (Galatea) and negative (Golem) consequences of teachers' expectancies as these were brought about by teachers especially selected for their bias or for their lack of bias.

Each teacher nominated three high-expectancy and three low-expectancy students and a third group of children was alleged to their teacher to have been assessed as showing unusual potential for gain. In this study expectations were not of intellectual but of physical ability. Not IQ this time, but the ability to do pushups and situps, and to run fast and jump far. Results of this study showed that the children alleged to have special physical potential performed (a) as well as did the children who had been nominated by the teachers as superior in physical education, and (b) significantly beiter than exected under the null hypothesis of no effect of manipulated teacher expectation.

Averaging over all the teachers, biased and unbiased, they treated children better if they had been led to expect more of them or if they already expected more of them than if they expected less of them. Thus, teachers were more friendly toward and less critical of the high-expectancy children than of the low-expectancy children. Friendly and critical behaviors presumably involve both verbal and nonverbal components. Finally, a major result of this study was that this differential treatment of the children was very much more the case for the high-bias teachers than for the unbiased teachers.

THE 10-ARROW MODEL

Since much of the rest of this chapter describes research relevant to the mediation of interpersonal expectancy effects, it will be helpful to have a framework or a model into which to cast the many studies bearing on the mediation of inter-personal self-fulfilling prophecies. In addition, the model is useful in pointing out areas in need of special attention before we can understand (a) the variables serving to moderate or alter the magnitude of interpersonal expectancy effects and (b) the variables serving to mediate the operation of interpersonal expectancy effects, including the role of various channels of nonverbal communication (Rosenthal, 1981).

The model, called the 10-arrow model, for the study of interpersonal expectancy effects utilizes an underlying dimension of time and, therefore, looks as though it might depend on a particular data analytic procedure called "path analysis," but that is not the case. The model does not imply any particular data analytic method. One purpose of the model is to make explicit the classes of variables that must be examined in relation to one another before we can achieve any systematic understanding of the social psychology of interpersonal expectation effects. The basic elements of the model include (A) distal and (B) proximal independent variables, (C) mediating variables, and (D) proximal and (E) distal dependent variables.

Distal independent variables refer to such more stable attributes of the expecter (e.g., teacher, therapist, experimenter) or expectee (e.g., pupil, patient, subject) as gender, status, ethnicity, ability, and personality. It should be emphasized that distal independent variables refer to stable attributes of the expectee as well as of the expector. That increases the power of the model by allowing us to make use of expectee attributes as moderating variables. The proximal independent variable in this model generally refers to the variable of interpersonal expectation—especially expectations that have been varied experimentally rather than those that have been allowed to vary naturally. When expectations are simply measured rather than varied experimentally, a correlation between distal and proximal variables is introduced (e.g., teachers usually expect superior performance from brighter students); this correlation makes it virtually impossible to disentangle the effects of interpersonal expectations from the effects of attributes of the expectee, so that the effects of interpersonal expectations per se become virtually unassessable.

Mediating variables refer to the processes by which the expectation of the expecter is communicated to the expectee. These, then, are like the process variables of the psychotherapy research literature, and our focus is on the behavior of the expecter during interaction with the expectee. By constraining the nature of the verbal communication permitted between expecter and expectee, many studies have shown that these mediating variables must, to a great extent, be nonverbal in nature.

Proximal dependent variables refer to the behavior of the expectee after interaction with the expecter has occurred. A significant relationship between these variables and the experimentally varied proximal independent variables is what we mean by an interpersonal expectancy effect. We should note that the behavior of the expectee (D), including the nonverbal behavior, may have important feedback effects on the behavior of the expecter (C) and the expectation of the expecter (B). Distal dependent variables refer to longer term outcome variables such as those obtained in follow-up studies, e. g., the one-year follow-up testing in the Pygmalion research by Rosenthal and Jacobson (1968). We can present the model diagrammatically as in Fig. 4.1

The 10 arrows of the model summarize some of the types of relationships that are to be examined before any claim to a thorough understanding of interpersonal expectancy effects can reasonably be made. As is shown, each of the arrows is usually of social psychological significance, with the exception of arrow AB, which is often of only methodological significance. An overview of the meaning of the 10 arrows follows.

AB.   These relationships are often large in studies not manipulating interpersonal expectations. Thus, in studies in which teachers are asked to state their expectancies for pupils' intellectual performance, high correlations between teacher

Classes of Variables

Independent		Mediating	Dependent	
A	B	C	D	E
Distal	Proximal	Process	Proximal	Distal

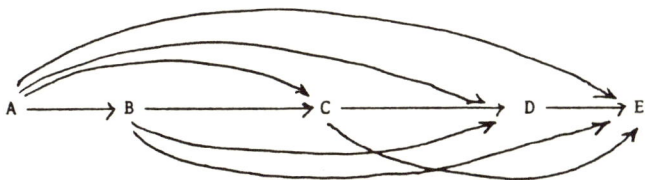

FIG. 4.1 The 10-arrow model for the study of interpersonal expectancy effects.

expectations (B) and pupil IQ (A) are inevitable. These high correlations make it difficult to conclude that it is the teacher's expectancy rather than the pupil's IQ that is "responsible" for subsequent pupil performance. Covariance analysis, cross-lagged panel analyses, and related procedures can be useful here, however, and have been creatively employed (e.g., Crano & Mellon, 1978). When expectancies are varied experimentally, the expected value of the AB correlations is zero since neither the attributes of the expecter nor of the expectee should be correlated with the randomly assigned experimental conditions. A non-zero correlation under these circumstances serves as a methodological warning of a "failure" of the randomization procedure.

AC.   These relationships describe the "effects" on the expecter's interactional behavior of various characteristics of the expecter, the expectee, or both. The joint "effects" of teacher susceptibiity to biasing information and pupil ability on the teacher's subsequent behavior toward the pupil serve as illustration.

AD.   These relationships describe the effects of (usually) the expecter's characteristics on the subsequent behavior of the expectee. A relationship between teacher attitude and/or ability and pupil learning would be an illustration.

AE.   These relationships are like those of AD except that behavior E occurs at some time in the future relative to D.

BC.   These relationships describe the effects on the expecter's behavior toward the expectee of the expectation that has (often) been induced experimentally in the expecter. An example is the four-factor "theory" of the mediation of teacher expectancy effects that summarizes several dozen studies of BC relationships (Rosenthal, 1974). (The four-factor "theory" is discussed later in this chapter.)

BD.   These relationships define the phenomenon of interpersonal expectancy effects when the expectancy has been experimentally manipulated. These relationships may be self-moderating over time, as when expectee behavior (D) affects the subsequent expectation of the expecter (B).

BE.   These relationships define the longer term effects of interpersonal expectations. There are very few studies of this type available.

CD.   These relationships provide suggestive clues to the type of expecter behavior that *may* have effects on the expectee behavior. It is often assumed that CD relationships tell us how teachers, for example, should behave in order to have certain desirable effects on pupil behavior. Except in those very rare cases where mediating variables are manipulated experimentally, such assumptions are unwarranted. Finding certain teacher behavors to correlate with certain types of pupil performance does not mean that teachers changing their behavior to emulate the behavior of the more successful teachers would show the same success with their pupils. These relationships may also be self-moderating over time, as when expectee behavior (D) affects the subsequent behavior of the expecter (C).

CE.   These relationships are like the CD relationships except that the outcome variables are of the follow-up variety.

DE.   These relationships may merely assess the stability of the behavior of the expectee, as when the measures employed for D and E are identical. When these measures are not very similar, the DE relationship may yield an index of predictive validity that is of substantive interest.

Of the 10 arrows of the model, 3 are clearly most important and should ideally be included in most studies of interpersonal expectancy effects: BC, BD, and CD.

The BD relationship tells us the degree to which interpersonal expectancy effects occurred. The BC relationship tells us the degree to which the (preferably experimental induction of) expectancy was a determinant of a particular type of behavior of the expecter toward the expectee. The CD relationship tells us the degree to which certain behaviors of the expecter are associated with changes in the behavior of the expectee. If the BC results show an increase in behavior X due to the induced expectations, and the CD results show that increases in behavior X by the expecter are associated with changes in the performance of the expectee, behavior X becomes implicated as a candidate for status as a mediating variable. Among the most outstanding investigations of these relationships are the studies of Brophy and Good (1974), (AC or BC); Jones and Cooper (1971), (CD); Snyder, Tanke, and Berscheid (1977), (BC, BD); and Word, Zanna, and Cooper (1974), (BC, CD).

MEDIATING MECHANISMS

Among the early hypotheses proposed to account for interpersonal expectancy effects, at least in laboratory situations, were the following:

1. Experimenters cheated and recorded the data they believed desirable rather than their subjects' actual respones.
2. Experimenters misrecorded their subjects' responses with errors tending to favor their expectations. These errors were "honest" errors, but they nevertheless meant that the subjects' actual responses were not being properly recorded.

3. Whenever subjects gave responses consistent with experimenters' expectations, experimenters unwittingly reinforced these responses by means of such small reinforcers as smiles, glances, or nods.

In a detailed consideration of these hypotheses, it was shown that although in any given study it might be difficult to rule out any of these occurrences, many studies found that none of these occurrences were necessary contributors to the mediation of interpersonal expectancy effects (Rosenthal, 1969). For example, cheating and recording errors could be ruled out in studies that (a) provided systems of automated data collection and (b) still showed substantial effects of interpersonal expectation. Unintended reinforcement of expected responses could be ruled out in studies showing that subjects' very first responses were more, rather than less, affected by the experimenters' expectations than were later responses.

Auditory Cues

That the very first response of an experimental subject can be affected by the expectancy of the experimenter suggests that the mediation of expectancy effects must occur, at least sometimes, during that phase of the data-collection situation in which the experimenter greets, seats, and instructs his or her subject. Some beginnings have been made to learn what the experimenter does unintentionally during this phase of the experiment to inform subjects of the expected response. These beginnings are not characterized by spectacular success (Rosenthal, 1966, 1976). Data of a more modest sort, however, are beginning to sketch some picture of the classes of cues likely to be involved in the mediation of expectancy effects. In what follows we cannot be exhaustive but we can be more than illustrative.

Auditory Cues as Sufficient Cues. There is considerable evidence to show that auditory cues alone may be sufficient to mediate expectancy effects. One source of evidence is the study by Adair and Epstein (1968) described earlier in which subjects heard only the instructions tape-recorded by experimenters given different expectancies. A more recent study, inspired in part by the work of Adair and Epstein, was conducted at Tartu State University in the Soviet Union by Läänesaar and Jaama (1976). They also employed photographs as stimuli, with experimenters asked to obtain ratings on the language aptitude of the persons pictured in the photos. Five experimenters were led to expect ratings of high language aptitude and five experimenters were led to expect ratings of low language aptitude. The interactions of these experimenters with their subjects were tape-recorded. In the next phase of the research, additional subjects listened to the tape-recorded instructions provided by the experimenters of the first phase of the experiment. Just as in the study of Adair and Epstein, subjects hearing instructions read by experimenters expecting higher photo ratings responded with higher photo ratings than did subjects hearing instructions read by experimenters expecting lower photo ratings. In terms of the 10-arrow model for the study of interpersonal expectancy effects, the studies by Adair and Epstein and by Lää-nesaar and Jaama involved the critical chain of variables BCD (see Fig. 4.1). The effect of the experimentally induced expectancy on the instruction-reading behavior of the experimenter is an example of a BC arrow. The effect of the experimentally induced expectancy on the photo-rating behavior of the phase 2 subjects is an example of a BD arrow, and the effect of the tape-recorded instructions on the photo-rating behavior of these phase 2 subjects is an example of a CD arrow.

Another study bearing on the importance of auditory cues in the mediation of interpersonal expectancy effects was by Troffer and Tart (1964) in which the experimenters were all experienced hypnotists. They read standard passages to subjects in each of two conditions that may have affected the expectation of the experimenters. When experimenters had reason to expect lower suggestibility scores, their voices were found to be significantly less convincing in their reading of the instructions to their subjects. This result was obtained despite the fact that experimenters were (a) cautioned to treat their subjects identically, (b) told their performances would be tape-recorded and (c) all aware of the problem of experimenter expectancy effects. This study provides an additional example of a BC arrow.

Auditory Versus Total Cues.   The studies previously described suggest that auditory cues may be sufficient to serve as mediators of expectancy effects. Other experiments support this proposition, with the next two having the additional merit of permitting estimates of the effects on the magnitude of expectancy effects of subjects' having available only auditory cues as compared to having access to both auditory and visual cues. The possibility of obtaining such estimates depends on having available at least three groups of experimenters. For two of these groups, subjects must have access to both visual and auditory cues from their experimenters, but each group of experimenters must have a different expectation for their subjects' responses. The difference between the mean response obtained by experimenters of these two groups is considered the base line of magnitude of expectancy effect when both channels of information are available. The third group of experimenters is given one of the two possible expectations but subjects' access to visual cues from these experimenters is cut off. The difference between the mean response obtained by experimenters in this condition and the mean response obtained by experimenters expecting the opposite response is considered the magnitude of expectancy effect when only auditory cues are available. This magnitude can be divided by the base line magnitude for an estimate of the proportion of expectancy effect obtained when only auditory cues were available.

Two experiments meeting these requirements have been reported elsewhere (Rosenthal & Fode, 1963b; Zoble & Lehman, 1969). The earlier study was originally a master's thesis by Fode. Fode's study employed the photo-rating task of Rosenthal and Fode (1963b) and his data showed that 47% of the total expectancy effect was obtained when subjects had access only to auditory cues from their experimenter. Zoble and Lehman's study employed a task requiring subjects to make tone-length discriminations, but their results were remarkably similar to Fode's. Their data showed that 53% of the total expectancy effect was obtained when subjects were restricted to purely auditory cues.

Differential Vocal Emphasis. Additional evidence for the importance of the auditory channel to the mediation of expectancy effects comes from an analysis by Duncan and Rosenthal (1968). Sound motion pictures were available of three male experimenters administering the standard photo-rating task to 10 different subjects. An analysis of the experimenters' vocal emphases showed that no subject was exposed to identical differential emphases of those portions of the instructions that listed the subject's response alternatives. All 5 subjects who heard relatively greater vocal emphasis on the response alternatives associated with high photo ratings subsequently assigned higher photo ratings than did any of the 5 subjects who heard relatively greater vocal emphasis on the response alternatives associated with low photo ratings.

The three experimenters on whose differential vocal emphases these para-linguistic analyses were made had been selected because they were known to have shown expectancy effects. We expect, therefore, by definition, to find a large correlation between the various expectancies given each experimenter and the mean photo rating given by the subject contacted under each different expectation. That correlation, a BD arrow, was + .60, a finding obviously not reported in support of the hypothesis of expectancy effect, but rather to establish a base line for comparison. The correlation between an experimenter's differential vocal emphasis on the various response alternatives in the instructions read to subjects and the subjects' subsequent response, a CD arrow, was + .72. That was a promising chain of correlations. The experimenters' expectancies predicted their subjects' responses, and the differential vocal emphasis of the experimenters also predicted their subjects' responses. It remained only to show that the experimenters' expectancies were a good predictor of how they read their instructions to their subjects. Then everything would fall nicely into place. Unfortunately, that is not what we found. The correlation between experimenters' expectancies and their instruction-reading behavior, a BC arrow, was only + .24, a correlation that is not significantly different from zero for this small sample. The correlation between experimenters' differential vocal emphases and their subjects' subsequent photo ratings with the effects of experimenter expectancy partialed out showed no shrinkage; it was + .74. Therefore, though this analysis gave further evidence of the importance of the auditory channel of communication, it did not turn out to provide the key to the specific signal employed by subjects to learn what it was their experimenter expected. Evidence for such a signal would have been provided only if the correlation between experimenters' expectations and their differential vocal emphasis during instruction reading (i.e., the BC arrow), had been substantial. (Fig. 4.2 illustrates the three arrows of the 10-arrow model that were employed in this study.) The basic finding of the importance of the auditory channel in the mediation of expectancy effects, however, has received still further support in the work of Duncan, Rosenberg, and Finkelstein (1969) who found that auditory cues alone could be sufficient mediators of expectancy effects.

In all the studies described so far it was possible to conclude that auditory cues were important, but it was not possible to isolate any particular aspect of the vocal cues as specifically effective in influencing subjects' responses. It was the purpose of an experimental series by Scherer, Rosenthal, and Koivumaki (1972) to learn whether one specific aspect of vocal emphasis, intensity (or volume), might be sufficient to function as a mediating cue in the communication of expectancy effects. Accordingly, a tape-recorded, balanced reading of instructions to subjects for the standard photo-rating task was re-recorded four times. In each recording the intensity, or volume, of the words describing the scale anchor points (success or failure response alternatives) was raised or lowered by manipulation of the recording level. This generated a 2 x 2 design in which two levels of loudness for the failure word anchor points were crossed by two levels of loudness for the success word anchor points.

In a series of studies, some subjects were exposed to audiotaped instructions giving relatively greater emphasis (loudness) to failure words, and other subjects were exposed to audiotaped instructions giving relatively greater emphasis (loudness) to success words. Results of these studies showed that subjects tended to

Classes of Variables

Independent	Mediating	Dependent
B	C	D
Proximal	Process	Proximal

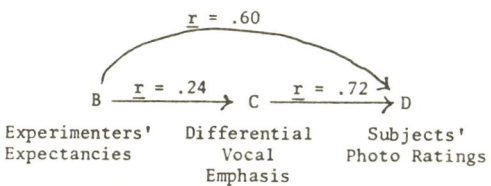

FIG. 4.2 Three arrows employed in the study by Duncan and Rosenthal.

rate photographs of others in accordance with the scale anchor points that had been read more loudly in the audiotaped instructions they had heard. This study illustrates a CD arrow in which the mediating variable (loudness) was varied experimentally.

With all the data available to suggest the importance of the auditory channel in the mediation of interpersonal expectancy effects, it should not surprise us that those studies of expectancy effects permitting the subject little or no auditory access to the experimenter often failed to obtain expectancy effects. That was the result in the two studies by Carlson and Hergenhahn (1968) and in that by Moffatt (1966). The same result occurred in one group of experimenters in the study conducted by Fode (Rosenthal & Fode, 1963b).

Visual Cues

So far we have focused on the auditory channel of communication, but data are also available to show the importance of the visual channel. One important finding comes from the research by Zoble and Lehman (1969) described earlier. As one of their many experimental groups, these investigators had one group of subjects with access only to visual cues from their experimenter. Although their results helped to support the importance of auditory cues, the data of Zoble and Lehman nevertheless showed that visual cues were even more effective than auditory cues in the mediation of expectancy effects. Whereas those subjects with access only to auditory cues were affected by their experimenters' expectancy only 53% as much as those subjects with access to both visual and auditory cues, those subjects with access only to visual cues were affected by their experimenter's expectancy 75% as much as those subjects with access to both information channels. Zoble and Lehman's results suggest a possible non-additivity of the information carried in the visual and auditory channel. It may be that when subjects are deprived of either visual or auditory information, they focus more attention on the channel that is available to them. This greater attention and perhaps greater effort may enable subjects to extract more information from the single channel than they could or would from that same channel if it were only one part of a two-channel information input system. The results of the experiment by Adair and Epstein (1968) strongly support this interpretation.

In an experiment by Kennedy, Edwards, and Winstead (1968) there was additional evidence for the importance of the visual channel. Significant effects of the experimenters' expectancies were found only when subjects had visual access to their experimenter. When subjects were deprived of the possibility of visual cues, no evidence for expectancy effects was obtained.

A recent study by Badini and Rosenthal (1982) employed graduate students to teach vocabulary and reasoning lessons to undergraduates. Half of the teaching situations provided the students with access to visual cues from their teacher and half provided no access to visual cues. In addition, following the Pygmalion paradigm, teachers were led to expect higher intellectual performance from some of their students than from others. Results showed that those students with access to visual cues from their teachers were more affected by their teachers' expectations than were those students with no access to visual cues from their teachers.

An interesting study was conducted by Burnham (1971) in which he videotaped the instruction reading behavior of experimenters who had been led to expect high versus low ratings of success in the standard photo-rating task. The videotaped instructions delivered by experimenters who had shown appreciable degrees of expectancy effects while in "live" interaction with subjects were then shown to fresh samples of subjects. These videotapes elicited substantial degrees of expectancy effects from the samples of subjects who never met the biased experimenters, only their biased videotapes. In this study we cannot ascribe mediation specifically to either visual or auditory cues since both were available to subjects. However, this study, like some of those described earlier, does show that personal contact between expecter and expectee is not a necessary condition for the mediation of interpersonal expectancy effects.

The studies described here suggest that visual cues may also be important for the mediation of expectancy effects, though the experiment by Fode (Rosenthal & Fode, 1963b) found mute but visible experimenters to exert no expectancy effect. Further indirect evidence for the importance of visual cues comes from the experiment by Woolsey and Rosenthal (1966). In the first stage of that experiment, subjects had no visual access to their experimenters but in the second stage they did. When the screens were removed from between experimenters and subjects, expectancy effects became significantly greater. This bit of evidence must be held very lightly, however, since experimenters contacting subjects with visual contact differed in several other ways from experimenters contacting subjects without visual contact. One difference was that experimenters with visual contact had gained greater experience, and more experienced experimenters appear to show greater expectancy effects, a topic to which we now turn.

Interpersonal Learning

For a number of laboratory experiments on expectancy effects, sound motion pictures were available, which had been obtained without the experimenters' or subjects' prior knowledge. The analyses of some of these films have been reported elsewhere (Rosenthal, 1966; Rosenthal, 1967; Rosenthal, Friedman, & Kurland, 1966). For all the hundreds of hours of careful observation, and for all the valuable things learned about experimenter-subject interaction, no well-specified system of unintentional cueing was uncovered. But if the students of experimenter behavior do not know how experimenters unintentionally cue their subjects to give the expected response, then how do experimenters themselves know how to cue their subjects? Perhaps they do not know but perhaps within the context of the given experiment, they can come to know. Expectancy effects may be a learned phenomenon and learned in interaction with a series of research subjects. Each experimenter may have some types of unintended signaling in common with other experimenters, but beyond that, each experimenter may have some unique unintended signals that work only for him or her. Whether this is so is a problem for the psycholinguist, the paralinguist, the kinesicist, the sociolinguist. But if there were this unique component to the unintentional cueing behavior of the experimenter, that might account for our difficulty in trying to isolate very specific but very widespread cueing systems.

The experimenters, who very likely know no more than we about their cueing behavior, may begin their experiment with little ability to exert expectancy effects. But all the time, in their interaction with their first subject, they are emitting a myriad of unprogrammed and unintended cues in the visual and auditory channels. If whatever pattern of cues they are emitting happens to affect the subject's response, so that experimenters obtain the responses they expect to obtain, that pattern of cues may be more likely to recur with the next subject. In short, obtaining an expected response may be the reinforcement required to shape the experimenter's pattern of unintentional cueing. Subjects, then, may teach experimenters how to behave kinesically and paralinguistically so as to increase the likelihood that the next subject's response will be more in the direction of the experimenter's expectancy. Our old friend Pfungst, the student of Clever Hans, had found that as experimenter-questioners gained experience in questioning Hans, they became better unintentional signalers to Hans.

If we are seriously to entertain the proposition that expectancy effects are learned in an interpersonal context, then we must be able to show that, in fact, experimenters are more successful in their unintentional influencing of subjects later, rather than earlier, in the sequence of subjects contacted. The evidence suggests that this is indeed the case, but more so in American as compared to Japanese studies of interpersonal expectancy effects (Rosenthal, 1969; Uno & Rosenthal, 1972).

Sensitivity to Nonverbal Cues

If nonverbal cues are implicated in the mediation of interpersonal expectancy effects, it seems reasonable to suppose that expectees who are more sensitive to the appropriate nonverbal cues might be more influenced by interpersonal expectations. The first study to investigate this question was a Pygmalion type of experiment conducted by Conn, Edwards, Rosenthal, and Crowne (1968). Although the overall magnitude of the teacher expectancy effect was smaller in this study than in the original Pygmalion study, it was found that those children who were more accurate in decoding the tone of voice of an adult female speaker were more affected by their teacher's expectation than were the children who were less accurate in decoding the tone of voice of an adult female. Since most of the children were taught by adult female teachers, and since the tone of voice has been strongly implicated as a mechanism serving to mediate interpersonal expectancy effects, these results were especially provocative.

Just as it seems reasonable to think that better decoders of nonverbal cues might be more affected by interpersonal expectancy effects, it seems reasonable to think that expecters who were better encoders of nonverbal cues might be more effective in bringing about interpersonal expectancy effects. Zuckerman, DeFrank, Hall and Rosenthal (1978) examined these hypotheses simultaneously. Employing the standard photo-rating task, experimenters were led to expect high ratings from some of their subjects and low ratings from their other subjects. Half the experimenters were exceptionally good encoders of nonverbal cues and half were exceptionally poor encoders. Half the subjects were above average in decoding nonverbal cues and half were below average in decoding. The measure of decoding skill was a standardized test of sensitivity to nonverbal cues, the *Profile of Nonverbal Sensitivity*, or PONS test (Rosenthal, 1979; Rosenthal, Hall, DiMatteo, Rogers, & Archer, 1979).

Results showed that the greatest effects of experimenters' expectations were obtained in the condition in which the best encoding experimenters were paired with the best decoding subjects. In a more recent experiment by Christensen and Rosenthal (1982) and in a set of six other studies reviewed in Rosenthal et al. (1979), however, there was no systematic relationship between subjects' nonverbal decoding ability and susceptibility to experimenter expectancy effect. For the present, then, it appears that only when the subjects are children or when the expecter is an especially good encoder of nonverbal cues can we use expectees' nonverbal decoding skill to predict susceptibility to interpersonal expectancy effects.

The Four-Factor "Theory"

Much of the recent work on the mediation of interpersonal expectancy effects has dealt with the mediation of teacher expectancy effects in particular. Early summaries of the research on the mediation of these Pygmalion effects include those by Brophy and Good (1974), investigators whose contributions to this area have been enormous, and by Rosenthal (1974). More recent summaries are those by Persell (1977), Brophy (1982, in press), and Harris and Rosenthal (in press, a, b).

Most of the research conducted in this area has not employed the full BCD chain described earlier, in which we can examine the BC, BD, and CD arrows individually. Most typically, it has been the BC arrow alone that has been studied. There is space here only to be illustrative of the type of research results that have been accumulating. A preliminary four-factor "theory" of the mediation of expectancy effects suggests that teachers (and perhaps clinicians, supervisors, and employers) who have been led to expect superior performance from some of their pupils (clients, trainees, or employees) tend to treat these "special" persons differently than they treat the remaining less special persons in the four ways shown below as the climate, feedback, input, and output factors (Rosenthal, 1974).

The Climate Factor. Based upon the earlier review of the literature (Rosenthal, 1974), teachers appear to create a warmer socioemotional climate for their "special" students. This warmth appears to be at least partially communicated by nonverbal cues. The bulk of the more recent evidence supports the operation of this factor. For example, in their research on camp counselors Blanck and Rosenthal (1984) found that counselors spoke in warmer tones about those campers for whom they held higher expectations for their social and athletic skills. Similarly, Babad, Inbar, and Rosenthal (1982) found that their especially biased teachers, those whose students were, for example, markedly less successful at doing pushups or situps when they were not expected to do many, treated these low-expectation students in a substantially less friendly manner. Also in a Pygmalion context, but with students now being military trainees, Eden and Shani (1979, 1982) found that trainees whose instructors had been led to expect high performance not only performed better on a subsequent test of military performance but also felt more supported by their instructors. Additional recent studies of interpersonal expectancy effects showing warmer climate provided to expectees of whom more favorable expectations were held include those by Heines (1980) and by Andersen and Bem (1981). The latter workers substitute the term *behavioral confirmation* for the term *interpersonal expectancy effect,* as did Snyder et al. (1977) whose work Andersen and Bem replicated and expanded.

The Feedback Factor. Based upon the earlier review of the literature (Rosenthal, 1974), teachers appear to give their "special" students more differentiated feedback, both verbal and nonverbal, about how they have been performing. There appear to be fewer studies bearing on this factor than on the climate factor, but there are some recent studies in support of this hypothesis, including a study of preexisting teacher expectations by Perry (1975) and a study of induced teacher expectations by Smith and Luginbuhl (1976).

The Input Factor. Teachers appear to teach more material and more difficult material to the students for whom they have higher expectations (Rosenthal, 1974). Recent studies providing additional support for this hypothesis include those of Badini and Rosenthal (1982) and Taylor (1979).

The Output Factor. Teachers appear to give their "special" students greater opportunities for responding. These opportunities are offered both verbally and nonverbally, for example, by giving a student more time in which to answer a teacher's question (Rosenthal, 1974). Studies not included in the earlier review of the literature but which support the hypothesis include those of Taylor (1979) and Wellons (1973).

CONCLUSION

More than three quarters of a century have elapsed since Clever Hans demonstrated in replication after replication the role of nonverbal cues in the mediation of interpersonal expectancy effects. Nearly a quarter of a century has gone by since behavioral researchers have looked for the mechanisms serving to mediate interpersonal expectancy effects for organisms other than Hans (Rosenthal, 1956, in press). That quarter of a century has not been wasted, but neither has it had quite the happy outcome that was given to Pfungst in his pursuit of the same question for Clever Hans.

But, though the sought-for answers are not at hand, much has been learned along the way. Some of what has been learned has been described in the pages that lie behind us, and some that is not so directly related to the present topic has been described elsewhere (Rosenthal, in press). Somewhat more related to our present topic is how much there is yet to be learned about what we can foretell about important social outcomes just from knowing about the tone of voice in which people speak to each other. Those people might be doctors, mothers, businesswomen, or college students, but from their content-filtered speech we can tell something about how well their patients (Milmoe, Rosenthal, Blane, Chafetz, & Wolf, 1967) or children (Milmoe, Novey, Kagan, & Rosenthal, 1968) did, how favorably they will be evaluated as executive women (Krasner, Snodgrass, & Rosenthal, 1982), or whether their tone and transparency are such that they have just been talking about men or about women (Green & Rosenthal, 1982).

As little as we know about the mediation of interpersonal expectancy effects, we at least know a lot more than we did. So there is cause for optimism; but there is also need for patience. There will not be an experiment to answer our questions; not one, not two, not ten. "The answers" in behavioral and social sciences do not come in sudden rushes, though the evidence sometimes does. Many studies are needed, conducted in various settings: in laboratories, in clinics, in schools, in the workplace; studies by different workers, working in different research centers. Some of these studies I hope to do; some of these studies I hope you'll do.

ACKNOWLEDGMENT

Preparation of this chapter and much of the research described was supported in part by the National Science Foundation.

REFERENCES

Adair, J. G., & Epstein, J. S. (1968). Verbal cues in the mediation of experimenter bias. *Psychological Reports, 22,* 1045–1053.

Allport, G. W. (1950). The role of expectancy. In H. Cantril (Ed.), *Tensions that cause wars.* Urbana: University of Illinois Press.

Andersen, S. M., & Bem, S. L. (1981). Sex typing and androgyny in dyadic interaction: Individual differences in responsiveness to physical attractiveness. *Journal of Personality and Social Psychology, 41,* 74–86.

Babad, E. Y. (1979). Personality correlates of susceptibility to biasing information. *Journal of Personality and Social Psychology, 37,* 195–202.

Babad, E. Y., Inbar, J., & Rosenthal, R. (1982). Pygmalion, Galatea, and the Golem: Investigations of biased and unbiased teachers. *Journal of Educational Psychology, 74,* 459–474.

Badini, A. A., & Rosenthal, R. (1982, May). *Visual cues and student gender as mediating factors in teacher expectancy effects.* Paper read at the meeting of the Eastern Communication Association, Hartford, CT.

Blanck, P. D., & Rosenthal, R. (1984). Mediation of interpersonal expectancy effects: Counselor's tone of voice. *Journal of Educational Psychology, 76,* 418–426.

Brophy, J. E. (1982, March). *Research on the self-fulfilling prophecy and teacher expectations.* Paper read at the meeting of the American Educational Research Association, New York.

Brophy, J. E. (in press). Teacher-student interaction. In J. B. Dusek (Ed.), *Teacher expectancies.* Hillsdale, NJ: Lawrence Erlbaum Associates.

Brophy, J. E., & Good, T. L. (1974). *Teacher-student relationships.* New York: Holt, Rinehart & Winston, 1974.

Burnham, J. R. (1971). *Experimenter bias and video tape: A methodological step forward.* Unpublished doctoral dissertation, Purdue University.

Carlson, J. A., & Hergenhahn, B. R. (1968). *Use of tape-recorded instructions and a visual screen to reduce experimenter bias.* Unpublished manuscript, Hamline University.

Christensen, D., & Rosenthal, R. (1982). Gender and nonverbal decoding skill as determinants of interpersonal expectancy effects. *Journal of Personality and Social Psychology, 42,* 75–87.

Conn, L. K., Edwards, C. N., Rosenthal, R., & Crowne, D. P. (1968). Perception of emotion and response to teachers' expectancy by elementary school children. *Psychological Reports, 22,* 27–34.

Crano, W. D., & Mellon, P. M. (1978). Causal influence of teachers' expectations on children's academic performance: A cross-lagged panel analysis. *Journal of Educational Psychology, 70,* 39–49.

Duncan, S., Rosenberg, M. J., & Finkelstein, J. (1969). The paralanguage of experimenter bias. *Sociometry, 32,* 207–219.

Duncan, S., & Rosenthal, R. (1968). Vocal emphasis in experimenters' instruction reading as unintended determinant of subjects' responses. *Language and Speech, 11,* Part 1, 20–26.

Eden, D., & Shani, A. B. (1982). Pygmalion goes to boot camp: Expectancy, leadership, and trainee performance. (Paper read at the meeting of the American Psychological Association, New York, September, 1979.) *Journal of Applied Psychology, 67,* 194–199.

Green, C., & Rosenthal, R. (1982). *On decoding noisy talk about women.* Unpublished manuscript, Harvard University.

Harris, M. J., & Rosenthal, R.(in press a). Four factors in the mediation of teacher expectancy effects. In R. S. Feldman (Ed.), *Social psychology applied to education.* New York: Cambridge University Press.

Harris, M. J., & Rosenthal, R. (in press b). The mediation of interpersonal expectancy effects: 31 meta-analyses. *Psychological Bulletin.*

Heines, B. A. (1980). *Pygmalion's sisters and brothers: The influence of sibling-related teacher expectancies on classroom behaviors and student achievement.* Unpublished manuscript, Lake Erie College.

Jones, R. A., & Cooper, J. (1971). Mediation of experimenter effects. *Journal of Personality and Social Psychology, 20,* 70–74.

Kennedy, J. J., Edwards, B. C., & Winstead, J. C. (1968). *The effects of experimenter outcome expectancy in a verbal conditioning situation: A failure to detect the "Rosenthal Effect."* Unpublished manuscript, University of Tennessee.

Krasner, S. Q., Snodgrass, S. E., & Rosenthal, R. (1982). *The executive woman's voice.* Unpublished manuscript, Harvard University.

Läänesaar, J., & Jaama, A. (1976). Experimenter's influence on the results of the experiment: An experimental investigation. *Perception and Communication,* Special Publication of Tartu State University, 66–73.

Merton, R. K. (1948). The self-fulfilling prophecy. *Antioch Review, 8,* 193–210.

Milmoe, S., Novey, M. S., Kagan, J., & Rosenthal, R. (1968). The mother's voice: Postdictor of aspects of her baby's behavior. *Proceedings of the 76th Annual Convention of the American Psychological Association, 3,* 463–464.

Milmoe, S., Roenthal, R., Blane, H. T., Chafetz, M. E., & Wolf, I. (1967). The doctor's voice: Postdictor of successful referral of alcoholic patients. *Journal of Abnormal Psychology, 72,* 78–84.

Moffat, M. C. (1966). Unpublished data. University of British Columbia.

Perry, E. (1975, August). Communication of teacher expectations over time. Paper read at the meeting of the American Psychological Association, Chicago.

Persell, C. H. (1977). *Education and inequality.* New York: Free Press.

Pfungst, O. (1911/1965). *Clever Hans (the horse of Mr. von Osten): A contribution to experimental, animal, and human psychology.* (Translated by C. L. Rahn) New York: Holt, 1911. Republished by Holt, Rinehart & Winston, 1965.

Rosenthal, R. (1956). *An attempt at the experimental induction of the defense mechanism of projection.* Doctoral dissertation, UCLA.

Rosenthal, R. (1966). *Experimenter effects in behavioral reearch.* New York: Appleton-Century-Crofts.

Rosenthal, R. (1967). Covert communication in the psychological experiment. *Psychological Bulletin, 67,* 356–367.

Rosenthal, R. (1969). Interpersonal expectations: Effects of the experimenter's hypothesis. In R. Rosenthal & R. L. Rosnow (Eds.), *Artifact in behavioral research.* New York: Academic Press.

Rosenthal, R. (1974). *On the social psychology of the self-fulfilling prophecy: Further evidence for Pygmalion effects and their mediating mechanisms.* New York: MSS Modular Publications, Module *53,* pp. 1–28.

Rosenthal, R. (1976). *Experimenter effects in behavioral research: Enlarged edition.* New York: Irvington Publishers, Halsted Press Division of Wiley.

Rosenthal, R. (Ed.) (1979). *Skill in nonverbal communication.* Cambridge, MA: Oelgeschlager, Gunn & Hain.

Rosenthal, R. (1981). Pavlov's mice, Pfungst's horse, and Pygmalion's PONS: Some models for the study of interpersonal expectancy effects. In T. A. Sebeok & R. Rosenthal (Eds.), *The Clever Hans phenomenon.* Annals of the New York Academy of Sciences, No. 364.

Rosenthal, R. (in press). From unconscious experimenter bias to teacher expectancy effects. In J. B. Dusek (Ed.), *Teacher expectancies.* Hillsdale, NJ: Lawrence Erlbaum Associates.

Rosenthal, R., & Fode, K. L. (1963a). The effect of experimenter bias on the performance of the albino rat. *Behavioral Science, 8,* 183–189.

Rosenthal, R., & Fode, K. L. (1936b). Three experiments in experimenter bias. *Psychological Reports, 12,* 491–511.

Roenthal, R., Friedman, N., & Kurland, D. (1966). Instruction-reading behavior of the experimenter as an unintended determinant of experimental results. *Journal of Experimental Research in Personality, 1,* 221–226.

Rosenthal, R., Hall, J. A., DiMatteo, M. R., Rogers, P. L., & Archer,D. (1979). *Sensitivity to nonverbal communication: The PONS test.* Baltimore, MD: Johns Hopkins University Press.

Rosenthal, R., & Jacobson, L. (1966). Teachers' expectancies: Determinants of pupils' IQ gains. *Psychological Reports, 19,* 115–118.

Rosenthal, R., & Jacobson, L. (1968). *Pygmalion in the classroom.* New York: Holt, Rinehart & Winston.

Rosenthal, R., & Lawson R. (1964). A longitudinal study of the effects of experimenter bias on the operant learning of laboratory rats. *Journal of Psychiatric Research, 2,* 61–72.

Rosenthal, R., & Rubin, D. B. (1978). Interpersonal expectancy effects: The first 345 studies. *The Behavioral and Brain Sciences, 3,* 377–386.

Scherer, K. R., Rosenthal, R., & Koivumaki, J. (1972). Mediating interpersonal expectancies via vocal cues: Differential speech intensity as a means of social influence. *European Journal of Social Psychology, 2,* 163–175.

Sebeok, T. A., & Rosenthal, R. (Eds.) (1981). *The Clever Hans phenomenon.* Annals of the New York Academy of Sciences, No. 364.

Smith, F. J., & Luginbuhl, J. E. R. (1976). Inspecting expectancy: Some laboratory results of relevance for teacher training. *Journal of Educational Psychology, 68,* 265–272.

Snyder, M., Tanke, E. D., & Berscheid, E. (1977). Social perception and interpersonal behavior: On the self-fulfilling nature of social stereotypes. *Journal of Personality and Social Psychology, 35,* 656–666.

Taylor, M. C. (1979). Race, sex, and the expression of self-fulfilling prophecies in a laboratory teaching situation. *Journal of Personality and Social Psychology, 37,* 897–912.

Troffer, S. A., & Tart, C. T. (1964). Experimenter bias in hypnotist performance. *Science, 145,* 1330–1331.

Uno, Y., & Rosenthal, R. (1972). Tacit communication between Japanese experimenters and subjects. *Psychologia, 15,* 213–222.

Wellons, K. W. (1973). *The expectancy component in mental retardation.* Unpublished D.S.W. dissertation, University of California, Berkeley.

Woolsey, S. H., & Rosenthal, R. (1966). Unpublished data, Harvard University.

Word, C. O., Zanna, M. P., & Cooper, J. (1974). The nonverbal mediation of self-fulfilling prophecies in interracial interaction. *Journal of Experimental Social Psychology, 10,* 109–120.

Zoble, E. J., & Lehman, R. S. (1969). Interaction of subject and experimenter expectancy effects in a tone length discrimination task. *Behavioral Science, 14,* 357–363.

Zuckerman, M., DeFrank, R. S., Hall, J. A., & Rosenthal, R. (1978). Accuracy of nonverbal communication as determinant of interpersonal expectancy effects. *Environmental Psychology and Nonverbal Behavior, 2,* 206–214.

5 Telling Lies: Verbal and Nonverbal Correlates of Deception

Miron Zuckerman, Robert E. Driver
University of Rochester

THE LEAKAGE HIERARCHY

The period of the last 15 years or so witnessed an explosion of interest in the nonverbal aspects of communication. Much of the fascination with this topic has to do with the assumption that nonverbal behavior is, at least in part, involuntary and unintended. Built on this assumption is the notion that nonverbal behaviors may leak information that people try to hide, as well as indicate whether a given message is truthful or deceptive. Freud (1905, 1959) expressed this idea best in a well-known quote: "if his lips are silent, he chatters with his fingertips; betrayal oozes out of him at every pore" (p. 94). The means by which people betray their emotions and thoughts is the topic of this chapter. First, however, it is necessary to examine the question of whether nonverbal behavior does in fact disclose hidden information and deception.

Folk wisdom makes a sharp distinction between the spoken intentional word and the less voluntary and thus more truthful nonverbal display. However, not all nonverbal channels are alike and some may be more controllable than others. Specifically, Ekman and Friesen (1969, 1974) suggested that relative to the face, the body is a better source of leakage and deception cues; leakage cues being defined as nonverbal acts that give away information the sender wishes to conceal, and deception cues being the nonverbal acts indicating that deception is occurring without revealing the concealed content of the message. More recently, researchers (e.g., Rosenthal & DePaulo, 1979) extended this analysis to other channels, particularly tone of voice. Several studies have shown that, like the body, the tone of a person's voice leaks information that is not revealed by the verbal content or facial expressions associated with the message (e.g., Bugental, Henker, & Whalen, 1976; Zuckerman, Amidon, Bishop, & Pomerantz, 1982). It thus appears that the dichotomy between verbal communications and nonverbal displays may be replaced with the concept of a leakage hierarchy—the proposition that all channels form a continuum indicating different degrees of controllability and leakage. Verbal content and face may be located in the controllable end of the continuum whereas the body and tone of voice may be classified as less controllable and more leaky channels.

Underlying the concept of the leakage hierarchy is the assumption that leaky channels are more likely to give away deception than are controllable ones. The empirical evidence relevant to this question has recently been summarized by Zuckerman, DePaulo, and Rosenthal (1981). It was found that accuracy of lie detection is above chance but low—from .45 to .60 in most studies when chance accuracy is .5. As predicted by the leakage model, detection accuracy of either body or tone of voice was higher than that of facial expressions. In fact, of all channels and channel combinations, only the accuracy of the facial channel was not significantly greater than chance. Unexpectedly, it was also found that accuracy of detecting deception from verbal content (transcript) was higher than the accuracy of any other single channel. This evidence is in direct contradiction to the belief that nonverbal channels are more likely to disclose deception than are verbal cues. Furthermore, it is difficult to reconcile this evidence with the proposition that verbal content is highly controllable. Perhaps one should distinguish between the content or theme of a transcript and its semantic structure. Speakers clearly control the general content of the message but may be less likely to monitor other aspects of what they say. Thus, the well-known distinction between what is said and how something is said may be reinterpreted. How something is said is usually understood as a reference to paralanguage aspects of the speech, e.g., tone of voice, speech errors, speech hesitations, and so forth. Perhaps how something is said should also refer to the semantic structure of the message which is independent of its content.

Since accuracy of detecting deception is generally above chance level, there must be some behavioral cues that distinguish between truth and deception. Furthermore, since deception can be detected from transcripts as well as from bodily movement and auditory cues, the behaviors associated with deception must be verbal as well as nonverbal. We now turn to the question of what these behaviors might be.

A FOUR-FACTOR MODEL OF BEHAVIORAL CUES TO DECEPTION

As discussed in this chapter, deception is an act that is intended to convince another person to believe in something that the deceiver considers false. It follows that an act may qualify as deception only when it is intentional, conscious, and

directed at another person. These criteria exclude several deception-related phenomena from the present discussion, including self-deception and intentionally
transparent lies. Self-deception occurs when the individual holds simultaneously
two contradictory beliefs and, for motivational reasons, is not aware of one of
them (Gur & Sackeim, 1979). Thus self-deception is not a conscious act and is
not directed at another person. Intentionally transparent lies occur when individuals are prevented by social norms or other factors from telling the truth and,
consequently, express their opinions nonverbally. Sarcastic remarks fit this
description. Since this form of lie telling is not meant to foster a false belief in
another person, it too is excluded from this discussion.

Even after the exclusion of the aforementioned phenomena we are still left
with a wide variety of lies and deceptive situations. Furthermore, by its very
nature the act of deception is not meant to be communicated and, unlike emotion,
should not have any distinctive pattern of either verbal or nonverbal expression.
That is, since lies are meant to be concealed rather than disclosed, we cannot
assume either an evolutionary process or some form of learning by which they
become associated with a particular behavior. On the other hand, deception does
involve various processes or factors that can influence behavior. Four such factors
are discussed: attempted control, arousal, felt emotion, and cognitive processing.

(a) *Attempted Control.*   Since deceivers try not to disclose what they really
think, they must exercise greater control over their behavior than do truth-tellers.
The attempted control may induce at least three behavioral cues to deception.
First, deceptive behavior may appear too planned, rehearsed, or lacking in spon-
taneity. Second, the deceivers may try to be too persuasive, presenting a too
slick and/or exaggerated performance. Third, since people cannot monitor all
aspects of their behavior and since some channels are leakier than others, deceptive communications may be characterized by discrepancy between the more
controllable and the less controllable components of the message.

(b) *Arousal.*   Research on psychophysiological detection of lying has clearly
shown that truth and lie telling are associated with different autonomic responses
(for reviews, see Lykken, 1974; Orne, Thackray, & Paskewitz, 1972; Waid &
Orne, 1981). Interestingly, there is no agreement on the precise interpretation
of this phenomenon. For example, Davis (1961) suggested three possibilities:
the conditioned response theory, the conflict theory, and the punishment theory.
According to the conditioned response theory, questions related to the concealed
information, which must be of some importance to the deceiver, act as conditioned stimuli and thus enhance autonomic responsivity. (A variant of this
explanation would be that lying rather than the question evoking it is conditioned
to previous deceptive communications, which sometimes led to unpleasant consequences.) The conflict theory suggests that the enhanced responsivity to lying
is a consequence of conflicting tendencies to tell the truth and lie. The punishment
theory proposes that lying enhances responsivity because of the anticipation of

punishment if the lie is discovered. Two other interpretations attribute the autonomic activity associated with deception to the concealed information (termed "guilty knowledge"), which is made salient by the crucial question in the interrogation procedure (Lykken, 1959, 1960); and to deceivers' motivation to succeed on the deception task (Gustafson & Orne, 1963, 1965).

The processes producing physiological arousal in response to deception may also produce several other behavioral reactions. For example, Hemsley (1977) suggested that arousal may cause an increase in the intensity and frequency of various nonverbal behaviors. Note that such an effect is almost the opposite of the planned and rehearsed impression predicted by the control deceivers must exercise over their behavior. This contradiction may be resolved if controllability of the channels is taken into account. Behavior in controllable channels may appear as more planned and organized whereas behavior in less controllable channels may appear more intense and less organized.

Apart from the general hypothesis of more intense behavior due to arousal, it is possible to make more specific predictions regarding behaviors that are generally considered to be associated with arousal. Five such behaviors can be mentioned here: pupil dilation, eyeblinks, fundamental frequency (voice pitch), speech errors, and speech hesitations. Several studies have shown that arousal-producing stimuli, such as a signal for the firing of a gun, trigger an increase in pupil dilation (Nunnally, Knott, Duchnowski, & Parker, 1967; Scott, Wells, Wood, & Morgan, 1967; Simpson & Hale, 1969). An increase in the rate of eyeblinks was viewed by Meyer (1953) as a correlate of general arousal. Two related reviews by Scherer (1980a, b) indicated that arousal induces higher pitch. In the first review, Scherer (1980a) showed that fundamental frequency increases with stress. A well-known example is the finding of higher fundamental frequency in pilots' voices (recorded by their radio transmissions) during flight difficulties as opposed to before they occur (Williams & Stevens, 1969). In the second review, Scherer (1980b) showed that emotions classified as high in arousal are characterized by vocal expressions of high fundamental frequency, whereas emotions low in arousal are characterized by low fundamental frequency. Finally, Kasl and Mahl (1965) reported that manipulation of the level of anxiety in an interview produced concomitant changes in speech errors and hesitations, which were also related to palmar sweat. The above evidence suggests that if deception is an arousal-producing stimulus, it may also produce increases in pupil dilation, eyeblink rate, fundamental frequency, speech errors, and speech hesitations.

(c) *The Affective Approach.* In general, deception is supposed to be associated with negative affects such as guilt and anxiety—guilt about engaging in deception and anxiety about being caught. Ekman (1980) added to this list the "duping delight," that is, the joy associated with meeting the challenge of a successful deception. It is easy to see that the above affects may account for the arousal associated with deception. In fact, anxiety about being caught is at the core of Davis's (1961) punishment theory and the duping delight is related to Gustafson and Orne's (1963, 1965) motivation to succeed on the deception task. Nevertheless, the predictions based on arousal and the affective approach are somewhat different. The latter views behavioral responses to deception as a direct reflection of specific affects rather than as a consequence of arousal.

The experience of guilt and anxiety under deception may result in direct expressions of negative affects, e.g., facial expressions may become less pleasant and verbal content may become more negative. Another indication of anxiety may be an increase in the frequency of adaptors (Ekman & Friesen, 1972)—behaviors that satisfy some self-needs or body-needs (e.g., grooming, scratching, etc.). Deceivers may also try to disassociate themselves from the deceptive messages so as to minimize the negative experience. Consequently, they may employ fewer self-references in the message and more nonimmediate expressions (cf. Wiener & Mehrabian, 1968). Nonimmediacy implies a less direct relationship between the communicator and the object of the message (e.g., "I like John's company" is a less immediate statement than "I like John"). Finally, withdrawal can also cause a decrease in the frequency of illustrators—hand movements that accompany and change (emphasize, augment, etc.) what is being , said verbally (Ekman, 1980).

(d) *Cognitive Factors in Deception.*   Lying can be considered a more difficult task than truth telling. The deceiver must construct a message from scratch and the content of the messge must be both internally consistent and compatible with what the listeners already know. To the extend that lying is a complex task, it may give rise to speech characteristics, pupillary responses, and gestures indicative of such complexity. Goldman-Eisler (1968) showed that when subjects are required to make verbal statements of greater cognitive complexity, they start the response later and pause more frequently. Pupil dilation has been related to mental effort in numerous investigations, particularly those conducted by Kahneman (1973). In fact, Kahneman has shown that the pupillary response was sensitive enough to indicate within a trial the second-to-second variation in the processing load imposed by the task (for a recent review of the relationship between pupil dilation and processing load, see Beatty, 1982). Finally, Ekman and Friesen (1972) suggested that a high level of concentration and absorption in a speech would lead to a decrease in the frequency of illustrators.

Thus, it may be proposed that the more complex nature of lie telling may result in longer latencies, more frequent hesitations, an increase in pupil dilation, and fewer illustrators. Note that changes in some of these behaviors have been previously predicted on the basis of other factors. Specifically, the increase in pupil dilation and frequency of speech hesitations was previously derived from the arousal associated with deception; and the decrease in frequency of illustrators was previously derived from the lower involvement of the speaker in the deceptive message. To the extent that the empirical data support these predictions, we have no way of isolating their exact causal antecedents. It is possible, of course, that some behavioral correlates of deception are multidetermined, having in fact more than one cause.

EMPIRICAL FINDINGS—A META-ANALYTIC APPROACH

Empirical data regarding the relationship between various behavioral cues and deception have been previously reviewed by Kraut (1980) and Zuckerman et al. (1981). Both Kraut and Zuckerman et al. conducted quantitative summaries that were designed to compute the overall level of significance for the association between each of the behaviors in question and deception. The Kraut review, based on 21 studies, showed that of 14 auditory and visual behaviors, 4 (29%) were significantly associated with deception—a percentage that is higher than the 5% expected by chance. The Zuckerman et al. review, based on 32 studies, showed that 8 out of 19 behaviors (42%) distinguished reliably between lie telling and truth telling. The present analysis was based on all the studies included in the Zuckerman et al. review as well as data from 13 additional studies that have now become available. The sum total of 45 studies includes published and unpublished papers as well as unpublished data that have come to the authors' attention.

Most of the studies that were analyzed involved judges who were required to count the frequency or measure the duration of the various behaviors. Sometimes, however, the measure of a behavior was based on readings of some mechanical device such as a pupillometer or, conversely, the subjective impressions of judges. Most investigators reported rates of occurrence for each behavior rather than absolute values, thus controlling for response length. Our impression was that potential distortion due to a lack of control of response length in few of the studies was minimal.

For a particular behavior to be included in the analysis it has to be examined in at least two studies. The list of behaviors to be presented plus a brief description of the measurement techniques follows. It goes without saying that sometimes investigators have used different techniques to measure the same or what appears to be the same behavior. Consequently, somewhat arbitrary decisions had to be made regarding the inclusion or exclusion of particular behaviors from the analysis. We attempted not to mix apples and oranges and at the same time not to exclude data that might have been relevant.

Visual Behaviors

1. Pupil Dilation: Measured by a pupillometer, which is designed to assess the pupil's diameter.
2. Gaze: Measured by duration or frequency of attempts to establish eye contact with the listener.
3. Blinking: Measured by frequency of blinks.

4. Smiling: Measured by duration or frequency of smiles; sometimes also measured by judges' ratings of overall facial pleasantness.
5. Facial Segmentation: Measured by the number of units or segments in the stream of behavior as identified by naive judges.
6. Head Movements: Measured by frequency of either head nods or any head movement.
7. Gestures or Illustrators: Measured by frequency or duration of hand movements designed to modify and/or supplement what is being said verbally.
8. Shrugs: Measured by frequency of hand and shoulder shrugs.
9. Adaptors: Measured by duration or frequency of self-manipulations (e.g., scratching); unlike gestures, adaptors are not related to what is being said verbally.
10. Foot and Leg Movements: Measured by frequency count of movements.
11. Postural Shifts: Measured by frequency count of shifts.
12. Bodily Segmentation: Measured in the same manner as facial segmentation except that judges are requested to segment bodily movement rather than facial expressions.

Paralanguage
13. Latency: Measured by the amount of time between the end of a question and the beginning of the answer.
14. Response Length: Measured by the duration or number of words associated with the response.
15. Speech Rate: Measured by the number of words divided by the duration of the message.
16. Speech Errors: Measured by frequency of nonfluencies, grammatical errors, word and/or sentence repetition, sentence change, sentence incompletion, slips of the tongue, and so forth.
17. Speech Hesitations: Measured by frequency of pauses, including those filled with "ahs," "ers," and "uhms."
18. Pitch: Fundamental frequency of the voice is extracted and analyzed by electronic devices.

Verbal
19. Negative Statements: Measured by frequency of negative and disparaging statements or by judges' overall ratings of the negativity of the message.
20. Irrelevant Information: Measured by frequency of statements judged as irrelevant to the theme of the message or by judges' overall ratings of the relevance of the message.
21. Self-References: Measured by frequency of references to the self (e.g., I, me, mine, etc.).
22. Immediacy: Measured by frequency of immediate indicators (e.g., "his manner bores me" is considered nonimmediate whereas "he bores me" is considered immediate).

23. Leveling: Measured by frequency of overgeneralized statements, which are characterized by leveling terms such as every, all, none, nobody, and so on.

General Variables

24. Discrepancy: Measured by judges' ratings of the overall perceived discrepancy between channels associated with the same massage or by the extent to which the message appears to communicate simultaneously several different emotions.

For each behavior that was included in the analysis we computed two test statistics. The first was the estimate of the effect size, expressed in terms of Cohen's d (1977), of the difference in the occurrence of the behavior in question between deceptive and truthful messages. Cohen's d is defined conceptually as the difference between the means of two groups (truth and deception in the present context) divided by their common standard deviation. As a rule of thumb, Cohen suggested that ds of .20, .50, and .80 should be viewed as small, medium, and large effects, respectively. Although studies do not generally provide d estimates, it is possible to compute this index using formulas given by Friedman (1968), Cohen (1977), and Rosenthal (1978). In the present analysis, d was computed most frequently as a $2\sqrt{F}/\sqrt{df}$, or equivalently as $2r/\sqrt{1-r^2}$. In most cases the ds were derived from statistics provided by the author(s) in the article or in personal communications; when no statistics were available, the ds were derived from the statement that the results were either significant or not significant (in the latter case, d was scored as 0). The ds were assigned positive values when the behavior in question occurred more frequently under deception. Finally, for each behavior we computed the mean d (across the relevant studies), which estimates the overall size of the relationship between the behavior in question and deception.

The second statistic was designed to compute the overall combined p or significance level of the average d. Combined ps were computed according to the procedure outined in Rosenthal (1978). For each study we first calculated the one-tail p and the associated standard normal deviate (z) of the difference in the occurrence of the behavior between truth and deception. zs were assigned positive values if the behavior occurred more frequently under deception. To calculate a combined z, all the zs associated with a behavior were added and then divided by the square root of the number of studies being combined.

Table 5.1 presents the results of the above analysis. The first column shows the number of studies measuring a particular behavior; the second column indicates the mean d for each of these behaviors; and the third column presents the combined z and the significance level associated with this z. It can be seen that 14 out of 24 (58%) behaviors distinguished reliably between truth and lie telling. Because this proportion exceeds substantially the 5% that would be expected by

TABLE 5.1
Behaviors Associated with Deception

Behavior	N	Mean d	Combined Z
Visual			
Pupil dilation	5	1.37	6.82***
Gaze	18	−.03	.13
Blinking	8	.50	1.96*
Smiling	19	−.09	−1.67
Facial segmentation	5	−.27	−2.00*
Head movements	10	−.18	−1.20
Gestures	12	−.12	−.19
Shrugs	4	.38	1.81
Adaptors	14	.34	3.50***
Foot and leg movements	9	−.03	−.22
Postural shifts	11	−.03	−.88
Bodily segmentation	3	.83	2.84**
Paralanguage			
Latency	15	−.02	.28
Response length	17	−.19	−1.98*
Speech rate	12	−.07	−1.36
Speech errors	12	.23	2.14*
Speech hesitations	11	.54	4.06***
Pitch	4	.68	2.26*
Verbal			
Negative statements	5	.95	5.34***
Irrelevant information	6	.40	2.17*
Self-references	4	.05	−.38
Immediacy	2	−.77	−3.37***
Leveling	4	.44	2.16*
General			
Discrepancy	4	.64	4.31***

Note: Positive values indicate that an increase in the behavior was associated with deception.

  *$p < .05$
 **$p < .01$
***$p < .001$

chance, it may be inferred that the different deceptive situations included in the analysis share some common elements or factors.

Earlier we proposed that deception may be associated with four such factors: control, arousal, negative affects, and cognitive complexity. Each of these is discussed below in relation to the empirical evidence.

It is hypothesized that deceivers' attempts to control their expressions may result in well-organized and less spontaneous behavior, exaggerated performance, and discrepancy between controllable and less controllable channels. Well-organized behavior may be more homogeneous and therefore less segmented.

Accordingly, Table 5.1 shows that deception was related to a smaller number of segments in a controllabe channel such as the face. Apparently the attempt to monitor one's facial expressions results in fewer changes in the stream of behavior and consequently a smaller number of identifiable units. Single studies of behaviors not included in the meta-analysis also provide evidence that is consistent with this aspect of the control factor. Thus, Zuckerman, DeFrank, Hall, Larrance, and Rosenthal (1979) found that deceptive answers gave rise to impressions of less personal involvement; and DePaulo, Lanier, and Davis (1983) reported that deceptive answers were viewed as less spontaneous. One behavioral cue presented in Table 5.1, leveling, is relevant to the second aspect of control, that of exaggerated performance. That deceivers are more likely to express their opinions in absolute leveling terms, barring any exception to the position presented, can be viewed as a form of exaggerated and extreme performance. Finally, in accordance with the third predicted aspect of the control factor, deceptive messages were judged as more discrepant than were truthful communications.

It was hypothesized that arousal may increase the intensity and frequency of behaviors in noncontrollable channels. An increase in the frequency of behavior may be associated with an increase in the number of identifiable units. Accordingly, Table 5.1 shows that deception was related to a higher number of segments in the body. It was also hypothesized that arousal may increase pupil dilation, frequency of blinking, voice pitch level, and frequency of speech errors and speech hesitations. As can be seen in Table 5.1, all five behaviors were reliably associated with deception.

Turning to the factor of felt emotion, it was hypothesized that the negative affect associated with deception may give rise to direct expressions of negativity, to behaviors that signal anxiety and discomfort, and to various forms of withdrawal from the content of the message. As can be seen in Table 5.1, deception was associated with a close to significant decrease in smiling ($z = -1.67$, $p < .10$), and a significant increase in verbal negative statements; deception was also associated with an increase in adaptors, a behavior that can serve as an indicator of discomfort. Finally, deceptive statements were more nonimmediate than truthful ones, perhaps signaling withdrawal from the content of the message.

It should be noted that originally, nonimmediacy was conceptualized as a communication mode of negative expressions. For example, it has been shown that nonimmediate statements were rated as more negative and that negative statements were judged as more nonimmediate (Mehrabian, 1966, 1967; Wiener & Mehrabian, 1968). Certainly, the interpretation of nonimmediacy as a negative expression is consistent with the finding that other negative expressions, both facial and verbal, appear associated with deception. Furthermore, since two other indices of withdrawal, self-references and illustrators, were not associated with deception, a parsimonious explanation of the relationship between deception and nonimmediacy is that the latter is an index of negativity rather than of withdrawal.

Perhaps the important point is that no matter how nonimmediacy is interpreted, its association with lie telling indicates that deception involves negative affects.

The conceptualization of deception as complex cognitive activity led to predictions of increase in latency of response, speech hesitations, and pupil dilation, as well as a decrease in the frequency of illustrators. Of these four behaviors, only speech hesitations and pupil dilation were related to deception and these relationships can be accounted for by the arousal factor. On the other hand, the two remaining correlates of deception in Table 5.1—a decrease in response length and an increase in irrelevant information—also suggest that deception involves more complex cognitive processing. Unlike truthful communications, deceptive messages are constructed in the deceiver's mind. Consequently, the deceiver has fewer things to say (shorter response length) and may use irrelevant information as a stopgap mechanism. It may be concluded, then, that the description of deception as a complex activity remains a viable hypothesis.

Although the empirical findings of the meta-analysis provide some support for the four-factor model of deception, they also raise a number of questions. Clearly, the meta-analysis of cues to deception is constrained by the empirical data that are available. Thus, a large number of behaviors are left out and the measurement of others leaves something to be desired. For example, the five verbal variables that are included in the analysis cannot possibly account for the semantic structure of the transcript. Thus, the means by which transcript leaks deception cues remain a mystery. In addition, variables such as gestures, adaptors, head movements, and so forth appear too global to be of use in detecting deception. Perhaps lie telling is characterized by more specific subcategories of these movements. Finally, a model of cues to deception may benefit from a factor-analytic approach. That is, the suggestion that behavioral cues are organized around particular factors may be tested by a factor analysis of these cues. The emerging factors will show how these variables may be grouped and thus indicate how deception is structured.

DIFFERENT TYPES OF LIES; THE EFFECTS OF MOTIVATION AND PLANNING

Although the association between behavioral cues and deception is substantially above chance, it is also far from perfect. Fully 42% of the behaviors presented in Table 5.1 were not related to deception. In addition, the relationships that had been found were not particularly strong; the median d of the significant relationships was .52, which is only slightly above what Cohen (1977) considered a medium effect. It is possible, however, that some of the variation in the association between behavioral cues and deception is accounted for by differences between different deceptive contexts and different lies. In an exploratory attempt to examine this issue, the studies included in Table 5.1 were classified according to two dimensions: motivation to succeed on the deception task and the amount of planning involved in the deception. Because of a relatively small number of available studies, these two dimensions could not be crossed and their effects on the behavioral correlates of deception are discussed separately.

Motivation

Studies were grouped into two levels of motivation, low and high. Motivation was considered high if subjects were promised some monetary rewards for doing well on the deception task or if the deception was described as a test of some skill. To the extent that motivation was manipulated in a single study as an independent variable and results were reported for each motivation level, we entered the appropriate data in the low- and high-motivation groups as if the study consisted of two separate experiments. If the results were not reported separately for each motivation level, the study was excluded from the present analysis.

Mean ds and combined zs of the relationship between each behavioral cue and deception were computed for each group of studies according to the procedures described previously. Table 5.2 presents the results of this analysis. For each level of motivation the table shows the number of studies, mean d, and the significance level derived from the combined z associated with this d. In addition, the right-hand column presents the zs of the difference between the significance levels associated with the low- and high-motivation ds (Rosenthal & Rubin, 1979). It can be seen that 9 out of 24 (38%) behaviors listed in the low-motivation group were significantly associated with deception compared with 10 out of 20 (50%) behaviors in the high-motivation group. Furthermore, there were 8 significant differences between the low- and high-motivation levels where only one would be expected by chance.

Although the differences between the two motivation levels appear substantial, their interpretation is speculative. With the exception of shrugs, visual behaviors associated with highly motivated deception show a decrease in frequency and/or intensity. Specifically, compared with the low-motivation condition, deception under high motivation was associated with less blinking, more neutral expressions ($p = .11$), fewer head movements, fewer adaptors ($p = .12$), and fewer postural shifts. With the exception of pitch, paralanguage behaviors also showed an association between highly motivated deception and a slower temporal pacing. Specifically, compared with the low-motivation condition, deception under high motivation was associated with shorter response length and slower rate of speech. Finally, the verbal behaviors showed only one significant difference between the two motivation levels—negativity of deceptive messages was greater in the high-motivation condition.

Most of the above differences appear counter-intuitive. To the extent that the highly motivated deceivers were more anxious about being detected or more highly motivated to succeed, they should have manifested a faster pattern of behavior, signaling higher arousal, rather than the slower pace that was actually

TABLE 5.2
Behaviors Associated with Deception by Level of Motivation

Behavior	Low Motivation		High Motivation		Z of difference
	N	Mean d	N	Mean d	
Visual					
Pupil dilation	2	1.65***	1	1.52**	1.31
Gaze	12	.13	6	−.33	2.33*
Blinking	6	.85***	2	−.57**	4.60***
Smiling	10	−.14*	9	−.02	1.65
Facial segmentation	5	−.27*	−	−	−
Head movements	5	.16	5	−.52**	3.01**
Gestures	6	.09	6	−.32	1.03
Shrugs	3	.14	1	1.10*	.71
Adaptors	7	.49***	7	.19	1.55
Foot and leg movements	4	.01	5	−.06	.10
Postural shifts	5	.22	6	−.24*	2.51*
Bodily segmentation	3	.83**	−	−	−
Paralanguage					
Latency	8	−.05	7	−.00	.20
Response length	7	.07	10	−.36***	2.92**
Speech rate	5	.35	7	−.38***	3.03**
Speech errors	4	.40	8	.15	.24
Speech hesitations	6	.55*	5	.52***	.63
Pitch	2	.08	2	1.27**	1.99*
Verbal					
Negative statements	3	.34	2	1.88***	3.50***
Irrelevant information	5	.42	1	.28	.60
Self-references	3	.22	1	−.44	1.13
Immediacy	2	−.77***	−	−	−
Leveling	2	.29	2	.60*	1.28
General					
Discrepancy	4	.64***	−	−	−

Note: Positive values indicate that an increase in the behavior was associated with deception.

*p < .05
**p < .01
***p < .001

obtained. How are we to explain the results? Zuckerman et al. (1981) suggested that the highly motivated deceivers tried harder to control their behavior and consequently moved less and displayed more behavioral rigidity. Similarly, Siegman (1982) proposed that in high-motivation studies, the deceivers try harder to cover up their lies, which has the effect of attenuating or even reversing the "natural" relationship between motivation and behavior. It should be noted that this explanation is somewhat inconsistent with the association between highly motivated deception and greater increases in shrugs, level of pitch, and frequency of negative statements. Since pitch is relatively uncontrollable, it is perhaps appropriate that it should increase under high motivation. However, the increases in shrugs and negative statements under high motivation remain without clear interpretation.

Planning

Studies were grouped into three levels of planning: low, medium, and high. Level of planning was considered high if the deceptive communication was rehearsed with the subjects or if subjects needed only to say no (or yes) in response to all questions; level of planning was considered medium if, after the question was asked, subjects were allowed to pause and prepare their answers; finally, level of planning was considered low if subjects did not know in advance the content of the questions and were not given time to prepare their answers. The association between behavioral cues and deception, expressed in terms of effect size and significance level, were computed for each level of planning. Table 5.3 presents the results as well as the zs of differences between the significance levels obtained in the low and high levels of planning.

Unlike motivation, planning seems to have relatively weak effects on the relationships between the behaviors in question and deception. Six out of 17 (35%) behaviors were related to deception in the low-planning condition; 5 out of 19 (26%) were related to deception in the medium-planning condition: and 9 out of 24 (37%) were related to deception in the high-planning condition. There were four significant differences between the low- and high-planning levels where only one would be expected by chance. Compared with deception under low level of planning, the highly planned deception was associated with more pupil dilation, somewhat more smiling ($p < .11$), somewhat fewer gestures ($p < .07$), more postural shifts, shorter response latencies, somewhat shorter answers ($p < .10$) and faster speech rate. Some of these effects are not hard to explain. For example, it stands to reason that well-prepared deceivers start to talk earlier and continue to talk faster compared to the unprepared liars. The association of planning with increase in pupil dilation, increase in frequency of postural shifts, and decrease in response length is more puzzling. It is almost as if preparing for deception intensified the anxiety of the would-be deceiver, thus resulting in an increase in arousal-related variables. Admittedly, such interpretation is somewhat tenuous and should be treated with a considerable degree of caution.

OTHER CORRELATES OF DECEPTION

The search for behavioral cues to deception led investigators to focus on somewhat more exotic possibilities than those that have been discussed so far. Two variables that may or may not be related to deception and in fact may or may

TABLE 5.3
Behaviors Associated with Deception by Level of Planning

Behavior		Low		Medium		High	Z of Difference
	N	Mean d	N	Mean d	N	Mean d	
Visual							
Pupil dilation	2	1.35**	–	–	3	1.38***	2.27*
Gaze	9	.13	2	−.42	7	−.12	.64
Blinking	1	.27	1	.38	6	.56	.61
Smiling	9	−.23*	5	−.06	5	.14	1.63
Facial segmentation	–	–	2	−.26	3	−.27	–
Head movements	2	−.25	5	−.29	3	.05	1.40
Gestures	4	.15	3	−.29	5	−.22	1.87
Shrugs	1	.11	–	–	3	.47	.98
Adaptors	7	.17*	2	.68*	5	.45*	.21
Foot and leg movements	2	−.03	3	.22	4	−.22	1.00
Postural shifts	6	−.13	1	−.78*	4	.31	2.40*
Bodily segmentation	–	–	–	–	3	.83**	–
Paralanguage							
Latency	8	.25**	1	0	6	−.40**	4.03***
Response length	8	.01	4	−.45**	5	−.28	1.65
Speech rate	4	−.38*	5	−.24	3	.61*	2.84**
Speech errors	5	.19	4	.25	3	.26	.05
Speech hesitations	3	.64***	3	.27	5	.64*	.66
Pitch	2	.80	–	–	2	.55	.30
Verbal							
Negative statements	–	–	3	.86***	2	1.09***	–
Irrelevant information	1	.28	1	−.72	4	.71*	1.14
Self-references	–	–	3	.12	1	−.15	–
Immediacy	–	–	–	–	2	−.77***	–
Leveling	–	–	2	.60	2	.30	–
General							
Discrepancy	–	–	3	.75***	1	.31	–

Note: Positive values indicate that an increase in the behavior was associated with deception.

$*p < .05$
$**p < .01$
$***p < .001$

not exist are discussed below: microexpressions and stress-related tremors in the voice.

Microexpressions (Ekman & Friesen, 1969), also termed micromomentary expressions (Haggard & Isaacs, 1966), and very brief muscular movements in the face that ordinarily can be detected only when the videotape is shown in slow motion. Haggard and Isaacs (1966) reported that in clinical interviews, microexpressions were associated with both denial statements and verbal blocking and also tended to be incompatible with the regular facial expressions that preceded or followed them. Consistent with the Haggard and Isaacs view, Ekman and Friesen (1969) proposed that microexpressions are the remnants of masked or squelched displays and consequently may provide deception and leakage cues. From the more popular literature, an interview with Bennet (1978) indicated that this investigator could detect microexpressions "in the faces of the speakers at the precise moment they laid a lie on their classmates" (p. 34). To our best knowledge, however, there have been no reports of actual evidence regarding the relationship between microexpressions and deception. At this point, then, we tend to consider this relationship as no more than an intriguing topic for future research.

Stress-related tremors in the voice are measured by the Psychological Stress Evaluator (PSE). Developers of the PSE, Dektor Counterintelligence and Security of Springfield, Virginia, claim that their instrument detects deception. It is not clear, however, just what is being measured in a PSE voice analysis (Podlesny & Raskin, 1977), and even the existence of voice tremors is considered problematic (Shipp & McGlone, 1973). Finally, Horvath (1978, 1979) reported controlled studies in which the PSE instrument failed to discriminate between truth and deception although a conventional GSR analysis did. At present there appears to be no evidence in support of the validity of the PSE as an instrument of lie detection (see also Podlesny & Raskin, 1977; Rice, 1978).

SUMMARY

When the truthfulness of a message is in doubt, folk wisdom tells us that the spoken word is not to be given as much credence as the nonverbal behavior of the speaker. However, empirical research has shown that some nonverbal channels are less likely to give away deception than others. These findings suggest that communication channels may form a leakage hierarchy—a continuum indicating the degree to which different channels leak involuntary information. Of the various nonverbal channels, face is relatively controllable whereas body and tone of voice are relatively leaky. Surprisingly, accuracy of detecting deception from verbal content (i.e., transcript) was found to be relatively high. It appears that although the content of the speech may be quite controllable, its semantic structure may be as leaky as the body and/or tone of voice. Consequently, the search for cues to deception must focus on both verbal and nonverbal behaviors.

A meta-analysis of data from 45 studies available to the authors suggested that lie telling is linked to four processes or factors: control, arousal, negative affects, and cognitive complexity. Deceivers' need to control their behavior and/or appear convincing seems to result in a more homogenous and less segmented facial behavior, signaling a higher level of control; a higher level of use of absolute verbal terms—a form of exaggeration; and discrepancy between channels, signaling inability to control simultaneously all of one's behavior. The arousal associated with deception appears to result in less homogeneous and more segmented bodily behavior as well as an increase in pupil dilation, frequency of blinking, level of voice pitch, frequency of speech errors, and frequency of speech hesitations. The negative emotions associated with deception appear to cause a decrease in smiling and an increase in the frequency of negative statements and adaptors. Deceptive messages were also characterized by a less direct and more nonimmediate verbal style, indicating withdrawal or negative feelings about the content of the message. Finally, lying appears to be a relatively complex cognitive activity as evidenced by shorter response length and more irrelevant information; both of these characteristics indicate the difficulties involved in creating a "new" reality by the deceiver. In this regard, the increase in pupil dilation and speech hesitations associated with deception may indicate a higher level of complexity rather than a higher level of arousal.

Of the 24 behaviors examined in the meta-analysis, 14 (58%) were reliably associated with deception, indicating that the different deceptive contexts, lies, and decievers examined in the studies shared some common elements. However, when the studies were classified according to the level of motivation and planning involved in the lying, different types of lies appeared associated with somewhat different behavioral cues. Unfortunately, the effects of motivation and planning on cues to deception were hard to interpret and are presented here as fruit for further thought rather than as results of a well-defined investigation.

REFERENCES

Beatty, J. (1982). Task-evoked pupillary responses, processing load, and the structure of processing resources. *Psychological Bulletin, 91,* 276–292.

Bennet, R. (1978). Micromoments. *Human Behavior, 7,* 34–35.

Bugental, D. B., Henker, B., & Whalen, C. K. (1976). Attributional antecedents of verbal and vocal assertiveness. *Journal of Personality and Social Psychology, 34,* 405–411.

Cohen, J. (1977). *Statistical power analysis for the behavioral sciences* (Rev. ed.) New York: Academic Press.

Davis, R. C. (1961). Physiological responses as a means of evaluating information. In A. D. Biderman & H. Zimmer (Eds.), *The manipulation of human behavior.* New York: Wiley.

DePaulo, B. M., Lanier, K., & Davis, T. (1983). Detecting the deceit of the motivated liar. *Journal of Personality and Social Psychology, 45,* 1096–1103.

Ekman, P. (1980, May). *Mistakes when deceiving.* Paper presented at the conference on the Clever Hans Phenomenon. New York Academy of Sciences, New York.

Ekman, P., & Friesen, W. V. (1969). Nonverbal leakage and clues to deception. *Psychiatry, 32,* 88–106.

Ekman, P., & Friesen, W. V. (1972). Hand movements. *Journal of Communication, 22,* 353–374.

Ekman, P., & Friesen, W. V. (1974). Detecting deception from the body or face. *Journal of Personality and Social Psychology, 29,* 288–298.

Freud, S. (1959). Fragments of an analysis of a case of hysteria. *Collected papers* (Vol. 3). New York: Basic Books. (Original work published 1905)

Friedman, H. (1968). Magnitude of experimental effect and a table for its rapid estimation. *Psychological Buletin, 70*, 245–251.

Goldman-Eisler, F. (1968). *Psycholinguistics: Experiments in spontaneous speech.* New York: Academic Press.

Gur, R. C., & Sackeim, H. A. (1979). Self-deception: A concept in search of a phenomenon. *Journal of Personality and Social Psychology, 37*, 147–169.

Gustafson, L. A., & Orne, M. T. (1963). Effects of heightened motivation on the detection of deception. *Journal of Applied Psychology, 47*, 408–411.

Gustafson, L. A., & Orne, M. T. (1965) Effects of perceived role and role success on the detection of deception. *Journal of Applied Psychology, 49*, 412–417.

Haggard, E. A., & Isaacs, K. S. (1966). Micromomentary facial expressions as indicators of ego mechanisms in psychotherapy. In L. A. Gottschalk & A. H. Auerbach (Eds.), *Methods of research in psychotherapy.* New York: Appleton.

Hemsley, G. D. (1977). *Experimental studies in the behavioral indicants of deception.* Unpublished doctoral dissertation. University of Toronto.

Horvath, F. (1978). An experimental comparison of the psychological stress evaluator and the galvanic skin response in detection of deception. *Journal of Applied Psychology, 63*, 338–344.

Horvath, F. (1979). Effect of different motivational instructions on detection of deception with the psychological stress evaluator and the galvanic skin response. *Journal of Applied Psychology, 64*, 323–330.

Kahneman, D. (1973). *Attention and effort.* Englewood Cliffs, NJ: Prentice-Hall.

Kasl, S. V., & Mahl, G. F. (1965). The relationship of disturbances and hesitations in spontaneous speech to anxiety. *Journal of Personality and Social Psychology, 1*, 425–433.

Kraut, R. E. (1980). Humans as lie detectors: Some second thoughts. *Journal of Communication, 30*, 209–216.

Lykken D. T. (1959). The GSR in the detection of guilt. *Journal of Applied Psychology, 43*, 385–388.

Lykken, D. T. (1960). The validity of the guilty knowledge technique: The effects of faking. *Journal of Applied Psychology, 44*, 258–262.

Lykken, D. T. (1974). Psychology and the lie detector industry. *American Psychologist, 29*, 725–739.

Mehrabian, A. (1966). Immediacy: An indicator of attitudes in linguistic communication. *Journal of Personality, 34*, 26–34.

Mehrabian, A. (1967). Attitudes inferred from non-immediacy of verbal communications. *Journal of Verbal Learning and Verbal Behavior, 6*, 294–295.

Meyer, D. R. (1953). On the interaction of simultaneous responses. *Psychological Bulletin, 50*, 204–220.

Nunnally, J. C., Knott, P. D., Duchnowski, A., & Parker, R. (1967). Pupillary response as a general measure of activation. *Perception and Psychophysics, 2*, 149–155.

Orne, M. T., Thackray, R. I., & Paskewitz, D. A. (1972). On the detection of deception: A model for the study of the physiological effects of psychological stimuli. In N. S. Greenfield & R. A. Sternbach (Eds.), *Handbook of psychophysiology.* New York: Holt.

Podlesny, J. A., & Raskin, D. C. (1977). Physiological measures and the detection of deception. *Psychological Bulletin, 84*, 782–791.

Rice, B. (1978, June). The new truth machines. *Psychology Today*, 61–78.

Rosenthal, R. (1978). Combining results of independent studies. *Psychological Bulletin, 85*, 185–193.

Rosenthal, R., & DePaulo, B. M. (1979). Sex differences in eavesdropping on nonverbal cues. *Journal of Personality and Social Psychology, 37*, 273–285.

Rosenthal, R., & Rubin, D. B. (1979). Comparing significance levels of independent studies. *Psychological Bulletin, 86,* 1165–1168.

Scherer, K. R. (1980a). Vocal indicators of stress. In J. Barby (Ed.), *The evaluation of speech in psychiatry and medicine.* New York: Grune & Stratton.

Scherer, K. R. (1980b). Speech and emotional states. In J. Darby (Ed.), *The evaluation of speech in psychiatry and medicine.* New York: Grune & Stratton.

Scott, T. R., Wells, W. H., Wood, D. Z., & Morgan, D. I. (1967). Pupillary response and sexual interest reexamined. *Journal of Clinical Psychology, 23,* 433–438.

Shipp, T., & McGlone, R. (1973, November). *Physiologic correlates of acoustic correlates of psychologic stress.* Paper presented at the meeting of the Acoustical Society of America. Los Angeles.

Siegman, A. W. (1982, February). *Tell-tale signs of anxiety, lies, and coronary heart disease.* Colloquium paper presented at the Psychologisches Institut of the University of Bern.

Simpson, H. M. (1969). Effects of a task relevant response on pupil size. *Psychophysiology, 6,* 115–121.

Simpson, H. M., & Hale, S. M. (1969). Pupillary changes during a decision making task. *Perceptual and Motor Skills, 29,* 495–498.

Waid, W. M., & Orne, M. T. (1981). Cognitive, social and personality processes in the physiological detection of deception. In L. Berkowitz (Ed.), *Advances in experimental social psychology* (Vol. 14). New York: Academic Press.

Wiener, M., & Mehrabian. A. (1968). *Language within language.* New York: Appleton.

Williams, C. E., & Stevens, K. N. (1969). On determining the emotional state of pilots during flight: An exploratory study. *Aerospace Medicine, 40,* 1369–1372.

Zuckerman, M., Amidon, M. D., Bishop, S. E., & Pomerantz, S. D. (1982). Face and tone of voice in the communication of deception. *Journal of Personality and Social Psychology, 43,* 347–357.

Zuckerman, M., DeFrank, R. S., Hall, J. A., Larrance, D. T., & Rosenthal, R. (1979). Facial and vocal cues of deception and honesty. *Journal of Experimental Social Psychology, 15,* 378–396.

Zuckerman, M., DePaulo, B. M., & Rosenthal, R. (1981). Verbal and nonverbal communication of deception. In L. Berkowitz (Ed.), *Advances in experimental social psychology* (Vol. 14). New York: Academic Press.

6 Vocal Paralanguage Without Unconscious Processes

Bruce L. Brown, C. Terry Warner, Richard N. Williams
Brigham Young University

INTRODUCTION

It is widely held that nonverbal aspects of verbal behavior contain potential information about the character and psychological state of the speaker, quite apart from the message that he himself thinks he is conveying. Because he is attending to his spoken message, he is not attending to these paralinguistic aspects of his speech. Hence, he is not disclosing to himself the information he paralinguistically discloses to others. This information may be consistent with his intended message or discrepant. Many have claimed that when it is discrepant it is more trustworthy information about him than anything he may be saying about himself. There is some research in the past decade that supports this view (Zuckerman, DePaulo, & Rosenthal, 1981). It is easy to understand the appeal that paralanguage has had for psychologists: potentially at least, it appears to be a "window into the soul." Presumably it can reveal information about motivation and personality that goes beyond any impression management on the part of the speaker.

In their classic paper on "nonverbal leakage," Ekman and Friesen (1969) state the proposal that "nonverbal behavior may escape efforts to deceive, may evade self-censoring, or may betray dissimulation." They show that this idea is by no means new, dating back at least to Darwin. As one might expect, one of the most colorful statements of the nonverbal leakage hypothesis comes from Freud (1905/1957a) himself:

> When I set myself the task of bringing to light what human beings keep hidden within them, not by the compelling power of hypnosis, but by observing what they

say and what they show, I thought the task was a harder one than it really is. He that has eyes to see and ears to hear may convince himself that no mortal can keep a secret. If his lips are silent, he chatters with his finger-tips; betrayal oozes out of him at every pore. And thus the task of making conscious the most hidden recesses of the mind is one which it is quite possible to accomplish. (p. 94)

Why doesn't the speaker himself have the information that he paralinguistically conveys to others? There may be different answers to this question, depending upon whether the paralinguistic information is compatible with his intended message or incompatible with it. If it is incompatible, then there is an obvious logical reason that the speaker cannot comprehend it: He cannot be taking himself to be doing one thing while simultaneously admitting that the incompatible information describes him accurately. For this case, there is a traditional way of describing the speaker's relation to the paralinguistic information: he is *self-deceived*. Even a cursory examination of the self-deception literature gives much evidence of knotty problems and conceptual traps, and the issues cannot be avoided by one who professes an interest in vocal paralanguage.

But even when the paralinguistic information is consistent with his intended message it is beyond the speaker's ken, at least in part. One is never aware of all of his paralanguage: He is never aware of all of the information that his behavior makes available to others. Much is always there waiting to be discovered. This kind of paralinguistic information is less problematic than the kind that contradicts the person's avowed intention, but it brings questions and difficulties of its own. For example, in our perception of another person we can have an impression of guile, yet not be able to identify a single cue in his behavior as evidence for the impression. How is this possible? This question is related to the problematic hypothesis of subliminal perception, where a stimulus or complex pattern of stimuli affects our response without rising above our limen of awareness. We ought to feel queasy with such explanations, and one of the principal burdens of this chapter is to explore better ways to handle such issues conceptually.

By speaking of paralinguistic information we are making assumptions about behavior that are important to examine. "Paralanguage" means information "around" the linguistic (verbal, propositional) message. It is information in addition to and perhaps even against this message.

How does the concept of paralanguage relate to other concepts like "nonverbal behavior" and "nonverbal communiction"? *Nonverbal behavior* is a subject matter just about as broad as psychology itself. It includes every aspect of behavior outside of the verbal propositional message. These may be intended nonverbal messages (like deliberate gestures) or unintended aspects of verbal or nonverbal messages (like nervousness in the voice or in a gesture). The intended nonverbal messages are referred to as *nonverbal communication*. This is a very small subject, because we intend only a fraction of the information that others gather when they observe us. The remainder of nonverbal behavior is a very large subject, comprising all of the potential information in our behavior that we do not actually intend.

Paralinguistic information is a subset of this more general nonintended nonverbal behavior, but it has special properties. Although it is not intentionally communicated by the speaker, it is not unrelated to the meaning of his behavior either. It is instead a manifestation of his purposes, motives and intentions in acting as he does. It can even divulge information about him that he would resist.

Not all paralanguage is nonverbal. Some aspects of the *verbal* message also provide paralinguistic information—for example, slips of the tongue. Wording and syntax choices also are manifestations of personality. The term *nonverbal leakage* as it has been used since it was coined by Ekman and Friesen refers to the nonverbal variety of paralanguage. It is this nonverbal leakage—the nonverbal kind of paralanguage—that is the major topic of interest in this chapter.

But what is this nonverbal paralinguistic information? What is being leaked nonverbally? It is information that the careful observer sees the agent must have in order to act as he does. That is, it is information that guides the agent's behavior. Yet he himself appears to not be aware of having this information. It is information about the purposive character of the act, information that the observer needs in order to understand the act adequately, such as information about its motives and aims. Paralinguistic information is very different from accidental nonverbal information (due to physical limitations of the speaker's musculature, etc.) In a sense, paralinguistic information allows us potentially to know more than the speaker about his own intentions.

It is easy to see why paralanguage has historically been bound up with what are usually thought to be questions of unconscious mental processes. But as we see in this chapter, historical versions of the unconscious have been either self-contradictory or inadequate. Until we can formulate an adequate, nonparadoxical explanation of paralanguage, we will not have made sense of it. We therefore cannot put off doing theoretical work in favor of doing empirical studies: a self-contradictory concept denotes an empty set, does not have the implications it is thought (by those who ignore its contradictoriness) to have, and hence cannot form the foundation for empirical work. We think that in the course of this chapter the reader will see that in the research program we describe these theoretical and empirical issues are tangled together. Even though it complicates one's task, progress in paralanguage research depends on dealing with both of them at once.

In the course of this chapter, then, we deal with theoretical questions like the ones already alluded to:

What is paralinguistic information *about*?

Is it about something separate from the overt nonverbal behavior, a message originating in "unconscious" processes?

Intimately linked with these theoretical questions are empirical ones:

What aspects of nonverbal behavior most reliably manifest paralinguistic information?

And what research techniques are the most fruitful for getting at this information?

For dealing with the empirical questions, it appears that the study of vocal paralanguage is a most promising avenue of research. As a way of investigating interpersonal perception and personality it has two advantages: it is natural and it is precise. Not only are vocal qualities rich in personal information, they are also, with the advances of the past two decades in acoustic analysis and synthesis technology, totally quantifiable (Brown, Strong, & Rencher, 1975). Many of the technological hurdles are behind us. Speech scientists have made impressive gains, not only in quantifying voice, but also in unraveling the correspondence between vocal tract movements and their acoustic realization (Laver, 1968, 1975, & 1978; Titze, 1973, 1974; see also Strong and Plitnik, 1983 for an up-to-date summary of the physics of speech). The speech part of the presonality-speech equation is coming along well. The major difficulties have been in conceptualizing and quantifying psychological dimensions such as personality and emotion. These raise many subtle theoretical questions which we will try to answer in this chapter. We shall even ask whether it is fruitful to approach the study of personality apart from paralinguistic research.

On the theoretical questions, we offer a view of paralanguage—of information not accessible to the speaker that he himself is conveying—that does *not* require the postulation of unconscious processes. For reasons we give later, we call this view "transparency theory." Building upon the work of others (Fingarette, 1969; Sartre, 1953) we have elsewhere shown (Warner, 1982) that every model of so-called unconscious mental processes—every model that splits the psyche into more than one level—cannot avoid being either explanatorily inadequate or else infected with conceptual paradoxes.

Where the paralinguistic information is compatible with the intended spoken message, the paradox may be expressed as follows. Suppose a person is in a job interview that she hasn't been worrying about. The interviewer asks why her voice is quivering. She is a little surprised and then says, "I didn't realize it, but I guess I'm nervous." This woman will have perceived the situation as risky or intimidating, but this perception was not a part of any perceptual experience she was aware of having. The "unconscious process" explanation of this is that she perceived the threat "unconsciously," i.e., below the lower limit of what the subject is aware of perceiving. Though there have been explanations of this "subliminal perception" paradox that have been widely accepted, we show there are problems with these explanations.

When we turn to the case in which the paralinguistic information is incompatible with the speaker's intended message, there are further complications. The paralinguistic information that expresses the supposed unconscious processes is not admitted when it is pointed out. The subject is *resistant* to it. This resist-ance, and the defensive irrationality and even obsessiveness and compulsivity that may accompany it, are commonly observed in the clinic and in everyday life. Here, the paradox is that for resistance to be possible, the subject would have to be aware of precisely what he refuses to admit. All the resolutions of this paradox that are based on a splitting of the psyche (such as the hypothesis of unconscious processes) only create other paradoxes or else make the paral-inguistic behavior impossible to explain. Transparency Theory is neatly free of both kinds of paradox.

In this chapter, then, we bring together several bodies of work, some of them theoretical and some empirical, that together form a promising conception of the nature of paralanguage. We suggest a program for future research on vocal paralanguage. Because of the issues involved—personality theory and measure-ment and the questions that historically have surrounded the concept of the unconscious—this conception of paralanguage and the associated research pro-gram have major implications for clinical psychology.

VOCAL PARALANGUAGE RESEARCH: A SELECTIVE SURVEY WITH PROPOSALS

In his review of personality markers in speech, Scherer (1979a) identifies two primary kinds of research: (1) externalization studies, or those that examine the relationship between personality dimensions and their vocal externalization, and (2) attribution studies, or those that examine the personality inferences that human judges make on the basis of speech characteristics. Brown and Bradshaw (in press) add to this a third kind of study: (3) accuracy studies. Most of the early personality/speech studies in the 1930s and the 1940s were of this kind. Like externalization studies, accuracy studies involve using some kind of personality test or other kind of measure or categorization of person characteristics. But then rather than correlating this with speech characteristics as externalization studies do, accuracy studies test whether judges can accurately identify the "highs" and "lows" on the personality dimension in question on the basis of hearing each person speak. We now will add to this list a fourth kind of study that is of interest in vocal paralanguage research: (4) speech psychophysics. In this study speech dimensions are varied, as in attribution studies, but then rather than having judges make personality trait attributions, they are asked to make judgments of the speech properties themselves.

Table 6.1 lists these four studies and the kind of independent and dependent variables characteristic of each. We can see from this that attribution and speech psychophysics studies have the possibility of giving more solid results, for the reason that the independent variable for both of them is an experimentally man-ipulable one, namely, speech characteristics. Both accuracy studies and also

TABLE 6.1
The Four Kinds of Vocal Paralinguistic Research and the Kind of
Independent Variable and Dependent Variable Characteristic of Each

The Four Kinds of Research:	Independent Variable (Antecedent)	Dependent Variable (Resultant)
① Externalization Studies	Personality	Speech Characteristics
② Attribution Studies	Speech Characteristics	Judged Personality
③ Accuracy Studies	Personality	Judged Personality
④ Speech Psychophysics	Speech Characteristics	Judged Speech Characteristics

externalization studies have been plagued by the problem common to all personality research, the unreliability of personality tests and the problem of test validity. However, there are some personal characteristics (such as age, years of education or occupational social class) that are much easier to establish or can be objectively measured, and some good accuracy and externaliztion studies have been done.

Vocal Paralanguage and Personality

Psychologists have long tried to establish a link between personality traits and speech characteristics. Brown and Bradshaw (in press) have traced the history of the early studies of personality and speech, which were primarily accuracy studies (the third type outlined in Table 6.1) (see Scherer, 1979a; Siegman, 1978 for additional reviews). These studies almost all relied on standardized psychological tests to define personality traits, and concluded that although judges have considerable agreement in their personality stereotypes from vocal properties, they were not very accurate. Brown and Bradshaw also reviewed a number of studies that show that when the characteristics of the person were objectively determined (things like social class or age), judges are very accurate in identifying them from voice. They have argued from this that the judgments of persons from voice are more to be trusted than the personality tests. The whole concept of personality itself is rooted in the perception of one person by another. The "personality" tests are a step removed, inferring personality from a person's answers to questions that are obvious and usually allow broadly for disseminating responses. Mischel (1973) has articulated the personality measurement dilemma. Personality measures are notably unreliable and lacking in cross-situational consistency, and this in the face of our obvious experience that personality is recognizable and stable through many situational variations.

We propose that perhaps the best way to unlock the science of personality is through studies of nonverbal communication, and particularly vocal paralanguage, but certainly not in the way studies have typically been done. Most of the studies relating personality to speech have used the externalization paradigm, the first one listed in Table 6.1. Scherer, in his review of the personality/speech research (1979a), describes the present state of research on externalization as "bleak" and the "amount of hard data negligible," and hastens to add that it isn't because of a lack of effort (more than 1500 references in Gorlitz's review, in German, which Scherer in turn reviews). A coherent pattern does not emerge from these massive proceedings. There have been two problems: inadequate measures of speech and inadequate measures of personality. The first of these is clearly soluable by the impressive advances in acoustics. Were this the only problem, it would be very productive to just go back and replicate some of the best of the old studies with improved speech-measuring methodology. The more serious problem is the correlative nature of the studies and the monumental problem of personality measurement.

In the past few years we have begun using a new strategy to deal with the problem of personality measurement for paralinguistic research: trait nomination. In one study (Dicks, Brown, & Wells, in preparation) we found that extreme high and low scorers on the Personal Orientation Inventory (P.O.I.), a test based upon self-actualization theory, did not differ in their ability to recognize portrayed emotions or in their ability to portray them, but when we switched to a nomination strategy comparing those who had been nominated as being unusually well adjusted to two control groups, the nominated group was significantly and substantially better at judging emotion portrayals.

We propose two ways to improve on the previous externalization studies of personality manifestations in speech: (1) We will examine unique or extreme exemplars of various traits to maximize chances of getting clear "ideal" patterns of vocal properties that differentiate one trait from another, rather than just correlating a bunch of vocal measures with a bunch of trait measures on a randomly varying sample. (2) We will use nomination to select exemplars of various traits rather than standardized tests. In interpreting results, then, we would say, "this vocal pattern is characteristic of those who are nominated by another person as being the most dominant person he knows," or "the most well-adjusted person he knows," rather than "characteristic of those who judge themselves to be high in dominance" or "characteristic of those who answer questions on a standardized test in a way that is scored (for whatever reasons, logical or empirical) as being dominant."

We have some early results (Bowen, Lacayo, Brown, & Jentz, 1983) that are encouraging. This study involved 6 female inmates at a state prison, half nominated to be very low in aggressiveness and half to be high, and 6 female non-prison controls, half of them nominated high in aggressiveness and half low. Each described into a tape recorder four significant others in her life ("someone who likes me," "someone who makes me feel uncomfortable," etc.). Because of the confidential nature of these recordings, we used a few of our faculty and student colleagues as judges (only four of each), and they attempted to judge which category of speaker each of the 12 belonged to. They first judged only from typed transcripts and later from recordings.

This kind of accuracy study is much stronger than the accuracy studies in the 1930s and 1940s. In an example study (Fay & Middleton, 1939) subjects were not particularly accurate in judging traits as measured by the Spranger test, but there was high agreement among judges in their ratings. One is left wondering whether judges were inaccurate (as was concluded) or whether the Spranger test can't be trusted. There is no defensible criterion. The Bowen et al. study has two criteria of accuracy. For the "prisoner vs. non-prisoner" categories the accuracy criterion is objective reality: each subject either is or is not a prison inmate. In the case of the "nominated high vs. nominated low aggressive" categories the criterion of accuracy is more complex. One could argue that it is a subjective determination whether a person is in fact aggressive. But the judge's task isn't to accurately determine whether the speaker *is* actually aggressive, but whether the speaker has been *nominated as* aggressive. In other words there is an assessable reality: either the subject was or was not nominated as aggressive. Therefore, the judge can be clearly correct or incorrect in his judgment. In the Fay and Middleton type of study there is no way to deterine whether judges are correct. In the nomination paradigm, if in fact we find that judges have a high level of accuracy, we have established the traits in question by the only way that personality exists—the perception of one person by anoher. And furthermore we can demonstrate how much of the information about the nomination categories gets transmitted through various channels such as "content only," "voice only," or "content plus voice."

In the Bowen et al. study, when judgments were made from typed transcripts (content only) the accuracy in identifying nominative categories was very low. For the prisoner versus nonprisoner categories the accuracy was only 58.3%, slightly above chance level (which is 50%). For the high versus low nominated aggressiveness category it was 47.9%, a little below chance level. But when judges heard the spoken answers (content plus voice) the accuracy for the prisoner versus nonprisoner categories was 91.7% and for aggressiveness was 87.5%

Now that it has been demonstrated that such information is communicated through vocal properties, the next question is just what features are communicating it and subjectively how each speaker is perceived by judges. We are now having the voices rated on linguistic and acoustic dimensions by judges, and also doing a computerized acoustical analysis of rate, pitch, intonation, pauses, and power spectrum. Also, we are having a small group of judges make adjective ratings of the voices for a phenomenological analysis of how the voices sound to judges, using the principal factors biplot as discussed in the next section and shown in Fig. 6.3.

The early personality/speech researchers made the mistake of building upon the shaky foundation of personality psychometrics (existing personality tests) to establish the personality-speech connection. Their strategy seemed to be to use personality tests to establish personality traits and then determine what vocal characteristics accompany various personality types. The vocal properties were seen as a kind of "sign" of the traits. But in the nomination paradigm there is no need to suppose that these traits are somehow separate from vocal and other paralinguistic properties. There is no need to think of them as standing behind these properties and correlated with them. They *are* these properties. And, as we try to establish in the Transparency Theory section of this chapter, there is no possibility that we shall find a more fundamental way to access these traits than by observation of the behaviors that evidenced them. Taylor (1964) has made a similar point with respect to nonverbal signs of intention: "Your angry expression or action, or my thoughts and feelings cannot usually be called "signs" of desire or intention. For there is no more direct way of observing or telling what we or others intend to do." (p. 47)

In abandoning the psychometric approach to defining personality traits we not only liberate the enterprise of personality/speech research, we also open the way for a new approach to the criterion problem in personality psychometrics. We can turn the tables on the old approach by using vocal paralinguistic research and the nomination paradigm as a way of evaluating and comparing personality tests. We are beginning a study in which we use nominations of extreme exemplars of "competitive" and "cooperative" to compare the accuracy of human judges (who read or hear subjects' responses to various questions) with personality tests (the CPI, the TAT, and the Kelly REP test) in terms of how well each can identify which subjects are of each nominative category. Although the categories are subjective, the question of whether a given stimulus person was or was not nominated to a given category is an established reality. It can be used to compare the accuracy of naive judges who are judging from vocal properties and content of speech to the "accuracy" of personality test scores (as well as to clinical judgment from the personality tests) in discriminating nominative categories.

Social Cognition Through Speech

Many of the personality/speech studies have been attribution studies, the second kind listed in Table 6.1. Whereas in externalization studies we examine the kinds of speech properties that are characteristic of various personality types, in this kind of study we use voices that vary along certain dimensions and determine the subjective reactions of judges to these voices. This kind of reserach lends itself well to an experimental paradigm, since speech is the independent variable. Speech properties can be precisely manipulated in controlled combinations to examine their effects upon personality trait attributions from the judges. This kind of study can be considered as a variety of person perception or social cognition research: the perception of persons as mediated by vocal properties. The first experimental studies of personality attribution from voice were in the late 1960s and early 1970s. The early ones (Addington, 1968; Kjeldergaard, 1968) were only quasi-experimental. Even though they involved manipulations of vocal qualities and then comparisons of the resultant evaluative reactions, the variations were accomplished through subjective manipulation by speakers. Scherer (1979b) refers to such as "cue manipulation" studies. He points out that the problem with such studies is that with subjective alteration of voice there is no assurance that other vocal features are not also being manipulated.

In the 1970s and 1980s a number of studies appeared that utilized the new acoustic techniques of speech synthesis and manipulation by computer to vary one parameter of speech at a time (such as rate, pitch, intonation, etc.) and examine the resultant effects on personality attributions (Apple, Streeter, & Kraus, 1979; Brown, 1980a; Brown, 1982; Brown, Strong, & Rencher, 1972a, 1972b, 1973, 1974, 1975; Scherer, 1979a; Scherer & Oshinsky, 1977; Smith, Brown, Strong, & Rencher, 1975). Scherer (1979b) refers to these as "cue synthesis" studies. He points out that the problem with this approach to personality attribution from speech is that such manipulations may be quite artificial and may not really tell us that much about the effects of natural manipulations. That is, computer alteration of rate is rigidly experimental: nothing other than rate is manipulated. But it may be that natural alterations in rate have side effects involving other vocal characteristics.

Most of the cue manipulation studies and cue synthesis studies previously listed were somewhat artificial in that they had judges listen to recordings of speakers reciting "standard passages" and then rate them on paired opposite adjectives. In other words, it was obvious to judges that they were not hearing natural speech but rather "posing," and that their task was to focus upon vocal properties.

The more natural situation is to have both content and vocal properties varying such that one makes a total judgment of the person with vocal properties being more in subsidiary awareness. A recent study (Stewart, Brown, & Stewart, in preparation) used a Greco-Latin Square design to counterbalance speaker and vocal rate manipulation so that natural speech, spoken answers to interview questions, could be used. (A summary of the preliminary results can be found in Brown, 1980a.) The study involved three replications using three different interview questions, and the voices were manipulated in rate, both subjectively ("cue manipulation") and by computer ("cue synthesis"). The results show that at least for the rate manipulation, Scherer's criticisms of both the "cue synthesis" studies as being too artificial and the "cue manipulation" studies as lacking in experimental control are not very serious. Virtually the same results were obtained whether the manipulation was subjective or computerized, and they were amazingly consistent with the cumulative findings with respect to rate from the many earlier rate synthesis studies using the more artificial standard passage method. Increased rate led to higher ratings on "competence"-related adjectives and lower ratings on "benevolence"-related adjectives. Decreased rate led to lower ratings on both kinds of adjectives (see Smith et al., 1975 for the most detailed demonstration of this).

If we broaden our conception of vocal paralanguage to include social markers in speech, such as regional or status-related dialect, the "matched guise" (Lambert, 1967) literature that began in the early 1960s has much to contribute to our understanding of tacit knowledge in interpersonal perception and its relevance as a reflection of the personality structure of the perceiver. In this method recordings of bilingual speakers are presented to judges both in their English and in their French "guise." The judges then rate them on paired opposite adjectives thinking that they are just rating a group of separate individuals. Since each speaker is his own control, appearing in both guises, any differences in personality ratings can be attributed to "covert prejudice."

The matched guise studies are a kind of "cue manipulation" study, one in which the "cue" that is manipulated (for example, French vs. English) is a very objective one. Historically, the matched guise studies were the beginning of the "cue manipulation" and "cue synthesis" approach. In fact, the first "cue synthesis" studies in the series by Brown et al. (1972a, 1972b, 1973, 1974, 1975) grew out of the Lambert "matched guise" tradition (Brown, 1980a).

Although the initial applications of this technique were to examine evaluative reactions toward different ethnolinguistic groups, particularly French Canadians and English Canadians in Quebec, it was soon expanded to explore the perceived personalities of speakers of many dialects, accents and sociolects in a wide variety of cultural settings (see Giles & Powesland, 1975; Lambert, 1967; and Ryan, 1979 for reviews). In a review of the French Canadian studies based on a factor analysis of similar data, Brown et al. (1975, Fig. 2) summarized the findings by stating that English Canadians rate French guises as less competent and less benevolent than the English counterpart. But what is surprising is that French Canadian respondents also rate the French guises as less competent. However, they do rate the French guises as more benevolent (kind) than English. And when French Canadian judges respond to Continental French voices, they rate them as highest on both competence and benevolence adjectives.

The French Canadians view the English Canadians as a threat (competent but not kind), but the Continental French are seen by them as a group to be both respected and trusted, both competent and kind. French Canadian males consistently rate speakers of their own dialect of French lower than both of these other groups on competence adjectives. It is interesting to note that if one explicitly asks French Canadian judges how they view the Continental French or the English Canadians with respect to themselves in terms of competence, they do not attribute to either of those groups a higher competence level than to themselves. They seem to not be aware of how they use the linguistic marker information in attributional judgments.

It is easy to appreciate how tempting it is to call this kind of self-derogation "unconscious." Lambert (1967) has not described it in that way, but as more "covert" or more "private reactions" than those called forth by a "direct attitude questionnaire" (p. 94). In transparency theory, which we will discuss later, the way a person appropriates and *uses* ethnic identity information, as part of the skill he employs in making competency judgments, is different from what he would *say* he is doing if called upon to describe his behavior explicitly. Nor does he need to be able to appreciate the "trait" components of his skillful behavior in order to engage in it. This is reminiscent of the studies reviewed by Nisbett and Wilson (1977) where it is shown that a person cannot accurately introspect how he will judge or why he did judge in a particular way. The matched guise technique is a good way to show how such inforamtion is actually used by a judge in the judgment process (when group identity is not necessarily highlighted) rather than directly asking what he thinks of groups. In other words, in the matched guise paradigm we have a clear example of what contemporary cognitivists refer to as "unconscious mental processes." But, as we argue later, those terms are theory laden and commit us to a way of understanding such things that is misleading and paradoxical.

Emotion and Speech

There has been much less emotion/speech research than personality/speech research. In this section we give a few examples of how speech scientists have studied the expression of emotion in speech and then make some proposals for future work. These proposals are given in much more detail in the review by Brown and Bradshaw (in press). We summarize only briefly the main points here. The studies of the past have been primarily of two types, externalization studies and accuracy studies. Although the "cue synthesis" attribution paradigm lends itself best to a solid experimental method (as outlined above), it has yet to be used here. Also, almost all of the studies, both externalization and accuracy ones, have utilized portrayals of emotions rather than naturally occurring emotion. (One notable exception is the report by Williams and Stevens [1972] of their acoustic analysis of the radio announcer who was witnessing and describing the Hindenberg disaster.) One of the primary characteristics of natural emotion is that it is subsidiary to the ongoing human drama, whereas portrayals involved explicit re-creation. There is some evidence, however (Williams & Stevens,

1972, for example), that the acoustic characteristics of emotion portrayals by actors are reasonably close to the acoustic characteristics of actual emotion. When actors tried to portray the appropriate emotion in reciting the Hindenberg protocol, their vocal characteristics were very similar to those of the radio announcer in the actual event.

In order to move one step closer to natural emotion in spontaneous speech, we conducted a study (Brown, Hamblin, & Bowen, in preparation; see also the partial report of it in Brown, 1980b) in which five undergraduate male students were recorded as they described (in Spanish) six films quite diverse in emotional impact, immediately after viewing them. Their purpose was to describe the films as clearly as possible, so that the emotion in the voice was a tacit accompaniment. Judges not familiar with Spanish were then given the task of rating the voices on 9 point emotion scales (for how much sadness there was in the voice, how much anger, etc.). Other similar judges were given the task of identifying, on the basis of the speakers' vocal qualities, the movie that led to each utterance. We found that judges could, on the basis of only the vocal qualities, identify the film with an accuracy almost as great as that for portrayed emotion in the earlier Davitz and Davitz (1959) and Kramer (1964) studies. In both the personality/speech and the emotion/speech research traditions, we propose that there is much to be gained from using all three kinds of studies (accuracy, externalization, and attribution) in coordination with one another. As was shown above, the accuracy paradigm can be effectively used to give a logical footing to the definition of personality categories by nomination, and then externalization can be used to identify the vocal properties that are characteristic of these nominative personality categories. Externalization studies are not experimentally tight, but they do allow one to examine the naturally occurring variations in speech. Finally, attribution studies can be used to test experimentally the hypotheses that grow out of externalization studies. That is, voices can be varied by computer in accord with the findings of naturalistic externalizaiton studies in order to determine whether the judges do in fact attribute the hypothesized characteristics to the voices. A similar approach can be taken to emotion/speech, but using situational definitions of emotions. For example, one could record the voices of doctoral candidates right before they take their oral exams and right after and test the accuracy of judges in identifying which speech sample is from before and which from after (Fuller, 1982). The linguistic externalization of "before" and "after" could then be determined with acoustic analysis of voice, and the major acoustic differences could be synthesized by computer and used in an attribution study to see if those parameters found to be characteristic of "before" are perceived as "nervous" (see Brown & Bradshaw, in press, for a much more detailed account of the rationale for using these three kinds of studies in concert as a way of solving the logical problems of defining personality and emotion).

TROUBLES WITH THE UNCONSCIOUS

Historically, the unconscious was postulated in order to account for the phenomenon of resistance as seen in clinical situations and everyday life. There was no preexisting body of experimental results which needed to be explained. Subsequently, empirical research on "unconscious phenomena" has been conducted in an attempt to validate a clinical concept. Where experimental studies are concerned, the theory came first and experimental attempts to confirm it afterward.

The Psychodynamic Version

Freud's "discovery" of the psychodynamic unconscious is the historical beginning of a divided consciousness approach to the explanation of behavior. In his earliest "hysterical" patients Freud encountered what seemed to him behavior that was resistant to his probing. In the case of Elisabeth von R., her pains, her forgetfulness of crucial experiences, and her satisfaction at his frustrations were opportune and persistent—so much so that he could only suppose that she suspected where his inquiries were leading and was misdirecting them. So, early on he came to believe these "symptoms" expressed wishes that she kept herself from being conscious of. Freud said she "fended them off" or "repressed" them away from consciousness because the symptoms were acceptable to her whereas the undisguised wishes were not. These aspects of her behavior were intentional, Freud said, but the intentions were unconscious.

Freud recognized that there were deep logical problems with this model. The immediate difficulty was that the idea of the unconscious as defined by this model made no sense. This "unconscious" supposedly possessed all the rational capacities required for the strategic behavior Freud observed in Elisabeth and for the strategic behavior of everyday life—only it is supposed to lack altogether the capacities that are inseparably bound up with consciousness, such as self-reflection, self-assessment, self-monitoring. But these capacities are absolutely essential for strategic behavior. Thus, as Freud (1915/1957b) recognized in his later writings, we ought not to think of the unconscious as "another, second consciousness which is united in myself with the consciousness I know" (p. 170). As he argues:

> . . . a consciousness of which its own possessor knows nothing is something very different from that of another person and it is questionable whether such a consciousness, lacking, as it does, its most important characteristic, is worthy of any further discussion at all. (p. 170)

Freud sought to remedy these problems in *The Interpretation of Dreams*. From this point on the unconscious became not an impossible hidden consciousness but a psychical realm with specifiable characteristics all its own (the Primary Processes) that are very different from the characteristics of consciousness. This story is well known. In course of time, to make an involved story short, Freud realized that aligning this unconscious exclusively with the Primary Processes would not work. It meant that the act of repression, which is a rational (secondary) process, would have to be conscious rather than unconscious. On a superficial level we might want to say that the model simply is false because we are manifestly not conscious of repressing. More deeply, we see that repression is logically impossible, since it means that we must be conscious of what we repress in order to repress it and to keep it repressed. As Sarte (1953) said:

> I must know the truth very exactly in order to conceal it more carefully—and this not at two different moments, which at a pinch would allow us to re-establish a semblance of duality—but in the unitary structure of a single project. (p. 89)

This is perhaps the most often quoted form of the classical critique of Freud's concept of an unconscious and of the idea of self-deception generally. It applies primarily to the earlier theories that Freud formulated. His mature theory was designed in part to escape this sort of critique. In it, he reconceived the Secondary Processes so that they extend deep into the unconscious. This model of the psyche (which he achieved with the creation of the tripartite Id, Ego and Super-ego) enabled him to say that repression is both a secondary and an unconscious process. It was in connection with this model that Freud spoke of a "censor" operating on the unconscious level that monitors mental contents to determine those to be repressed.

However satisfied Freud may have been with this model, the problems inherent in the idea of unconscious processes were not conquered. In this model as in the previous ones, there are two kinds of unconscious mental contents: the dynamically unconscious ones, and the descriptively unconscious ones. The dynamically unconscious contents are those that cannot be brought to consciousness because they are being repressed. The descriptively unconscious ones can be brought to consciousness (they are not being repressed) but simply happen not to have been. In this model the only way to define repression is this: It is the act by which certain mental contents and not others are kept unconscious. We have no other reason except this one for supposing that repression exists; it is needed in order to explain resistance. There are absolutely no other properties we can ascribe to the dynamic unconscious other than that it explains resistance. On the other hand, the only properties that dynamically unconscious contents can have that descriptively unconscious contents lack is this: They are the ones that are being repressed. The idea of dynamically unconscious processes and the idea of repression are wholly defined in terms of each other and in terms of the observations of resistance they were invented to explain. They have no observable implications other than these observations. They are therefore empirically empty ideas. Talk of repression or of the psychodynamic unconscious is simply another way to state Freud's original enigmatic observations: that his patients engaged in purposive behavior the motives of which were unknown to them. (A thorough treatment of Freud's futile wrestle with this problem is found in Warner, 1982.)

The classical critique (given in Sartre's words) applies primarily to the early form of psychodynamic theory, but this second critique shows that even in the mature theory the concepts of repression and the unconscious are vacuous. For our purposes this second critique is interesting because it enables us to see that it is impossible in principle to verify by independent means the existence or functioning of these unconscious contents or processes. In other words, the only evidence we have of unconscious processes is the observation of resistant behavior. The primary data is paralinguistic nonverbal behavior, which may be explainable in much simpler ways than the positing of special kinds of cognition.

There is a contemporary Freudian treatment of these matters by the philosopher Herbert Fingarette (1969) that tries to get around some of the problems. Instead of thinking that it takes a special mental action to make mental contents dynamically unconscious, he proposes that it takes a special mental act to make them conscious. Consciousness is a kind of "spelling out" to oneself or avowal of a mental content. Unconscious contents result when one refuses to spell out such a content (because it is inconsistent with the image of himself he has been assembling in the course of his experience). There are consequently three possible states of mental contents: avowed, unavowed, and, as a result of this refusal, disavowed. Fingarette thinks that this formulation avoids the logical problem of self-deception because, as he supposes, disavowal does not require spelling out. But instead it makes Freud's earliest error all over again, because disavowal, like avowal, presupposes recognition and assessment—in his words "spelling out"—of contents to be disavowed. Here again, seeing to it that one is not conscious of something requires that one be conscious of it.

The Splitting of the Psyche in
Contemporary Cognitive Psychology

The major body of empirical work on the unconscious has been within the perceptual defense research tradition. Dixon (1971) and Erdelyi (1974) argue that the combined sum of all this research has firmly established the existence of unconscious mental processes. In his review and resuscitation of the "new look in perception" Erdelyi (1974) sampled the over 1000 research publications on perceptual defense and vigilance, "gargantuan proceedings" as he called them, and argued that the disillusionment with this research topic in the late 1950s was premature and mistaken. He goes to great length to meet the methodological criticisms and to show that even when giving the critics the benefit of the doubt, there is still ample evidence to establish the perceptual defense and vigilance phenomena.

Most interesting for the thrust of this chapter is his way of dealing with what Howie (1952) calls the most serious criticism of all—the conceptual one. This criticism holds that perceptual defense cannot be established empirically because it makes no sense conceptually—it is paradoxical. The paradox Howie has identified is a version (in the context of perception) of the self-deception paradox. In order to defend against a threatening input, the perceiver must already know enough of its content to be intimidated. He therefore hides from himself what he already knows. Worse yet, he also must hide from himself the act of hiding the content, since the act includes his motive or reason for hiding it.

Erdelyi attempts to deal with the perceptual defense version of the paradox from his point of view as an information processing cognitivist. To an information processing theorist there is nothing at all surprising about parallel processors, even one called "conscious" and another that is not conscious. Nor need any feel threatened by animism in admitting unconscious processing in this day and age (Erdelyi, 1974). His argument closely parallels one given a few years earlier by Dixon (1971), also a defender of the perceptual defense faith. For both theorists there seems to be an implicit acceptance that reduction to mechanistic entities, either in physiological or computer logic terms, makes the two-agent explanation acceptable. A paper by Dennett (1978) entitled "Why the Law of Effect Will Not Go Away" demonstrates how compelling this kind of argument can be at its best. In this view the artificial intelligence theorist can proceed in his computer program to posit agents, demons, and all kinds of animistic entities, as long as it is remembered that all such things will finally be reducible to "and gates," "or gates," and so forth, in the hardware language. The old behaviorism insisted upon both parsimony and the mechanistic thesis. The new information processing psychology (closely associated with the artificial intelligence establishment) is content with the mechanistic thesis. They are willing to sacrifice parsimony and multiply agents as long as those agents are ultimately reducible to mechanistic elements.

These same kinds of phenomena have appeared in a much more recent tradition, selective attention. The development of the evidence and the debates are generally known and are only briefly alluded to here. The controversy centers on the fate of unattended items in a dichotic listening task: Are they processed semantically or are they somehow "filtered" from semantic processing and rejected on the basis of superficial features? Some (Corteen & Dunn, 1974; Corteen & Wood, 1972; Deutsch & Deutsch, 1963; Inouye, 1975; Lewis, 1970) claim to have evidence for full semantic processing of the unattended channel. Others (Treisman, 1964; Treisman & Geffen, 1967; Treisman & Gelade, 1980; Treisman & Riley, 1969; Treisman, Squire, & Green, 1974) claim that unwanted information from the unattended channel is rejected on the basis of features of the input, without full semantic processing. Dixon (1971) and Erdelyi (1974) have both recognized that the conceptual machinery used by attention theorists is essentially equivalent to their own accounts of perceptual defense, and on that basis have claimed a rightful place for perceptual defense theory in contemporary cognitive psychology. A major thrust of Dixon's book is the question of why the multitude of subliminal perception studies and perceptual defense studies have been ignored and spurned by academic psychologists while the closely related demonstrations of selective attention have been received as some of the most important cognitive research of the past 20 years. That these attentional theories would eventually be pushed to posit a splitting of the psyche (comparable to the Freudian one) was anticipated early by Deutsch and Deutsch (1963):

> . . . such evidence as the above would require us, on filter theory, to postulate an additional discriminative system below or at the level of the filter, perhaps as complex as that of the central mechanism to which information was assumed to be filtered. (p. 82)

Evidence such as that given by Lewis (1970) indicates that the filtering must be done on the basis of the meaning of the input—full semantic processing of the unattended channel. We then ask what the "central mechanism" can do that the "filter" can't. If, as Dixon and Erdelyi suggest, this filter is also implicated in perceptual defense, then it must have knowledge of the whole personality structure of the person in order to discriminate threatening from non-threatening inputs. How ironic it is that the academic psychology that spurned the "Freudian fictions" a generation ago now posits similar entities. But they are made respectable by the promise that they are reducible to Boolean logic and can be modeled on a computer. It seems acceptable to multiply "processors" to the extent necessary to account for the phenomena (with little concern for elegance or parsimony) as long as each one is ultimately reducible to physicalistic entities interacting with each other.

There have been objections within mainstream cognitive psychology to this kind of theorizing. Neisser criticizes the attentional theories of the past decade, primarily on the basis of their mechanical passivity. As he said in the introduction to *Cognition and Reality* (1976):

> The last of the questions that generated this book concerns the conceptions of attention, capacity and consciousness. In writing cognitive psychology a decade ago, I deliberately avoided theorizing about consciousness. It seemed to me that psychology was not ready to tackle the issue, and that any attempt to do so would lead only to philosophically naive and fumbling speculation. Unfortunately, these fears have been realized; many current models of cognition treat consciousness as if it were just a particular stage of processing in a mechanical flow of information. Because I am sure that these models are wrong, it has seemed important to develop an alternative interpretation of the data on which they are based. (pp. xii–xiii)

Neisser's 1976 work was strongly influenced by the perceptual theory of J. J. Gibson. In his classic 1966 treatise, *The Senses Considered as Perceptual Systems*, Gibson argues that to divide human action into discrete stimulus and response units is much too glib. There is motor action in the service of perception and much perceptual feedback needed for skillful motor action. The passive "camera model" of perception comes from basing theory primarily upon visual perception. The motoric component is much more obvious in haptic perception. He also opposes "atomism," the isolation of single stimulus (or response) units, arguing instead for an active search and sampling of an "optic array" (or auditory or haptic array).

Self-Deception in Social Psychology

Social psychologists have also studied self-deception and related phenomena but not under that name. Cognitive dissonance (Festinger, 1957) is an example of these phenomena. One of the typical experiments (Festinger & Carlsmith, 1959) is to have subjects perform a very boring task such as turning over spools for half an hour and then paying them either $1 or $10 to convince incoming subjects that it is an interesting task. Contrary to behavioristic predictions, the subjects who are reinforced less (the $1 subjects) actually come to believe their own statements, that the task was interesting, more than the $10 subjects. The usual explanation is that the $10 subjects have adequate explanations for why they would deceive incoming subjects, but that the $1 subjects must do some rationalizing to "reduce the dissonance" by convincing themselves that it really was an interesting task.

In the era when cognitive dissonance theory was invented there was much less concern about experimenter ethics. The experimental design is a curious one for many reasons. The experimenter deceives subjects in order to catch them in a self-deception. In order for the study to "work," the subjects must be deceived about the true purpose of their participation. The most interesting thing about this whole line of experimentation is that the cognitive dissonance theorists do not mention or seem to notice the paradoxical nature of their subjects' actions. Certainly at some point in time the subjects notice that the task is boring. What could they possibly say to themselves to later be convinced otherwise? And even if they could somehow successfully "repress" the contradiction, would they not also have to repress the repressive act, to an infinite regress. A few years ago Gur and Sackeim (1979) published a paper entitled "Self-Deception: A Concept in Search of a Phenomenon" in which they set as their task to give adequate empirical evidence to support the self-deception concept as it exists in the philosophical literature. But we would argue that there has been adequte empirical precedent for the concept for some time now, even in some of the most major traditions of cognitive and social psychology. What is still missing in the psychological literature is a noncontradicotry *theoretical* treatment of the phenomenon.

Although Festinger did not discuss his "forced compliance" studies in terms of their relevance for the concept of unconscious mental processes, later developments in that kind of research did. Festinger accounted for his findings in terms of "dissonance," as an aversive motivational state that the person will seek to reduce. Bem (1967) argued that the hypothesized drive was an unnecessary one, that all of the findings could be explained more simply in terms of environmental contingencies. He maintained that a person observes his own actions and then attributes cognitive and emotional states to himself just as he would in explaining the actions of an observed other. In several simple studies he demonstrated a very obvious thing: Not only will a person believe his own statement more when paid less for giving it, but a second person observer will also believe the person more when he sees that the person was paid less for saying it.

But it was not Bem who saw the implications of his work for unconscious mental processes. In a 1977 *Psychological Review* paper entitled, "Telling More Than We Can Know: Verbal Reports on Mental Processes," Nisbett and Wilson picked up on Bem's point: that we have no private access to the causes for our own actions but rather infer those causes from our observations of those actions, just as we would do in explaining the behavior of another person. In the intervening 10 years between Bem's 1967 *Psychological Review* paper and Nisbett and Wilson's 1977 one, Tversky and Kahneman's (1974) demonstration of the irrationality of decision making under uncertainty became well known and Kelley's attribution theory (1967, 1972) called attention to attributional bias in social judgment. The case against accurate introspection of one's mental processes was growing. Nisbett and Wilson (1977) reviewed an impressive number of studies in the cognitive dissonance tradition, the learning-without-awareness literature, helping behavior research, and other areas—all demonstrating that people are not aware of the processes and reasons underlying their judgments. Altogether, they give impressive evidence for Mandler's (1975, p. 241) statement that "the analysis of situations and appraisal of the environment . . . goes on mainly at the nonconscious level."

Nisbett and Wilson (1977) are aware that the studies they review converge with the subliminal-perception/perceptual-defense research. They give a brief summary of that literature and comment that Dixon and Erdelyi were successful in obtaining a new acceptance for perceptual defense phenomena on the grounds of convergence with the selective attention and filtering research. They also mention the logical paradox problem of this literature, but like Dixon and Erdelyi they erroneously conclude that an information processing account resolves the paradox. The computer metaphor is a seductive one. Somehow it seems that if a computer "filters out" threatening information that we don't have to worry about how it could have been recognized as threatening without first being received. But, the problem is not to be easily dismissed by saying the person perceived it and forgot, as Nisbett and Wilson do (p. 240): to continue defensively means to *continue* to perceive.

TRANSPARENCY THEORY

Perhaps the single most important unresolved matter in psychology is the kind of phenomena that "unconscious mental processes" were invented to explain. It is important because, as recognized by the "new look in perception" theorists of the 1950s, it is a matter that brings together areas of psychology as diverse as psychophysics and psychodynamic theory. It extends to the central problems of attention theory in cognitive psychology, to recent directions of social psychology having to do with how we judge the actions of ourselves and others, to conceptual issues pertaining to the nature of emotion, self-deception, and self-knowledge, and to the discovery of better strategies for therapy. And besides all this, we are proposing in this chapter that the explanation of this kind of behavior is central to an understanding of nonverbal communication.

The theory, or the outline of it that now exists, is compounded of the work of several individuals who are discussed in this section.

Warner's Self-Deception Theory

The self-contradiction that seems to inhere in the idea of self-deception is this. If we are self-deceived about something, then we disbelieve (do not know) it is the case. But also, we must believe (know) or at least suspect it is the case in order to feel any need to deceive ourselves. Since we can't both believe and disbelieve the same thing at the same time, we cannot deceive ourselves. Standardly, this contradiction is dissolved by saying that the way in which the self-deceiver believes a thing is different from the way in which he disbelieves it. Most often these two ways of believing (or knowing) are made possible by the postulating of a duality of cognitive processing or a duality of cognitive structure, or both. For example, some have said that a self-deceiver believes (knows) the thing unconsciously but disbelieves (or does not know it) consciously. As we have seen in the discussion of Freud, this won't work. So, if the contradition is to be overcome, and the validity of the phenomena preserved, there must be some other sense in which one can believe the thing and yet disbelieve it in the same act.

What might this be? We know that there can be no mental act that converts a mental content from one status (conscious) to another (unconscious). Therefore, there can be no mental content that is the same whether the individual deceives himself about it or not. A belief about which one is self-deceived must be different *intrinsically* from a straightforward belief. In other words, it cannot be straightforwardly believed. Self-deception cannot be a matter of the status of a belief relative to consciousness at all; it is a matter of the intrinsic character of certain beliefs. An analogy may help: deceiving oneself is not like hiding a coin in a purse and publicly denying one has done so. It is more like doing business with a counterfeit coin and being insulted at the suggestion that the coin is false, and thereby giving the appearance that one has something to hide. Whether it is hidden or in plain view, the counterfeit coin cannot—because of its own intrinsic character—have the value stamped on its face.

What sort of belief can it be that has this intrinsically false character? And what sort of paralinguistic information will be available about the holder of this belief? How can it be information about her behavior and at the same time be inaccessible to her unless it is unconscious? To construct a theory of paralanguage without an unconscious we must answer these questions satisfactorily.

Warner (1982) has shown that what we must look for is nonmendacious behavior (the self-deceiver is not simply lying) that gives the *appearance* of being a denial of hidden knowledge, or "protesting too much," but *only* the appearance. A theory of self-deception must explain how the self-deceiver can give this appearance of resisted, hidden knowledge without simply faking or possessing unconscious knowledge. Because nothing unseen will be involved, we must look for previously overlooked features of commonplace phenomena that will help us understand why the behavior gives off this appearance. We must arrive at a reappraisal of this commonplace subject matter.

This is what Warner has done. For example, he has shown (paper in preparation) that there is a class of emotions that have all the properties of which we have spoken. We first give an example of such an emotion, showing some of its features when regarded from a different point of view than our usual one, and then gradually indicate why it is a self-deception. We show how it can appear to be resistant to unconscious knowledge, without there actually being any unconscious knowledge.

Here is one example of such an emotion. In most varieties of anger the angry person feels that she is aroused or provoked to anger by another and that she is acting self-protectively and justifiably. Yet what seems to her to be self-protection seems to the individual at whom her anger is directed to be aggresive and accusing. In other words, the angry person does accuse the person who angers her, but of abuse, so that in her own mind she is merely coping with the situation thrust upon her by the other. If the other reciprocates the anger, he in turn feels that he is the blameless one and regards her as abusively accusing. Each holds the other responsible—malicious and only pretending to be abused—and himself or herself passive in relationship to his or her feelings. But neither is correct. The anger is something both are doing[1] but, in doing, cannot understand themselves as doing. Because being angry *is* regarding oneself as being made angry and not as doing something purposefully, it is impossible to be angry and to believe otherwise. Because the angry person lacks this understanding, she is not malicious as her accuser's interpretation has it. Yet, because her anger is something she is doing, she is not passive as her interpretation has it.

This way of looking at emotions such as anger makes connection with much work on paralanguage, for example, that of Ernst Beier (1966):

> As an illustration of the evoking message we can consider an individual who thinks of himself as lonely and without any friends. In a careful analysis of his messages, we discover the coding of very subtle cues that are likely to create an emotional

---

[1]Tavris (1983) has reviewed social psychological studies of anger and shown that they corroborate this claim that anger is active, not passive.

climate in the people he addresses, resulting in negative and angry feelings. The sender evokes this negative response but is nevertheless able to see himself as the victim of circumstances. As he was not aware that he coded this information, he does not have a feeling of responsibility for the response he obtained. Indeed, the evoking message seems to be the type of communication which maintains the patient's present state of adjustment. With this message he helps to create those responses in his environment which confirm his view of the world. Through the responses he elicits, he constantly obtains proof that the world is exactly the place he thinks it is! . . . The evoking message is probably one of the basic tools used by individuals to maintain their consistency of personality. . . . The person with emotional conflict . . . creates a world in which he typically feels victimized by others, in which he experiences great unhappiness, though he has little awareness that he is often the creator of this world. (pp. 12–13)

The behavior of one with the type of emotion we are discussing can be seen by an observer to be both strategic and sincere. As Beier says, this paralinguistic information is abundantly available to others, but not to the agent, who believes himself sincere and not strategic, or to his accusers, who believe him strategic but not sincere. Thus we have an act that paralinguistically leaks information about itself that is not available to the agent. But we do not yet understand why the agent would be resistant to admitting the truth if it were suggested to him. The first step to understanding his resistance is to realize that what he resists— namely, the possibility that he is not a victim but is instead maliciously trying to provoke the person he is angry at—is not the truth. (Remember that from his viewpoint the only two conceivable possibilities are that he is genuinely angry and victimized, or that he is pretending and malicious, whereas neither of these interpretations of his behavior is the truth.) In other words, the possible unwelcome interpretation of his conduct that he resists is not something that would ever occur to him if he were not angry. This possible interpretation is an artifact necessarily accompanying the equally false interpretation that someone else is causing the anger. It is this unwelcome interpretation that he resists; as we show in a moment, it is as if this interpretation is always there, nagging at him and challenging the conception of his anger that he insists upon. Yet, if he were to admit that he were malicious, the self-deception would not end, but only undergo a transformation. Fore example—and this is but one of many variations on a theme—if the self-deceiver comes to believe that it is not good to have her "ugly" feelings about others, she can only think that she is not good for having them. The reason is that, being self-deceived, she does not believe they are merely something she is doing. Therefore, she can only believe they are something that she *is*. She will think she has a "bad real self"—even though no such self exists. On the other hand, if the undistorted truth about what she is doing were admitted, the individual wouldn't continue to be angry while confessing her malice. She would instead cease living the lie that her anger entails. She would cease being angry altogether.

The counterfeit truth (passive innocence) and the other equally false alternative interpretations of the self-deceiver's conduct (malicious pretense) came into being together. Indeed, in a series of arguments too intricate to replicate here, Warner shows that the anger is *intrinsically* resistant; it is at once the raising of the possibility that it is insincere and the denial of this very possibility. In fact, what convinces the self-deceiver of the unassailability of her position depends, ironically, upon her preoccupation with this very possibility. This preoccupation is, therefore, not incidental to her anger, it is essential. It serves her purposes in the following way. Because she does not perceive the truth (which is that she is neither passively innocent nor maliciously pretending), every clue that might suggest she is not absolutely justified can only be understood by her as charging her with pretense and malice. But since she actually feels attacked and hurt, she is certain that she is not just "making up" her anger. Hence, in her mind, the perceived charge that she is malicious has got to be preposterous. What makes her certain that she is right about her anger is the preposterousness, in her eyes, of every alternative interpretation of her anger. In other words, the threat to her position she feels from others is an *essential* part of her position. Her resistance does not require an independently perceived threat.

What Warner has done is to dissociate what the self-deceiver resists (the distorted alternatives to his claim about his own passivity and the other's malice) from what he deceives himself about (the undistorted view of the situation paralinguistically available). The truth is, the self-deceiver is neither passively innocent not pretending and malicious, but what he resists is the possibilty that he is pretending and malicious, which is just as false as his claim that he is a pure victim. What we have here, then, is the appearance, but not the reality, that an object exists in the psyche in another level of consciousness and is being resisted. We have, then, an explanation of the resistant behavior that we call self-deception that does not reduce to mere pretense and that does not invoke a hidden belief that is unconsciously repressed and overtly denied.

Let us step back and comment upon the relation of Warner's work, and of this paper generally, to the question of empiricism. Historically theories of the unconscious (and repudiations of the unconscious) developed as natural, perhaps even logically necessary, outgrowths of prevailing ways of looking at behavior. For example, the educated in our culture have shared a certain assumption about beliefs. The assumption is that the content of a belief is dissociable from the psychological state of belief. This means that a content can be the same for many psychologically different states of belief. One form of this assumption is the idea that the content of a belief exists independently of the people who may be said to have this belief. Not only is it common to say, e.g, "George and Harry believe the same thing," but also common to suppose that there is some thing that has a metaphysical existence independent of George's and Harry's states of belief. Another form of the assumption is the idea that the content of a belief will be the same whether one is deceived about it or undeceived, i.e., that this content is invariant through the process of self-deception. Once this invariance is assumed it is natural to suppose that deceiving oneself about some situation, which requires a belief that the situation exists, can *only* be a matter of "hiding" the content of this belief from oneself in a special "unconscious" status. Given this entire outlook, our observations of paralinguistic phenomena will unavoidably be "theory-laden;" they will irresistibly indicate unconscious processes. The only way out of such unexamined theoretical commitments—which in the case of observations of paralanguage lead to self-contradictions—is to see the phenomena, such as nonverbal leakage and resistance, differently. This is the value of Warner's treatment of self-deception. It does not postulate a new set of explanatory processes in rivalry to the unconscious. Instead, it comprehensively reappraises the phenomena in a manner that makes the postulation of such processes unnecessary.

The principle of parsimony suggests that this is the course we always should take. Choosing the theory with the fewest kinds or numbers of postulated explanatory entities is a secondary consideration. Prior to that we should seek the simplest reading of the phenomena themselves—the one that least encumbers us with the necessity to postulate unobservable entities at all. This is not a process of discovery as much as what Hanson, following Wittgenstein, called the "dawning of an aspect" (Hanson, 1961). From the Ptolemaic astronomers' geocentric viewpoint, they *observed,* or thought they observed, epicycles—retrogressive movements of the heavenly bodies—and Copernicus' work was predictalby unwelcome to any who held on to the old outlook. Regarding the heavens under the Copernican aspect changed the observations themselves. This kind of reappraisal of the subject matter "may be difficult, but should not obscure the fact that nothing less than this may do" (Hanson, 1961, p. 19).

When such reappraisal is what we mean by theory, theoretical work is inseparable from empirical scrupulousness. No amount of data gathering can substitute when a transformation of vision is required.

The material of this chapter, and the work of Michael Polanyi we discuss below, are like Warner's theory in the following way. They offer not armchair generalizations that could and should be tested empirically within the old point of view; they offer instead the conceptual connections that make up a new point of view and allow us to reappraise the significance of previous empirical work. No less than physics, psychology needs constantly to be on the lookout for new observational perspectives that allow for the casting aside of heavy, occult, explanatory burdens like unconscious processes.

Polanyi's Varieties of Knowledge

Polanyi's account (1962) of information that appears to be subliminally perceived but is not, shares this with Warner's account: What is thus perceived is originally and in its nature not specifiable by the speaker—yet it *is* perceived. So with

Polanyi too, no unconscious process is required to explain how the perceived can exist as a guide to behavior and still not be known to the speaker.

In exploring the limits of scientific knowledge Polanyi was led to distinguish two kinds of knowing: *tacit* and *explicit*. Science is explicit knowledge—knowledge that can be completely articulated, verbally transmitted, and publicly verified. But this is not the only kind of knowledge that is of value to a culture. Indeed, even the art of science itself—the way in which effective science is conducted—cannot always be made explicit, but must be learned by apprenticeship.

An example of tacit knowing is a craft. The half-literate Stradivarius created violins superior to anything that can be produced today, despite our technological advances. One who has this skill cannot put it into words—not because he lacks a second skill, namely, the skill of verbal description, but because the skill is itself ineffable. In British Common Law the decision of the judge is often of greater value than any reasons he can give for that decision, for he has no way to access the plethora of intricately interrelated aspects of the "know-how" by which he actually arrive at it. If it is proper to speak of an "unconscious" here, it is nothing like the unconscious of psychodynamic theory. Polanyi's maxim is, "We know more than we can say." Tacit knowledge is unspecifiable because it is *ineffable*.

There is another kind of unspecifiable knowledge, and it is unspecifiable for a different reason. It is called *subsidiary* knowledge. An example of this is a skilled pianist's awareness of the individual chords that he plays in the course of playing an entire piece of music. In order for his performance to proceed, his focus must be on the totality of the piece. Its particulars, such as the chords, he is aware of subsidiarily. A skilled pianist can identify each of the chords that he plays in a given piece, but cannot do so, even to himself, while he is playing the piece. If he were to focus upon any part, the performance would falter. He can focus on the whole performance or on a part, but not on both at the same time. So, of any particular in the perceptual array, he can have *focal awareness* or *subsidiary awareness*. Subsidiary knowledge is *logically unspecifiable* because if it is specified it is no longer subsidiary, and the entire activity of which it is a part is altered.

What role in behavior does the subsidary awareness play? When a skilled carpenter hammers a nail (Polanyi, 1962), he is aware of the nail focally and hammer subsidiarily. He attends *through* the hammer to the nail. The hammer is an extension of his body; he takes no focal notice of the texture of the handle against his palm or its heft as he swings it. If he were to focus on these things, his activity would change; he could no longer drive the nail effectively. Contact with the nail is the object of attention; awareness of the hammer is the instrument of this attention.

Again, when we read, words are the instruments of attention and their message is the object. If we focus instead on the individual words, we fail to apprehend their message. It is thus possible to read too slowly. Identifying each word focally robs the whole of its coherence; and we can go over and over the text this way without comprehension. In Polanyi's words, "all particulars become meaningless if we lose sight of the pattern which they jointly constitute." This he calls "the transparency of language."

> My correspondence arrives at my breakfast table in various languages, but my son understands only English. Having just finished reading a letter I may wish to pass it on to him, but must check myself and look again to see in what language it was written. I am vividly aware of the meaning conveyed by the letter, yet know nothing whatever of its words. I have attended to them closely but only for what they mean and not for what they are as objects. If my understanding of the text were halting, or its expressions or its spelling were faulty, its words would arrest my attention. They would become slightly opaque and prevent my thought from passing through them unhindered to the things they signify. (p. 57)

Some Implications of Transparency Theory and Support for Them.

Perceptual Atomism.   This transparency view of knowledge that the speaker cannot access, but that he betrays himself as having by his speech, is free of many assumptions that are either empirically unsupportable or conceptually incoherent. One of these assumptions—one that leads directly to the invention of unconscious processes—is perceptual atomism. This is the proposition that the entire sensory array consists of discrete stimulus units and that human action can be understood in terms of discrete response units. Once this assumption is made, then each bit of information, if it does guide or influence behavior, must be explicit and focal (in Polanyi's sense). If a person knows that she knows such information (i.e., is aware of it) it is in the conscious mind. If she does not know the information consciously, she can know it only in an unconscious part of the mind. Paralanguage, by its very nature, is behavior which manifests unacknowledged information. Hence, only if we eliminate atomism can we conceive paralanguage without an unconscious.

We saw that in Warner's critique of classical self-deception theories he specified the assumption that cripples them. It is the assumption that the contents of beliefs are independent of the psychological states of the people who have them and are invariant through the self-deception process. We are now in a position to point out that this is but another version of the atomistic assumption. It requires that if a belief is to be unacknowledgable by its holder, it can only be because it is in a special status inaccessible to him.

The major opponent of atomism in mainstream academic psychology is Gibson (1966). In a paper dealing with Gibson's "ecological optics" theory, Neisser (1977) argues that the revolutionary nature of Gibson's idea has not been fully appreciated, that "his innocent-sounding suggestion that we make a new description of the stimulus would render that whole century of theory obsolete" (p. 17).

It seems natural enough, he continues, for psychologists to first consider the simplest experimental situation, a single stimulus and response. He goes on to show that in the case of perception (as well as the learning of nonsense syllables and animal conditioning) the strategy has backfired in that the unnatural and impoverished "punctate stimulus" situation has led to unnecessarily complex perceptual theory.

In transparency theory, perception involves what Gibson calls active "information pick-up" from a total optic array (or auditory array, etc.); the apprehension of parts as discrete requires special mental effort. This idea combines Gibson's holistic theory of perception with Polanyi's account of subsidiary awareness. It suggests that most of what we perceive at any one time is in the background, subsidiarily apprehended in the service of a focus. (Fingarette too tries to make this sort of point about the "natural state" of our perceptual experience, but his atomism makes his version incoherent.)

Tranparency theory rejects atomism as unnecessary, not only for the actor (speaker) but also for the observer. Atomistically viewed, the properties of vocal paralanguage express a meaning for which they are "signs"—a meaning that "stands behind them" in the speaker's unconscious. If a property is considered in and of itself it can *only* mean something extra-linguistic and independently existing. But on the transparency theory, when an observer perceives the paralinguistic information, she is "looking through" the vocal properties to a focus they contribute to, i.e., the pattern which they jointly constitute. The properties considered in and of themselves are mere properties; the pattern they together form is the information. When the observer "looks through" these properties, it is not something independent of them that she perceives, but this pattern. In regard to this pattern, they play a subsidiary role. If they were focused on individually and directly, the meaning would not be perceived. In other words, what the paralinguistic behavior means is not separate from the behavior itself, but *is* that behavior seen holistically.

Perceptual Thresholds.   Closely connected with the idea of unconscious mental processes is the psychophysical notion of a perceptual threshold. The concept of 'subliminal perception' implies that information below the level of the usual sensory threshold somehow affects behavior. There has been a great deal of evidence against the classical concept of a sensory threshold since the 1950s. We briefly review this evidence and then show with other more recent data, that one can under proper conditions, find empirical support for a kind of threshold. But it is a discontinuity in perception that is predictable from the structure of the task being carried out and the strategy of the perceiver rather than "hardware" physiological structures. We hope to show that—just as the psychodynamic unconscious and the unconscious mental processes of the contemporary cognitivists are an error of stipulating physiological or mentalistic structure where the empirical observations could be much more easily explained in terms of the *observable* structure of the psychological task—so too the threshold can be more properly understood as being a function of the observable spatial and temporal structure of the perceptual context and of the person's perceptual strategy. We argue that the threshold, when seen in this way, is a very useful and empirically supportable concept that fits with the holistic transparency theory view of person perception articulated in this chapter.

One of the major contributions of contemporary psychophysics in the 1950s and 1960s was to find a productive way of quantifying the step function hypothesized by threshold theory and the opposing continuous function hypothesized by signal detection theory. The psychophysical functions for these two models are shown in Fig. 6.1. The signal detection theorists (Green & Swets, 1966; Swets, Tanner, & Birdsall, 1961; Tanner & Swets, 1954) demonstrated that the "two-state" model gives rise to an ROC curve ("receiver operating characteristic curve") that has two facets with inflection at the "ideal" decision point, while the multistate model gives rise to a smooth continuous ROC curve (which is under certain conditions an "isosensitivity" curve). They found no perceptual data that would fit the two-state ROC curve, but rather all that they tested fit the multistate continuous curve. In other words, when the threshold model is made mathematically precise in this way, there are no data to support it.

In a classic study of the minimum amount of light necessary to be detected, Hecht, Shlaer and Pirenne (1942) demonstrated that 10 quanta absorbed by the retina are sufficient for detection. In a recent update of this work in terms of signal detection theory, Sakitt (1972, 1974) has demonstrated that retinal absorption of a single quantum is sufficient for detection to take place. Actually this could have been anticipated in the signal detection theory demonstration that there is no psychophysical evidence for a threshold. If detection of a weak

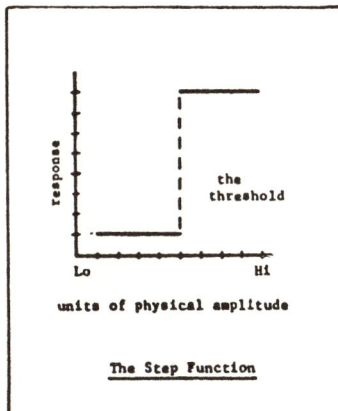

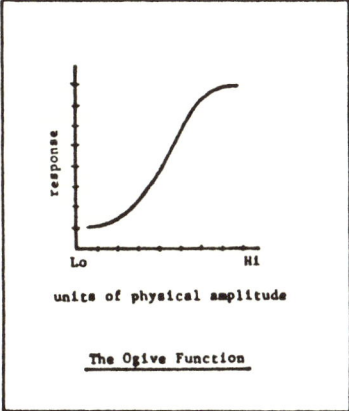

FIG. 6.1 A comparison of the step function of threshold theory with the ogive function of multistate theory.

stimulus is a continuous function of amplitude rather than the step function posited by threshold theory, *any* increase is enough to be detected given enough signal and noise trials. It becomes a statistical problem of probability to show detection of a weak stimulus rather than a perceptual one.

But the classical psychophysicists had good reason to take the concept of a threshold seriously. When one arranges weak stimuli in an ascending or descending series (the method of limits), it subjectively *seems* that there is a point of discontinuity, a place where the present stimulus seems noticeably louder than the ones before, even though the series are equidistant in amplitude. The ascending series has a different "threshold" or point of discontinuity than the descending series. For years psychophysicists have just averaged these, but the distance between the two is in fact much more interesting than their mean. Using a three-dimensional model called the "cusp," one of the seven fundamental surfaces in Thom's (1975) topological system, called Catastrophe Theory, Inouye (1978) has demonstrated that the distance between the ascending discontinuity (or "catastrophe," as Thom calls them) and the descending one is much different for schizophrenics than for normals. (Earlier psychophysical studies of schizophrenia, using the traditional techniques, had failed to show that schizophrenics' thresholds would differ from normal.) Schizophrenics perseverate more than normals. The distance between their ascending and descending points of discontinuity is greater. It has also been demonstrated that a normal person under stress has a greater interpoint distance than when not under stress.

The cusp catastrophe is nothing more than a three-dimensional surface with an ogive "lazy S" curve at one end and a "hard S" at the other as shown in Fig. 6.2. It is geometrically the general case of which both the threshold model and the continuity model (shown in Fig. 6.1) are special cases (Brown, Ferguson, Williams, & Barrus, 1976). The continuity model is, of course, identical with the lazy S end of the surface, and the hard S end has two thresholds, one for ascending from left to right (as shown in Fig. 6.2) and one descending from right to left. The "high-stress" function (a cross-section from the surface) shown in Fig. 6.2 is characteristic of schizophrenics and the "low-stress" function (the second cross-section behind the first in Fig. 6.2) is characteristic of normals.

We amend our position, then, to say that there is a threshold (or rather there are multiple thresholds), but thresholds are cognitive rather than sensory. Thresholds are a mirror of emotive state and cognitive style. What has been discovered is no more than an example of the complementary perceptual processes of assimilation and contrast put forth years ago by the Gestalt psychologists, but this time with a topological way of predicting when assimilation (not noticing a difference) will occur. And it becomes a useful index of personality and psychological state.

Gibson has made a profound contribution by providing the concept to begin the work of a holistic analysis of perception, but it is not altogether clear how to turn this concept into experiments. The topological surfaces of Catastrophe

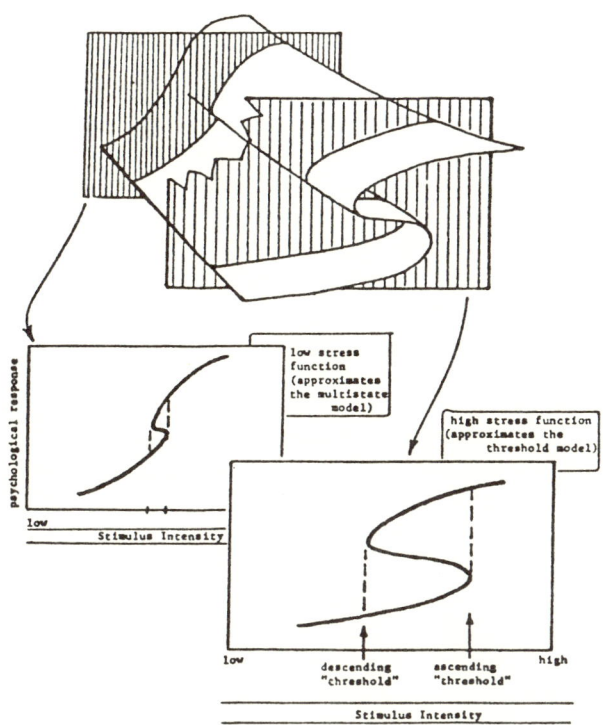

FIG. 6.2 The cusp catastrophe as the general case incorporating both the multistate model and the threshold model.

Theory provide a way of making precise predictions about the ways in which judgments are predictable from spatial and temporal context. They are qualitatively precise parables, or "canonical forms" that can be directly tested in perception research as well as in person perception from voice research as suggested below.

Passive Information Processing.   Gibson has rejected the traditional typification of perception as sensation colored by conception or past experience. We do also, but our proposed alternative premise differs from Gibson's and Neisser's. Gibson does move us forward from "information processing" (as though information were pushed through us) to "information pickup" (an active selecting perceiver), but he doesn't specify how this happens. As Hamlyn (1977) has pointed out, although Gibson moves in the direction of active holistic perception, he finally leaves the self, the agent, the perceiver out of perception. In his description of information pickup Hamlyn (1977) claims that the senses functioning as perceptual systems "can obtain information about objects in the world without the intervention of an intellectual process" (p. 13). This leaves one hard pressed to extrapolate Gibson's theory to abnormal psychology, and even to everyday self-deception—unless, of course, he invokes unconscious processes. Neisser (1976) also admits the Piagetian concept of a perceptual process of accommodation (altering schemata to fit incoming information), but not the complementary process of assimilation (altering incoming information to make it fit preexisting schemata), and is also therefore not able to account for self-deceived or pathological perception.

But the transparency alternative does more than just include Piaget's concept of assimilation. A person's perceptions are not only *altered* according to existing intentions, beliefs, and so forth, but they are *acquired* in the first place in a form that reflects intentions, beliefs, and the like. Our perceptions are a reflection of personality; they are aspects of our actions. They are not stimuli passively received, but responses. So we agree with Gibson in rejecting the view that perceptions are merely sensations colored by past experience and bias, but we differ in holding that the particular information that will be picked up and the way that it is most rudimentarily experienced are different for different persons. These matters are reflections of intention, personality and cognitive style. The perceptual or sensory experience in its rawest experienced form is already an expression of the person and the person's state. Inouye (1978) demonstrated this in the psychophysical studies referred to above.

This proposal, though radical, is not without precedent in the clinical and philosophical literature. A number of theorists (Kelly, 1955; Rychlak, 1981; Warner, 1982) have also proposed that we can choose to construe our circumstances in a number of ways ("constructive alternativism," Kelly calls it). Kelly's personality test, the REP test, is based upon the idea that we can best understand a person by understanding how he views significant others. This kind of perception, the way a person perceives another person, is at the highest level of what could be referred to as perception, whereas the psychophysical demonstration is at the lowest; nevertheless, at both levels and everywhere in between, the person and his intentions are paralinguistically manifest.

The Passivity of Emotion.   Another assumption that transparency theory can do without is that of emotions as causes of responses. Rather than considering all emotions as biologically based reactions that cause behavior in some necessary fashion, we propose that many emotions, like perceptions, are themselves responses rather than causes of behavior (Warner, 1982). Although we will concede that many emotions, such as grief, or certain kinds of fear, are very much like automatic reactions, and have a strong biological basis, others like most anger and much depression can be better understood as a kind of intentional nonverbal, manipulative message. We have already seen what instrumental efficacy anger can have. The implications of this conception of emotions for research on nonverbal behavior are very promising.

The fragmentation of the psyche by the "information processing" psychologists had become quite complete by the 1980s. Not only do they posit conscious and unconscious processors, but also separate systems for cognition and affect, and evidence has it that the affective system is faster (Zajonc, 1980). The same results can be explained alternatively in terms of a part/whole distinction and that what Zajonc has demonstrated is that the most primitive and fundamental kind of perception is holistic, that it takes mental work to notice parts. The Gestalt psychologists noticed this phenomenon long ago and referred to it as "physiognomic perception." The basic idea is that we do not look at a face and notice the glaring eyes, the grinding teeth, the red flush and conclude that the person is angry, but rather the impression of anger is immediate and unmediated and the component parts are only noticed afterward if at all. "We must assume that features like 'threatening' or 'tempting' are more primitive and more elementary contents of perception than those we learn of as 'elements' in the textbooks of psychology" (Koffka, 1928, p. 150). Likewise, the statistician Chernoff (1973) has shown that complex multivariate data can be apprehended much more quickly in the form of stylized human faces than in traditional graphs. The gestalt of a human face has an immediate, tacit meaning that precedes any notice of parts.

Rather than positing a fast emotion-processing system and a slow cognitive one, the empirical evidence can be explained by saying that perception is tacitly monitored skill directed upon a holistically apprehended field, and that explicit notice of the elements and parts of the field requires special mental work. In a voice study Feldstein and Bond (1981) demonstrated that when subjects are given the task of judging the speech rate of voices that are in fact equivalent in rate but vary in terms of frequency and intensity, they will judge higher frequency voices to be faster and higher intensity voices also to be faster (see also Bond & Feldstein, 1982). But it seems to us that judging rate or intensity or any other single feature of voice is not a very natural thing for a person. The impression from voice is much more global. When pressed for a judgment we can make it, but the dimension we think we are judging may not be the one the experimenter is varying at all. Such attention to a part requires mental work, but it will not be very accurate without practice and feedback.

Selective Attention.   We are now ready to deal with the contradictory results of the dichotic listening studies mentioned above. Whereas Treisman (1964) provides evidence that the subject cannot even accurately identify the language in which the unattended words are spoken, Lewis (1970) gives evidence of full semantic processing of the unattended channel. The two seem contradictory, but this is exactly what Polanyi would expect on the basis of his concept of the transparency of language. It is not necessary to notice words or even the language identity of the words to have an apprehension of the meaning. Skilled reading involves attending through the words (the instruments of attention) to the message (the object of attention). (See Brown, Inouye, Barrus, & Hansen, 1981.) In the Lewis (1970) study the subject is not able to identify specific words from the unattended channel (they are not in focal awareness) but rather it is shown that synonyms slow down his reaction time. On an atomistic analysis of the situation the results are mysterious. We have evidence of a stimulus affecting the person's response without the usual awareness of having been perceived, and if we are atomists we presume it was processed unconsciously. On a holistic analysis the account is simpler: The presence of a part helps determine the apprehension of the whole, even though that part is not noticed focally. The fragmentation of the psyche into conscious and unconscious processes is the natural result of considering perception in terms of discrete stimuli rather than as a patterned whole. One can argue that the whole cognitive enterprise called "attention theory" is a way of patching up the mistaken premises of 50 years of behaviorism. As Kahneman (1973) has confessed, "Indeed, the main function of the term 'attention' in post-behavioristic psychology is to provide a label for some of the internal mechanisms that determine the significance of stimuli and thereby make it impossible to predict behavior by stimulus considerations alone" (p. 2).

Likewise, we need not conclude from the evidence reviewed by Nisbett and Wilson (1977) that because our attributions of reasons for our choices and actions are in error, the actions are in some way "caused by behavioral contingencies" or otherwise nonintentional. Most intentional action is tacitly monitored and the circumstantial features that guide it are subsidiarily known. To try to articulate what we have done or why we have done it requires mental work, which always involves distortion.

APPLICATIONS OF TRANSPARENCY THEORY TO PARALINGUISTIC RESEARCH

In transparency theory paralinguistic behavior is meaningful in itself without reference to an unconscious. We have seen why this is not true for atomists. Thus it is that a transparency theorist will see personality *in* paralinguistic behavior whereas an atomist will tend to look for it *behind* this behavior, and see it as more reliably accessible in some other way (as with a "personality test"). As far as the paralinguistic evidence of personality is concerend, the atomist considers objectively specifiable paralinguistic cues and tries to correlate these with independently discovered "personality traits" and characteristics. The meaning of the cues is established by reference to these traits and characteristics in terms of modern cognitive psychology. This means that we can trace the flow of information outward from internal processes to particular components of behavior. But on transparency theory, personality *is* paralanguage—not seen atomistically as a set of discrete cues, but holistically, as a pattern. There is no need, on this view, to validate paralinguistic research by means of personality tests. Personality can be studied by the more precise and reliable methods of paralanguage research.

In this section we review some empirical research that cannot be correctly understood apart from the transparency point of view, and that in turn supports this view.

Paralinguistic Studies of Social Cognition

The matched guise studies have almost without exception had the speakers recite standard passages, and in many cases half of the voices are of one language and half of another. In other words, the information about ethnic identity is not nearly as "subsidiary" as it could be. The judges are focusing upon voice and language, the only two things that vary, since content of the utterance is constant.

Barlow (1983) conducted a study using the Latin-Square methodology of the Stewart, Brown, and Stewart (in preparation) study previously mentioned to study the effects of standard English versus Pidgin (as well as intonation manipulations) on attributions of the relative adequacy of answer given to interview questions. This is a matched guise study (standard vs. Pidgin English), but one that uses natural speech. Rather than using standard passages, each speaker's actual answer to the question "What do you think of racial quotas for graduate school admission?" is used, but the same set of speaker answers appears in different guise manipulations for each judging group. To each judge it seems that he is just hearing the answers of 12 different people, but the counterbalancing allows us to have each answer presented in each of the "guises." In this way we can identify how much of judge ratings is attributable to each manipulation (as in the matched guise method), but with very natural speech samples that vary in content (an improvement over matched guise standard passages). Rather than rating the personality of the speaker, Barlow had judges rate the adequacy of the answer itself. In this way he was able to assess how ethnic and intonation information was used tacitly by the judges in assessing answer content quality.

The most important factor in accounting for how adequate the answer sounded was the dialect. The answer sounded much more competent when given in standard English than in Pidgin. Barlow also had judges indicate the reason for the rating whenever they gave a very high or very low rating. The low rating was almost never attributed to dialect, but almost always to content, "because he seemed to not understand the issues," and so on. In transparency theory terms, the judges make a holistic evaluation of the spoken answer, and it requires mental work to identify why they judge it as they do. But "why" is a question that they cannot adequately introspect; the rating process is a tacit "skill," not introspectable. As Bem (1967) and as Nisbett and Wilson (1977) have said, in answering such a question, they seem to ask themselves, "What would be a likely reason for judging the answer as incompetent?"

This demonstration has the fundamental elements of the "processing without awareness" studies, where it is shown that manipulation of a part of the stimulus array can profoundly affect the response without the person having any awareness of what was altered. But this kind of research is much closer to what happens in actual human action and interaction than the artificial experimental paradigms of taboo word studies and dichotic listening.

In addition to these studies that demonstrate tacit reactions and can be used to illustrate transparency theory, we are also conducting some direct tests of implications of the theory. For example, we have used a variant of the Latin-Square method to examine the differences in rating style of those found to be "accurate perceivers" and those who are "inaccurate." The voices are given in ascending and in descending order of rate, but each answer is different and from a different person so that judges will not notice the organization with respect to rate. But we average over many such path-dependent tapes to show the effects only of rate. In this way we will demonstrate that inaccurate perception is not haphazard or random, but is predictable from the temporal gestalt, as Inouye (1978) found in his comparison of schizophrenic and normal subjects. In other words, we expect the competence ratings as a function of rate to have the "low-stress" function shown in Fig. 6.2 above for the accurate perceivers and the "high-stress" function in that figure for the inaccurate perceivers.

Before leaving the "social cognition" aspect of personality/speech research we examine one other technique for assessing tacit knowledge. In his dissertation, Brown (1969) used factor analysis to give a geometric summary in a two-dimensional space of the ratings given to voices on 15 to 20 adjective pairs. This method has evolved over the past 15 years as it has been applied to many "cue synthesis" studies. It is referred to as the "principal factors biplot" (Brown, Williams & Barlow, 1984; Everitt, 1978). It provides a way of making a structural description of a person's or group's "implicit (tacit) personality theory."

Brown, Barlow, and Williams (in preparation) recently reviewed the matched guise literature and used the biplot method to compute secondary analyses comparing all of the studies that published the means for their adjective ratings. The biplot for the reanalysis of data from El-Dash and Tucker's (1975) matched guise study of the significance of various English dialects in Egypt is given in Fig. 6.3. The figure shows two biplots, one for the ratings given to each of the three dialects of English (British, American and Egyptian) when the respondents correctly recognized the dialect identity of the speaker, and one for when the identity was not recognized. Notice that grade school Egyptian respondents rate the British dialect as considerably higher on competence adjectives than the other two dialects, as do the high school respondents, but the American University of Cairo respondents rate the British lower in competence than the other two dialects (as shown in the bipilot on the left, for "dialect recognized"). But when dialect is not explicitly recognized, the university respondents agree with the other respondents that British dialect sounds more competent. It seems that at the

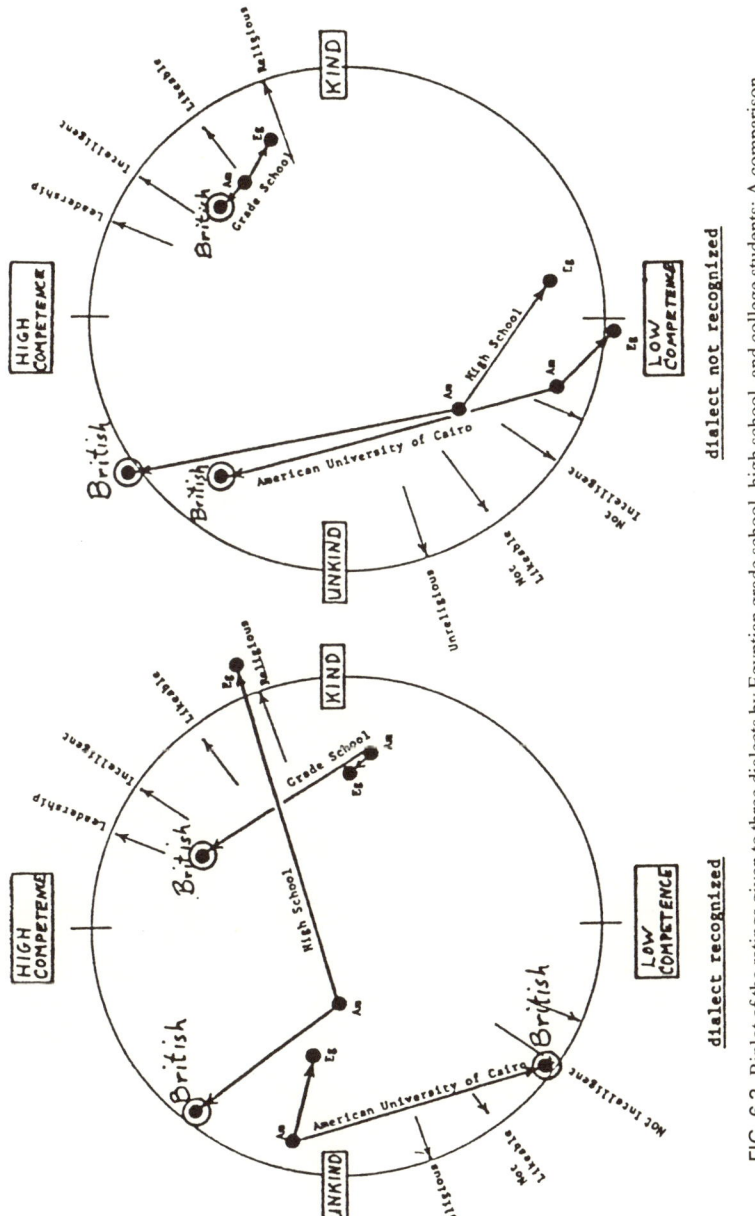

FIG. 6.3 Biplot of the ratings given to three dialects by Egyptian grade school, high school, and college students: A comparison of the ratings when dialect identity of the speaker is recognized and when it isn't. (From Brown, Barlow, & Williams' reanalysis of El-Dash & Tucker, 1975).

American University of Cairo it is fashionable to downgrade the British, but that when identity is not recognized the British dialect is still judged as high in competence. (It was shown in a reanalysis of the data of Anisfeld, Bogo, and Lambert, 1962, that even when a Jewish-accented voice is not explicitly recongized as Jewish, it still receives the typical Jewish rating: shorter, kinder, good sense of humor, etc.)

We have argued that much of what is called "unconscious processing" is nothing more than the experimenter focusing on a particular part of the available paralinguistic information while the subject is responding to the gestalt. But the biplot is a way of looking at another kind of "unconscious," with the subjects giving responses to speakers one at a time, and the biplot showing the implications of all of the ratings as a gestalt. In that sense, a biplot can show the totality of the person's "implicit personality theory" in a way that the person herself is not aware of. The person only notices the judgments one at time (the parts) wheras the experimenter, with the aid of a biplot, can see the totality implied by the judgments and in this way can apprehend more of a subject's thinking than the subject can explicitly report.

The biplot method also allows the investigator to look at a kind of "group unconscious process." That is, the experimenter can compare the responses of two or more groups to see how their tacit use of dialect markers, vocal markers, and so forth, differ. The El-Dash and Tucker (1975) data (Fig. 6.3) are an illustration of this.

Brown et al. (in preparation) computed this same kind of reanalysis of Tucker and Lambert's (1969) matched guise study of northern white, southern white and southern black reactions to six white and six black dialects. The biplots for these data show an interesting group gestalt. Whereas southern whites rated southern black dialect speakers as being equal to southern white dialect speakers on the competence factor, the southern black respondents rated the southern white dialect speakers as being way below every other type of speaker on the benevolence or kindness factor. It seems that the dominant culture may have been very much affected by the civil rights movement of the 1950s and 1960s and that perhaps much of the bias and discrimination has been corrected even on the tacit level, but that there is till some mistrust and resentment for past wrongs on the part of the plaintiffs.

Emotion, Mental Illness and Nonverbal Language

Whereas some emotions like sadness, joy, and so on, can be thought of as tacit accompaniments of human interaction woven into the total gestalt of an experience, we propose (in concert with Solomon, 1977, and Warner, 1982) that other emotions, like anger and most depressions, are often a kind of response, intended to bring about a particular state of affairs—a paralinguistic operant. This approach to studying the relationship between emotion and speech has yet to be explored in the research literature, but we suggest that it provides a crucially important direction for future investigation. Such investigation will have important implications for an understanding of "mental illness."

Vocal paralanguage research carried out within the framework of transparency theory could be of great importance to clinical psychology in providing a basis for the definition of "mental illness." Thomas Szasz has been one of the most outspoken critics of psychiatry and clinical psychology and the whole concept of mental illness. His approach has been seen by many as primarily destructive and cynical, but in his book, *The Myth of Mental Illness* (1974), he makes an analysis of psychopathology that may be a very productive one. He argues that the illness metaphor is a mistaken and misleading one, the primary purpose of which is to promote psychiatry as a medical discipline. His counterproposal is that "mental illness" be considered as a kind of nonverbal language. This proposal is not unrelated to the approach to abnormal behavior seen in the work on self-deception by Warner, which was discussed above. Many who work in clinical settings find his suggestions offensive and would maintain that such an approach could not begin to account for the variety of extreme behaviors that can be observed in such settings. But few would argue for the validity and reliabilty of clinical categories as they now exist, and his proposal has merit at least as a fresh point of departure that may provide new insights into the nature of psychopathology.

Consider the ontogeny of vocal paralanguage in the human infant. We propose that much of the nonverbal communication of the infant is instrumental in its purpose, intended to bring about a desired state of affairs. Perhaps these nonverbal operants in the beginning months are quite innocent and connected primarily with seeking nourishment, affection and attention. But as the child matures and interpersonal conflicts become a part of life, other kinds of "evoking messages" develop. Some are assertive, some accusatory. Some are intended primarily to irritate: to evoke hostility or retaliation from a sibling. It is subtle, intentional action, a manifestation of skill. The child is certainly not ignorant of what is happening, yet the child certainly cannot acknowledge what he is doing, not even to himself. At least he cannot both acknowledge it and continue to do it. It is inherent in the structure of the act that it cannot both be continued and be acknowledged. It is unspecifiable in Polanyi's second way: logically unspecifiable. We propose that these nonverbal "habits" constitute in large measure what we think of as personality, and are at the root of psychopathology.

Braginsky, Braginsky, and Ring (1969) describe a study in which 30 male schizophrenic patients all living on an open ward of the institution were recorded during an interview with the staff psychologist. One third of the patients were told by the person who escorted them to the inteview that the purpose of the interview was to determine whether they should be discharged from the hospital. One third were told the purpose was to determine who should be in open wards and who in closed. The last third was the control group who were told that the purpose was just to see how they were feeling and getting along in the hospital. (In earlier studies they had demonstrated the hypothesis that "old timers" like these were actually adjusted to the hospital setting and did not wish to be discharged.) The recorded interviews were played to three staff psychiatrists who had no knowledge of the design or purpose of the experiment (nor did the interviewer). The psychiatrists rated each speaker on the degree of psychopathology, and the amount of hospital control needed (with interjudge reliabilities of .89 and .74 respectively). In addition, ratings were made of the vocal properties of speakers and the content of the interview. Those who were "threatened" with discharge had the highest ratings of degree of pathology and those "threatened" with a closed ward had the lowest ($F = 9.38$, $p < .01$). These results were consistent with the hypothesis that schizophrenics are very good at impression management, and that these patients wanted to stay where they were. Also consistent with the hypothesis, the highest ratings for amount of hospital control needed was for the discharge-threatened patients and the lowest for those threatened with a closed ward ($F = 3.85$, $p < .05$).

The results of the analyses of the speech of the three groups were disappointing in comparison to what could have been done. Essentialy what they found was that the closed-ward, threatened group had substantially more positive self-references and the discharge-threatened group had more negative self-references. This makes it appear that the major aspect of impression management was the content of the interview. From the studies we have done, we would expect that the major part of the impression is from vocal qualities. This kind of study is a difficult one in terms of ethical issues such as "informed consent," adequate debriefing (which these authors did), and so forth, but it has considerable potential as a way of understanding the nonverbal management of impressions in psychopathology. It would be important to compare content with vocal qualities (by using typed transcripts and in some way masking intelligibility) in order to determine how much effect each has in creating the impression of pathology. The next step would be to do a thorough acoustical analysis of the voices to obtain hypotheses about the particular voice qualities that are instrumental in that impression and then to test such hypotheses experimentally with a cue synthesis attribution study.

SUMMARY

The currently dominant psychological paradigm strongly suggests that unconscious processes are required to explain paralanguage. But the idea of such processes is self-contradictory. What is required is a comprehensive outlook on behavior that without recourse to an unconscous, can explain how we reveal more about ourselves and our actions than we ourselves can know, and even things that we would resist. We have sketched some features of a theory, transparency theory, that seems able to do this job and we have shown with example vocal paralinguistic studies how it can be applied.

The topic of paralanguage is central to psychology, in fields ranging from information processing to psychopathology. We have outlined a program here for studying vocal paralanguage, but its implications are not limited to voice research. They extend to personality, cognition, learning theory, perception, developmental psychology, abnormal psychology, and clinical psychology.

Work is beginning on the application of this theoretical approach to second langauge acquisition (Brown & Williams, 1983) and expansion of learning theory to account for the acquisition of listening and reading skills from a gestalt perspective (Brown, 1985).

REFERENCES

Addington, D. W. (1968). The relationship of selected vocal characteristics to personality perception. *Speech Monographs, 35,* 492–503.

Anisfeld, M., Bogo, N., & Lambert, W. E. (1962). Evaluational reactions to accented English speech. *Journal of Abnormal and Social Psychology, 65,* 223–231.

Apple, W., Streeter, L. A., & Kraus, R. M. (1979). Effects of pitch and speech rate on personal attributions. *Journal of Personality and Social Psychology, 5,* 715–727.

Barlow, C. D. (1983). *The effects of manipulating several linguistic parameters on judge ratings of answers.* Doctoral dissertation, Brigham Young University, Provo, Utah.

Beier, E. (1966). *The silent language of psychotherapy.* Chicago: Aldine.

Bem, D. J. (1967). Self-perception: An alternative interpretation of cognitive dissonance phenomena. *Psychological Review, 74* (3), 183–200.

Bond, R. N., & Feldstein, S. (1982). Acoustical correlates of the perception of speech rate: An experimental investigation. *Journal of Psycholinguistic Research, 11* (6), 539–557.

Bowen, K. L., Lacayo, M., Brown, B. L., & Jentz, J. (1983). *Person-characteristic judgment from content and from vocal properties plus content.* Paper presented at the 1983 Meetings of the Rocky Mountain Psychological Association, Salt Lake City, Utah.

Braginsky, B. M., Braginsky, D. C., & Ring, K. (1969). *Methods of madness: The mental hospital as a last resort.* New York: Holt, Rinehart & Winston.

Brown, B. L. (1969). *The social psychology of variations in French Canadian speech styles.* Doctoral dissertation, McGill University, Montreal Canada.

Brown, B. L. (1980a). Effects of speech rate on personality attributions and competency evaluations. In H. Giles, W. P. Robinson, & P. M. Smith (Eds.), *Social psychology and language* (pp. 293–300). Oxford: Pergamon Press.

Brown, B. L. (1980b). The detection of emotion in vocal qualities. In H. Giles, W. P. Robinson, & P. M. Smith (Eds.), *Social psychology and language* (pp. 237–245). Oxford: Pergamon Press.

Brown, B. L. (1982). Experimentelle untersuchungen zur personwahrnehmung aufgrund vokaler hinweisreize. In Klaus Scherer (Ed.), *Vokale kommunikation: Nonverbale aspekte des sprachverhaltens.* Weinheim: Beltz Verlag.

Brown, B. L. (submitted for publication). An expansion of learning theory and its implications for the language laboratory. In Jerry W. Larson (Ed.), *Contemporary developments in the language learning laboratory.*

Brown, B. L., Barlow, C. D., & Williams, R. N. (in preparation). *A principal components biplot meta-analysis of selected matched guise studies*. Unpublished manuscript, Brigham Young University, Provo, Utah.

Brown, B. L., & Bradshaw, J. M. (in press). Towards a social psychology of voice variations. In H. Giles & R. St. Clair (Eds.), *Recent advances in language, communication and social psychology*. London: Lawrence Erlbaum Associates.

Brown, B. L., Ferguson, H. R. P., Williams, R., & Barrus, K. B. (1976). *A catastrophe theory account of dichotic listening*. Paper presented at the 84th Annual Convention, American Psychological Association, Washington, DC.

Brown, B. L., Hamblin, D. L., & Bowen, D. E. (in preparation). *The recognition of film-induced emotion from vocal qualities*. Unpublished manuscript, Brigham Young University, Provo, UT.

Brown, B. L., Inouye, D. K., Barrus, K. B., & Hansen, D. M. (1981). A social psychology of rapid reading. In J. R. Edwards (Ed.), *The Social Psychology of Reading*. Language and Literacy Monograph Series. Silver Spring: Institute of Modern Languages.

Brown, B. L., Strong, W. J., & Rencher, A. C. (1972a). Acoustic parameters of personality. *Journal of the Acoustical Society of America, 15* (1), 121.

Brown, B. L., Strong, W. J., & Rencher, A. C. (1972b). Manipulation of vocal qualities by speech synthesis: A new way to study person perception. *Proceedings of the 80th Annual Convention of the American Psychological Association, 7*, 197–198.

Brown, B. L., Strong, W. J., & Rencher, A. C. (1973). Perceptions of personality from speech: Effects of manipulations of acoustical parameters. *Journal of the Acoustical Society of America, 54* (7), 29–35.

Brown, B. L., Strong, W. J., & Rencher, A. C. (1974). Fifty-four voices from two: The effects of simultaneous manipulations of rate, mean fundamental frequency and variance of fundamental frequency on ratings of personality from speech. *Journal of the Acoustical Society of America, 55* (2), 313–318.

Brown, B. L., Strong, W. J., & Rencher, A. C. (1975). Acoustic determinants of perceptions of personality from speech. *International Journal of the Sociology of Language, 6*, 11–32.

Brown, B. L., & Williams, R. N. (1983). Transparency theory and second language acquisition. *Nagoya Gakuin Daigaku Gaikokugo Kyoiku Kiyo, 9*, 7–25.

Brown, B. L., Williams, R. N., & Barlow, C. D. (1984). PRIFAC: A Pascal Factor Analysis Program. *Journal of Pascal, Ada and Modula-2, 3* (2), 18–24.

Chernoff, H. (1973). Using faces to represent points in k-dimensional space graphically. *Journal of the American Statistical Association, 68*, 361–368.

Corteen, R. S., & Dunn, D. (1974). Shock-associated words in a non-attended message: A test for momentary awareness. *Journal of Experimental Psychology, 102*, 1134–1144.

Corteen, R. S., & Wood, B. (1972). Autonomic responses to shock-associated words in an unattended channel. *Journal of Experimental Psychology, 94*, 308–313.

Davitz, J. R., & Davitz, L. J. (1959). The communication of feelings by content-free speech. *Journal of Communication, 9*, 6–13.

Dennett, D. C. (1978). Why the law of effect will not go away. In D. C. Dennett, *Brainstroms: Philosophical essays on mind and psychology*. Montgomery, VT: Bradford Books.

Deutsch, J. A., & Deutsch, D. (1963). Attention: Some theoretical considerations. *Psychological Review, 70* (1), 80–90.

Dicks, R. H., Brown, B. L., & Wells, M. G. (in preparation). *A comparison of groups differing in mental health in their ability to judge and portray emotions*. Unpublished manuscript, Brigham Young University, Provo, UT.

Dixon, N. F. (1971). *Subliminal perception: The nature of a controversy*. London: McGraw-Hill.

Ekman, P., & Friesen, W. V. (1969). Nonverbal leakage and clues to deception. *Psychiatry, 32* (1), 88–106.

El-Dash, L., & Tucker, G. R. (1975). Subjective reactions to various speech styles in Egypt. *International Journal of the Sociology of Language, 6,* 33–54.

Erdelyi, M. H. (1974). A new look at the new look: Perceptual defense and vigilance. *Psychological Review, 81* (1), 1–25.

Everitt, B. (1978). *Graphical techniques for multivariate data.* New York: North-Holland.

Fay, P. J., & Middleton, W. C. (1939). Judgment of Spranger personality types from the voice as transmitted over a public address system. *Character and Personality, 8,* 144–155.

Feldstein, S., & Bond, R. N. (1981). Perception of speech rate as a function of vocal intensity and frequency. *Language and Speech, 24* (4), 387–394.

Festinger, L. (1957). *Cognitive dissonance.* Stanford, CA: Stanford University Press.

Festinger, L., & Carlsmith, J. M. (1959). Cognitive consequences of forced compliance. *Journal of Abnormal and Social Psychology, 58,* 203–210.

Fingarette, H. (1969). *Self-deception.* London: Routledge & Kegan Paul.

Freud, S. (1957a). Fragment of an analysis of a case of hysteria. In J. Strachey (Ed. and Trans.), *The standard edition of the complete psychological works of Sigmund Freud* (Vol 7, pp. 77–78). London: Hogarth Press. (Original work published 1905).

Freud, S. (1957b). The unconscious. In J. Strachey (Ed. and Trans.), *The standard edition of the complete psychological works of Sigmund Freud* (Vol. 14, p. 170). London: Hogarth Press (original work published 1915).

Fuller, B. (1982). *Reliability and validity of an interval method for scoring vocal stress.* Unpublished manuscript, University of Colorado Health Sciences Center, Denver, CO.

Gibson, J. J. (1966). *The senses considered as perceptual systems.* Boston: Houghton Mifflin.

Giles, H. & Powesland, P. F. (1975). *Speech style and social evaluation.* London: Academic Press.

Green, D. M., & Swets, J. A. (1966). *Signal detection theory and psychophysics.* New York: Wiley.

Gur, R. C., & Sackeim, H. A. (1979). Self deception: A concept in search of a phenomenon. *Journal of Personality and Social Psychology, 37* (2), 147–169.

Hamlyn, D. W. (1977). The concept of information in Gibson's theory of perception. *Journal of Theory of Social Behavior, 7* (1), 5–16.

Hanson, N. R. (1961). *Patterns of discovery.* Cambridge: Cambridge University Press.

Hecht, S., Shlaer, S., & Pirenne, M. H. (1942). Energy, quanta and vision. *Journal of General Physiology, 25,* 819–840.

Howie, D. (1952). Perceptual defense. *Psychological Review, 59,* 308–315.

Inouye, D. K. (1975). *Memory for unattended items.* Unpublished first-year project, Stanford University, Stanford, CA.

Inouye, D. K. (1978). *The identification and representation of catastrophic interactions.* Doctoral dissertation, Stanford University, Stanford, CA.

Kahneman, D. (1973). *Attention and effort.* Englewood Cliffs, NJ: Prentice-Hall.

Kelley, H. H. (1967). Attribution theory in social psychology. In D. Levine (Ed.), *Nebraska Symposium on Motivation* (Vol. 15). Lincoln: University of Nebraska Press.

Kelley, H. H. (1972). Attribution in social interaction. In E. E. Jones et al. (Eds.), *Attribution: Perceiving the causes of behavior.* Morristown, NJ: General Learning Press.

Kelly, G. A. (1955). *The psychology of personal constructs* (Vol. I). New York: W. W. Norton.

Kjeldergaard, P. M. (1968). *Changes in perceived personality traits as a function of manipulation of vocal characteristics.* Unpublished manuscript, Harvard University, Cambridge, MA.

Koffa, K. (1928). *The growth of the mind* (2nd ed.) New York.

Kramer, E. (1964). Elimination of verbal cues in judgments of emotion from voice. *Journal of Abnormal and Social Psychology, 68* (4), 390–396.

Lambert, W. E. (1967). The social psychology of bilingualism. *Journal of Social Issues, 23,* 91–109.

Laver, J. (1968). Voice quality and indexical information. *British Journal of Disorders Communciation, 3,* 43–54.

Laver, J. (1975). *Individual features in voice quality.* Doctoral dissertation, University of Edinburgh, Edinburgh, Scotland.

Laver, J. (1978). The concept of articulatory settings; An historical survey. *Historiographia Linguistica, 5,* 1–14.

Lewis, J. L. (1970). Semantic processing of unattended messages using dichotic listening. *Journal of Experimental Psychology, 85,* 225–228.

Mandler, G. (1975). Consciousness: Respectable, useful and probably necessary. In R. Solso (Ed.), *Information processing and cognition: The Loyola Symposium.* Hillsdale, NJ: Lawrence Erlbaum Associates.

Mischel, W. (1973). Toward a cognitive social learning reconceptualization of personality. *Psychological Review, 80,* 252–283.

Neisser, U. (1967). *Cognitive psychology.* New York: Appleton-Century-Crofts.

Neisser, U. (1976). *Cognition and reality: Principles and implications of cognitive psychology.* San Francisco: W. H. Freeman.

Neisser, U. (1977). Gibson's ecological optics: Consequences of a different stimulus description. *Journal for the Theory of Social Behavior, 7* (1), 17-28.

Nisbett, R. E., & Wilson, T. D. (1977). Telling more than we can know: Verbal reports on mental processes. *Psychological Review, 84* (3), 231–259.

Polanyi, M. (1962). *Personal knowledge: Towards a post-critical philosophy.* New York: Harper & Row.

Ryan, E. B. (1979). Why do low-prestige language varieties persist? In H. Giles & R. N. St. Clair (Eds.), *Language and social psychology.* Baltimore: University Park Press.

Rychlak, J. F. (1981). *A philosophy of science for personality theory* (2nd ed.). Malabar, FL: Robert E. Krieger.

Sakitt, B. (1972). Counting every quantum. *Journal of Physiology, 223,* 131–150.

Sakitt, B. (1974). Canonical ratings. *Perception and Psychophysics, 16* (3), 478–488.

Sartre, J. P. (1953). *Being and nothingness.* H. E. Barnes (Tr.). New York: Washington Square Press. (Originally published as L'Etre et le Neant in 1943).

Scherer, K R. (1979). Acoustic concomitants of emotional dimensions: Judging affect from synthesized tone sequences. In S. Weitz (Ed.) *Nonverbal communication.* New York: Oxford University Press.

Scherer, K. R. (1979a). Personality markers in speech. In K. R. Scherer & H. Giles (Eds.), *Social markers in speech.* Cambridge: Cambridge University Press.

Scherer, K. R. (1979b). Voice and speech correlates of perceived social influence in simulated juries. In H. Giles & R. N. St. Clair (Eds.), *Language and social psychology.* Baltimore: University Park Press.

Scherer, K. R. & Oshinsky, J. (1977). Cue utilization in emotion attribution from auditory stimuli. *Motivation and Emotion, 1,* 331–346.

Siegman, A. W. (1978). The tell-tale voice: Nonverbal messages of verbal communication. In A. W. Siegman & S. Feldstein (Eds.), *Nonverbal behavior and communication.* Hillsdale, NJ: Lawrence Erlbaum Associates.

Smith, B. L., Brown, B. L., Strong, W. J., & Rencher, A. C. (1975). Effects of speech rate on personality perception. *Language and Speech, 18* (2), 145–152.

Solomon, R. C. (1977). *The passions: The myth and nature of human emotion.* Garden City, NY: Anchor Press.

Stewart, M., Brown, B. L., & Stewart, S. (in preparation). *A comparison of computer manipulated speech rate with subjectively manipulated speech rate in effects upon personality attributions.* Unpublished manuscript, Brigham Young University, Provo, Utah.

Strong, W. J., & Plitnik, G. R. (1983). *Music speech high-fidelity.* Provo: Sound Print.

Swets, J. A., Tanner, W. P., & Birdsall, T. G. (1961). Decision processes in perception. *Psychological Review, 68,* 301–340.

Szasz, T. S. (1974). *The myth of mental illness: Foundations of a theory of personal conduct. (Revised ed.)* New York: Harper & Row.

Tanner, W. P., & Swets, J. A. (1954). A decision-making theory of visual detection. *Psychological Review, 61,* 401–409.

Tavris, C. (1983). *Anger: The misunderstood emotion.* New York: Simon & Schuster.

Taylor, C. (1964). *The explanation of behavior.* New York: Humanities Press.

Thom, R. (1975). *Structural stability and morphogenesis: An outline of a general theory of models.* D. H. Fowler (Tr.). Reading, MA: W. A. Benjamin.

Titze, I. R. (1973). The human vocal cords: A mathematical model. *Phonetica, 28,* 129–170.

Titze, I. R. (1974). The human vocal cords: A mathematical model, Part II. *Phonetica, 29,* 1–21.

Treisman, A. M. (1964). Selective attention in man. *British Medical Bulletin, 20,* 12–16.

Treisman, A. M., & Geffen, G. (1967). Selective attention: Perception or response? *Quarterly Journal of Experimental Psychology, 19,* 1–17.

Treisman, A. M., & Gelade, G. (1980). A feature-integration theory of attention. *Cognitive Psychology, 12* (1), 97–136.

Treisman, A. M., & Riley, J. G. R. (1969). Is selective attention selective perception or selective response? A further test. *Journal of Experimental Psychology, 79,* 27–34.

Treisman, A. M., Squire, R., & Green, J. (1974). Semantic processes in selective listening? A replication. *Memory and Cognition, 2,* 641–646.

Tucker, G. R., & Lambert, W. E. (1969). White and Negro listeners' reactions to various American-English dialects. *Social Forces, 47,* 463–468.

Tversky, A., & Kahneman, D. (1974). Judgment under uncertainty: Heuristics and biases. *Science, 184,* 1124–1131.

Warner, C. T. (in preparation). *Anger and other delusions.* Unpublished manuscript, Brigham Young University, Provo, UT.

Warner, C. T. (1982). *Bondage and emancipation: A conceptual introduction to the study of motivation.* Unpublished manuscript, Brigham Young University, Provo, UT.

Williams, C. E., & Stevens, K. N. (1972). Emotions and speech: Some acoustical correlates. *Journal of the Acoustical Society of America, 52,* 1238–1250.

Zajonc, R. B. (1980). Feeling and thinking: Preferences need no inferences. *American Psychologist, 35* (2), 151–175.

Zuckerman, M., DePaulo, B. M., & Rosenthal, R. (1981). Verbal and nonverbal communication of deception. In L. Berkowitz (Ed.), *Advances in experimental social psychology* (Vol. 14). New York: Academic Press.

7

Male and Female Nonverbal Behavior

Judith A. Hall
Harvard University

With a moment's reflection, one can think of many differences in the way men and women seem to express themselves through nonverbal behavior. Even young children can imitate "masculine" and "feminine" styles of moving, talking, gesticulating, and using facial expression. Stereotype says that women are interpersonally sensitive and "intuitive." How *do* males and females of our species differ in their nonverbal behaviors and skills?

This question has certainly been asked before. Empirical research on nonverbal sex differences goes back very far in the history of social psychology. In the past decade, the pace of this research has increased dramatically, partly because of psychology's new interest in sex differences of all sorts. A number of reviews of nonverbal sex differences have been published, which either take a broad view (Frieze & Ramsey, 1976; Harper, Wiens, & Matarazzo, 1978; Henley, 1977; LaFrance & Mayo, 1978), or concentrate on individual topics such as interpersonal distance (Evans & Howard, 1973; Hayduk, 1978), touch (Major, 1981), and decoding/judging and encoding/sending skill (Hall, 1978, 1979).

With this much scholarly attention to the subject, why do another review? Perhaps the best answer is that existing reviews tend to be very far from complete. To give some illustrations, two recent summaries of ability to judge others' emotions named only a handful of sex difference results each (Hoffman, 1977; Maccoby & Jacklin, 1974). In their book on gaze, Argyle and Cook (1976) named only 10 studies concerned with sex differences. Two reviews on personal space published in 1973 (Evans & Howard) and 1978 (Hayduk) mention 12 and 35 studies, respectively, and give only a few paragraphs to sex differences. The present review covers many more studies for all these topics, as a glance at the tables will reveal. Of course not all of the studies I have found were available to previous reviewers, and it was probably not always those reviewers' intention to name all the studies they knew of. The main point is that many studies with data on nonverbal sex differences seem to be forgotten, ignored, or undiscovered.

One reason for incomplete coverage is that findings cross traditional disciplinary lines within psychology. A reviewer who concentrates on social psychology journals, where the bulk of the studies are to be found, will miss studies on infants and children in developmental psychology journals and studies on face recognition in experimental psychology journals, to name just two examples. Another reason for studies being overlooked is that nonverbal sex differences are often examined by investigators who are not primarily interested in that topic. Instead, they may be studying nervous mannerisms as a clue to psychopathology, infant attachment to caretakers, children's response to humorous stimuli, or skill at telling lies. Sometimes a researcher who is primarily concerned with neither sex differences nor nonverbal behavior will include a nonverbal dependent measure along with paper-and-pencil responses or other kinds of behavior. Because sex is so often examined routinely by psychologists (and is sometimes introduced into an analysis only to increase statistical precision, not because the sex difference per se matters to the investigator), findings of interest to a student of sex differences are often available, although mentioned in passing and sometimes only for the sake of completeness.

Another reason for incompleteness is that null results tend to be less memorable than significant ones. If five well-known studies find women to gaze more than men, those studies will tend to be the ones cited regularly as demonstration of the effect. What if there were 40 null results hiding on the library shelves?

Yet another problem emerges where sex differences are concerned. People tend to be strongly committed to certain interpretations of sex differences. One prevalent interpretation ties sex differences in nonverbal behavior to differences in the sexes' power and status in society. Nancy Henley (1973, 1977) has been the major theorist in this tradition. Many other writers either have cited her theory as demonstrated truth or have fitted their findings into her framework without always mentioning other possible explanations. When authors are theoretically committed, selective literature reviews are particularly problematic because of the danger that only those studies that fit a theory best will be cited.

This review is not based on the conviction that any existing theory or summary statement about nonverbal sex differenes is wrong, but rather on the belief that a thorough review is required before any conclusions can be reached. By analyzing many studies, it is also possible to make more fine-grained comparisons. To give but two examples, one can ask not only how being male or female is related to a person's behavior, but also how the sex of an interactant is related to the first person's behavior; or, one can ask how the channel of communication (e.g., face versus voice) relates to sex differences in skill at decoding nonverbal cues. Such questions can be, and are frequently, asked within a given study, but they can also be addressed in the analysis of a collection of studies, often more persuasively.

One chapter cannot possibly include all the topics that should be discussed, and cannot give credit to all the studies that bear importantly on nonverbal sex differences, nor all the writers who have offered interpretations. The approach taken here is (1) to summarize sex differences in several categories of research in which a reasonable number of more or less comparable studies exist, these categories being attention, decoding skill, face recognition skill, encoding skill, facial expressiveness, positive and negative facial behavior, gaze, interpersonal distance, body orientation, touch, and body movement and gesture;[1] and (2) to mention some research on correlates of nonverbal skill and behavior that bears directly on the interpretation of sex differences. In the process, various interpretations of the sex differences are discussed.

METHODS EMPLOYED IN THIS REVIEW

This review is a "meta-analysis" (Glass, McGaw, & Smith, 1981; Rosenthal, 1980), which means that results are summarized quantitatively rather than impressionistically, at least to the extent that the designs of the studies and their data analyses permit. With only one exception (see section on encoding skill), only published studies are included. This means, of course, the sacrifice of a number of useful studies, and the danger that null or counter-trend results are underrepresented in the data set. On the other hand, because sex differences are so frequently *not* the main focus of a research report, but rather are analyzed and reported incidentally, it is probable that publication often does not depend on the strength of the sex difference results. Consequently, one would hope that such results would appear in the published reports regardless of their direction and magnitude, thus reducing the threat of bias in the published literature.

Within each major category of behavior, results are classified according to key theoretical questions asked in the literature, and also on the basis of major methodological differences (such as age of subjects, or whether an investigator used paper-and-pencil, staged, or unobtrusive observation of interpersonal distance). A *complete* cross-classification of independent variables (i.e., attributes of the studies) is ideal but is not possible without many more studies.

---

[1]Excluded from this chapter because of space constraints are studies on infants and studies of the voice (such variables as speech disturbances, voice quality, speech rate, and total speech production). Both of these topics are covered in Hall (1984), which is a much longer review of nonverbal sex differences. That review also contains more studies and interpretations, a listing of which studies contributed results to the statistical summaries of each nonverbal variable, complete bibliographic information, and quantitative comparisons between nonverbal and other psychological sex differences.

Dependent variables for the sex difference comparisons—that is, results of studies—are of three kinds: (1) *Direction of difference*, coded (for example) as unknown, no difference (literally), females more, or males more. Direction was coded regardless of whether a result was statistically significant. (2) *Effect size*, if known, expressed in the point biserial correlation, *r*, between an independent variable such as sex (coded as 0 for males and 1 for females) and whatever behavior is measured. The standardized effect size index *r*, or some other index of effect size, is very important for comparing studies that use different scales of measurement and also for ascertaining the overall magnitude of a phenomenon. Using it, one can also ask such comparative questions as, is the sex difference for gaze larger than the sex difference for decoding skill? By convention, an *r* of .10 is to be considered "small" and an *r* of .50 or more "large" (Cohen, 1969). Effect size is nonredundant with significance level in a very important way: a given *r*, say .30, would be nonsignificant if based on 35 people but would be significant if based on 100 people. Thus effect size tells about the size of a difference without reference to how many people were measured.[2] Following Eagly and Carli (1981), wherever possible both a minimum and a maximum *r* were computed. The minimum was the average *r* over all the studies in the group, with all unknown *r*'s given the value of zero; this is a very conservative procedure that almost certainly underestimates the true effect size. The maximum was the average *r* over only that subset of studies for which *r* was given or could be estimated; this procedure possibly overestimates the true effect size because of the likelihood that smaller effect sizes were unreported or unretrievable. (3) *Statistical significance*, coded as unknown, "not significant" (if that was all that was known), or with whatever more exact *p*-value was known.[3]

With these three outcome measures the following summaries could be made: (1) Proportion of results showing higher means for males versus females, or for whatever comparison was being made; if there were no sex difference, we would expect this proportion to be about .50 (or 50%). (2) Mean effect size (*r*); if there were no difference, this value would be about zero. (3) Proportion of studies showing significant differences; if there were no difference, we would expect this value to be about 5% of *n* (number of studies being summarized for that

---

[2] These *r*'s were rarely given in research reports. They were calculated using a variety of formulas available in Cohen (1969), the choice of formula depending on the nature of the data provided. The most common formula was $r = \sqrt{t/(t + df)}$. Often *t* was derived from *F* ($t = \sqrt{F}$ for two-group comparisons); in many such cases the magnitude of *r* benefited from the added precision of a factorial analysis of variance.

[3] In some instances I was able to provide an estimate of *r* or *p* when one of those values was not provided in the published report. Knowing only *n* and *r* enables one to calculate *t*, using the formula $t = (r\sqrt{n-2})/\sqrt{1-r^2}$; then *p* is derived in the usual way. Knowing only *n* and *p* enables one to calculate *r* (or, when *p* is not exact, as in "*p* < .05," to calculate a minimum value for *r*), using standard tables. In some studies, neither *r* nor *p* was easily ascertained without performing a new analysis of variance. Although it was possible in principle to do this, I did not, due to the number of studies involved.

comparison). If as many as a third or so of the results are significant in one direction, it is ample evidence of a real sex difference, since only 2.5% would be expected to be significant by chance alone. (4) Mean Z (mean of the standard normal deviates associated with the p's for the results being summarized), with an associated *combined* probability—that is, the probability that the whole group of studies came out as it did; if there is no difference we would expect the combined p (two tail) to be about 1.00.[4]

Almost always, the results were based on the entire number of people in a sample. In many studies, the samples could have been broken down by age or experimental conditions, yielding many more independent results for summary. The disadvantages of doing this are that often investigators provided complete statistical results only for the whole sample, and that the results for these smaller subsamples would be more unstable because of sampling fluctuations.

SUMMARY OF SEX DIFFERENCES

Attention

I use the word *attention* to subsume several concepts, including attention, responsiveness, and knowledge of meanings or occurrences of nonverbal cues (studies not describable either as decoding or encoding skill, summarized later). Although there are not enough of these studies for a quantitative summary, they shed light on male and female styles of information processing in the social arena.

1. Attention.   Females gave more attention to visual than vocal cues, and to facial than body cues, compared to males (DePaulo, Rosenthal, Eisenstat, Rogers, & Finkelstein, 1978; Zuckerman, Blanck, DePaulo, & Rosenthal, 1980). Females remembered more action cues after seeing a film of interaction, whereas males remembered more of the verbal content (Mazanec & McCall, 1976). However, no sex differences were found for using expression as a grouping concept in a concept-formation task (Savitsky & Izard, 1970).

2. Responsiveness.   Females were more influenced by nonverbal than verbal cues, relative to men, in the studies of Argyle, Salter, Nicholson, Williams, and

---

[4]To test the mean Z one calculates a combined probability using the formula: combined $Z = \Sigma\ Z/\sqrt{N}$, where N is the number of studies involved (Rosenthal, 1980). Rarely was an exact p easily ascertained from the published reports. Because of this, in combining p's I employed the *very* conservative procedures of entering the Z for whatever p was offered (e.g., "$p < .05$") and of entering an estimated Z of 0.00 (i.e., no difference whatever) for any result labeled "not significant," unless, as explained in footnote 3, I was able to compute p on the basis of r and n. These are conservative procedures because in a case such as "$p < .05$," the real p is actually *less* than .05, and in the case of "not significant," p is probably less than 1.00 (that is, if there actually is a sex difference on the average, which in this review there usually was).

Burgess (1970), and Zahn (1973, 1975), but not in that of Brooks, Brandt, and Wiener (1969). Females were more responsive than males to hearing their own voice (Rousey & Holzman, 1968; Weston & Rousey, 1970).

3. Knowledge. Females drew eye pupils larger for a "happy" face and smaller for an "angry" face than did males (which reflects correct understanding of pupil size-affect relationship) (Williams & Hicks, 1980). Females noted occurrences of eye contact better than males (Kleck & Nuessle, 1968).

On balance, these studies suggest that females take notice of nonverbal behavior more than men, and take differential notice of certain kinds of nonverbal cues (visible cues, especially the face). These results are consistent with data from other realms, such as self-report of interests and personality and small-group behavior, which point to sex differences in socio-emotional versus task orientation. More discussion of the attention data appears in the next section.

Decoding Skill

One impetus for attempting the present review of a variety of nonverbal behaviors was the outcome of an earlier meta-analysis I did on skill in decoding the meanings of nonverbal cues. Most summary statements I found in the literature were to the effect that no sex difference existed, that the literature was entirely contradictory, or that women *might slightly* exceed men in such skills. Some conclusions like this have been both recent (Hoffman, 1977; Maccoby & Jacklin, 1974), and confident, as in this quote from Westbrook (1974): "The belief about women's greater sensitivity . . . defined as accuracy of judgment [of nonverbal cues] . . . appears to be a cultural myth" (p. 388).

The literature warrants a very different conclusion, however. In my first review (Hall, 1978, 1979) I located many more results than previous reviewers had mentioned, 75 in all, dating from 1923. In all of the studies, groups of subjects served as judges of nonverbal expressive stimuli that consisted of face, body, or vocal cues (alone or in combination). These cues were presented via drawings, photos, films, videotapes, standard-content speech (one or more people reading standard passages or the alphabet while trying to express various emotions), scrambled speech (an audiotape that is cut up and reassembled in a random sequence so as to make the verbal message unintelligible), or electronically filtered speech (higher frequencies are removed from the voice, making the words unintelligible). The nonverbal behavior captured in these various channels was usually deliberate, a method known commonly as "posed encoding," though the word "posed" probably suggests more artificiality than was sometimes the case. "Spontaneous" cues were elicited in some studies by exposing encoders to emotion-provoking circumstances such as pleasant or unpleasant slides or films, and secretly videotaping their facial responses. Details on a few other miscellaneous methods are in Hall (1978).

With the exception of one study included in the earlier review, all of the decoding skill studies as well as the encoding studies (reviewed later on) are based on cues that are assumed to be truthful. An additional group of studies is based on *deceptive* cues. These are not included here because their results are not always based on strictly nonverbal cues. Sex differences in skill at detecting and encoding deception have recently been reviewed by Zuckerman, DePaulo, and Rosenthal (1981).

Subjects judging the nonverbal stimuli usually responded in a multiple-choice style, choosing among various emotions or situational descriptions such as the description of the emotion-eliciting circumstance in the case of spontaneous encoding. A few other judgment approaches were used (for example, pointing to a facial photo after hearing a story), and for a list of these the reader should see Hall (1978).

Since the time my first decoding meta-analysis was published, I have found 45 additional independent results. These studies were basically like the preceding group in design, but included tasks that were somewhat more varied, such as judging emotions in a chimpanzee's face, judging age or personality traits from nonverbal cues, decoding the meanings of infant cries, and decoding the meaning of proxemic (interpersonal distance) cues.

A summary of the overall results of both groups of studies appears in Table 7.1. All in all, the two groups told the same story: females were better at decoding nonverbal cues than males. Another similarity between the two groups of results was that both tended to show a more pronounced female advantage on visual

TABLE /.1
Sex Differences in Decoding Skill

Index	Analyzed before 1978 ($n = 75$)	Analyzed after 1978 ($n = 45$)
Direction of Effect (excluding no difference or unknown)	84% (51/61) favor females	80% (24/30) favor females
Mean Effect Size $(r)^a$	between .12 ($n = 75$) and .20 ($n = 46$)	between .10 ($n = 45$) and .27 ($n = 16$)
Statistical Significance (all studies)	31% (23/75) favor females significantly, 1% (1/75) favor males significantly	22% (10/45) favor females significantly, none favors males significantly
Combined p	$p = 10^{-6}$, two tail ($n = 75$)	$p = 10^{-4}$, two tail ($n = 38$)

^{a}Positive values indicate female advantage.

(face, body, arms) cues than on vocal cues. The first group showed mean known effect sizes (r) for visual and auditory cues of .16 $(n = 29)$ and .09 $(n = 10)$, respectively, and the second group showed analogous effects of .29 $(n = 12)$ and .09 $(n = 1)$. In addition, the vocal cue studies showed a smaller proportion of significant studies, which suggests that the effect sizes were small when unreported, other things (such as n's) being equal. This difference in the sex difference between visual and vocal cues has been amplified in further research by Rosenthal and DePaulo (1979a, 1979b), whose interpretations are discussed later.

An important result of the earlier review was that the difference between females' and males' decoding skills did not depend on which sex of encoder they were judging; the difference was about the same, regardless of whether the encoders were male or female, or were both represented in the stimuli. The new group of studies did not have enough studies with only male or female senders to make such a comparison worthwhile.

Several hypotheses have been offered to explain sex differences in decoding skill. Three hypotheses based on social roles or adaptation have been tested. These were (1) the *empathy hypothesis,* tested by Hall (1979), which states that women judge nonverbal cues well by virtue of an empathic disposition that makes them experience others' emotions vicariously; (2) the *masculinity-femininity hypothesis,* tested by Hall & Halberstadt (1981) and Isenhart (1980), which states that women are good decoders because they are "feminine" (and not "masculine")—that is, they have traits of being considerate, gentle, and wanting to develop harmonious relations with others; and (3) the *oppression hypothesis,* tested by Hall & Halberstadt (1981), which states (as in Weitz, 1974) that women decode well because oppressed people are forced to develop such skills in order to cope in society. Put briefly, the research found little support for these hypotheses. Though I do not doubt that future research could test these hypotheses more adequately, several additional avenues are worth pursuing.

One direction for future research is attentional processes and, relatedly, the effects of practice. These ideas rest on data reviewed earlier and later in this chapter that indicate that women attend more than men to nonverbal cues and in particular to visual cues (in gazing at others, for example). Attention to nonverbal cues has been shown to be positively correlated with accuracy at decoding those cues (DePaulo & Rosenthal, 1979; DiMatteo & Hall, 1979). Although differential attention could conceivably *follow* from existing skill (that is, women use certain attentional patterns because they know where their skills are), it seems more likely that women's extra skill for face and body cues develops as a *consequence* of focusing their decoding effort on those channels.

Why do women concentrate on certain channels? One possibility for focusing on the face is that the face may be the most informative channel overall. Or, the face may be a better source of certain kinds of information. The face probably conveys positivity-negativity especially well compared to other channels, and perhaps women are especially interested in this dimension of expression. Some evidence suggests that the voice, by contrast, may convey degrees of assertion more effectively (reviewed in DePaulo & Rosenthal, 1979). Perhaps women are somewhat less concerned with such cues, compared to men.

A major theoretical synthesis of data on skill and attention patterns has been offered by Rosenthal and DePaulo (1979a, 1979b) and their colleagues (Blanck, Rosenthal, Snodgrass, DePaulo, & Zuckerman, 1981). Briefly, they note that the pattern of women's advantage in decoding several kinds of nonverbal cues corresponds to the degree to which those cues are likely to be "leaked" or inadvertently revealed by an expressor. The face is most easily controlled, the body less so, the voice less so, and so on. Rosenthal and DePaulo propose that because women are brought up to be socially accommodating, they attend most to, and decode best, those cues that are the most controlled, thus pleasing the expressor by interpreting the mesage that he or she wanted to send. Conversely, women ignore "leaked" cues because it would be graceless to note emotions that the expressor is concealing or is unaware of.

Though Rosenthal and DePaulo base their hypothesis on a diverse and well-analyzed data base, it is still necessary to note that it is not demonstrated that women's skill and attention patterns are *caused* either by accommodatingness (an unobserved trait in their research) or by the "leakiness" of various kinds of cues. The authors' argument is based on observed parallelism between the magnitude of the sex difference over channels and the ordering of those channels according to their leakiness (which may not be the only label that could be applied to the same ordering of channels). But the data could be explained in other ways. As suggested earlier, perhaps women's attention and skill pattern relative to men reflects not women's awareness of the damaging social consequences of "eavesdropping" on nonverbal cues but rather their awareness of the relative informativeness of various channels in the course of everyday life. The voice may leak a lie every once in a while, but the face is telling the truth most of the time. Perhaps men, because they are not as attuned to nonverbal behavior as women, simply do not learn the properties of channels as well and therefore allocate attention diffusely over channels. By the same token, men's decoding patterns may reflect the same kind of lack of specialization or differentiation of channels. Therefore, though intriguing and plausible, the accommodation hypothesis requires further research.

Face Recognition

Unwisely repeating other people's assertions, I stated in an earlier paper (Hall, 1979) that there is no sex difference for recognition of faces (that is, knowing whether you have seen a face before). Now I must retract that. In concluding that a sex difference does exist for this skill, I concur with Haviland and Malatesta (1981). I located 28 studies of children, adolescents, and adults in which subjects were asked to state whether photos of faces (usually both sexes) had been seen earlier in the study. For children the results were sparse but suggested only a weak sex difference: none significant, and the effect size known only for one (girls better, effect size = .06), though in direction all three studies with a known direction favored girls. For adolescents and adults a sex difference emerged more clearly: 12 of 17 (70%) of results of known direction favored women; the mean effect size was between .06 (n = 22) and .16 (n = 9); 3 of 22 (14%) favored women significantly, 1 of 22 (4%) favored men significantly; and the combined p was .02, two tail, favoring women. Additional findings from this literature were that female faces were not more easily recognized than male faces (there were significant results in both directions), and that same-sex recognition was higher than opposite-sex recognition, a trend that was significant in five out of eight studies.

No one has correlated face decoding skill with face recognition skill to see how overlapping they are. Although both involve analysis of the face, they would seem distinct in that decoding involves analyzing the face's dynamic aspects, whereas face recognition involves analyzing and remembering the facial features themselves. Perhaps, though, in remembering a face one also remembers the expressive configuration. In any case, no one has explained the face recognition sex difference. As with decoding skill, a plausible explanation centers on social focus; women may pay more attention to the face than men do and this, combined with practice effects, may account for the skill difference. Further support for this hypothesis comes from the data on attention and on gaze.

Encoding Skill

My earlier review of accuracy of expression via nonverbal cues (Hall, 1979) turned up 26 results, from 22 independent studies, dating from 1938. Encoding skill is more laborious to measure than decoding skill, and this probably is a major reason why fewer studies have been done. To measure decoding skill, one need only have expressive stimuli, a group of subjects, and a scoring procedure for determining how many items each subject identifies correctly. The measurement of encoding skill, by contrast, is much less standardized and less efficient. This is because accuracy is determined not with reference to a set of established right and wrong answers, but instead is almost always determined by the accuracy with which *each* sender (encoder) is judged by a group of judges. For reliability, these groups are often large (60, for example). The task of recording each sender's face, body, or voice, preparing these photos, films, or tapes for presentaion to judges, obtaining judgments, and scoring the judges' accuracy for each encoder is a large one indeed. One additional consequence of this seems to be that the number of encoders in a typical study of encoding skill is smaller than the number of decoders in a typical study of decoding skill.

In the 26 results originally analyzed (Hall, 1979) and the 20 results located since then, the methods for producing expressive stimuli were much the same as in the decoding studies, except that the number of encoders in an encoding study was often larger than the number of encoders in a decoding study.[5]

Table 7.2 summarizes the overall results for both groups of studies. In both, females were better expressors. Both groups, however, showed pronounced inter-channel differences. In the first group, the average known effect size for visual (mainly facial) cues was .40 ($n = 11$) and the average known effect size for vocal cues was .00 ($n = 7$). In the later group, the analogous effects were .29 ($n = 7$) and $-.05$ ($n = 4$). In other words, female visual cues were considerably easier to judge than male visual cues, but for vocal cues there was no difference. The vocal category presents an interesting additional puzzle: vocal-cue findings were extremely variable, showing *both* large positive (female advantage) *and* large negative (male advantage) effects. This was true in both groups of studies.

As with decoding, we are also interested in age effects. Most studies of children showed nonsignificant results. But Buck, Baron, Goodman, and Shapiro (1980) found a very large superiority of preschool *boys'* spontaneous facial expressions. Without this one result, the average known effect size for visual

TABLE 7.2
Sex Differences in Encoding Skill

Index	*Analyzed before 1979* ($n = 26$)	*Analyzed after 1979* ($n = 20$)
Direction of Effect (excluding no difference or unknown)	71% (15/21) favor females	57% (8/14) favor females
Mean Effect Size (r)[a]	between .25 ($n = 26$) and .31 ($n = 20$)	between .11 ($n = 20$) and .17 ($n = 13$)
Statistical Significance (all studies)	31% (8/26) favor females significantly, 4% (1/26) favor males significantly	35% (7/20) favor females significantly, 10% (2/20) favor males significantly
Combined p	$p = .0072$, two tail ($n = 26$)	$p = .019$, two tail ($n = 20$)

[a]Positive values indicate female advantage.

[5]In both the earlier and present reviews of encoding skill, there is a small amount of nonindependence because in a few studies a given sample of subjects produced both visual and auditory accuracy scores. Because of the small data set I have treated these nonindependent results as though they came from separate samples. Some of the results for body movement are also nonindependent.

cues in the later group of studies (all for adults) jumps to .47, a substantial sex difference. Buck (1977) has also found dramatic decreases in preschool boys' facial sending accuracy spanning the ages 4–6 (cross-sectional finding). These results suggest that socialization pressure is exerted on boys during this time period to reduce their expression of emotion via the face.

Sex role socialization thus seems to be one possible explanation of the encoding skill sex difference, and indeed Zuckerman, DeFrank, Spiegel, and Larrance (1982) in three studies found evidence that "femininity" as measured via a paper-and-pencil self-report measure was correlated with encoding skill for both sexes (though Hall & Halberstadt [1981] did not find this). Zuckerman also found that femininity was able to account statistically for some of the sex difference in skill. Relatedly, Rosenthal and DePaulo (1979b) suggested that "accommodatingness" could account for women's encoding skill, especially their notable skill via the face, which is the most polite, non-"leaky" channel. According to them, an accommodating person wants to be easily read by others. It is also possible that generalization of knowledge from the decoding modality contributes to women's encoding skill.

Facial Expressiveness

The finding that women's faces are more easily judged than men's when they are posing or reacting to films or other visual stimuli, as in spontaneous encoding (e.g., Buck, Miller, & Caul, 1974), leads us to ask whether women's faces are more expressive than men's. Accuracy of encoding must reflect changeability from one mood or stimulus to the next, though changeability per se would not account for accuracy since those changes must be appropriate to the mood or stimulus conditions. The available literature does indicate that women's faces are more expressive than men's. The one study of preschool children's faces (while slide viewing) showed no overall sex difference, but four out of the five studies with adults showed women to have significantly more facial activity, reactions, movement, or "breakpoints" while slide-viewing or in social interaction than men (mean known effect size = .41, $n = 4$).

Smiling and Laughing

Many people believe, and a number of authors have stated, that women smile more than men. These assertions are generally backed up by only a handful of findings, at most. Various distinctions can be drawn in the many studies I located, such as social versus nonsocial situation, laboratory versus field, age of subjects and recipients, and the nature of the dependent variable—that is, how "smiling" was measured. Most studies measured smiling as distinct from laughing, but some measured "smiling and laughing" as one variable or measured both on a common scale that went from no expression or frown (lowest rating) through smile to laugh (highest rating). In Table 7.3, studies that combined smiling and laughing are included with the studies that measured laughing by itself.

Table 7.3, which shows the data for social situations only, reveals that the sex difference data for children for both the smiling and laughing categories were equivocal. There was actually a suggestion, contrary to common belief, that girls smile and laugh *less* than boys. For adults (college and older), the picture is different: all smiling and laughing indices favored women. In three smiling studies of adults, within-study comparison of male versus female recipients was also made. Two of these were nonsignificant (direction unknown), and one showed significantly ($p < .05$) more smiling *at* women by male and female subjects as a group (effect sizes unknown).

An additional smiling comparison was made for males with males versus females with females. This particular comparison was not included in the preceding discussion. For children, only 62% (5/8) of the results favored female-female smiling, with most p values and effect sizes unknown. For adults, however, all four of the results of known direction favored females, three of which were significant, and with an average known effect size of .40 ($n = 3$). Thus, the pattern for same-sex smiling for children and adults is similar to the pattern in Table 7.3: not totally clear for children but clear for adults. Also, the large effect size for female-female versus male-male smiling is just what we would expect on the basis of the foregoing evidence for main effects: women smile more and tend to be *smiled at* more than men. These two tendencies converge to make the male-male and female-female mean levels of smiling maximally different.

It is interesting to note that a gap exists in the smiling literature (as well as for most other topics reviewed in this chapter) for studies on adolescents. This is unfortunate because developmental trends are therefore hard to discern. The only smiling data I found for adolescents was a study of yearbook photos (Ragan, 1982), which found more smiling in girls' photos (as well as in three samples of adult photos, overall effect size $= .11, p < .001$). This study was not included in the preceding discussion because it seemed to be neither social nor completely nonsocial.

Most studies of *nonsocial* situations were of subjects' behavior while watching or listening to cartoons or funny stories (e.g., Chapman, 1973; Cupchik & Leventhal, 1974). Over both the smiling and laughing categories for children, 6 of 10 studies with a known direction favored girls (60%), with an average known effect size of only .04 ($n = 5$), but with three results of $p < .05$ or better, all favoring girls. For adults the same comparison yielded only one out of four studies favoring women, with a mean known effect size of $-.18$ ($n = 2$), and none significant. Thus the nonsocial data were much weaker for adults than the social data, but should not be overinterpreted because of the small number of nonsocial studies. With age, then, there appears to be a growing sex difference for social, but not nonsocial, smiling and laughing.

TABLE 7.3
Sex Differences in Social Smiling and Laughing in Children and Adults

Index	Smile[a]	Laugh[b]
Children		
Direction of Effect (excluding no difference or unknown)	27% (3/11) favor females	73% (11/15) favor females
Mean Effect Size $(r)^c$	between −.02 ($n = 12$) and −.08 ($n = 4$)	between −.05 ($n = 20$) and −.36 ($n = 3$)
Statistical Significance (all studies)	17% (2/12) favor females significantly, none favors males significantly	none favors females significantly, 10% (2/19) favor males significantly
Combined p	$p = .43$, two tail ($n = 11$)	$p = .27$, two tail ($n = 15$)
Adults		
Direction of Effect (excluding no difference or unknown)	92% (12/13) favor females	100% (5/5) favor females
Mean Effect Size $(r)^c$	between .18 ($n = 18$) and .30 ($n = 10$)	between .29 ($n = 5$) and .36 ($n = 4$)
Statistical Significance (all studies)	56% (10/18) favor females significantly, none favors males significantly	80% (4/5) favor females significantly, none favors males significantly
Combined p	$p = 10^{-8}$, two tail ($n = 17$)	$p = 10^{-6}$, two tail ($n = 5$)

[a] $n = 12$ for children, $n = 18$ for adults.
[b] $n = 19$ for children, $n = 5$ for adults.
[c] Positive values indicate more female smiling (laughing).

208

Of course, the reader may have been wondering by now what "smiling" and "laughing" *mean*. We all know that one can smile out of pleasure, out of nervousness, deliberately to please someone, or to deflect aggression. Psychologists are well aware of this fact and have not failed to conduct studies to ascertain such meanings (e.g., Rosenfeld, 1966). One exceptionally detailed study included in the present review points up the importance of trying to determine the affect that lies behind a smile. Stern and Bender (1974), instead of coding "smile" as a global variable, coded both "common" and "ambivalent" smiles to adults by children ages 3–5. Boys made more common smiles at all three ages (significant at age 3), but girls made more ambivalent smiles (compressed, or with lip in) at all three ages (significant at ages 3 and 5). (Only the common smile result was entered in the summary in Table 7.3.) The obvious suggestion that girls were more nervous is supported by the fact that they also showed more apprehensive mouth behavior. Thus, smiling may not always mean the same thing from situation to situation, and differences in males' versus females' affect within the same situation may lead to different kinds of smiles being exhibited.

Several authors have suggested that female smiling may reflect submission and appeasement behavior (e.g., Frieze & Ramsey, 1976). Though such an interpretation may be correct in some circumstances, it is far too simple. It neglects such other interpretations as situational anxiety, social enjoyment (admittedly these two may work at odds with one another), or sheer habit stemming from learning of sex-appropriate behavior. Sex-appropriate behavior, or any behavior that differentiates the sexes, may certainly have its roots in many centuries of male dominance and female submission. This does not mean, however, that a *given* instance of sex-appropriate behavior reflects these distant origins in any way besides the form of the behavior itself. In other words, if I smile, it may be because I learned that habit in my youth, and not because I am seeking either to deflect aggression or to please anyone. Nevertheless, if smiling gives the general impression of weakness or sycophancy, then women's tendency to smile could work to their detriment no matter what kind of emotion or motive it reflected. On the other hand, women's smiling may have the very desirable effect of facilitating positive social interaction and encouraging trust, outcomes that are certainly not to be belittled.

Negative Facial Expression

Though many studies have measured positive facial expression, few have measured negative expressions. For measures of frowning, grimacing, and the like (but not crying) I found four studies for children, none with significant or known-significance results; one showed more male negativity, one showed the reverse. For adults, there were only four studies, split 2:2 in direction. One result was significant; one effect size (that one) was available, and it was .30 showing more female frowning. It is impossible to draw conclusions from this tiny literature.

Why have investigators not measured negative expressions more often? Is it because people don't scowl very often in public or in laboratory settings, making efforts to measure such behavior unprofitable? Or could it be because stereotype regarding women is stronger for smiling than frowning? What if women actually frown nearly as much as they smile? This would be consistent with the facial expressivity data. If this were so, authors would surely not talk so much about women's affiliative and/or submissive tendencies, but would have to develop a somewhat different theory to account for sex differences across a wide range of facial expressions.

Gaze

Many authors have referred to women's tendencies to gaze at others more than men do. On balance such statements are correct. This is one of the larger literatures, but reviews that I know of have listed relatively few studies, and generally it is the same few well-known studies that are cited. Further, no careful breakdown of the literature by age, dependent measure, or sex of other has been attempted.

Let us first talk about measures of total gaze, measured for an individual in interaction, virtually always in the laboratory. Total gaze was commonly measured as total duration of gaze or proportion of time spent in gazing at the other, and it was almost always measured for all parts of the interaction (in a small number of cases it was measured just for gazing while speaking or while listening). This is the most plentiful category of results (shown in Table 7.4). Over all sexes of recipient except same-sex (to be discussed below), studies on children gazing at peers or adults showed 67% (4/6) of the results to favor girls in direction, with an average known effect size of .18 ($n = 4$) and with 38% (3/8) of the results significantly favoring girls (none significantly favoring boys). For adults, as Table 7.4 shows, the results also favored women. Among the 38 results for sex of gazer, the largest sex differences occurred when the targets of gaze were female (mean known effect size = .46), a finding I return to shortly.

Turning now to which sex was gazed at more, the data for children were sparse: I found only two studies, both showing more gaze at girls (one by peers, one by parents), but both nonsignificant and effect sizes not known. For adults, for being gazed at by other adults (and in one study by toddlers) the data were stronger, as Table 7.4 shows. Women are gazed at more than men, averaging over male and female gazers.

Our next question is about same-sex versus opposite-sex gazing (still for total gaze). A synonym for this effect is the sex of gazer X sex of recipient interaction. The children's data, not in the table, were again unclear, with one very large effect for more same-sex gazing to peers (effect size = .74, $p < .01$), but two others showing more for opposite-sex (one to peers, effect size and p not known; one to adults, effect size = $-.17$, $p = .28$). This time the adult data were

TABLE 7.4
Sex Differences in Total Gaze (Adults)

Index	Sex of Subject (n = 38)	Sex of Other (n = 17)	Same-Sex vs. Opposite-Sex (n = 16)	Female-Female vs. Male-Male (n = 16)
Direction of Effect (excluding no difference or unknown)	77% (17/22) favor females	91% (10/11) favor females	54% (7/13) show more same-sex gaze	93% (13/14) favor female-female
Mean Effect Size (r)	between .14 (n = 38) and .32 (n = 16)[a]	between .15 (n = 17) and .34 (n = 7)[a]	between .10 (n = 16) and .20 (n = 8)[b]	between .18 (n = 16) and .38 (n = 7)[a]
Statistical Significance (all studies)	29% (11/38) favor females significantly, 3% (1/38) favor males significantly	18% (3/17) favor females significantly, none favors males significantly	12% (2/16) show more for same-sex, 19% (3/16) show more for opposite-sex	31% (5/16) favor female-female significantly, none favors male-male significantly
Combined p	p = .000005, two tail (n = 37)	p = .003, two tail (n = 16)	p = .37, two tail (n = 12) (favoring same-sex)	p = .0005, two tail (n = 10)

[a] Positive values indicate more gaze by or at females.
[b] Positive values indicate more gaze in same-sex dyads.

211

unclear, too, as Table 7.4's third column shows. There were significant results showing *both* more same-sex *and* more opposite-sex gazing. An examination of the research methods involved does not hint at an explanation. The significant more-opposite-sex-gazing results were for gazing at the other while passing on the sidewalk (two results), and gazing at another subject while waiting for an experiment to begin; the significant more-same-sex-gazing results were for gazing at confederates in a laboratory setting (two studies). On balance, Table 7.4 suggests slightly more same-sex gazing, as does the comparatively large effect size noted earlier showing women to gaze relatively more when the women were the targets ($r = .46$).

Finally, we ask about female-female versus male-male gazing. The data were fairly clear on this. For children gazing at peers or adults, 89% (8/9) of the results favored female-female pairs, with a mean known effect size of .14 but with none known to be significant. For adults (see Table 7.4), all indices favored female-female pairs, with a strength and consistency greater than for any other comparison in the table. As with smiling, this effect is not surprising given the existence of main effects for sex of gazer and sex of recipient. Such a pattern would tend to produce a comparatively large disparity between the male-male and female-female combinations.

The literature on gazing provides more than just total gaze. For adults, at least, investigators have measured frequency of gazes, average duration of gazes, total *mutual* gaze (a dyadic rather than individual measure), frequency of mutual gaze, and average duration of mutual gazes, and have sometimes subdivided results according to gazing while speaking versus gazing while listening. It is impossible to present all of these results here. Although there were fewer results in each of these categories than there were for total gaze, the overall picture was very much the same. Women gazed more and were gazed at more; the same-sex versus opposite-sex comparison was mixed but the balance tipped toward more same-sex gaze; and the female-female versus male-male comparison showed the strongest and most consistent results (for mean duration of individual gazing, for example, the effect size was .50 [$n = 3$], and for total mutual gaze was also .50 [$n = 3$]).

Just one new result emerges from these additional measures. On frequency of gaze for sex of gazer, the data were more mixed, with more results favoring men than expected on the basis of the other comparisons: two of three (67%) showed men to gaze more frequently, as did three of seven (43%) of the female-female versus male-male comparisons. This result is consistent, of course, with the tendency of women to use *longer average* glances, since the longer the glance, the fewer the glances that can occur during a fixed length of time. Thus, men may gaze relatively, and sometimes absolutely, more frequently as a consequence of sustaining glances for shorter periods.

Sex differences in gaze are often interpreted in terms of affiliation. Exline (1963) found that more affiliative people of both sexes gazed more than less affiliative people , at least in a noncompetitive situation. (The reverse was actually true under competition.) But gaze is also thought of in terms of dominance. Several authors have looked at a gazing while speaking versus gazing while listening. The theoretical basis of such comparisons lies in an understanding of gaze *patterns* as expressions of degrees of dominance (Ellyson, Dovidio, & Fehr, 1981; Exline, Ellyson, & Long, 1975). These authors have established that relatively more gazing while speaking and relatively less gazing while listening occur in individuals of either dominant personality or dominant social standing within the dyad. If women were to show the same sort of gaze pattern as do less dominant individuals in such experiments, it would suggest that sex differences in dominance and/or social standing also lie behind this (and other) sex differences in gaze. I located 15 results for which I could calculate the direction of this effect, which is a sex of gazer X gaze measure (listen/speak) interaction, in which one contrasts men's gaze while speaking and women's gaze while listening to men's gaze while listening and women's gaze while speaking. Here, unlike almost all other summaries in this chapter, I counted naturally occurring subsamples (by experimental condition or age), because of the small number of studies. Nine of the 15 results (60%) showed women to gaze relatively more while listening (and men to gaze relatively more while speaking). Rarely, if ever, were these comparisons backed up by appropriate statistical tests, so we lack much-needed information. Nevertheless, the trend in terms of direction did not support very strongly the hypothesis of a sex difference in this dominance-related gaze pattern.

Though the preceding analysis indicates that women's tendencies to gaze more than men do not vary appreciably with the look-versus-speak gaze measures, one important set of studies does indeed force us to qualify any statements about the consistency of sex differences in gaze. Aiello (1972, 1977a, 1977b) has shown that women's gaze *decreases,* sometimes abruptly, with increased interpersonal distance, whereas men's gaze *increases* linearly with distance, the latter as predicted by intimacy equilibrium theory (Argyle & Dean, 1965). Aiello has even found men to gaze significantly more than women when at larger conversational distances. In Aiello's (1977a) view, interaction at a distance of some 10 feet or more makes women uncomfortable, and perhaps they decide they aren't in a "real" interaction at all. But is there good reason to expect women to prefer smaller distances? That is the topic of the next section.

Interpersonal Distance

The literature on distance is large and complex. In addition to age and various sex comparisons (sex of subject, sex of other, etc.), there are three distinct methodologies: (1) unobtrusive observation, (2) staged measures, and (3) paper-and-pencil measures. In the first, subjects are observed either in natural settings or in the laboratory, in both cases without their knowledge, while they approach or pass others, seat themselves near others, or engage in a conversation in progress (in which case the distinction between sex of subject and sex of other cannot be made). In the staged approach, subjects are generally asked to approach another person, usually in the laboratory (or to let themselves be approached, or both), and to indicate when they start to feel discomfort. In the paper-and-pencil approach, subjects either place felt figures or other representations of people on a surface (sometimes being asked to imagine that they are one of the figures); or they imagine, in an analogue to the staged approach, that someone in a schematic drawing is approaching them, and then they mark on the paper at what distance discomfort would occur.

Because our greatest interest in this chapter is in how men and women "really" behave, a detailed summary is presented only for unobtrusive observation. As indicated earlier, I decided generally against breaking studies up into subsamples (by grade in school or experimental treatments, for example) as a way to minimize sampling fluctuation, even though the total number of independent results would have been considerably increased had I done so. I have made an exception, however, for distance, and have treated cultural/ethnic subgroups as separate samples. The cultural/ethnic groups represented here are Caucasian (Anglo or European), black, Mexican-American, Puerto Rican, Filipino, Israeli, Costa Rican, Panamanian, Venezuelan, Colombian, Italian, Chinese, and Japanese.

For subjects' sex, the children's data were inconclusive: Two results showed girls to place less distance between themselves and others of both sexes (neither significant, one with an effect size of .16), and four others had unknown direction (all nonsignificant). For adults, shown in Table 7.5, the data were, as usual, clearer. By all indices, women approached others more closely than men did.

For sex of the other person in the dyad, there were still few children's results, but they were somewhat clearer: Two results showed children to approach female others closer than male others (both significant, mean effect size = .66), and three had unknown direction and were nonsignificant. For adults (Table 7.5), the data were very consistent in showing women to be approached closer than men.

For the same-sex versus opposite-sex comparison, the data were highly inconsistent. For children, three results showed same sex to be closer (with one significant result, effect size = .34), while four showed opposite sex to be closer (nonsignificant or significance unknown). For adolescents, all three results showed opposite sex to be closer (no other information available). For adults, shown in Table 7.5, the results were also mixed, with no clear trend for either sex combination. A possible resolution of the inconsistency stems from Heshka and Nelson's (1972) finding that same sex were closer when the dyad members were strangers, but opposite sex were closer when they were acquaintances. Indeed, for the data in Table 7.5, the two significant same-sex-closer results were for strangers, and the one significant opposite-sex-closer result was for acquaintances (these are in addition to Heshka & Nelson's result). The hypothesis that distance

TABLE 7.5
Sex Differences in Interpersonal Distance (Unobtrusive Observation, Adults)

Index	Sex of Subject (n = 29)	Sex of Other (n = 22)	Same-Sex vs. Opposite-Sex (n = 27)	Female-Female vs. Male-Male (n = 34)
Direction of Effect (excluding no difference or unknown)	in 73% (11/15), females approach closer	in 87% (13/15), females are approached closer	in 63% (12/19), same-sex are closer	in 81% (26/32), female-female are closer
Mean Effect Size (r)	between .06 (n = 29) and .22 (n = 8)[a]	between .20 (n = 22) and .38 (n = 11)[b]	between .02 (n = 27) and .20 (n = 2)[b]	between .10 (n = 34) and .32 (n = 10)[a]
Statistical Significance (all studies)	in 6 of 29 (21%), females approach significantly closer; in 2 of 29 (7%), males approach significantly closer	in 7 of 22 (32%), females are approached significantly closer; in none are males approached significantly closer	in 2 of 27 (10%), same-sex are significantly closer; in 1 of 27 (4%), opposite-sex are significantly closer	in 11 of 34 (32%), female-female are significantly closer; in none are male-male significantly closer
Combined p	p = .01, two tail (n = 27)	p = 10⁻⁶, two tail (n = 22)	p = .80, two tail (n = 17)	p = 10⁻⁹, two tail (n = 15)

Combined p row values: $p = .01$, two tail ($n = 27$); $p = 10^{-6}$, two tail ($n = 22$); $p = .80$, two tail ($n = 17$); $p = 10^{-9}$, two tail ($n = 15$)

[a]Positive values indicate smaller distances for women.
[b]Positive values mean same-sex distance larger than opposite-sex.

215

is a function of same- versus opposite-sex composition *and* acquaintanceship is attractive. Unfortunately, the whole group of studies yielded a more equivocal result: Although 71% (5/7) of the results showing smaller distances for opposite-sex dyads were for acquaintances (in support of the hypothesis), only 45% (5/11) of the results showing smaller distances for same-sex dyads were for strangers.

Turning to the female-female versus male-male comparison, all of the data pointed to females keeping smaller distances among themselves than men do. For children, 70% (12/17) of the studies showed this; five were significant (four of which showed smaller female distances), and the mean known effect size was .13 ($n = 4$). For adolescents, all three results showed smaller female distances (no other data available). For adults, shown in Table 7.5, the same trend was very persuasive. As in earlier analyses, the strength of the female-female versus male-male comparison was consistent with the sex-of-subject and sex-of-other main effects already noted.

We turn now to the results for staged and paper-and-pencil measures. Correlations among the three methods have been generally, but not always, positive and sometimes as large as .60 or more (Duke & Kiebach, 1974; Duke & Nowicki, 1972; Gottheil, Corey, & Paredes, 1968; Pedersen, 1973; Price & Dabbs, 1974; Tennis & Dabbs, 1975), though it is also evident that unobtrusive measures correlate weakest with the two other more reactive measures. Staged studies showed the following results (over adults and children): (1) a weak subject-sex effect, showing women to prefer smaller distances with others of both sexes than men; (2) a very consistent sex-of-other effect showing that subjects are more comfortable with female others at closer distances than male others; (3) an equivocal same-sex versus opposite-sex effect; and (4) a consistent tendency for female-female dyads to be comfortable at smaller distances than male-male dyads. Thus, staged measures paralleled unobtrusive measures with regard to sex differences.

Studies using paper-and-pencil measures showed a remarkably similar pattern, with the exception of the same-sex versus opposite-sex comparison. There, children put same-sex people closer in 70% (7/10) of studies, and adults put opposite-sex people closer in 100% (6/6) of studies where direction was known. The latter result is different from the mixed results obtained for unobtrusive measures and staged measures. In responding in a paper-and-pencil format, adults may register a stereotype of heterosexual attraction (and a reluctance to appear homophilic), or else they may imagine more intimate relationships than those observed in the naturalistic studies.

Authors have interpreted the trends reviewed here in the usual two ways: that women are more affiliative than men and therefore prefer the positive-affect connotations of closer distance, and that women have lower social status than men and therefore cannot command as large interpersonal spaces. When writing in the latter vein, authors are likely to refer to "violations" of women's personal space.

To these interpretations can be added a third, which has only rarely been mentioned, perhaps because it is less arresting theoretically. Women are smaller than men, and smaller individuals *within* a sex seem to experience closer interpersonal distances than larger individuals. This has been shown experimentally for height, using both a staged task with adults (Hartnett, Bailey, & Hartley, 1974) and unobtrusive observation of adults (Caplan & Goldman, 1981). An additional study that used 6'5'' confederates in a staged task (Frankel & Barrett, 1971) obtained larger than usual approach distances. (Bailey, Caffrey, & Hartnett, 1976, however, experimentally varied confederate height and failed to get a significant effect.) Further, among children using paper-and-pencil tasks, researchers have found that obese-looking others of both sexes are given larger distances (Lerner, Iwawaki, & Chihari, 1976; Lerner, Karabenick, & Meisels, 1975a; Lerner, Venning, & Knapp, 1975b). Though the latter results are easily conceptualized as a stigma effect, they can also be thought of in terms of sheer size. Consistent with such results, research has found that personal space increases with age (e.g., Price & Dabbs, 1974; Tennis & Dabbs, 1975). Height also increases with age. Further, in these two studies, which used same-sex pairs in a staged task in Grades 1, 3, 9, and 12, the male-male versus female-female difference in interpersonal distance grew steadily larger as age advanced, starting from virtually none in Grade 1. This increase in the sex difference for distance parallels increasing height differences between the sexes over this age span.

Theoretically, therefore, the size hypothesis may account for observed sex differences in distance as well as the affiliation and social status hypotheses can. They are not necessarily independent hypotheses, however; for example, small size may connote weakness, or smaller people may feel more affiliative with each other because their physical threat potential is less. The point is (here as elsewhere in this chapter) that all sensible interpretations should be considered. I would add that it is not necessary to invoke *one* explanation for all nonverbal sex differences. This would be needed only to the extent that various nonverbal skills and behaviors are empirically shown to covary. In fact, we do not know very much about such relationships. Even encoding and decoding skills, which seem to draw on similar knowledge, are only weakly positively correlated (DePaulo & Rosenthal, 1979). As long as we do not know that nonverbal behaviors are substantially positively correlated, we do not *have* to find a single grand explanation for sex differences.

Body Orientation

Closely associated with the study of distance is the assessment of people's angle of orientation toward each other—face-to-face, for example, or at an angle. On this question there were not a large number of studies, especially not that allowed the separation of sex-of-subject and sex-of-other effects. The only category worth summarizing is for unobtrusive observation of male-male versus female-female dyads. For children, two of three studies with known direction showed girls to be more direct, with two significant. For adults, 92% (11/12) of the studies with known direction found more direct orientation in women (three significant, two of which showed females to be more direct; mean known effect size = .18, n = 5).

Touch

For no nonverbal behavior has a theory coalesced as much as it has for touching. Henley (1973, 1977) has reasoned, in an argument persuasive to many, that touch is a prerogative of the socially powerful, and that because men are more socially powerful than women, men have, and exercise, a touching privilege over women—that is, they touch women more than vice versa. Henley (1977) has also hypothesized that men do more touching in general and women receive more touch in general.

This argument has such appeal that psychologists have seemed ready to accept it without much evidence. Henley (1973) did find male-female asymmetry in a ground-breaking study. Since then relatively few researchers have tried to test or replicate Henley's work, and only one reviewer besides ourselves has made a serious attempt to search the literature for additional results (Major, 1981).

A detailed analysis of sex differences in touch appears in Stier and Hall (1984). We found 40 observational results reporting on sex differences in touch, from preschool to elderly. The same set of comparisons by sex are possible for the observational studies as for the other nonverbal behaviors summarized in this chapter, with the additional interesting comparison of "asymmetry," that is, males touching females versus vice versa. The touch data did not allow very extensive quantitative summary, however, because the results were in a variety of forms and significance levels were very often not known.

For the asymmetry question, we found 19 independent results. Of these, males touched females more in only 37% (7/19) of the results where there was any asymmetry. Excluding children as touchers, that difference was 43% (6/14). Of the three statistically significant results, two showed more male touching of females and one showed the reverse. It seems that on balance Henley's asymmetry hypothesis is unsupported. A qualification must be made, however. Most studies did not distinguish between intentional and unintentional touch. The two studies showing significant asymmetry favoring men both coded only *intentional touch with the hand*. Thus, Henley's hypothesis may indeed be correct for more deliberate and focused touches.

For sex of toucher, only 32% (6/19) of results where the direction was known showed males to touch more. One found males to touch significantly more, but four found women to touch significantly more. It appears, then, that females tended to do more touching overall. For sex of recipient, the results were split

(54%, or 7/13, of results showing females to be touched more, with none significant either way, as far as I know).

For same- versus opposite-sex touch, 73% (19/26) of the results showed more for same sex. Six were significant showing more for same sex, but three were significant showing more for opposite sex. Results showing more opposite-sex touch tended to be based on more intimate dyads and/or contexts. Interestingly, in self-report studies people generally have said they experience more opposite-sex touch (Andersen & Leibowitz, 1978; Henley, 1977; Jourard & Rubin, 1968; Lomranz & Shapira, 1974). As with distance, noted earlier, people may remember more intimate (mainly heterosexual) encounters when responding to a paper-and-pencil task. Research on touch is especially prone to bias toward observation of the relatively casual, formal, or accidental touches that occur in public. The more psychologically significant, and memorable, touches may occur at times when researchers are not observing.

For male-male versus female-female touch, a full 84% (16/19) showed more female-female touch, though significance levels were rarely available.

Thus, women seem on average to be the touchers. In fact, one study (Berkowitz, 1971), which was entered as one result in this summary, was actually based on four age groups in six scattered areas of the world. Of these 24 samples (over 20,000 people), *all but one* showed females to initiate touch more than males. Women seem especially likely to touch other women, as we have seen. These results fit naturally with women's closer interaction distances, documented earlier.

Body Movement and Gesture

The last set of behaviors to be summarized is quite varied: head movements, hand movements, lean, gross body movements, foot and leg movements, and carrying behavior. Within some of these—hand gestures, for example—numerous individual behaviors have been examined. Rekers and his colleagues have routinely measured at least eight different kinds of hand gestures (Rekers, Amaro-Plotkin, & Low, 1977; Rekers & Rudy, 1978; Rekers, Sanders, & Strauss, 1981). A neat summary is difficult because there are many categories, and each has few results.

Head Movements.   Up-and-down head nods provided the most data. In two studies, women nodded more than men (both were significant); in six studies there was no difference at all or it was unknown. The average known effect size was .22 ($n = 4$). One study found significantly more "head movement" for women (effect size = .29). One study using photos (mainly yearbook) found significantly more head tilt for women (effect size = .09).

Hand Movements.   Rekers and his colleagues, in observing children and adolescents while alone playing a tossing game, have documented several gestures that show early sex differences. Girls in these studies did more hand clasping, holding the wrist limp, fluttering the hands, putting palm to head, and flexing the elbows. By adolescence (cross-sectionally), these differences were all much diminished. Hand "gesticulations" of all sorts, for adults in social settings, showed somewhat mixed results, but women showed more on the average (62%, 5/8 of known results).

Behaviors that are called sometimes "adaptors" and sometimes nervous habits—basically, fidgety and probably unconscious hand movements that reflect inner needs more than any direct aspect of *interpersonal* communication—mainly appeared in women. Females touched their hair more (four of four studies), touched ears more (two of three studies), touched face more (four of six studies), and used more general self-adaptors (four of seven studies). But there were some instances of significantly more male behavior of this sort.

Lean.   The data showed that males lean forward, to the side, or back more than females (83%, 5/6 of results with known direction).

Body Movements.   Large body movements, especially bodily fidgeting and shifting, seemed very much to be the province of males (88%, 7/8 of results with known direction). Perhaps men exhibit nervousness more with gross movements, women more with finer movements. Consistent with this hypothesis, Frances (1979) found that men's body, foot, and arm movements decreased relative to women's as an apparent function of increased comfort in dyadic interaction, and women's smiling and laughter decreased relative to men's. Finally, men kept their arms more open and/or more relaxed in both of the two studies located that measured these variables.

Foot and Leg Movements.   Consistent with the results for large movements, men moved their feet and legs more in the majority of studies, social and nonsocial, where the direction was known (80%, 4/5). They also kept their legs in more open positions (2/2).

Carrying.   A well-established finding is that males carry things (mainly schoolbooks in the studies done) at their side, whereas females carry them at their chest. This difference appears after kindergarten. Scheman, Lockard, & Mehler's (1978) evidence suggests that hip protrusion may be a physiological basis for the difference; but widespread observation of the difference in prepubescent children indicates modeling and generalization effects as well.

CONCLUSIONS

Very persuasive sex differences exist in the research literature for almost every behavior summarized. Sex-of-subject effects parallel sex-of-other effects, with the latter occasionally being slightly larger. This is very interesting because it suggests that the other person's sex is sometimes more salient than one's own when deciding how to act. Indeed, we are usually acutely aware of another's sex, whereas our own is simply a fact of life. The correlations calculated as a measure of effect size were not overwhelming in magnitude but were often impressively consistent and not trivial in size. Average correlations larger than .30 or so are not very often found in social psychological research. The sex differences documented here are often big enough to be "visible to the naked eye" (i.e., r greater than about .25; Cohen, 1969). Considering that nonverbal behavior is known to vary with age, race, affect, culture, role, personality, and relationship, it would in fact be surprising if sex, or any other single factor, were capable of explaining a large amount of variance.

Our concern for where nonverbal sex differences come from naturally makes the children's data especially important. Here the results are hard to interpret because the quantity of research on children is much smaller than is available for adults. The present review suggests that some nonverbal sex differences are observable in young children, whereas others—smiling being the most striking example—seem to develop some time later, before college age. The dearth of studies covering adolescence is regrettable. And, of course, infant data are important. Haviland and Malatesta (1981) and Hall (1984) both review sex differences in infants' nonverbal behavior.

Most authors assume that nonverbal sex differences are learned and, consequently, ask what it is about males' and females' histories that is responsible. Although conjecture abounds, there have not been many attempts to see whether affiliation-warmth, dominance-submission, or any other variable can account for the differences. Some efforts to do so have yielded potentially important data. LaFrance and Carmen (1980), for example, found that sex differences in gazing, smiling, and filled pauses (one nonverbal behavior on which men exceed women) were pronounced, but were even more pronounced when very "feminine" females were contrasted with very "masculine" males. This sort of research points in the direction of sex-typed personality traits.

In addition to looking for male and female traits as explanations for nonverbal sex differences, one can look at situational variables. Hall and Halberstadt (in press) asked whether situational and role variables are related to the magnitude of sex differences in smiling and gazing, using a meta-analytic approach. They found that sex differences in smiling (but not gazing) were much larger when the circumstances were judged to evoke more social tension. They found some evidence, although it was rather weak, that sex differences in smiling (but not gazing) increased when the circumstnces were judged to evoke more warmth and affiliation. They found no evidence that dominance-submission as defined by the circumstances was related to sex differences in either smiling or gazing.

Efforts at developing an understanding of causal factors, although fraught with problems, are clearly the direction in which the study of nonverbal sex differences should go. Ample descriptive evidence is at hand for many questions about sex differences, and it is time that investigators mounted serious empirical studies of explanatory factors, rather than simply offering interpretations based on theoretical arguments, as has happened so much in the past.

REFERENCES

Aiello, J. R. (1972). A test of equilibrium theory: Visual interaction in relation to orientation, distance and sex of interactants. *Psychonomic Science, 27,* 335--136.

Aiello, J. R. (1977a). A further look at equilibrium theory: Visual interaction as a function of interpersonal distance. *Environmental Psychology and Nonverbal Behavior, 1,* 122–140.

Aiello, J. R. (1977b). Visual interaction at extended distances. *Personality and Social Psychology Bulletin, 3,* 83–86.

Andersen, P.A., & Leibowitz, K. (1978). The development and nature of the construct touch avoidance. *Environmental Psychology and Nonverbal Behavior, 3,* 89–106.

Argyle, M., & Cook, M. (1976). *Gaze and mutual gaze.* Cambridge: Cambridge University Press.

Argyle, M., & Dean, J. (1965). Eye-contact, distance and affiliation. *Sociometry, 28,* 289–304.

Argyle, M., Salter, V., Nicholson, H., Williams, M., & Burgess, P. (1970). The communication of inferior and superior attitudes by verbal and non-verbal signals. *British Journal of Social and Clinical Psychology, 9,* 222–231.

Bailey, K. G., Caffrey, J. V., III, & Hartnett, J. J. (1976). Body size as implied threat: Effects on personal space and person perception. *Perceptual and Motor Skills, 43,* 223–230.

Berkowitz, W. R. (1971). A cross-national comparison of some social patterns of urban pedestrians. *Journal of Cross-Cultural Psychology, 2,* 129–144.

Blanck, P.D., Rosenthal, R., Snodgrass, S. E., DePaulo, B. M., & Zuckerman, M. (1981). Sex differences in eavesdropping on nonverbal cues: Developmental changes. *Journal of Personality and Social Psychology, 41,* 391–396.

Brooks, R., Brandt, L., & Wiener, M. (1969). Differential response to two communication channels: Socioeconomic class differences in response to verbal reinforcers communicated with and without tonal inflection. *Child Development, 40,* 453–470.

Buck, R. (1977). Nonverbal communication of affect in preschool children: Relationships with personality and skin conductance. *Journal of Personality and Social Psychology, 35,* 225–236.

Buck, R., Baron, R., Goodman, N., & Shapiro, B. (1980). Unitization of spontaneous nonverbal behavior in the study of emotion communication. *Journal of Personality and Social Psychology, 39,* 522–529.

Buck, R., Miller, R. E., & Caul, W. F. (1974). Sex, personality, and physiological variables in the communication of affect via facial expression. *Journal of Personality and Social Psychology, 30,* 587–596.

Caplan, M. E., & Goldman, M. (1981). Personal space violations as a function of height. *Journal of Social Psychology, 114,* 167–171.

Chapman, A. J. (1973). Social facilitation of laughter in children. *Journal of Experimental Social Psychology, 9,* 528–541.

Cohen, J. (1969). *Statistical power analysis for the behavioral sciences.* New York: Academic Press.

Cupchik, G. C., & Leventhal, H. (1974). Consistency between expressive behavior and the evaluation of humorous stimuli: The role of sex and self-observation. *Journal of Personality and Social Psychology, 30,* 429–442.

DePaulo, B. M., & Rosenthal, R. (1979). Ambivalence, discrepancy, and deception in nonverbal communication. In Rosenthal, R. (Ed.), *Skill in nonverbal communication: Individual differences.* Cambridge, MA: Oelgeschlager, Gunn & Hain.

DePaulo, B. M., Rosenthal, R., Eisenstat, R. A., Rogers, P. L., & Finkelstein, S. (1978). Decoding discrepant nonverbal cues. *Journal of Personality and Social Psychology, 36,* 313–323.

DiMatteo, M. R., & Hall, J. A. (1979). Nonverbal decoding skill and attention to nonverbal cues: A research note. *Environmental Psychology and Nonverbal Behavior, 3,* 188–192.

Duke, M. P., & Kiebach, C. (1974). A brief note on the validity of the Comfortable Interpersonal Distance Scale. *Journal of Social Psychology, 94,* 297–298.

Duke, M. P., & Nowicki, S., Jr. (1972). A new measure and social-learning model for interpersonal distance. *Journal of Experimental Research in Personality, 6,* 119–132.

Eagly, A. H., & Carli, L. L. (1981). Sex of researchers and sex-typed communications as determinants of sex differences in influenceability. *Psychological Bulletin, 90,* 1–20.

Ellyson, S. L., Dovidio, J. F., & Fehr, B. J. (1981). Visual behavior and dominance in women and men. In Mayo, C., & Henley, N. M. (Eds.), *Gender and nonverbal behavior.* New York: Springer-Verlag.

Evans, G. W., & Howard, R. B. (1973). Personal space. *Psychological Bulletin, 80,* 334–344.

Exline, R. V. (1963). Explorations in the process of person perception: Visual interaction in relation to competition, sex, and need for affiliation. *Journal of Personality, 31,* 1–20.

Exline, R. V., Ellyson, S. L., & Long, B. (1975). Visual behavior as an aspect of power role relationships. In Pliner, P., Krames, L., & Alloway, T., *Nonverbal communication of aggression.* New York: Plenum Press.

Frances, S. J. (1979). Sex differences in nonverbal behavior. *Sex Roles, 5,* 519–35.

Frankel, A. S., & Barrett, J. (1971). Variations in personal space as a function of authoritarianism, self-esteem, and racial characteristics of a stimulus situation. *Journal of Consulting and Clinical Psychology, 37,* 95–98.

Frieze, I. H., & Ramsey, S. J. (1976). Nonverbal maintenance of traditional sex roles. *Journal of Social Issues, 32* (3), 133–141.

Glass, G. V., McGaw, B., & Smith, M. L. (1981). *Meta-analysis in social research.* Beverly Hills: Sage.

Gottheil, E., Corey, J., & Paredes, A. (1968). Psychological and physical dimensions of personal space. *Journal of Psychology, 69,* 7–9.

Hall, J. A. (1978). Gender effects in decoding nonverbal cues. *Psychological Bulletin, 85,* 845–857.

Hall, J. A. (1979). Gender, gender roles, and nonverbal communication skills. In Rosenthal, R. (Ed.), *Skill in nonverbal communication: Individual differences.* Cambridge, MA: Oelgeschlager, Gunn & Hain.

Hall, J. A. (1984). *Nonverbal sex differences: Communication accuracy and expressive style.* Baltimore: Johns Hopkins University Press.

Hall, J. A., & Halberstadt, A. G. (1981). Sex roles and nonverbal communication skills. *Sex Roles, 7,* 273–287.

Hall, J. A., & Halberstadt, A. G. (in press). Smiling and gazing. In J. S. Hyde and M. C. Linn, (Eds.), *The psychology of gender: Advances through meta-analysis.* Baltimore: Johns Hopkins University Press.

Harper, R. G., Wiens, A. N., & Matarazzo, J. D. (1978). *Nonverbal communication: The state of the art.* New York: Wiley-Interscience.

Hartnett, J. J., Bailey, K. G., & Hartley, C. S. (1974). Body height, position, and sex as determinants of personal space. *Journal of Psychology, 87,* 129–136.

Haviland, J. J., & Malatesta, C. Z. (1981). The development of sex differences in nonverbal signals: Fallacies, facts, and fantasies. In Mayo, C., & Henley, N. M. (Eds), *Gender and nonverbal behavior.* New York: Springer-Verlag.

Hayduk, L. A. (1978). Personal space: An evaluative and orienting overview. *Psychological Bulletin, 85,* 117–134.

Henley, N. M. (1973). Status and sex: Some touching observations. *Bulletin of the Psychonomic Society, 2,* 91–93.

Henley, N. M. (1977). *Body politics: Power, sex, and nonverbal communication.* Englewood Cliffs, NJ: Prentice-Hall.

Heshka, S., & Nelson, Y. (1972). Interpersonal speaking distance as a function of age, sex, and relationship. *Sociometry, 35,* 491–498.

Hoffman, M. L. (1977). Sex differences in empathy and related behaviors. *Psychological Bulletin, 84,* 712–722.

Isenhart, M. W. (1980). An investigation of the relationship of sex and sex role to the ability to decode nonverbal cues. *Human Communication Research, 6,* 309–318.

Jourard, S. M., & Rubin, J. E. (1968). Self-disclosure and touching: A study of two modes of interpersonal encounter and their inter-relation. *Journal of Humanistic Psychology, 6,* 39–48.

Kleck, R. E., & Nuessle, W. (1968). Congruence between the indicative and communicative functions of eye contact in interpersonal relations. *British Journal of Social and Clinical Psychology, 7,* 241–246.

LaFrance, M., & Carmen, B. (1980). The nonverbal display of psychological androgyny. *Journal of Personality and Social Psychology, 38,* 36–49.

LaFrance, M., & Mayo, C. (1978). *Moving bodies: Nonverbal communication in social relationships.* Monterey, CA: Brooks/Cole.

Lerner, R. M., Iwawaki, S., & Chihara, T. (1976). Development of personal space schemata among Japanese children. *Developmental Psychology, 12,* 466–467.

Lerner, R. M., Karabenick, S. A., & Meisels, M. (1975a). Effects of age and sex on the development of personal space schemata towards body build. *Journal of Genetic Psychology, 127,* 91–101.

Lerner, R. M., Venning, J., & Knapp, J. R. (1975b). Age and sex effects on personal space schemata toward body build in late childhood. *Developmental Psychology, 11,* 855–856.

Lomranz, J., & Shapira, A. (1974). Communicative patterns of self-disclosure and touching behavior. *Journal of Psychology, 88,* 223–227.

Maccoby, E. E., & Jacklin, C. N. (1974). *The psychology of sex differences.* Stanford: Stanford University Press.

Major, B. (1981). Gender patterns in touching behavior. In Mayo, C., & Henley, N. M. (Eds.), *Gender and nonverbal behavior.* New York: Springer-Verlag.

Mazanec, N., & McCall, G. J. (1976). Sex factors and allocation of attention in observing persons. *Journal of Psychology, 93,* 175–180.

Pedersen, D. M. (1973). Developmental trends in personal space. *Journal of Psychology, 83,* 3–9.

Price, G. H., & Dabbs, J. M., Jr. (1974). Sex, setting, and personal space: Changes as children grow older. *Personality and Social Psychology Bulletin, 1,* 362-363.

Ragan, J. M. (1982). Gender displays in portrait photographs. *Sex Roles, 8,* 33–43.

Rekers, G. A., Amaro-Plotkin, H. D., & Low, B. P. (1977). Sex-typed mannerisms in normal boys and girls as a function of sex and age. *Child Development, 48,* 275–278.

Rekers, G. A., & Rudy, J. P. (1978). Differentiation of childhood body gestures. *Perceptual and Motor Skills, 46,* 839–845.

Rekers, G. A., Sanders, J. A., & Strauss, C. C. (1981). Developmental differentiation of adolescent body gestures. *Journal of Genetic Psychology, 138,* 123–131.

Rosenfeld, H. M. (1966). Approval-seeking and approval-inducing functions of verbal and nonverbal responses in the dyad. *Journal of Personality and Social Psychology, 4,* 597–605.

Rosenthal, R. (Ed.) (1980). *Quantitative assessment of research domains.* San Francisco: Jossey-Bass.

Rosenthal, R., & DePaulo, B. M. (1979a). Sex differences in eavesdropping on nonverbal cues. *Journal of Personality and Social Psychology, 37,* 273–285.

Rosenthal, R., & DePaulo, B. M. (1979b). Sex differences in accommodation in nonverbal communication. In Rosenthal, R. (Ed.), *Skill in nonverbal communication: Individual differences.* Cambridge, MA: Oelgeschlager, Gunn & Hain.

Rousey, C., & Holzman, P. S. (1968). Some effects of listening to one's own voice systematically distorted. *Perceptual and Motor Skills, 27,* 1303–1313.

Savitsky, J. C., & Izard, C. E. (1970). Developmental changes in the use of emotion cues in a concept-formation task. *Developmental Psychology, 3,* 350–357.

Scheman, J. D., Lockard, J. S., & Mehler, B. L. (1978). Influences of anatomical differences on gender-specific book-carrying behavior. *Bulletin of the Psychonomic Society, 11,* 17–20.

Stern, D. N., & Bender, E. P. (1974). An ethological study of children approaching a strange adult: Sex differences. In Friedman, R. C., Richart, R. M., & Vande Wiele, R. L. (Eds.), *Sex differences in behavior.* New York: Wiley.

Stier, D. S., & Hall, J. A. (1984). Gender differences in touch: An empirical and theoretical review. *Journal of Personality and Social Psychology, 47,* 440–459.

Tennis, G. H., & Dabbs, J. M., Jr. (1975). Sex, setting and personal space: First grade through college. *Sociometry, 38,* 385–394.

Weitz, S. (1974). *Nonverbal communication: Readings with commentary,* 2nd ed. New York: Oxford University Press.

Westbrook, M. (1974). Judgement of emotion: Attention versus accuracy. *British Journal of Social and Clinical Psychology, 13,* 383–389.

Weston, A. J., & Rousey, C. L. (1970). Voice confrontation in individuals with normal and defective speech patterns. *Perceptual and Motor Skills, 30,* 187–190.

Williams, S. L., & Hicks, R. A. (1980). Sex, iride pigmentation, and the pupillary attributions of college students to happy and angry faces. *Bulletin of the Psychonomic Society, 16,* 67–68.

Zahn, G. L. (1973). Cognitive integration of verbal and vocal information in spoken sentences. *Journal of Experimental Social Psychology, 9,* 320–334.

Zahn, G. L. (1975). Verbal-vocal integration as a function of sex and methodology. *Journal of Research in Personality, 9,* 226–239.

Zuckerman, M., Blanck, P.D., DePaulo, B. M., & Rosenthal, R. (1980). Developmental changes in decoding discrepant and nondiscrepant nonverbal cues. *Developmental Psychology, 16,* 220–228.

Zuckerman, M., DeFrank, R. S., Spiegel, N. H., & Larrance, D. T. (1982). Masculinity-femininity and encoding of nonverbal cues. *Journal of Personality and Social Psychology, 42,* 548–556.

Zuckerman, M., DePaulo, B. M., & Rosenthal, R. (1981). Verbal and nonverbal communication of deception. In L. Berkowitz (Ed.), *Advances in experimental social psychology* (Vol. 14). New York: Academic Press.

8

Race, Socioeconomic Status, and Nonverbal Behavior

Amy G. Halberstadt
Vassar College

The effects of two sociological variables, race and socioeconomic status, on nonverbal communiction skill and nonverbal communicative behavior are examined in 58 studies. Class seems to be a potent moderator of the relationship between race and nonverbal skill and behavior, and hypotheses attempting to explain why class may be a moderating variable are generated. The effect of culture on the relationship between race and nonverbal skill and behavior is also recognized. The literature is critically examined in an attempt to provide guiding points for future research. Some of the most serious problems found are the confounding of socioeconomic status and race, the paucity of multivariate research, and the failure to identify and measure carefully the variable constructs. Finally, it appears that investigators often overlook sociological variables in designing their research and thus build in bias in their results.

It is almost a truism that misunderstandings develop with regularity between groups of people that differ by race, class or culture. Despite this general knowledge, misunderstandings or miscommunications still seem to persist with tenacity. The ethnography of verbal communication, i.e., the study of race, class, and cultural components of performance in the verbal domain, has begun the process of examining precisely how sociocultural structural differences create these miscommunications (Gumperz, 1982; Hymes, 1977). In the same ethnographic spirit, this chapter attempts to document the differences between blacks and whites in the domain of nonverbal communication skill and behavior, and when the research allows, to look at class and culture as moderating variables for occurring differences.

In nonverbal communication, differences between ourselves and others are not often consciously noted, but are incorporated into our assessments of those others and into our evaluations of our interactions with them. In these situations a form of self-serving bias tends to surface; we tend to think that if all has not gone well, then there must be something wrong with the other person. After all, we were on our best behavior. Although we all know that "people are different," we rarely incorporate that concept into our implicit understanding of nonverbal communication.

The premise of this chapter is that styles of communication exist in the nonverbal domain, much like the accents and dialects found in the verbal domain. Instead of interpreting others' behaviors within the structure of our own nonverbal style system, it is important to distinguish between these stylistic differences in communication and the actual messages being conveyed.

Until recently, the scientific community has not been able to provide much guidance in this matter of interpreting behaviors outside of one's own style of communication. The first research on race and socioeconomic differences in nonverbal communication was conducted in the 1930s (Justin, 1932; Kellogg & Eagleson, 1931), but interest in these issues was not sustained until the early 1970s. Even now, an initial glance at this body of research suggests a series of occasionally contradictory results. When examined carefully, however, these studies reveal an important and discernible pattern.

The research is divided into two broad categories, nonverbal communication skill and nonverbal communicative behavior. Because these two areas have different intents, strengths and difficulties, they must be reviewed separately.

The first category, differences in skill, investigates differential ability to recognize or decode communications by others, and to transmit or encode communications to others.[1] The second category, differences in behavior, investigates how the patterns, frequency, or style of transmitted cues differ because of cultural differences or differential treatment of individuals by society. This area is a collection of research that must be analyzed according to the particular behavior employed. Three or more studies were found for four types of nonverbal behavior; these were proxemics (interpersonal distance and body orientation), touch, eye gaze, and interactions between the verbal and nonverbal systems. Whenever possible, developmental trends are examined in an attempt to understand how and when race and class differences evolve.

The variable of race, in the 44 studies on race that are summarized, refers only to black and white people. Race appears to be an implicitly defined variable (Duncan & Fiske, 1977) that is easy to measure (all of the studies assume that the presence of any pigmentation defines an individual as "black") and, thus, is often employed in research without much consideration as to its meaning. As is described later, many studies examine the variable of race without regard for

---

[1] Although the proverb "You can have too much of a good thing" fits the very good decoder who may recognize messages not meant for her or him and the very good encoder in a poker game, the dimension of skill remains a valid one. However, the relationship between skill and other variables may not always be linear.

the effects of socioeconomic status. Since socioeconomic status varies considerably between blacks and whites in the United States, according to any status index, it is important to distinguish between the effects of class and race. Also, very few studies examine cultural differences between blacks and whites; in fact, most references to this type of explanation will be descriptive reports.

Class, in the 37 studies that report or examine socioeconomic status, is a more explicitly defined variable. Nevertheless, as is also described later, the majority of studies do not give this variable careful consideration, in terms of either measurement or relevance.

Evidence of similar patterns of race and class differences appear in both nonverbal skill and nonverbal behavior; when black subjects appear less skilled or show evidence of greater frequency of a behavior, relative to white subjects, lower class subjects also appear less skilled or show evidence of greater frequency of that behavior. When socioeconomic status is controlled in studies of race and skill or of race and behavior the black/white differences are often reduced. Nevertheless, some behavior patterns cannot be claimed as related to social class so much as unique aspects of black culture.

The first category, differences in skill, and each of the four sections in the second category, differences in behavior, are accompanied by tables that contain a brief description of each relevant study and, whenever possible, three outcome indices. The first outcome is the level of statistical significance; p is nonsignificant (ns) or at some level of significance (.10, .05, .01, or .001). The second outcome is the direction of the effect. Results are signed positively (+) or negatively (−) dependent upon the data supporting or rejecting the hypothesis identified in that section. Three of the studies are virtually directionless and remain unsigned. The third outcome is the size of the effect, disregarding significance level and N. The effect size estimate (d) reports the size of the effect without influence of sample size, and is defined as the difference between the means of the two groups, divided by their common standard deviation. An effect size of .20 is considered small, an effect size of greater than .50 is considered visible to the naked eye, and an effect size of greater than .80 is considered large (Cohen, 1977). Often, an index was not reported but enough information was provided in the text of the article to accurately calculate the desired index.

Chapter sections begin with a description of the studies as a whole, continue with descriptions of methods or peculiarities in specific studies, and conclude with verbal summaries of group results and meta-analyses of the outcome indices.

NONVERBAL SKILL

The criteria for inclusion in this first major area were the following: (a) the studies were published or else presented at a conference, (b) the studies measured ability to accurately decode (judge) or encode (send) visual or audio nonverbal communications, and (c) subjects were classified by their race and/or socioeconomic status (SES).

Fourteen studies fit these criteria (summarized in Table 8.1 with 7 race studies followed by 7 studies of socioeconomic status, and organized by age of subjects).[2] All of these studies focus on ability to decode nonverbal cues. The types of cues judged were emotions (e.g., happiness, anger, sadness), scenarios of expression (e.g., nagging a child, expressing gratitude, talking about death), or emblems (nonverbal communications with exact verbal translations [Ekman & Friesen, 1969], e.g., be quiet, come here, hello). Two studies (Michael & Willis, 1968, 1969) also investigated the sending of nonverbal cues (emblems).

For the second outcome index, the direction of the effect, no one hypothesis predominated in the area of skill prior to this examination. The direction of the effect was determined, therefore, by a coin toss, and is positive when blacks or lower class subjects show an advantage and negative when whites or middle-class subjects show an advantage.

Race

For the summary analysis of race differences in nonverbal communication skill, data were unavailable for one study reporting nonsignificant results. The meta-analysis for the six remaining visual and audio studies indicated no significant race difference (weighted mean $r = .03$, Stouffer's $z = .92$), however the negative effect sizes for the youngest groups were cancelled out by the positive effect sizes of the older college groups. This suggested a correlation of the race/skill relationship with age.

Scoring samples as children (1) and adults (2), the correlation of race/skill with age neared significance with a very large effect ($r(4) = .71$, ns, $d = 2.01$). Whereas black children appear less skilled at decoding visual cues than white children, in adulthood blacks appear to surpass the skill of whites.

A possible explanation for this finding is the "oppression hypothesis" (see Weitz, 1974), which posits that oppressed people are better at decoding nonverbal communications. Decoding skill is functional in that oppressed people must become especially good at recognizing what more powerful people think in order to "survive" in a social and political sense. Samples 5 and 6, in which black undergraduates did better on a visual decoding task than white undergraduates, may be examples of this process; or some selection process may be occurring such that only the most able black students can make it to college.

---

[2]When two or more independent samples were reported within one publication the samples have been treated as separate studies. Visual and audio data from the same samples are reported separately in Table 8.1 but are averaged for meta-analyses including both of these skills. Studies where multiple measures were obtained (e.g., interpersonal distance and eye gaze) are reported in each appropriate table, but are only counted once in summaries of the entire sample.

TABLE 8.1

Research on Nonverbal Communication Skill

Sample Number	Author(s) year; N	Age	SES	Nonverbal channel	Major findings	p	d
RACE							
1	Gitter & Quincy, 1968; $N = 80$	4–6	all low[b]	V: 4 emotions (3/4 figure)	No differences were found in decoding 3 black and 3 white actresses.	ns	−.04
2	Kellogg & Eagleson, 1931; $N = 739$	5–14	all[b]	V: 6 emotions (face)	Blacks are slightly worse decoders of a white female than whites (Rosenthal et al. analysis).	ns	−1.17
3	Izard, 1971; $N = 151$	5–7	all low[b]	V: 9 emotions (face)	No differences were found in judging a variety of mostly or all white decoders.	ns	—
4	Rosenthal, Hall, DiMatteo, Rogers, & Archer, 1979; $N = 316$	9–11	—	V: 4 expressions (face, body) A: 4 expressions (spliced & filtered)	(a) Blacks are slightly worse at decoding a white female than whites. (b) Blacks do worse on random splicing, better on filtered speech, compared to whites.	.10 ns	−.21 .00
5	Gitter, Black, & Mostofsky, 1972a; $N = 48$	college	—	V: 7 emotions (3/4 figure)	Blacks are better decoders of 10 black and 10 white actors and actresses than whites.	.05	+.71
6	Gitter, Black, & Mostofsky, 1972b; $N = 160$	college	—	V: 7 emotions (3/4 figure)	Blacks are better decoders of 10 black and 10 white actors and actresses than whites.	.05	+.42
7	Rosenthal et al., 1979; $N = 39$; 328	adults	—	V: 4 expressions (face, body) A: 4 expressions (spliced, filtered)	(a) No differences were found for decoding a white female ($N = 39$). (b) Blacks do slightly worse on random splicing, slightly better on filtered speech.	ns ns	.00 −.01

TABLE 8.1 (continued)

Sample Number	Author(s) year; N	Age	SES	Nonverbal channel	Major findings	p	d
SOCIOECONOMIC STATUS							
8	Michael & Willis, 1968; N = 80	4–7	low & middle, possibly confounded by race[b]	V: 12 emblems (gestures)	For a racially mixed group, middle class is better at decoding, and at encoding, compared to lower class.	.01 .01	−1.00 −.89
9	Michael & Willis, 1969; N = 80[d]	5–7	low & middle, possibly confounded by race[b]	V: 12 emblems (gestures)	For a racially mixed group, middle class is better at decoding, and at encoding, compared to lower class.	— —	— —
10	Izard, 1971; N = 168	5–7	lower-lower, upper-lower, lower-mid.[b]	V: 9 emotions (face)	Decoding of a variety of mostly or all whites improves with increases in SES level.	.01	−.55
11	Izard, 1971; N = 381	6–11	lower-lower, upper-lower, lower-mid.[b]	V: 9 emotions (face)	Decoding of a variety of mostly or all whites improves with increases in SES level.	.01	−.34
12	Gottman, Gonso, & Rasmussen, 1975; N = 198	9–10	lower-mid.[b]	V: 9 emotions	Decoding of a variety of mostly or all whites improves with increases in SES level.	.01	−.64
13	Pfaff, 1954; N = 103	junior high	above & below[a]	A: 10 emotions (standard content)	Higher SES are better decoders of a male encoding emotions in his voice than lower SES.	—	—

| 14 | Rosenthal et al., 1979; $N = 303$ | high school | all, possibly confounded by race[b] | V: 4 expressions | (a) For video and audio channels combined, decoding of a white female and SES are related positively for females, but negatively for males. | .001 | −.27 |
| | | | | | (b) For audio, SES and decoding are positively related for both females and males. | .10 | −.33 |

Note. The findings include explanation of the results and three outcome indices: p, the direction of the effect ($+$, $-$), and d. The effect size estimate, d reports size of the effect without influence of the sample size, and is defined as the difference between the means of the two groups divided by their common standard deviation (Cohen, 1977). An effect size of .20 is considered small, an effect size of .50 is considered visible to the naked eye, and an effect size of .80 is considered large.

[a]No information regarding how the SES classifications were made was provided in the original text.

[b]One criterion (father occupation, neighborhood, Head Start. or family income) determined the SES classifications.

[c]Two criteria determined the SES classifications.

[d]These studies examined other cultures as well as blacks and whites. Outcome measures in the tables exclude results concerning those additional samples. For the sake of simplicity only black/white contrasts were made in this chapter. Those interested in extending comparisons to other cultural groups may refer to studies designated with this superscript to obtain the appropriate data.

[e]V = Visual, A = Audio.

[f]This sample included nonwhites who were predominantly but not exclusively blacks.

These race differences are attenuated, however, by two confounds in several of the studies. First, the black subjects in Samples 2, 3, 4, and 7 had the disadvantage of having only a different-race encoder to judge, despite the consistent reports from recognition research that persons discriminate faces and voices of their own race better (Brigham & Barkowitz, 1978; Brigham & Williamson, 1979; Chance, Goldstein, & McBride, 1975; Coleman, 1976; Cross, Cross, & Daly, 1971; Feinman & Entwisle, 1976; Luce, 1974; Malpass, 1974; Malpass & Kravitz, 1969; and Malpass, Lavigueur, & Weldon, 1973). The three studies that did employ both black and white encoders reported no differences by race for 4- to 6-year-olds and greater skill in black college students than in white college students.

Second, Samples 2, 4, 5, 6, and the larger subsample in 7 never controlled for socioeconomic status. Kellogg and Eagleson (1931) did attempt to test "similar groups of negroes" to whites but, given the socioeconomic realities of blacks and whites in the 1920s, it seems hardly likely that such an attempt could have succeeded. Considering the inequities of our present-day American society, it is also highly unlikely that a random sample of black and white elementary school students (Rosenthal, Hall, DiMatteo, Rogers, & Archer, 1979, Sample 4) would be evenly distributed across socioeconomic background. All three studies that attempted to control for SES reported no racial differences in decoding ability. The differences across race may actually be differences due to socioeconomic background, such that children of higher SES levels have greater nonverbal decoding skill. When SES was not carefully controlled, differences did occur in that direction.

Finding a difference due to methodological artifact, such as unequal numbers of different-race encoders for subjects to judge, is important, but it is not a very interesting theoretical discovery. Finding that racial differences may be confounded by SES, however, is quite interesting; for this discovery leads us to a new question: why skill in nonverbal communication would be related to socioeconomic status. But first we must explore further the hypothesis that SES is confounding the race/skill relationship. Though no studies analyzed the effects of race and class on skill simultaneously, we can examine the relationship between just SES and nonverbal communication skills in the seven studies present in the literature.

Socioeconomic Status

All seven of the studies concur; lower class individuals are not as skilled at decoding as more privileged individuals. The unweighted mean effect size for both visual and audio decoding studies was moderate ($N = 5$, mean $d = .56$). For a summary analysis, data could not be generated for two studies not reporting a test of significance. Though using the highly conservative procedure of setting the zs for these studies at zero, the effect of an advantageous background on nonverbal decoding skill was apparent (weighted mean $r = .22$, Stouffer's $z = 6.51$, combined $p \leq .0001$). Two of these studies, however, may have been confounded by race. Despite setting a third and a fourth z at zero, the result was still powerful for the remaining three studies (Stouffer's $z = 4.15$, combined $p \leq .0001$). Thus, these studies support the hypothesis suggested earlier: SES appears related to nonverbal decoding skill.

The pattern of decreasing effect sizes with age again suggested an interaction with age. Samples were scored as nursery school (1), elementary school (2), and high school (3). The correlation of the SES/skill relationship with age was nonsignificant because of the small N, but showed a very large effect ($r(3) = -.76$, ns, $d = 2.35$). Whereas lower class children are less skilled at decoding cues than middle-class children, with age they seem to improve considerably more than middle-class individuals. This class/skill interaction with age is similar to the race/skill interaction with age described earlier.

Yet to be performed is the most appropriate (and difficult!) test of all these effects, an analysis of variance contrasting race, class, and age. Despite the absence of this analysis, the 14 studies that are available continue to suggest two clear patterns for race and class differences in nonverbal communication skill: (a) young white and middle-class individuals are better decoders than young black and lower class individuals and (b) these race and class differences are attenuated and possibly even reversed by adulthood. Why white and middle-class individuals' advantages are attenuated over time is not yet clear. Before discussing this matter further, it will be interesting to discover whether race and class differences found for nonverbal communicative skill also hold for nonverbal communicative behavior.

NONVERBAL BEHAVIOR

Studies in differential skill (ability) account for only a portion of the research on the nonverbal system. Thirty-seven additional studies related race to at least one category of nonverbal behavior. Three of these studies, one study that also examined skill, and seven others examined SES.

The criteria for inclusion in this second major area were the following: (a) the studies were published or presented at a conference, (b) the nonverbal behaviors were observed or recorded, as opposed to being tapped solely through projective measures, and (c) subjects were classified by their race and/or social class (see Footnote 2).

Again, for each study, a brief description and the three outcome indices, p, direction of effect ($+$, $-$), and d, are provided wherever possible.

Nonverbal behavior encompasses a huge range of cues, many of which have not been examined by race or socioeconomic status. Much of the wealth of nonverbal cues actually present and available in these studies was neglected. As usual, what was measured reflects the concern of particular researchers and this review, like any other is therefore limited to those concerns. The four areas researched with any frequency are proxemics (interpersonal distance and body orientation), touch, eye gaze, and interactions between the verbal and nonverbal systems. Each area is discussed separately.

Proxemics

The hypotheses concerning racial differences in spatial behavior are derived from Hall (1966), whose general thesis is that people from different cultures inhabit what Hall calls "different sensory worlds." Because of the cultural differences between blacks and whites in the United States, Hall hypothesized that the spatial relations of these groups are dissimilar. Twenty-one of the 22 studies mentioned in Table 8.2 test the validity of this hypothesis.

All studies in Table 8.2 (with race studies followed by one social class study, and organized by age of subjects) investigated interpersonal distance. Eight also investigated the body orientation (directness of axis) of subjects. Body orientation refers to the directness with which people face each other while interacting, generally forming an acute angle with their bodies (e.g., one o'clock formation) or an obtuse angle (e.g., five o'clock formation).

Ten of the samples include only same-sex pairs. Contrasts in the table are of same-race pairs with two exceptions. Booraem, Flowers, Bodner, and Satterfield (1977, Sample 10) employed only one white confederate, a methodological weakness. In Thompson and Baxter's (1973, Sample 13) clever study, however, mixed-race pairs were essential. Thompson and Baxter predicted if individuals in mixed-race pairs did indeed prefer different spatial relations they would move forward or away, thereby creating the interpersonal distance they preferred. Consequently, they observed not the static personal distance (one moment in time) but the actual movement of mixed-race pairs as individual members tried to obtain the personal distance most comfortable for themselves. The conceptualization of interpersonal distance as a dynamic process is a creative and new idea.

Sixteen of the studies were observational, though several observations were under controlled but unobtrusive conditions (e.g., in a classroom or laboratory playroom). The other six studies employed invasion-oriented procedures which were obtrusive and probably reactive as well. For example, two studies (Samples 7 and 10) had a confederate approach a subject until the subject requested that he halt, and two studies (Samples 7 and 12) required subjects to advance up to a confederate as closely as was comfortable for the subject. As another example, Leibman (1970, Sample 16) employed a forced-choice intrusion task; female workers had to decide which confederate to intrude upon while waiting in their personnel department.

TABLE 8.2
Proxemic Differences

Sample number	Author(s) & year; N	Age	SES	Major findings	p	d
RACE						
1	Aiello & Jones, 1971;[d] N = 140 pairs	6–8 years	low & middle confounded by race[b]	(a) Blacks stood closer together than whites, in school playground observations.	.05	+
				(b) Blacks stood less directly than whites.	.05	+
2	Duncan, 1978; N = 96 pairs	5, 7, 9 years	mostly upper-lower[b]	(a) Blacks stood closer together than whites, in school playground observations.	.001	+.53
				(b) A developmental trend showed this to be true only at the earlier ages.	.001	—
				(c) Blacks stood less directly than whites.	.001	+.50
				(d) A developmental trend suggests whites are becoming more direct in stance.	.01	—
3	Jones & Aiello, 1973; N = 96 pairs	6, 8, 10 years	upper-low & middle-middle confounded by race[b]	(a) Blacks stood closer together than whites, while discussing their favorite commercial.	ns	+
				(b) A developmental trend reversed (a).	.05	—
				(c) Blacks stood less directly than whites.	.001	+.75
				(d) A developmental trend showed this to be true only at the earlier ages.	ns	—
4	Scherer, 1974; N = 33 pairs	6–10 years	low[b]	Blacks stood closer together than whites, in a playground setting.	ns	+.26
5	Scherer, 1974; N = 68 pairs	6–10 years	low & middle[b]	(a) In playground behavior, blacks stood closer together than whites.	ns	+.39
				(b) Lower-class subjects stood closer together than middle-class subjects.	.05	+.62
6	Willis, Carlson, & Reeves, 1979;[c] N = 641	5–12 years	low to upper-middle confounded by race[b]	Blacks seemed to stand closer together than whites, while on a cafeteria line.	—	+

TABLE 8.2 (continued)

Sample number	Author(s) & year; N	Age	SES	Major findings	p	d
7	Severy, Forsyth, & Wagner, 1979; N = 144	7, 11, 15 years	specific levels not reported, but matched across race[b]	(a) In a meta-analysis of four measures blacks desired less personal space than whites, overall. (b) A developmental trend reversed (a).	ns .05	+ —
8	Zimmerman & Brody, 1975; N = 78	11–12 years, male	low & middle confounded with race[b]	(a) Unfamiliar whites played closer to each other than unfamiliar blacks, in a laboratory playroom. (b) Blacks played less directly than whites.	.01 .10	−1.00 +.40
9	Baxter, 1970;[d] N = 699 pairs	5–10, 10–20, ≥ 20 years	—	(a)Whites stood closer together than blacks while at a zoo. (b) No developmental interaction occurred.	.001 ns	−.56 —
10	Booraem, Flowers, Bodner & Satterfield, 1977;[d] N = 60	delinquent male youths	—	Whites stopped an approaching white confederate at a closer distance than did blacks.	.001	−1.16
11	Aiello & Jones, 1978; N = 114 pairs	16 years	low & middle[b]	(a) Whites stood closer together than blacks while discussing their favorite T.V. program. (b) Middle-class subjects stood closer together than lower class subjects. (c) Blacks stood less directly than whites.	.05 .10 .01	−.45 −.32 +.56
12	Bauer, 1973; N = 60	college	—	Blacks approached a black confederate more closely than whites approached a white confederate.	.05	+.60
13	Thompson & Baxter, 1973;[d] N = 10 pairs	high school & adult	—	In mixed-race pairs observed in high schools and in a hospital, whites advanced to decrease distance; blacks retreated to increase distance.	.05	−1.96
14	Rosegrant & McCroskey, 1975; N = 240	college	—	Whites sat closer together than blacks in an interview situation; when subjects were asked to move closer to the interviewers this difference disappeared.	—	—

	Study	Age	SES	Result	p	r
15	Tennis & Dabbs, 1976; N = 28 pairs	college females	—	Whites approaching or approached by other whites maintained closer distances than did black pairs.	ns	−.64
16	Leibman, 1970; N = 64	17–59, mean = 28 yrs. female	—	Blacks who chose to intrude on black confederates sat closer than did whites choosing to intrude upon a white confederate.	—	+
17	Willis, 1966; N = 60	adult	—	Whites stood closer together than blacks, in different settings.	.10	−.45
18	Jones, 1971;[d] N = 41	adult	low[b]	(a) No racial difference was observed, in street settings.	ns	.00
				(b) Blacks stood less directly than whites.	ns	+
19	Jones, 1971;[d] N = 151	adult	low[b]	(a) Whites stood closer together than blacks, in street settings.	ns	—
				(b) Blacks stood less directly than whites.	ns	+
20	Hall, 1974[d]; N not reported	adult, mostly male	lower-low & middle confounded by race[b]	(a) Blacks stood closer together in street settings than whites did at a convention.	.05	+
				(b) Blacks stood less directly than whites.	.10	+
21	Maines, 1977; N = 249	—	—	Whites sat less than 6 inches apart in subway cars slightly more often than did blacks.	ns	−.17

SOCIOECONOMIC STATUS

22	Schmidt & Hore, 1970; N = 30 pairs	5 years & mothers	low & high[a]	No social class difference was observed in mother-child pairs while copying designs or telling each other stories.	ns	—

[a]No information regarding how the SES classifications were made was provided in the text.

[b]One criterion (generally neighborhood) determined the SES classifications.

[c]Two criteria (generally neighborhood and father occupation) determined the SES classifications.

[d]These studies examined other cultures as well as blacks and whites. Outcome measures in the tables exclude results concerning those additional samples. For the sake of simplicity only black/white contrasts were made in this chapter. Those interested in extending comparisons to other cultural groups may refer to studies designated with this superscript to obtain the appropriate data.

[e]Children in this study appear to be drawn from the Willis and Hofmann (1975) sample reported in Table 8.3.

In addition to the one study investigating socioeconomic status, the researchers of only two studies (Samples 5 and 11) thought to examine socioeconomic status as well as race, and only five other studies controlled for class differences.

Hall (1966) hypothesized that blacks in the United States engage in a closer, more sensorially involved culture, relative to whites. Predictions follow, then, that blacks would be more likely to maintain closer interpersonal distances and to orient their bodies more directly toward each other. As in most puzzles, however, the pieces don't fit as simply as expected.

Interpersonal Distance.   Four of the five studies testing for age effects (Samples 2, 3, 6, 7, and 9) and other studies of white children (e.g., Aiello & Aiello, 1974; Lomranz, Shapira, Choresh, & Gilat, 1975; and Tennis & Dabbs, 1975) show that interpersonal distances increase as white children grow up. The same four of those five studies and another study of black preschoolers (Langlois, Gottfried, & Seay, 1973) contribute the information that this pattern is true for black children as well. Thus, the pattern in black and white children's development of interpersonal distance appears fairly similar in that interpersonal distance increases with age.

Information about a similar pattern of development, however, does not inform as to whether the interpersonal distances themselves are similar across races. As the first step in making this comparison, all the studies in Table 8.2 are signed in accordance with the original hypothesis (Hall, 1966). When blacks maintained a closer interpersonal distance than whites, the effect was signed positively. When whites maintained a closer interpersonal distance, the effect was signed negatively.

Of the 20 studies that showed any difference at all (including 8 for which the effect was not significant and 3 which did not perform a test of significance), 50% found closer distances in blacks than in whites, exactly what we would expect by chance. Of the 10 significant studies, 4 reported closer distances in blacks but 6 reported closer distances in whites. The unweighted mean effect size was small ($N = 15$, mean $d = -.23$) and the meta-analysis was just significant (Stouffer's $z = -1.80$, combined $p = .04$).

It appears that the two groups are not participating in different spatial relations at all. An eyeball analysis of the signs, however, suggests that subjects' age is interacting with the difference in distance maintained by the racial groups. Studies were therefore characterized as "younger" (subjects in elementary school, $N = 8$) or "older" (adolescents or adults, $N = 12$). In the sample involving younger subjects 87.5% of the studies confirmed Hall's hypothesis: black children interacted more closely with their peers than did white children. In the samples involving older subjects 75% of the studies disconfirmed the hypothesis: adolescent and adult blacks interacted at further distances than did adolescent and adult whites.

A chi-square analysis with two factors, age and direction of effect, was performed. To increase the N and the precision of this analysis, the samples reporting means for several age groups (Samples 2, 3, 7, and 9) were broken down by age. A large effect resulted; black children do appear to maintain closer interpersonal distances than do white children, as predicted by Hall (1966), but by adulthood blacks appear to prefer greater distnces than whites ($X^2(1) = 6.24$, $p = .05$, $d = 1.10$). A correlation between subject age and direction of the effect was also significant ($r(26) = .41$, $p = .05$, $d = .89$).

Three studies examined the interaction of age and the direction of the effect (Samples 2, 3, and 7) and one more study provided enough information for this author to compute the interaction (Sample 9). Three significant interactions (ages 5 through 15) indicated that the findings of closer interpersonal distances for blacks were attenuated with age, exactly what we would now expect for that age group. The fourth study (Sample 9) investigated a much larger age span extending into adulthood. Although no significant interaction occurred, the means indicated that the finding of blacks preferring larger distances was weakest for the youngest groups, again as would be predicted. The mean effect size for the four studies was moderate (mean $d = .48$), and a meta-analysis of these studies shows the interaction to be highly significant (Stouffer's $z = 3.50$, combined $p \leq .0002$).

In summary, these studies suggest (a) blacks and whites share a developmental pattern of increasing interpersonal distance, (b) young black children interact more closely with each other than do young white children, (c) by junior high school, black children outdistance white children, and (d) the greater interpersonal distance of blacks relative to whites is a difference persisting through adolescence and adulthood.

We can now see that different proxemic behavior is clearly occurring for the two observed groups. A racial interpretation is too quickly assumed, however, and it is not entirely correct. Two thirds of the studies failed to tease out the confound of social class from the relationship between proxemics and race. It is not unreasonable to wonder whether the class distinctions are what cause the correlations with race.

As mentioned earlier, one study investigated just class differences and two studies investigated the relationship of both race and class. Schmidt and Hore (1970, Sample 22) asked low-income and high-income (based on census records) 5-year-olds and their mothers to perform two fun tasks together and observed no distance differences between the two groups.

Scherer (1974, Sample 5) photographed same-sex, same-race pairs of first-through-sixth graders from a lower-SES neighborhood school and a middle-SES neighborhood school in their respective playgrounds during recess and lunch. The conversational and environmental contexts were not controlled in this study but the two environments were described as similar (in size, density, and aesthetic dullness). Interpersonal distance did not vary significantly by race, but did vary by class. Lower class children stood closer together than middle-class children. There was also an interaction between race and class; the differences in interpersonal distance between lower and middle-class blacks were not as pronounced as for lower and middle-class whites. Unfortunately, Scherer (1974) did not analyze the data by age; an interaction of greater distance between lower class children in later grades relative to middle-class children would have made an even more powerful argument for social class as the causal factor of proxemic differences.

Aiello and Jones (1980, Sample 11) also investigated race and class differences in an adolescent sample. Students discussed their favorite television programs. Again, the environmental contexts were similar. In this sample, interpersonal distance varied significantly by both race and class. Whites stood closer together while conversing than blacks. Also, middle-class adolescents stood closer together than lower class adolescents. This finding was contrary to Scherer's findings, but was appropriate for this age group if the age interaction just described for race is also related to SES.

Of these 2 studies and 5 other studies controlling for SES in at least a rudimentary fashion (Samples 2, 4, 7, 18, and 19), 71% reported no significant race differences, compared with 27% of the remaining 11 samples that tested for significance. Though a small sample, this was nearly significant (using Fisher's exact test, $p = .08$), suggesting that SES may well be influencing the spatial relations of the two cultures. Jones (1971) suggests that the surprising cultural homogeneity of distance scores among the several ethnically different but similarly lower class subcultures he studied reflects the existence of a "culture of poverty." These findings all tie together to suggest that the proxemic race differences are at least partially mediated by social class.

Body Orientation. The eight studies reporting data for body orientation all agree that blacks are less direct in their stance than whites, contrary to what would be expected based on Hall's (1966) original hypothesis. For five of the studies the difference was significant. An effect size could be generated for only four studies; the resulting mean effect was moderate in size (mean $d = .55$). For a summary analysis, data for the three nonsignificant results could not be generated and zs for these studies were set at zero. Despite this highly conservative procedure the result was powerful (Stouffer's $z = 4.16$, combined $p \leq .0001$). In these studies, blacks were significantly less direct in their body orientation than whites were.

One might predict that the two age × race interactions for body orientation would parallel the age × race interactions for interpersonal distance discussed earlier. A similar trend did occur, though not significantly, in Sample 3 (Jones & Aiello, 1973). The race difference was attenuated from first to fifth grade, with blacks becoming increasingly more direct in body orientation. In Sample

2 (Duncan, 1978), however, the opposite occurred, and the race difference significantly increased with age. More research must be conducted to identify whether a developmental interaction for race differences in body orientation exists.

In summary, these studies show clearly that blacks engage in less direct body orientation than whites. Whether this difference is attenuated by age is not yet known.

Of the studies (Samples 2, 11, 18, and 19) controlling for SES in even a rudimentary fashion, 50% reported significant race differences, compared with 100% of the remaining four samples. Though not significant in this very small sample, it appears, again, that SES may be influencing the different spatial relations of blacks and whites.

Thus, the proxemic differences seem to reflect the different sensory worlds that different classes inhabit. They also suggest why social class might affect nonverbal skill (discussed in the first section), making a class interpretation of the racial differences in skill more plausible. If lower class subjects are immersed in a different nonverbal communication system then it is unlikely that they will be as good as middle-class subjects at decoding cues sent by a middle-class encoder. The converse should also be true.[3]

Why different sensory experiences are associated with these particular cultures is another matter entirely, and largely a matter of speculation. The results with mixed-race dyads (therefore also mixed-SES dyads, in this case) (Thompson & Baxter, 1973) suggest that proxemic behavior is flexible, and can be somewhat adapted to the customs of the dyad partner. However, it does not appear to be the case that black and poor children are learning the nonverbal cues of the majority group since their interpersonal distances become significantly greater than distances maintained by whites and their less direct body orientation persists through adulthood. The differences in proxemic norms across classes may be due to the differential density being experienced on a day-to-day basis by the classes. The idea here is that lower class individuals have less personal space (less spacious housing and urban life) which leads to a sense of crowdedness, which, in turn, leads to a need for a greater personal space whenever possible. Some tentative support can be garnered for this drive model, which proposes that continued crowding creates an intolerance to crowding rather than habituation to it (an adaptation model). Baron, Mandel, Adams, and Griffen (1976) found a lower tolerance for crowded college dormitory conditions in students who came from high density homes. These students perceived their overcrowded quarters (double rooms that were turned into triples) as more cramped and perceived

---

[3]Some research on cross-cultural decoding skill may concur with this hypothesis. In several analyses of cross-cultural samples Rosenthal et al. (1979) found a large relationship between ratings of cultural similarity to Americans and scores on their measure of nonverbal decoding skill (encoded by an American woman), thus indicating that different cultures may have their own cue systems.

TABLE 8.3
Differences in Touch

Sample number	Author(s) & year; N	Age	SES	Major findings	p	d
RACE						
1	Williams & Willis, 1978; N = 274	3–5 years	low & middle[b]	(a) Blacks touched each other more than did whites during free play.	.001	+.65
				(b) Low-income subjects touched each other more than did middle-income subjects.	.001	+.42
2	Willis & Hofmann, 1975; N = 890	5–12 years	low to upper-middle confounded by race[b]	Blacks touched each other more than did whites while on a cafeteria line.	.001	+.36
3	Willis & Reeves, 1976;[d] N = 915	junior high	probably low to upper-middle confounded by race[a]	Blacks touched each other more than did whites while on a cafeteria line.	.001	+.29
4	Willis, Reeves, & Buchanan, 1976; N = 1051 pairs	senior high	probably low to upper-middle confounded by race[a]	Blacks touched each other more than did whites while on a cafeteria line.	.001	+.27
5	Willis, Rinck, & Dean, 1978; N = 811 pairs	college	probably low to middle confounded by race[a]	Blacks touched each other more than did whites while on a cafeteria line.	.001	+.40
6	Hall, 1974;[d] N not reported	adult, mostly male	lower-low & middle confounded by race[b]	Blacks in street settings touched each other more than did whites at a convention.	—	+

244

7	Smith, Willis, & Gier, 1980; N = 93	adult	low to upper probably confounded by race[a]	(a) Blacks touched each other more than did whites while bowling.	.001	+.93
				(b) Blacks were more likely to touch each other following a successful bowl than whites.	.001	.85
				(c) Hand touches were more frequent among blacks than other body (e.g., arm or shoulder) touches compared to whites.	.001	1.13
8	Rinck, Willis, & Dean, 1980; N = 490	elderly	—	(a) Blacks touched each other more than did whites, in nursing homes.	ns	—
				(b) Personal touch (e.g., hand touch, hugging) was more frequent among blacks than other body touch (e.g., arm or shoulder) compared to whites.	.05	.46

SOCIOECONOMIC STATUS

9	Clay, 1968; N = 45 pairs	0-4 years & mothers	low, middle, & high[c]	Lower class mothers touched their children more frequently than other mothers, but middle-class mothers touched their children the longest while copying designs and telling each other stories.	—	—
10	Schmidt & Hore, 1970; N = 30 pairs	5 years & mothers	low & high[b]	Lower class mother-child pairs engaged in more physical contact than middle-class mother-child pairs.	.10	+.67

[a]No information regarding how the SES classifications were made was provided in the text.

[b]One criterion (generally neighborhood) determined the SES classifications.

[c]Two criteria (generally neighborhood and father occupation) determined the SES classifications.

[d]These studies examined other cultures as well as blacks and whites. Outcome measures in the tables exclude results concerning those additional samples. For the sake of simplicity only black/white contrasts were made in this chapter. Those interested in extending comparisons to other cultural groups may refer to studies designated with this superscript to obtain the appropriate data.

themselves as less in control and less cooperative than did students who reported having more space prior to college. Controlling for ethnic groups, Booraem et al. (1977) found that delinquent youths from higher density families requested significantly more personal space than subjects from lower density families. These studies support a drive model, such that "past high density sensitizes persons to future crowding experiences" (Baron et al., 1976).

Touching

Levels of tactile communication are occasionally presented as a proxemic analysis since some researchers regard body contact as another index of sensory involvement. Although some kinds of touches, such as body brushes, may provide evidence of greater immediacy or sensory involvement, other kinds of touch may be communicating entirely different and specific messages. In the white culture, touch can implicitly convey general feelings of friendship and positivity, such as holding hands or hugging someone, or attempts to control and anger, such as grabbing someone on the shoulder (Major, 1981). Henley (1973, 1977) additionally suggests that reciprocal touch indicates solidarity whereas nonreciprocal touch indicates status. These messages may appear equally valid in the black culture, but touch also seems to convey a special message of community and selectivity.

Examples of black touch that explicitly communicate shared experiences and brotherhood include the "dap," a two-person ritual of touching hand movements developed in the military (Shuter, 1979); "giving skin," a slap on the hand or palm-to-palm contact (Cooke, 1972); and the Black Power handshake. Cooke (1972) describes five components of this "soul shake:" (a) mutual encircling of the thumbs, symbolizing togetherness, (b) grasping each other's hands with curved fingers, symbolizing strength, (c) mutual grasping of wrists and hands, symbolizing solidarity, (d) placing hands on each other's shoulders with slight pressure, symbolizing comradeship, and (e) raising the arm, flexing the biceps and making a fist; incorporating the meanings of the first four, this gesture symbolizes black pride, solidarity, and power.

Emphasis on the hands is also reported by Hall (1974). In Hall's black sample of 18- to 24-year-olds discussing filmed job interviews, the hands appeared to be the single most important nonverbal cue for interpreting the interaction; certainly, hand movements were referred to more than any other specific nonverbal behavior.

Therefore, because touch may be a proxemic cue, but may also be a symbol for unity and brotherhood, studies on touch are examined independently.

Ten studies (with race studies followed by two class studies, and organized by age) are reported in Table 8.3. With the exception of all-male Sample 6, the studies include same-sex and cross-sex pairs. All contrasts in the table are of same-race pairs, and all studies were observational.

In addition to the two studies investigating class, the researchers of one other study (Sample 1) examined socioeconomic status as well as race. All of the other studies appear to have class and race confounded in their samples; only two bother to report the possibility.

The samples span the entire age range, but no study investigated age trends in touch. The pattern indicated across the studies is one of decreasing touch with age, for both blacks and whites, with white children reducing their touch rates slightly earlier than black children (Smith, Willis, & Gier, 1980).

This similar pattern of development does not inform whether the touch rates themselves are comparable across race. To make this comparison the studies in Table 8.3 are signed positively when blacks exhibit greater rates of touch and negatively when whites touch more. The direction of these signs is in accordance with both Hall's (1966) original hypothesis of greater sensory involvement by blacks and my hypothesis that blacks employ touch to develop and maintain a sense of solidarity and pride.

Seven of the eight studies found blacks exhibiting greater levels of touch than whites. This finding was significant in six studies. The mean effect size for these studies was moderate (mean $d = .48$). For a summary analysis, data could not be generated for two studies. Despite the conservative procedure of setting zs for these studies at zero, the meta-analysis proved highly significant (Stouffer's $z = 6.92$, combined $p \leq .0001$). These eight studies clearly reveal that blacks engage in more touch behavior than whites, and also suggest that this is a stable difference lasting at least from early childhood through adulthood.

The two studies investigating socioeconomic status and touch were primarily concerned with mothering behavior. Socioeconomic status was based on choice of beach or club, corroborated by father's occupation and education in Sample 9 and by census reports in Sample 10. Both studies reported greater frequency of physical contact in their lower class mother-child pairs, though Clay (1968, Sample 9) reported that middle-class mothers maintained the longest duration of touch.

The one study investigating class and race (Williams & Willis, 1978, Sample 1) found that low-income preschoolers touched each other more than did middle-income preschoolers. In fact, in similar indoor play settings, both black and white children in the low-income schools exhibited more than twice as much touching behavior as black and white children in the middle-income schools. Their finding that black children communicated by touch more than white children when SES is "equated" may be due to cultural differences in the shared meanings of touch. Unfortunately, the confound with SES was not eliminated, as the median family incomes of the two schools were still somewhat disparate (means of $10,058 for the black middle-income school and $13,065 for the white middle-income school). Overall, the findings of these 10 studies suggest that both social class and culture have power as explanations for the differences in interpersonal touch.

TABLE 8.4
Eye Gaze Differences

Sample number	Author(s) & year; N	Age	SES	Major findings	p	d
	RACE					
1	Zimmerman & Brody, 1975; N = 78	11, 12 years, male	low & middle confounded by race[b]	Unfamiliar blacks looked at each other slightly less than did whites in a laboratory playroom.	ns	+
2	Aiello & Jones, in Aiello & Thompson, 1980; N = 114	16 years	low & middle[b]	Blacks looked at each other less than did whites while discussing their favorite T.V. program.	.01	+.61
3	Exline, Jones & Maciorowski, 1977; N = 88	High school & adult, male	—	(a) Blacks looked at each other less than did whites during a laboratory discussion varying in intimacy.	—	+
				(b) Blacks (N = 40) looked more while listening than speaking, similar to the white pattern.	.001	1.14
4	Fehr & Exline, 1978; N = 50	college	—	(a) Blacks looked less at a black and a white interviewer than did whites in a laboratory discussion.	.001	+1.96
				(b) Blacks (N = 22) looked more while listening than speaking, similar to the white pattern.	.001	3.97
5	Fehr & Exline, 1978; N = 56	college, female	—	(a) Blacks looked less at a black and a white other than did whites in a laboratory discussion.	.05	+.69
				(b) Blacks (N = 28) looked more while listening than speaking, similar to the white pattern.	.001	3.24
6	Fugita, Wexley, & Hillery, 1974; N = 40	college, female	—	Blacks looked at a black or a white interviewer less than did whites.	.10	+.65
7	Hall, 1974; N = 60[c]	18–24	lower-low[b]	Blacks looked down or away from an interviewer while middle-class whites gazed at the interviewer and the room.	—	+

#	Study	Age	SES	Outcome	p	Effect
8	LaFrance & Mayo, 1976; N = 2 pairs[f]	adult, male	—	(a) Blacks looked less than did a white in a black-black and a black-white conversation.	.10	+.22
				(b) Blacks looked more while speaking than listening, contrasting the white pattern.	.01	.35
9	LaFrance & Mayo, 1976; N = 126 pairs	variety of ages	variety of levels[a]	Blacks looked at each other less while listening than did whites, seated at a table in several settings.	.05	+.38
10	Hall, 1974;[d] N not reported	adult, mostly male	lower-low & middle confounded by race[b]	(a) No gaze differences were observed between blacks in street settings and whites at a convention.	ns	—
				(b) Blacks were using peripheral vision primarily; whites used foveal (direct) vision.	—	—
11	Dorch & Fontaine, 1978; N = 138	adult	—	Witnesses received less frequent gazes from 2 black judges than 2 white judges.	.001	+.61

SOCIOECONOMIC STATUS

#	Study	Age	SES	Outcome	p	Effect
12	Schmidt & Hore, 1970; N = 30 pairs	5 years & mothers	low & high[b]	Lower-class mother-child pairs engaged in less mutual gaze than upper-class pairs, while copying designs and telling each other stories.	.01	+1.05
13	Robbins, Devoe, & Wiener, 1978; N = 30	14 years	lower & middle[b]	Middle-class adolescents gazed less at an adult than lower class adolescents during a conversation in an experiment.	.10	−.72

[a]No information regarding how the SES classifications were made was provided in the text.

[b]One criterion (generally neighborhood) determined the SES classifications.

[c]Two criteria (generally neighborhood and father occupation) determined the SES classifications.

[d]These studies examined other cultures as well as blacks and whites. Outcome measures in the tables exclude results concerning those additional samples. For the sake of simplicity only black/white contrasts were made in this chapter. Those interested in extending comparisons to other cultural groups may refer to studies designated with this superscript to obtain the appropriate data.

[e]It is not clear whether middle-class whites were actually subjects in this study.

[f]One pair in this study appears to be drawn from a portion of the LaFrance (1974) sample reported in Table 8.5.

Two more findings shed some additional light on the use of touch by blacks and whites. Smith et al. (1980, Sample 7) reported an interaction of race and success (strike or spare versus less successful bowl) in their sample of adult bowlers. Blacks were much more likely to touch each other following a successful bowl than whites were ($p \leq .001$, $d = .81$). This study and two others (Samples 2 and 8) also reported on the relative frequency of hand touches versus other touches among blacks and whites. Although no difference was found for elementary school children, adult and elderly blacks showed many more hand touches than other body touches, compared to whites. The mean effect size for the three studies was moderate (mean $d = .51$), and the combined analysis was significant (Stouffer's $z = 3.20$, combined $p \leq .001$). That the sharing of success and other communications are being tactilely expressed, probably via handshakes or slaps, provides evidence supporting Cooke's (1972) and Hall's (1974) observations. Whether this more developed use of the tactile system is based in black culture or, in Jones' (1971) term, the "culture of poverty" cannot be presently ascertained. Future researchers would do well to extend the boundaries of tactile studies to include style of touch as well as frequency and to do so while contrasting the effects of race and class.

Eye Gaze

Several descriptive reports on nonverbal behavior in both children and adults suggest differences by class and/or by race in eye gaze (e.g., Byers & Byers, 1972; Goffman, 1971; Johnson, 1971; Kozol, 1967; and Williams, 1972). Reports of racial differences include (a) frequency, e.g., blacks gaze at others less than whites do, particularly in the presence of an authority; (b) patterns of gaze, e.g., blacks gaze at different times than whites do; and (c) styles, e.g., blacks roll their eyes to express disapproval and negativity toward a dominant person, a communication uncommon in white behavior.

The first two of these described differences have been examined in research. Eleven studies on race followed by two studies on class (organized by age) are reported in Table 8.4. Four of these studies also examined patterns of gaze while looking and speaking.

Six samples include only same-sex pairs. About half of the contrasts are same race; Samples 4, 5, 6, 8, and 11 included same-race and cross-race pairs, and Sample 7 appeared to employ only a white male interviewer. Sample 12 also employed only one interviewer, of unidentified race and class.

Three samples on race and one on class (1, 3, 6, and 12) may not have controlled for conversation length. If blacks talk less than whites in the settings under study (MacCombie, 1977, and Zimmerman & Brody, 1975 suggest they do), their unadjusted rates of gaze may be artifactually reduced, making a greater difference than actually exists in real life. Samples 3, 4, 6, 7, and 12 employed interviewers or confederates but only Sample 3 and possibly Sample 4 trained them to emit consistent amounts of eye gaze to all subjects.

No samples examined race and class simultaneously. Of the studies on race, only four samples reported the SES levels of the participants, and all of these appear to be confounded with race.

Hall's (1966) prediction that blacks experienced a more highly involved and immediate sensory world would include higher rates of eye gaze between blacks than between whites. As mentioned, however, the gaze of blacks has been anecdotally described as less frequent than that of whites. Also, amount of eye contact and direction of shoulder orientation are related (Mehrabian, 1968a, 1968b), and we have already found that blacks are less direct in their body stance. Thus, studies are signed positively when reporting less frequent gaze by blacks (or lower class individuals) relative to whites (or middle-class individuals), and negatively when reporting less frequent gaze by whites (or middle-class individuals) relative to blacks (or lower class individuals).

Ten of the 11 studies on race reported that blacks gazed less frequently in conversations than whites did. This is a significantly greater number of studies than could be expected by chance ($\chi^2(1) = 5.82$, $p \le .02$, $d = 2.12$). The mean effect size was moderate-large ($N = 7$, mean $d = .73$). For the summary analysis, data could not be generated for three studies and for the sample reporting nonsignificance. Despite the highly conservative procedure of setting zs for these studies at zero, the meta-analysis proved highly significant (Stouffer's $z = 4.40$, combined $p \le .0001$).

No differences in effect size occurred between samples that may have failed to control for conversation length compared to those samples that were known to do so. The difference in effect size between samples employing interviewers or confederates versus samples using only naive participants was not significant, although there was a trend for larger effects in samples employing interviewers or confederates ($t(7) = 1.88$, $p = .11$, $d = 1.42$). Since d is considered to be a good signal-to-noise index—that is, it indicates the size of a difference relative to uncontrolled variation in the study (Hall, 1979)—this is not surprising. Interviewers were either increasing precision in the study by their constant presence or were instilling experimenter bias into the results. A third possibility is that interviewers are perceived as authorities, and this perception was affecting subjects' eye gazing differentially by race. Based on our anecdotal evidence, black eye gaze is most minimal when interacting with a superior, as a means of showing respect. Black children, for example, are socialized to lower their eyes when an older person or teacher is talking to them, particularly when they are being scolded (Johnson, 1972). In contrast, white children are commanded, "Look me in the eye when I'm talking to you!" and several studies indicate that white eye gaze tends to *increase* in the presence of higher status individuals (Exline, 1971; Exline, Ellyson, & Long, 1975; and Mehrabian, 1968a). A repeated measures study, in which blacks and whites would interact with both peers and authority figures, would help define the range of this difference.

All in all, that blacks gaze less frequently than whites do in conversation appears as a robust difference that spans many different settings and many different subjects beyond the usual college population. A continuation of this series of research would be a developmental analysis to discover whether or not differences in eye gaze frequency follow a pattern similar to interpersonal distance differences.

The two studies reporting class differences in eye gaze (Samples 12 and 13) found opposite relationships between lower and middle-class subjects, so it is impossible at present to evaluate whether or not class is a contributing factor in the race/eye gaze relationship. Unfortunately, there simply is not sufficient evidence to hypothesize whether or not class is a contributing factor in the race/eye gaze relationship.

Regarding patterns of gaze while looking and speaking, previous studies on eye gaze by white adults (e.g., Argyle & Ingham, 1972; Exline, 1963; and Kendon, 1967) have repeatedly found greater frequency and mean length of other-directed gaze during listening relative to speaking. However, in a microanalysis of two encounters of a black male student with another black male and a white male (both of higher status than the student), LaFrance and Mayo (1976, Sample 8) found a complete reversal of eye gaze; the two black subjects looked more while speaking than listening. In their follow-up study of listening only (Sample 9), LaFrance and Mayo found that eye gaze by black conversants was significantly less than by white conversants, in a wide variety of settings.

This difference of less black eye gaze during listening, however, is very likely due just to the main effect of blacks gazing less overall than whites. Further, three other studies found a pattern in blacks similar to that found in whites, and these studies all reported tremendous effects. Consequently, despite the one study countering these results, the mean effect size was still very large (mean $d =$ 2.00). Additionally, the meta-analysis of the four studies was highly significant (Stouffer's $z = 3.70$, $p = .0002$). The most accurate analysis has yet to be done; a race by conversation mode (listen, speak) analysis of variance would directly test race differences in gaze patterns during conversation.

In summary, these studies contribute the information that during interactions blacks gaze less frequently than whites do and that whereas rates of gaze differed by race, patterns of looking more while listening than speaking are shared interracially. Since no developmental research has been conducted, it is impossible to determine when racial differences in gazing behavior develop. If these racial differences do appear to be a function of class, they may fit nicely with the drive model hypothesized to explain the proxemic data. Decreasing levels of gaze is another way lower class or crowding-sensitive individuals may be psychologically increasing interpersonal distance, thereby creating a more spacious personal bubble for themselves (Argyle & Cook, 1976; Argyle & Dean, 1965). Obviously, more research must be conducted.

Regarding the third aspect of eye gaze differences, that of style, no studies have been conducted to assess the different behaviors or even the accuracy of different-race observers. Johnson (1972) reports that rolling the eyes occurs as an expression of general disapproval or during stress or conflict situations, particularly as an insolent, hostile message from someone in the subordinate role being lectured or reprimanded. Johnson describes the movement as very quick, and one that may be missed, especially by a nonblack. Thus, a study of such eye movements would have to include same-race judges.

Hall (1974) also cautions very strongly about the "sensory bias" judges may have, that we see only that with which we are familiar, and that we are constrained by our own narrow cultural perceptions. Hall discovered that black subjects were able to discern from photographs whether a black peer was talking to another black or a white. Further, they could determine whether the *photographer* was black or white, based on what aspects of the interaction the photographer focused on.

These descriptive reports indicate that Hall (1966) is correct in hypothesizing that blacks and whites inhabit different sensory worlds. The data, however, reverse the direction of the effects he predicted.

Verbal Versus Nonverbal System

Schatzman and Strauss (1955), Bernstein (1962a, b), and many others suggest a correlation between social class and the use of elaborated codes. Usually these are understood mainly as terms referring to verbal communication, although there is little reason, except convenience, for this limitation. That is, only difficulties in data collection and conceptualization stand in the way of doing work in the extension of these codes to nonverbal channels, and even the definitions of the codes suggest that nonverbal components are critical.

The restricted code is a communication system of limited scope, with ritualistic and predictable form, and with a low degree of verbal planning (Bernstein, 1962a). It is used in a fairly close-knit group whose members draw upon a long period of shared identifications and experience, and is context-dependent. The elaborated code, on the other hand, is much more far-ranging in scope, and is oriented toward complex, detailed, and planned verbal communication. It enables the speaker to encode precisely and fully his or her own experience and is context-independent. The restricted code is perceived as a means of reinforcing group membership, keeping out new members and yet getting the gist of the matter across. The elaborated code is seen as a means of abstracting and analyzing experience and conceptions in a purely verbal way. Speakers of the restricted code, therefore, are thought to depend largely on role prescriptions, and more

TABLE 8.5
Verbal/Nonverbal Differences

Sample number	Author(s) & year; N	Age	SES	Major findings	p	d
	SOCIOECONOMIC STATUS					
1	MacCombie, 1977; N = 64	3, 4 years	low & middle[b]	Middle-class "teachers" (4 yr. olds) used more verbal communication relative to lower class "teachers," who used more visual nonverbal communication when teaching 3-yr.-olds.	.05	+
2	Brooks, Brandt, & Wiener, 1969; N = 108	mean = 5.9 years	low & middle[c]	Lower class subjects responded better to positive tone & words than neutral tone & positive words, relative to middle-class subjects in a reinforcement paradigm (game).	.01	+.69
3	Brooks, Brandt, & Wiener, 1969; N = 168	mean = 5.7 years	low & middle[c]	(a) Findings of Sample 1 were replicated in a similar design adding negative tone.	.001	+.43
				(b) Tone, especially positive, may be an information marker for lower class subjects directing the subject to the semantic message.	.001	+.47
4	Kashinsky & Weiner, 1969; N = 120	mean = 5.8 years	low & middle[c]	(a) Lower class subjects responded much better to positive tone than either neutral or negative tone with a set of game instructions, whereas middle-class subjects did not differentiate between conditions in a nonreinforcement paradigm.	.05	+.48
				(b) Lower class subjects responded more quickly to positive, neutral, and negative tone, respectively, whereas middle-class subjects did not differentiate.	.05	+.48
5	Gottman, Gonso, & Rasmussen, 1975; N = 198	9–10 years	low & upper middle[b]	For middle-class subjects, dispensing verbal reinforcement related to popularity; for lower class subjects, dispensing visual nonverbal reinforcements related to popularity.	.05	+

6	Robbins, Devoe, & Wiener, 1978; $N = 30$	14 years	low & middle[b]	When subjects conversed with an adult experimenter about a previously viewed cartoon, type & frequency of turn-taking regulators varied by class; lower class subjects used more speaker-shift regulators (e.g., unfilled pauses and upward inflection) whereas middle-class subjects used more continuation regulators (e.g., filled pauses and downward inflection).	.05	+.85
RACE						
7	LaFrance, 1974; $N = 1$ pair	adult, male	—	In conversation, several different turn-taking regulators not commonly found among whites were used by two blacks, e.g., less variable intonation at a turn termination and unfilled pauses between termination and a new turn.	—	+

[a]No information regarding how the SES classifications were made was provided in the text.
[b]One criterion (generally neighborhood) determined the SES classifications.
[c]Two criteria (generally neighborhood and father occupation) determined the SES classifications.

on nonverbal signals such as intonation, stress, and other expressive features since there is a paucity of verbal signals.

Until recently, black children were thought to be limited in the restricted code. This was because nonstandard black English, a dialect, has been confused with the restricted code, a mode of viewing and interacting with the world. However, in a study in which black children were given a topic of personal interest to themselves (and thus were motivated to communicate with a strange experimenter) they did indeed give detailed and complex communications, and did so using nonstandard English (Labov, 1968, reported in Cazden, 1971). It is clearly possible for the elaborated code to be employed when speaking in nonstandard black English, just as in any other dialect or language. Social scientists' inability to recognize the legitimacy of black English, as a dialect, against the backdrop of "normative" majority usage of standard English, is a basic example of the discipline's ethnocentrism (Baratz & Baratz, 1972). Bernstein (1971a, b) suggests that usage of the nonverbal and verbal systems may be inversely related and that restricted code users rely more on nonverbal communications than elaborated code users. He thus places the entire nonverbal system in the restricted code, and fails to account for the possibility that elaborated and restricted codes in the nonverbal domain might parallel those in the verbal domain.

As has been shown with nonstandard black English, Jancovic, Devoe, and Wiener (1976) clarify that the nonverbal system also sustains a substantial degree of communicative complexity. They found that communicative complexity (semantic modifying gestures) increased with age, suggesting that an elaborated code is being learned.

If the restricted and elaborated codes extend to the nonverbal system, how they do so can only be studied in light of the relationship between the verbal and nonverbal systems.

Six studies on class and one study on race (organized by age) assessed some of these hypotheses. No study examined race and class simultaneously. Studies in Table 8.5 were signed positively when black or lower class individuals were relatively more responsive to or used more specific nonverbal cues than verbal cues, compared to white or middle-class individuals. Studies were signed negatively when the opposite occurred.

These studies employed diverse methods. In a teaching task, with 4-year-old "teachers" and 3-year-old "pupils," MacCombie (1977, Sample 1) found that middle-class children used more positive reinforcers than lower class children, and an equivalent amount of negative reinforcement, when controlling for verbal frequency (middle-class children talked more). Also, the lower class "teachers" transmitted more nonverbal communications; i.e., pointing, moving, and touching. Since MacCombie did not code the nonverbal communications into positive, negative, and neutral evaluations like the verbal communications, we do not know if different class children emitted similar amounts of positive, negative, and neutral nonverbal reinforcers. It can be concluded, however, that the two communication systems were used in a compensatory way—those who were high in verbal communication were low in nonverbal communication and vice versa.

In Samples 2, 3, and 4, experiments were conducted, using different game situations and varying positivity of voice tone and words uttered by an experimenter. These samples used both the Wiener and Mehrabian (1968) framework of independent channels and the restricted versus elaborated code hypothesis to develop their predictions; "the lower-class child's greater use of the 'restricted' code . . . of language, as compared to the use of verbal content, should lead to the child's greater use of information transmitted tonally than of information transmitted in the verbal channel. The middle-class child should be expected to make use of information transmitted in either channel (i.e., tonal or verbal)" (Kashinsky & Wiener, 1969).

In all three studies, albeit with some variations on the theme, the middle-class children responded fairly equivalently to the game instructions across all conditions and with the same latency. As predicted, the lower class children did better with, and responded more quickly to, the positive voice tone as compared to neutral voice tone, but, not as predicted, responded to negative voice tone to the same degree as, and more slowly than, neutral voice tone. The effect sizes for these interactions were very similar with a moderately sized mean effect (mean $d = .53$). The summary analysis was highly significant (Stouffer's $z = 4.01$, $p \le .0001$). The total findings were supportive of the predictions that lower class children are more responsive to variations in voice tone than middle class children, and that for lower class children positive intonation acts as the most effective reinforcer.

In a study of social skills, Gottman, Gonso, and Rasmussen (1975, Sample 5) assessed children's classroom behavior and popularity. For middle-class children, verbal reinforcements (giving approval or verbally complying with a request) accounted for the most variance in the relationship of dispensed reinforcement and popularity. For lower class children, nonverbal reinforcement (giving a token, giving affection, or nonverbally complying with a request) accounted for the most variance in this relationship. Though actual frequency of verbal and nonverbal reinforcements by class were not reported, the data suggest, again, that verbal and nonverbal reinforcements are differentially valued by lower and middle-class children.

In a study investigating frequency and type of reinforcement received by students, middle-class students received significantly more reinforcement overall from their teachers than did lower class students (Friedman, 1976). Separate analyses for verbal and nonverbal reinforcements indicated that middle- and lower class students received similar amounts of verbal reinforcement, but middle-class students received more nonverbal reinforcement than lower class students. Thus, the reinforcement techniques that Brooks, Brandt, & Wiener et al.

(1969), Kashinsky and Wiener (1969), and Gottman et al. (1975) have shown to be most efficacious with lower class students appear to be those used least frequently with them.

In Sample 6 (Robbins, Devoe, & Wiener, 1978), class differences emerged in the usage of nonverbal communications in conversational turn taking. Returning to the concept of restricted versus elaborated codes, Schatzman & Strauss (1955) and Bernstein (1971a) have noted that members of the lower class seem to talk more frequently about the "here and now," or shared events, compared to members of the middle class who seem to talk more frequently about not-here, not-now, and not-shared events. Robbins et al. (1978, Sample 6), predicted that these differences in the verbal domain would be reflected in the variety and frequency of usage of nonverbal regulators in turn taking. In exchanges where the content of a communication is shared, the speaker needs only to signal the beginning and the end of a comment (speaker-shift regulator). In more elaborated exchanges, however, the speaker needs to signal as above, but also will wish to (a) elicit responses from the listener indicative of his or her degree of comprehension of the speaker's message (monitoring decoding regulator) and (b) to signal continuation of the message (speaker-continuation regulator). Thus, if lower class children do employ a restricted code in their verbal communications, they should emit more speaker-shift regulators than middle-class children who, due to their use of the elaborated code, should emit a greater variety of types of regulators.

As predicted, lower class children emitted more unfilled pause and open inflection behaviors and more speaker-shift regulators than middle-class children, who emitted more filled pause and closed inflection behaviors and more speaker-continuation regulators.

Also, upwardly inflected voice tone predominated among the lower class children whereas middle-class children used more downward inflection. Robbins et al. (1978) suggested that upward inflection may be identified as "uncertain" or "tentative" voice tone by middle-class listeners (e.g., teachers) while being classified as "appropriate" voice tone by the lower class senders. On the other hand, lower class listeners might find the downward inflection of middle-class children to be too assertive, and not what would be acceptable for information exchange.

One can conclude from all of these findings that the regulator patterns favored by the two classes rarely overlap. Not only are lower class children more responsive to and more frequent senders of nonverbal communication than middle-class children, but their patterns of usage of nonverbal regulators appear to be quite different.

Returning for a moment to the first category on differences in skill, it may be remembered that most, if not all, of the studies on skill employed middle-class senders only. These studies on children's verbal versus nonverbal behavior, however, employed almost all same-class pairs. Also, all of the studies on skill were clearly tests and required verbal identifications of the nonverbal expressions. All of the studies on behavior were more ecologically valid, including games and actual peer interactions. It is certainly conceivable (and did occur in the Gottman et al. [1975] sample) that lower class children are not as skilled as middle-class children at explicitly identifying nonverbal expressions in testing situations, or as motivated to do so as middle-class children, but, as shown in these studies of natural social situations, lower class children place greater emphasis on and are more responsive to communications in the nonverbal domain. It seems likely that lower class individuals have weaker nonverbal decoding skills because they are tested on understanding middle-class patterns of behavior.

The one study on race differences (LaFrance, 1974, Sample 7) described turn-taking behaviors of only one black pair. Though both individuals were presently engaged in middle-class occupations, they also employed unfilled pauses to a noticeable extent, comparable to the lower class children in Sample 6. This descriptive sample hints at different turn-taking patterns by race as well as by class. Like lower class individuals, blacks may have weaker nonverbal decoding skills because they are tested on understanding white patterns of behavior.

In summary, these seven studies suggest two conclusions. First, nonverbal cues are powerful messages for lower class chidren relative to middle-class children. Second, since nonverbal cues play a more significant role in the communications of lower class children than middle-class children, the paucity of verbal communication reported for lower class speakers does not mean a paucity of total communication. Rather, lower class children may be employing the restricted code in the verbal domain and an elaborated code in the nonverbal domain, versus the pattern of middle-class children.

The ethnocentric perspective of middle-class researchers may have precluded their conception of the nonverbal channel as capable of sustaining sufficient communicative complexity and of lower class conversants as capable of employing the nonverbal channels for elaborated communications.

SUMMARY

The meta-analysis of the 58 studies within the broad category of nonverbal communication skill and within the four subcategories of nonverbal communicative behavior indicate clear race and class differences. These studies also suggest the power of social class as an explanation for race differences.

One final calculation of the effect of social class can be made by examining all of the studies on race differences together and contrasting the number of significant studies found when SES was or was not matched across race. Of the 10 studies controlling for SES in at least a rudimentary fashion, 70% reported no significant race differences, compared with 19% of the remaining samples that tested for significance. This was a significant difference, using Fisher's exact probability test, $p = .02$. This, again, suggests that at least some of the black-white differences are attributable to differences in social class. It is unfortunate that similar analyses cannot yet be conducted on a culture explanation for race differences, and future research will have to rectify this problem.

To summarize present hypotheses and to advise future researchers:

1. Several hypotheses regarding differences in nonverbal communication skill and behavior were identified in this review. These are (a) that racial differences in nonverbal skill are mediated by social class differences; (b) that "oppressed" people may become better at decoding nonverbal communication in order to survive politically, socially, and economically (Weitz, 1974); (c) that racial differences in proxemic behavior, in particular, appear to be mediated by social class differences and develop over time; (d) that a drive model (Baron et al., 1976) may account for proxemic and other nonverbal differences by class and race; (e) that some nonverbal differences (e.g., touch) have developed out of a sense of black pride, solidarity, and power; (f) that there are restricted and elaborated codes within the nonverbal domain which relate to these codes in the verbal domain; (g) that there are class differences in usage and responsivity to nonverbal relative to verbal behaviors; (h) whereas blacks/lower class individuals and whites/middle-class individuals do appear to experience different sensory worlds, the behavioral results are counter to Hall's (1966) original hypothesis; and (i) the different styles of nonverbal behavior used and experienced by black and lower class individuals, compared to white and middle-class individuals, may explain the apparent race and class differences in nonverbal skill. More theoretically oriented research needs to be conducted, and testing of these hypotheses should be a guiding force in future research.

2. Of the 44 studies on race differences in nonverbal communication, 22 did not report the SES of the subjects. Although not all of these studies were concerned with the effects of class on nonverbal behavior, this review shows that such a concern is necessary, particularly when examining variables (e.g., race) confounded with SES.

3. Of all the studies on both race and class that do report the SES of subjects, 31 employ only one criterion in determining subjects' SES classifications, and 6 more failed to report the criterion altogether. Even when the type of criterion was mentioned, the specific classifications were often omitted. Socioeconomic status is a complex construct, which can probably be best described by a heterogeneity of measurement. However, if a researcher is limited to only one criterion of SES, special care should be taken in fully describing that particular measurement. Obviously, use of only one criterion per study and poor descriptions of criteria make comparisons between studies more difficult, since it is not clear that the studies even partially share definitions of SES. Additionally, the consensus among sociologists is that the best single indicators of SES are occupation-based measures (Mueller & Parcel, 1981). In this review, occupation-based decisions were infrequent; neighborhood was the most common choice.

That so many social class differences emerged despite the abuses in measurement of SES points to the robustness of the effects.

4. The construct validity of socioeconomic status and race is actually more complex than generally considered. Researchers sometimes use race and class as factors simply because of their presumed convenience of measurement and because they usually can be depended upon to provide at least main effects if not interactions. After finding an effect for race or class, however, it is not often clear what actually has been found—is there a relationship with heredity, cognitive ability, achievement, motivation, social expectation, oppression, isolation, or something else? It is not enough to say that race or class and nonverbal variables are correlated. The mediators of these relationships must be explored.

One must also beware of minimizing the impact of black culture when pointing to class as an explanation of race differences. Assimilation into the middle class may require not only economic and occupational changes but also middle-class values and middle-class behaviors. That middle-class blacks evidence white middle-class patterns of nonverbal behavior may be a function of having to repudiate the black ethnic behaviors shunned by many middle-class whites, in order to maintain their new positions in mainstream culture.

The interview situation is the clearest example of the need created by whites for blacks to adopt white, middle-class behaviors. Black interviewees must adopt middle-class patterns of greater eye gaze, to denote honesty as opposed to untrustworthiness to the white interviewer; and closer interpersonal distances and more direct body orientation, to indicate friendliness as opposed to hostility. Thus, in the middle class, anyway, race differences may be attenuated due to the pressures by the white, majority culture.

5. The habit of splintering the nonverbal domain into single channels and studying them one at a time, while simplifying matters for the researcher, seriously decreases the value of the results. Only six studies investigated more than one nonverbal behavior simultaneously. Nonverbal channels interact with each other as well as with the verbal system and multivariate research must be attempted. Additionally, in the area of skill, emotional expression was generally the only type of affect judged. Expressions of power, familiarity, and so forth, are also valuable communications to test.

6. The construct validity of skill can also be questioned. Researchers must be aware that though skill may be a fixed point on the continuum of nonverbal communication, the continuum itself may change depending on who is encoding, what is being encoded, and who is the judge. We know that spatial behavior differs depending on the race, culture, or class of the sender. Likewise, the nuances of emotional expression may also vary. Skill in recognition and transmission of emotion exemplify agreed-upon definitions of nonverbal skills. But the vast majority of the people who agree upon and encode the measures are of the middle class. If the tests of judging skill are employed to discover how differentially skillful races, cultures, or classes are in decoding the majority

group (i.e., white middle class) then these tests are acceptable. Most of the research so far (with the exceptions of Gitter and his associates), however, has involved attempts to study ability per se, and these researchers must be aware that their definitions probably emphasize middle-class communications.

The research of behavior differences is vital to the research on skill, because it points to areas where operational definitions of skill are biased toward middle-class communications. Research on differential interpretation and expression of emotions, status, familiarity, and so on, by race and class is needed.

In closing, of utmost importance for both research and application is an awareness of differences rather than the assumption of sameness. As stressed earlier, there are differences in nonverbal behavior across race, class, and culture. The unstated assumption that there are no differences is a dangerous one. At the very least, research on skill which assumes no differences can lead to misleading results (e.g., when lower class subjects are asked to decode a middle-class encoder) and the ethnography of communication will be sadly incomplete. At the worst, responses to day-to-day interaction, which assume no differences in nonverbal behavior, will continue to create miscommunications and misunderstandings (e.g., "She kept her distance from me," and "Don't look at me in that tone of voice!") and negative attitudes (e.g., "He wouldn't look me in the eye," "You know, that know-it-all voice"). Precisely because they crop up in the nonverbal domain, which everybody uses but few discuss, these misunderstandings persist. Thus, until we are able to recognize, respect, and understand differences in nonverbal behavior, we are helping to perpetuate the status quo of social and economic inequities by race and class.

ACKNOWLEDGEMENTS

The author would like to thank Doris Entwisle for her valuable encouragement, and to thank her, Judith Hall, Bruce C. Milligan, and Kathleen Pike for criticisms of various drafts of the paper. Thanks are also due to Jack Aiello for additional references and to Frank N. Willis, Jr. for hunting down unpublished details in his research.

REFERENCES

Aiello, J. R., & Aiello, T. (1974). The development of personal space: Proxemic behavior of children 6 through 16. *Human Ecology, 2,* 177–189.

Aiello, J. R., & Jones, S. E. (1971). Field study of the proxemic behavior of young school children in three subcultural groups. *Journal of Personality and Social Psychology, 19,* 351–356.

Aiello, J. R., & Thompson, D E. (1980). Personal space, crowding, and spatial behavior in a cultural context. In I. Altman, A. Rapaport, & J. F. Wohlwill (Eds.), *Human behavior and environment: Advances in theory and research: Vol. 4. Environment and culture.* New York: Plenum Press.

Argyle, M., & Cook, M. (1976). *Gaze and mutual gaze*. New York: Cambridge University Press.

Argyle, M., & Dean, J. (1965). Eye-contact, distance and affiliation. *Sociometry, 28,* 289–304.

Argyle, M., & Ingham, R. (1972). Gaze, mutual gaze and proximity. *Semiotica, 6,* 32–49.

Baratz, J., & Baratz, S. (1972). Black culture on black terms: A rejection of the social pathology model. In T. Kochman (Ed.), *Rappin' and stylin' out*. Chicago: University of Illinois Press.

Baron, R. M., Mandel, D. R., Adams, C. A., & Griffen, L. M. (1976). Effects of social density in university residential environments. *Journal of Personality and Social Psychology, 34,* 434–446.

Bauer, E. A. (1973). Personal space: A study of blacks and whites. *Sociometry, 36,* 402–408.

Baxter, J. C. (1970). Interpersonal spacing in natural settings. *Sociometry, 33,* 444–456.

Bernstein, B. (1962a). Linguistic codes, hesitation phenomena and intelligence. *Language and Speech, 5,* 31–46.

Bernstein, B. (1962b). Social class, linguistic codes and grammatical elements. *Language and Speech, 5,* 221–240.

Bernstein, B. (1971a). *Class, codes and control: Vol. 1. Theoretical studies towards a sociology of language*. London: Routledge & Kegan Paul.

Bernstein, B. (1971b). A sociolinguistic approach to socialization: With some reference to educability. In F. Williams (Ed.), *Language and poverty: Perspectives on a theme*. Chicago: Markham.

Booraem, C. D., Flowers, J. V., Bodner, G E., & Satterfield, D. A. (1977). Personal space variations as a function of criminal behavior. *Psychological Reports, 41,* 1115–1121.

Brigham, J. C., & Barkowitz, P. (1978). Do "they all look alike"? The effect of race, sex, experience, and attitudes in the ability to recognize faces. *Journal of Applied Social Psychology, 8,* 306–318.

Brigham, J. C., & Williamson, N. L. (1979). Cross-racial recognition and age: When you're over 60, do they still "all look alike? *Personality and Social Psychology Bulletin, 5,* 218–222.

Brooks, R., Brandt, L. J., & Wiener, M. (1969). Differential response to two communication channels: Socioeconomic class differences in response to verbal reinforcers communicated with and without tonal inflection. *Child Development, 40,* 453–470.

Byers, P., & Byers, H. (1972). Nonverbal communication and the education of children. In C. B. Cazden, V. P. John, & D. Hymes (Eds.), *Functions of language in the classroom*. New York: Teachers College Press.

Cazden, C. B. (1971). The neglected situation in child language research and education. In F. Williams (Ed.), *Language and poverty: Perspectives on a theme*. Chicago: Markham.

Chance, J., Goldstein, A. G., & McBride, L. (1975). Differential experience and recogniton memory for faces. *The Journal of Social Psychology, 97,* 243–253.

Clay, V. S. (1968). The effect of culture on mother-child tactile communication. *The Family Coordinator, 17,* 204–210.

Cohen, J. (1977). *Satistical power analysis for the behavioral sciences (rev. ed.). New York: Academic Press*.

Coleman, L. M. (1976). Racial decoding and status differentiation: Who hear what? Journal of Black Psychology, *3,* 34–46.

Cooke, B. G. (1972). Nonverbal communication among Afro-Americans: An initial classification. In T. Kochman (Ed.), *Rappin' and stylin' out*. Chicago: University of Illinois Press.

Cross, J. F., Cross, J., & Daly J. (1971). Sex, race, age and beauty as factors in recognition of faces. *Perception and Psychophysics, 10,* 393–396.

Dorch, E., & Fontaine, G. (1978). Rate of judges' gaze at different types of witnesses. *Perceptual and Motor Skills, 46,* 1103–1106.

Duncan, B. L. (1978). The development of spatial behavior norms in black and white primary school children. *Journal of Black Psychology, 5,* 33–41.

Duncan, S., Jr., & Fiske, D. W. (1977). *Face-to-face interaction: Research, methods, and theory*. Hillsdale, NJ: Lawrence Erlbaum Associates.

Ekman, P., & Friesen, W. V. (1969). The repertoire of nonverbal behavior: Categories, origins, usage, and coding. *Semiotica, 1,* 49–98.

Exline, R. V. (1963). Explorations in the process of person perception: Visual interaction in relation to competition, sex, and need for affiliation. *Journal of Personality, 31,* 1–20.

Exline, R. V. (1972). Visual interaction: The glances of power and preference. In J. K. Cole (Ed.), *Nebraska Symposium on Motivation,* 1971. Lincoln: University of Nebraska Press.

Exline, R. V., Ellyson, S. L., & Long, B. (1975). Visual behavior as an aspect of power role relationships. In P. Pliner, L. Krames, & T. Alloway (Eds.), *Advances in the study of communication and affect* (Vol. 2). New York: Plenum Press.

Exline, R. V., Jones, P. & Maciorowski, K. (1977, August). *Race, affiliation-conflict theory and mutual visual attention during conversation.* Paper presented at the meeting of the American Psychological Association, San Francisco, CA.

Fehr, B. J. & Exline, R. V. (1978). *Visual interaction in same- and interracial dyads.* Paper presented at the meeting of the Eastern Psychological Association, Washington, DC.

Feinman, S., & Entwisle, D. R. (1976). Children's ability to recognize other children's faces. *Child Development, 47,* 506–510.

Friedman, P. (1976). Comparison of teacher reinforcement schedules for students with different social backgrounds. *Journal of Educational Psychology, 68,* 286–292.

Fugita, S. S., Wexley, K. N., & Hillery, J. M. (1974). Black-white differences in nonverbal behavior in an interview setting. *Journal of Applied Social Psychology, 4,* 343–350.

Gitter, A. G., Black, H., & Mostofsky, D. (1972a). Race and sex in the communication of emotion. *Journal of Social Psychology, 88,* 273–276.

Gitter, A. G., Black, H., & Mostofsky, D. (1972b). Race and sex in the perception of emotion. *Journal of Social Issues, 28,* 63–78.

Gitter, A. G., & Quincy, A. J., Jr. (1968). Race and sex differences among children in perception of emotion. *CRC Report No. 27.* Boston: Boston University.

Goffman, E. (1971). *Relations in public.* New York: Harper Colophon Books.

Gottman, J., Gonso, J., & Rasmussen, B. (1975). Social interaction, social competence, and friendship in children. *Child Development, 46,* 709–718.

Gumperz, J. J. (1982). *Discourse strategies.* Cambridge: Cambridge University Press.

Hall, E. T. (1966). *The hidden dimension.* New York: Doubleday.

Hall, E. T. (1974). *Handbook for proxemic research.* Washington, DC: Society for the Anthropology of Visual Communication.

Hall, J. A. (1979). Gender, gender roles, and nonverbal communication skills. In R. Rosenthal (Ed.), *Skill in nonverbal communication: Individual differences.* Cambridge, MA: Oelgeschlager, Gunn & Hain.

Henley, N. M. (1973). Status and sex: Some touching observations. *Bulletin Psychonomic Society, 2,* 91–93.

Henley, N. M. (1977). *Body politics: Power, sex, and nonverbal communication.* Englewood Cliffs, NJ: Prentice-Hall.

Hymes, D. (1977). *Foundations in sociolinguistics: An ethnographic approach.* London: Tavistock Publications.

Izard, C. E. (1971). *The face of emotion.* New York: Appleton-Century-Crofts.

Jancovic, M. A., Devoe, S., & Wiener, M. (1976). Age related changes in hand and arm movements as nonverbal communication: Some conceptualizations and an empirical exploration. *Child Development, 46,* 922–928.

Johnson, K. R. (1971, 1972). Black kinesics—some non-verbal communication patterns in the black culture. *Florida FL Reporter, 9,* 17–20. Also in L. A. Samovar & R. E. Porter (Eds.), *Intercultural communication: A reader.* Belmont, CA: Wadsworth.

Jones, S. E. (1971). A comparative proxemics analysis of dyadic interaction in selected subcultures in New York City. *The Journal of Social Psychology, 84,* 35–44.

Jones, S. E., & Aiello, J. R. (1973). Proxemic behavior of black and white first-, third-, and fifth-grade children. *Journal of Personality and Social Psychology, 25*, 21–27.

Justin, F. (1932). A genetic study of laughter provoking stimuli. *Child Development, 3*, 114–136.

Kashinsky, M., & Wiener, M. (1969). Tone in communication and the performance of children from two socioeconomic groups. *Child Development, 40*, 1193–1202.

Kellogg, W. N., & Eagleson, B. M. (1931). The growth of social perception in different racial groups. *Journal of Educational Psychology, 22*, 367–375.

Kendon, A. (1967). Some functions of gaze-direction in social interaction. *Acta Psychologica, 26*, 22–63.

Kochman, T. (1969). "Rapping" in the black ghetto. *Trans-action, 6*, 26–34

Kozol, J. (1967). *Death at an early age*. New York: Bantam Books.

LaFrance, M. (1974). Nonverbal cues to conversational turn taking between black speakers. *Personality and Social Psychology Bulletin, 1*, 240–242.

LaFrance, M., & Mayo, C. (1976). Racial differences in gaze behavior during convensations: Two systematic observational studies. *Journal of Personality and Social Psychology, 33*, 547–552.

Langlois, J. H., Gottfried, N. W., & Seay, B. (1973). The influence of sex of peer on the social behavior of preschool children. *Developmental Psychology, 8*, 93–98.

Leibman, M. (1970). The effects of sex and race norms on personal space. *Environment and Behavior, 2*, 208–246.

Lomranz, J., Shapira, A., Choresh, N., & Gilat, Y. (1975). Children's personal space as a function of age and sex. *Developmental Psychology, 11*, 541–545.

Luce, T. S. (1974). The role of experience in inter-racial recognition. *Personality and Social Psychology Bulletin, 1*, 39–41.

MacCombie, D. J. (1977, March) *Social reinforcement in a communication network: A reanalysis of teaching styles of lower- and middle-class children*. Paper presented at the Biennial Meeting of the Society for Research in Child Development, New Orleans.

Maines, D. R. (1977). Tactile relationships in the subway as affected by racial, sexual, and crowded seating situations. *Environmental Psychology and Nonverbal Behavior, 2*, 100–108.

Major, B. (1981). Gender patterns in touching behavior. In C. Mayo & N. M. Henley (Eds.), *Gender and nonverbal behavior*. NY: Springer-Verlag.

Malpass, R. S. (1974). Racial bias in eyewitness identification? *Personality and Social Psychology Bulletin, 1*, 42–44.

Malpass, R. S., & Kravitz, J. (1969). Recognition of faces for own and other race. *Journal of Personality and Social Psychology, 13*, 330–334.

Malpass, R. S., Lavigueur, H., & Weldon, D. E. (1973). Verbal and visual training in face recognition. *Perception and Psychophysics, 14*, 285–292.

Mehrabian, A. (1968a). Inference of attitudes from the posture, orientation, and distance of a communicator. *Journal of Consulting and Clinical Psychology, 32*, 296–308.

Mehrabian, A. (1968b). Relationship of attitude to seated posture, orientation, and distance. *Journal of Personality and Social Psychology, 10*, 26–30.

Michael, G., & Willis, F. N., Jr. (1968). The development of gestures as a function of social class, education, and sex. *Psychological Record, 18*, 515–519.

Michael, G., & Willis, F. N., Jr. (1969) The development of gestures in three subcultural groups. *The Journal of Social Psychology, 79*, 35–41.

Mueller, C. W. & Parcel, T. L. (1981) Measures of socioeconomic status: Alternatives & recommendations. *Child Development, 52*, 13–30.

Patterson, M. L. (1978). The role of space in social interaction. In A. W. Siegman & S. Feldstein (Eds.), *Nonverbal behavior and communication*. Hillsdale, NJ: Lawrence Erlbaum Associates.

Pfaff, P. L. (1954). An experimental study of the communication of feeling without contextual material. *Speech Monographs, 21*, 155–156.

Rinck, C. M., Willis, F. N., Jr., & Dean, L. M. (1980). Interpersonal touch among residents of homes for the elderly. *Journal of Communication, 30,* 44–47.

Robbins, O., Devoe, S., & Wiener, M. (1978). Social patterns of turn-taking: Nonverbal regulators. *Journal of Communication, 28,* 38–46.

Rosegrant, T. J., & McCroskey, J. M. (1975). The effects of race and sex on proxemic behavior in an interview setting. *The Southern Speech Communication Journal, 40,* 408–418.

Rosenthal, R., Hall, J. A., DiMatteo, M. R., Rogers, P. L., & Archer, D. (1979). *Sensitivity to nonverbal communication: The PONS test.* Baltimore: Johns Hopkins University Press.

Schatzman, L., & Strauss, A. (1955). Social class and modes of communication. *American Journal of Sociology, 60,* 329–338.

Scherer, S. E. (1974). Proxemic behavior of primary school children as a function of their socioeconomic class and subculture. *Journal of Personality and Social Psychology, 29,* 800–805.

Schmidt, W., & Hore, T. (1970). Some nonverbal aspects of communication between mother and preschool child. *Child Development, 41,* 889–896.

Severy, L. J., Forsyth, D. R., & Wagner, P. J. (1979). A multimethod assessment of personal space development in female and male, black and white children. *Journal of Nonverbal Behavior, 4,* 68–86.

Shuter, R. (1979). The dap in the military: Hand-to-hand communication. *Journal of Communication, 29,* 136–142.

Smith, D. E., Willis, F. N., & Gier, J. A. (1980). Success and interpersonal touch in a competitive setting. *Journal of Nonverbal Behavior, 5,* 26–34.

Tennis, G. H., & Dabbs, J. M., Jr. (1975). Sex, setting and personal space: First grade through college. *Sociometry, 38,* 385–394.

Tennis, G. H., & Dabbs, J. M., Jr. (1976). Race, setting, and actor-target differences in personal space. *Social Behavior and Personality, 4,* 49–55.

Thompson, D. J., & Baxter, J. C. (1973). Interpersonal spacing in two-person cross-cultural interactions. *Man-Environment Systems, 3,* 115–117.

Weitz, S. (Ed.). (1974). *Nonverbal communication: Readings with commentary.* New York: Oxford University Press.

Wiener, M., & Mehrabian, A. (1968). *Language within language: Immediacy, a channel in verbal communication.* New York: Appleton-Century-Crofts.

Williams, A. P. (1972). Dynamics of a black audience. In T. Kochman (Ed.), *Rappin' and stylin' out.* Chicago: University of Illinois Press.

Williams, S. J., & Willis, F. N., Jr. (1978). Interpersonal touch among preschool children at play. *The Psychological Record, 28,* 501–508.

Willis, F. N., Jr. (1966). Initial speaking distance as a function of the speakers' relationship. *Psychonomic Science, 5,* 221–222.

Willis, F. N., Carlson, R., & Reeves, D. (1979). The development of personal space in primary school children. *Environmental Psychology and Nonverbal Behavior, 3,* 195–204.

Willis, F. N., & Hoffman, G. E. (1975). Development of tactile patterns in relation to age, sex, and race. *Developmental Psychology, 11,* 866.

Willis, F. N., & Reeves, D. L. (1976). Touch interactions in junior high students in relation to sex and race. *Developmental Psychology, 12,* 91–92.

Willis, F. N., Reeves, D. L., & Buchanan, D. R. (1976). Interpersonal touch in high school relative to sex and race. *Perceptual and Motor Skills, 43,* 843–847.

Willis, F. N., Rinck, C. M., & Dean, L. M. (1978). Interpersonal touch among adults in cafeteria lines. *Perceptual and Motor Skills, 47,* 1147–1152.

Zimmerman, B. J., & Brody, G. H. (1975). Race and modeling influences on the interpersonal play patterns of boys. *Journal of Educational Psychology, 67,* 591–598.

Author Index

Subject Index